Our Hulshoff and Kerchner Ancestors

A short history of our Hulshoff ancestral line beginning with my 6th great-grandfather Johannes David Hulshoff, who lived from about 1667 to 1717, through the death of my grandmother Anna Gertrude Hulshoff Gonce in 1983.

Also included in this book are reproductions of two self-published booklets about the Kerchner, Kern, and Kunkel families by Fr. Frank Kunkel (9 JUL 1870 - 15 JUN 1951) that overlap in many areas with our own Kerchner and Kern ancestry. These are each prefaced with my commentary and, where appropriate, corrections and additional material.

Frank Oberle

Our Hulshoff and Kerchner Ancestors

Copyright © 2010, 2011 by Frank Oberle
Revised March 2016

Cover Painting: Watercolor by my first cousin JoAnn Iglehart,
also a granddaughter of Anna Gertrude Hulshoff Gonce.

ISBN-13: 978-0692650578
ISBN-10: 0692650571

Rev. III

(Engenthal Press)

Preface

This book consists of three separate, but related, sections.

Section One – Our Hulshoff Ancestors

My maternal grandmother Anna Gertrude Hulshoff $^{\text{ID 44}}$ [1] was the 4th great-granddaughter of Johannes David Hülshoff $^{\text{ID 1602}}$ and Margareta Thoben $^{\text{ID 1603}}$. Grandmom married Charles R. Gonce $^{\text{ID 43}}$, whose oldest daughter Rosalie Gonce $^{\text{ID 242}}$ and her husband Cornelius Oberle $^{\text{ID 196}}$ are my parents.

This Section concentrates on the direct line from Johannes David Hulshoff $^{\text{ID 1602}}$, my 6th great-grandfather, through my grandmother Anna Gertrude Hulshoff Gonce; this line is diagrammed on page 5 for reference. Siblings and spouses of each of these ancestors are discussed to varying degrees.

Because existing records of our early Hülshoff ancestors are mostly found in church records, the names I've used for them are often the Latin forms as they appear in the parish registers or, in later cases, the Germanic forms used on civil (mostly travel) records. Obviously these forms were not used in their daily lives, but it seemed more convenient to use the names as documented rather than attempting to determine their "real" names. In most cases, however, names such as "Joannes Gerhardus," "Johann Gerhard", and "John Gerard" are similar enough that this should cause no undue confusion, particularly since each individual is identified by a unique ID number. Likewise, the umlaut in the name "Hülshoff" does not always appear consistently in the records, but I've tried to follow what the records show.

Section Two – Our Kerchner Ancestors

Anna Gertrude Hulshoff Gonce's mother, my great-grandmother, was Mary Regina Kerchner $^{\text{ID 8}}$, the wife of Herman R. Hulshoff $^{\text{ID 7}}$.

In the summer of 1939, my mother Rosalie Gonce assisted Fr. Frank[2] Kunkel $^{\text{ID 432}}$, her first cousin twice removed, by typing many of the notes he had been assembling for many years about his Kunkel and Kerchner ancestry. These were self-published on the 21st of November that same year as "John Nepomucene Kunkel & Mary Rosina Kerchner – A Short Sketch of their Lives" after being approved by the Catholic Church[3]. Because of the

---

[1] The ID numbers are from my genealogy database and are provided to permit correlation with various different reference material and other publications and documents I have created.

[2] See more about "Fr. Frank," as he was called by our family, on page 63. My mother's early 1930s-vintage manual Royal typewriter remains in the possession of my second daughter.

[3] A process resulting in a designation of "nihil obstat," Latin for "nothing stands in the way." Since Fr. Kunkel was a Catholic priest, this was a necessary requirement whether a publication had anything to do with religion or not.

relationship between my mother and Fr. Frank[4], the majority of his research into the Kerchner family reflects part of our family's genealogy as well.

Although I spent time validating his research as far as it related to our own line, it seemed appropriate to reproduce his original document[5] here rather than attempting to rewrite this history myself. I've added some commentary and copies of a few other documents where appropriate, and identified the very few areas where I suspect his conclusions were in error. Reproducing Fr. Kunkel's original has the added benefit of presenting some of this family history from the perspective of a "different time" – even though his document is less than one hundred years old, it is interesting to view this history through the lens of depression-era American viewpoints.

Section Three – Our Kern Ancestors

Just prior to World War II, my mother also assisted Fr. Frank Kunkel with the typing of his second genealogical effort – this time about his Kern and Kerchner ancestry. Although this book "The Descendants of (John) Dominic Kern and his wife Margaret Vaeth," self-published in August of 1941, covers more of the Kern family and its many branches than is relevant to our own history, it didn't seem appropriate to truncate or otherwise edit the document in any way. Fr. Kunkel's earliest Kern ancestors[6] are ours as well.

In his second document, much of the perspective is from an even earlier time than in the first. Some of the correspondence Fr. Kunkel presents here is between the first generation of his nineteenth century American immigrant ancestors and the families they left behind in Europe, and provides a detailed, albeit indirect, picture of some of the political and economic conditions that caused so many pioneers to flock to America in that century. For that reason alone, this manuscript is also reproduced in its entirety rather than attempting to rewrite it.

The following page shows the descendant tree for Johannes David Hülshoff [ID 1602] and Anna Margareta Thoben [ID 1603], our earliest documented Hulshoff ancestors.

---

[4] Mary Rosina Kerchner, Fr. Frank's mother, was the younger sister of my great-great grandfather Ferdinand Kerchner (my great-grandmother Mary Regina Kerchner's father).

[5] Because of the age of the document, as well as the fact that there are only a few known copies surviving, there appear to be no copyright issues with reproducing Fr. Kunkel's documents here.

[6] The last of these was my 3rd great-grandmother Anna Maria Kern Kerchner [ID 91] (21 Jan 1806 - 5 May 1879).

Lineage: Johannes David Hülshoff to Anna Gertrude Hulshoff Gonce

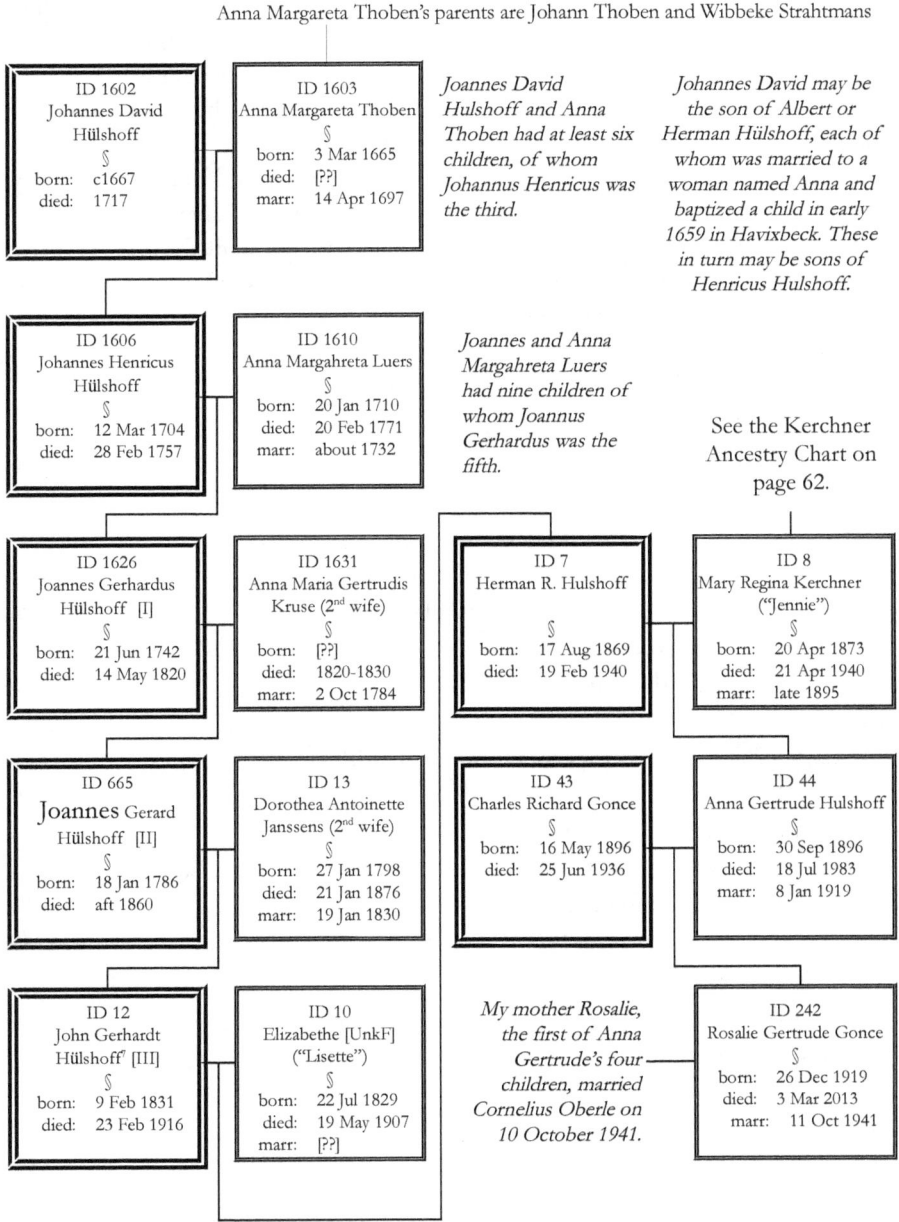

---

[7] Johann Gerhardt and Lisette Hulshoff (bottom left) arrived at New Orleans on 8 Nov 1855 on the ship Eberhard from Bremen along with their first child. Of their seven children, at least three died in childhood.

Ancestors of Anna Gertrude Hulshoff Gonce

The table below lists the known ancestors of my maternal grandmother Anna Gertrude Hulshoff[8], daughter of Herman R. Hulshoff and Mary Regina Kerchner. The number preceding each line identifies the generation relative to Gert (as she was known), who is considered generation 1 in this table. Her paternal ancestors are listed above her in the table, and her maternal line is listed below her. Her father Herman R. Hulshoff, for instance, can be found by locating generation 2 above, and her mother Mary Regina Kerchner by finding generation 2 below. The number at the end of each line is the person's identification number in my genealogical database that is used to reference documents and other material relating to that person. The "a" number preceding the identification number is my Ahnentafel Number[9].

................7. Joannes David HULSHOFF (b.1667;m.1697;d.1717)......a448 id 1602
..............6. Joannes Henricus HULSHOFF (b.1704;m.1732;d.1757)....a224 id 1606
................8. Johann THOBEN (b.1645)..a898 id 1660
................7. Anna Margareta THOBEN (b.1665)...............................a449 id 1603
................8. Wibbeke STRAHTMANS (b.1649).................................a899 id 1661
............5. Joannes Gerhardus HULSHOFF (b.1742;m.1784;d.1820)......a112 id 1626
................7. Heinrich Albers LUERS...a450 id 2980
..............6. Anna Margahreta LUERS (b.1710;d.1771).........................a225 id 1610
................7. Gertrud Tole THOBEN...a451 id 2981
..........4. Joannes Gerard HULSHOFF (b.1786;m.1830)........................a56 id 665
............5. Anna Maria Gertrud KRUSE (d.1820)...............................a113 id 1631
........3. John Gerhart HULSHOFF (b.1831;d.1916)..............................a28 id 12
............5. Victor JANSSENS (b.1755;d.1820)....................................a114 id 2384
..........4. Dorothea Antoinette JANSSENS (b.1798;d.1876)..................a57 id 13
............5. Anna Catharina MEYER..a115 id 2385
......2. Herman R. HULSHOFF (b.1869;d.1940)..................................a14 id 7
........3. Elisabethe UNKF (b.1829;d.1907)..a29 id 10
1. Anna Gertrude HULSHOFF (b.1896;d.1983)..................................a7 id 44
........married to Charles Richard Gonce (b.1896;d.1936)....................a6 id 43
................7. Johannes Michael KERCHNER (b.1709)........................a480 id 1178
..............6. Francis Caspar KERCHNER (b.1750)..............................a240 id 107
................7. Gertrude GROOS (b.1717)...a481 id 1179
............5. Paul KERCHNER (b.1782;m.1802;d.1856).........................a120 id 82

---

[8] If it is not obvious, this table is identical to what would be created for any of her siblings Rose Easter, Dorothy Hulshoff, Mary Agnes Hausman, or Gerard Hulshoff.

[9] That is, an Ahnentafel number based on me as number 1, my father Cornelius Oberle as number 2, etc. See an explanation of Ahnentafel numbers on page 53.

................7. Andreas RAUCH..a482 id 1174
...............6. Anna Katharina RAUCH (b.1756)...a241 id 1169
...............7. Margaret HOSKIN..a483 id 1175
..........4. Michael Anthony KERCHNER (b.1804;m.1828;d.1857)..............a60 id 100
...............7. Johann MÜSSIG..a484 id 1171
...............6. Anton MÜSSIG (b.1741)...a242 id 1170
...............7. ?Female? UNKF...a485 id 1176
.............5. Maria Rosina MUSSIG (b.1778;d.1853)................................a121 id 83
...............7. Michael ARNOLD...a486 id 1172
...............6. Maria Anna ARNOLD...a243 id 1173
...............7. ?Female? UNKF...a487 id 1177
........3. Ferdinand KERCHNER (b.1835;m.1860;d.1918)..............................a30 id 38
.............5. John Dominic KERN , Sr. (b.1781;m.1805;d.1826)...................a122 id 84
..........4. Anna Maria KERN (b.1806;d.1879)..a61 id 91
.............5. Margaret VAETH (b.1780;d.1820)...a123 id 85
......2. Mary Regina KERCHNER (b.1873;d.1940)...a15 id 8
.............5. ?Male? LINNENKEMPER..a124 id 87
..........4. Henry LINNENKEMPER (b.1806)...a62 id 98
.............5. Mary Rosina UNKF...a125 id 88
........3. Anna B. LINNENKEMPER (b.1839;d.1914)....................................a31 id 39
.............5. ?Male? UNKM...a126 id 89
..........4. Annie UNKF (b.1805)...a63 id 99
.............5. ?Female? UNKF...a127 id 90

Table of Contents

Preface iii
   Section One – Our Hulshoff Ancestors iii
   Section Two – Our Kerchner Ancestors iii
   Section Three – Our Kern Ancestors iv
   Lineage: Johannes David Hulshoff to Anna Gertrude Hulshoff Gonce v
   Ancestors of Anna Gertrude Hulshoff Gonce vi
Table of Contents viii
SECTION ONE – OUR HULSHOFF ANCESTORS 1
   Signature of Johann Gerhart Hulshoff (9 Feb 1831 - 23 Feb 1916) 1
   Map of Northern Germany in the time of our Hulshoff Ancestors 2
The History of our Hulshoff Ancestors 3
   The Hulshoff Name and Earliest References to the Family 3
   Anna Margareta Thoben – the Woman from Dingel (3 Mar 1665-) 5
   Johannes David Hülshoff (circa 1667 - 1717) 5
      Children and Grandchildren of Johannes David Hülshoff & Anna Margareta Thoben ... 6
   The Luers and Anna Margahreta Luers (20 Jan 1710 - 20 Feb 1771) 7
   Joannes Henricus Hülshoff (12 Mar 1704 - 28 Feb 1757) 7
      1771 entries in St. Andreas Katholisch Kirchenbuch 8
      Children of Joannes Henricus Hülshoff & Anna Margahreta Luers 8
   Joannes Gerhardus Hülshoff [I] – Button-Maker (21 Jun 1742 - 14 May 1820) 9
      Child of Joannes Gerhardus Hulshoff & Anna Maria Macke 9
      Child of Joannes Gerhardus Hulshoff & Anna Maria Gertrud (Maria) Kruse ... 11
   The Janssens and Dorothea Antoinette Janssens (27 Jan 1798 – 21 Jan 1878) 11
      January 27, 1798 St. Andreas Kirchenbuch entry for Dorothea Antonetta Janssens ... 11
   Joannes Gerard Hulshoff [II] (18 Jan 1786 – >May 1830 / >1860) 11
      Segment of January 18, 1786 entry for the birth of "Joannes Gerardus" [ID 665] ... 12
      23 January 1820 entry in St. Andreas Katholische Kirchenbuch (Cloppenburg) ... 12
      Children of Joannes Gerard Hülshoff & Maria Angela Klaus 13
      19 January 1830 entry in St. Andreas Katholische Kirchenbuch (Cloppenburg) ... 13
      Child of Joannes Gerard Hülshoff & Dorothea Antoinette Janssens 14
   Northern Europe in the mid-nineteenth Century 14
      Banhofstrasse (Train Station Road) in Kloppenburg, late 19th century ... 15
      Corner of the 11th century Hüls Castle in Burg Hülshoff, Havixbeck 15
      An early "Passenger Bill of Rights" passed by the U.S. Congress in May 1848 ... 16
   Elizabethe (Lizette) [Surname Unknown] (22 Jul 1829 - 19 May 1907) 16
   John Gerhardt Hülshoff [III] (9 Feb 1831 - 23 Feb 1916) 17
      9 February 1831 entry in St. Andreas Katholische Kirchenbuch: 17
      Sections of the 8 Nov 1855 New Orleans arrival manifest for the bark Eberhard ... 18
      1860 U.S. Census extract showing Gerhard Hulshoff's family and Dorie Johnson ... 19
      Page from the 20 April 1858 arrival manifest for the Saxonia 20
   American Citizenship 22
      1870 U.S. Census extract showing George (sic) Hulshoff's family 23
      Page 293 of the 1873 Baltimore City Directory 25
      Only known photograph of Johann Gerhardt Hulshoff, first of our Hulshoff ancestors
      to come to the United States 26

► viii ◄

The Hulshoff Cemetery Plot..27
  Obelisk face showing John G. (Johann Gerhard) and Lizette (Elisabethe) Hulshoff in
  Holy Redeemer Cemetery, Baltimore, MD..27
  Obelisk face showing Dorothea Antoinette Hulshoff and her great-granddaughter
  Dorothy Antoinette Hulshoff at Holy Redeemer Cemetery, Baltimore, MD................29
  1887 Baltimore City Directory, page 640, showing John G. Hulshoff and his sons........30
  Extract from 1900 U.S. Census Series t623, reel 617, page 242..............................31
  Extract from 1910 U.S. Census Series t624, reel 559, page 164..............................32
  Children and Grandchildren of John Gerhardt & Lisette Hülshoff..........................32
The Kerchners and Mary Regina Kerchner (20 Apr 1873 - 21 Apr 1940)..............33
  Needlepoint made by Jennie Kerchner..33
Herman R. Hulshoff (17 Aug 1869 - 19 Feb 1940)..34
  Mary Regina (Jennie) Kerchner ID 8..34
  Herman R. Hulshoff ID 7..34
  Extract from 1900 U.S. Census Series t623, reel 612, pages 45a & b showing the family
  of Herman H. Hulshoff, age 30, living at 1005 Biddle Street in Baltimore. Regina's year
  of birth is actually 1873..35
  Extract from 1910 U.S. Census Series t624, reel 556, page 165 showing the family of
  Herman R. Hulshoff, age 40, living at 932 Biddle Street in Baltimore with his wife
  Regina and their first four children...36
  Charles Gonce and Gertrude Hulshoff in about 1917...36
  Extract from 1920 U.S. Census Series t625, reel 662, page 147 showing the family of
  Herman I. Hulshoff, age 50, living at 932 Biddle Street in Baltimore with his wife Regina
  M. and five remaining children. Alfrieda had died and Gertrude married since 1910......37
  Settlement Papers for Herman and Jennie Hulshoff's purchase of their new home at 602
  Springhill Terrace (later known as Springfield Avenue). Aunt Dot (Dorothy Hulshoff)
  continued to live in this house until the mid-1970s..38
  Hulshoff Children and Grandchildren taken in Spring (Easter, April 8?) 1928............39
The Stock Market Crash...39
  Extract from 1930 U.S. Census Series t626, reel 0869, page 134a showing the Hulshoff
  family, now living at 602 Springfield Avenue. Rosalie had since married Frank Easter and
  moved out..40
  Herman Hulshoff in the back yard of 602 Springfield Avenue – probably late 1930s....41
  Jennie Hulshoff on the front porch of 602 Springfield Avenue – probably late 1930s...41
  Children and grandchildren of Herman Hulshoff & Mary Regina (Jennie) Kerchner....42
More Details about Herman and Jennie's Children...42
  Alfrieda Hulshoff..43
  Rose and Alfrieda Hulshoff circa 1906..43
  Clara Rosalia (Rose) Hulshoff...43
  Cathy and Donald Easter..44
  Mary Easter...44
  The Hospital Ship Repose..45
  Dorothy Antoinette (Dot) Hulshoff..45
  Aunt Dot with her siblings before leaving for Italy..46
  Aunt Dot and Uncle Jerry after her retirement..46
  Mary Agnes (Ag) Hulshoff...47
  Ag and Bill Hausman on their wedding day...47
  Gerard Herman Hulshoff..48
  Gerard Hulshoff – circa 1930..48
  Helen Polianski (later Hulshoff) in about 1943 at Camp Meade, Maryland..............49
The Gonces and Charles R. Gonce (16 May 1896 - 25 Jun 1936).........................49

Anna Gertrude Hulshoff (30 Sep 1896 - 18 Jul 1983)..49
   Ring given to Agnes by her father on her 18th Birthday in May 1929........................50
   Receipt for my Grandmother Anna Gertrude Hulshoff Gonce's 18th birthday gift from her father Herman..50
   Obituaries for my grandmother Anna Gertrude Hulshoff Gonce...............................51
   Herman and Jennie's children Gerard, Gertrude, Dorothy and Agnes (late 1950s or early 1960s)...52
Descendants of Joannes David Hulshoff...53
   Modern day entrance bridge to Gut Swede near Kappeln..53

SECTION TWO – OUR KERCHNER ANCESTORS....................................61

   Signature of Fr. Kunkel from a January 31, 1951 letter to Rosalie (Gonce) Oberle.........61
   Five Generations of Kerchners from Johannes Michael to Ferdinand..................62
   About Father Frank Kunkel..63
The Kerchner and Kunkel Families..64
   "John Nepomucene Kunkel & Mary Rosina Kerchner – A Short Sketch of their Lives"...64
   The Kerchner Name...64
   Errata..64
   Supplemental Information..65
   Ferdinand Kerchner and his Hulshoff Grandchildren; Spring 1915............................69
Holy Redeemer Cemetery..70
   Holy Redeemer Cemetery; Section V, Lot 70..70
John Brown's Papers from Harpers Ferry...117
   Disposition of John Brown's papers recovered by Lt Francis William Kerchner at Harpers Ferry..117
   Details of John Brown's Sharps Rifle presented to Lt. Kerchner..............................118
ID Number Cross-Reference...119

SECTION THREE – OUR KERN ANCESTORS....................................143

The Kern Family..144
   "Descendants of (John) Dominic Kern and his wife Margaret Vaeth"...............144
   The Kern Name..144
   Errata..144
   Fr. Kunkel's Interesting Omission..145

SECTION ONE

—

OUR HULSHOFF ANCESTORS

The Hulshoff Family

Signature of Johann Gerhart Hulshoff (9 Feb 1831 - 23 Feb 1916)

Johann Gerhart, the first of our Hulshoff ancestors to come to America, here signing the deed for the cemetery plot he purchased in 1880 with the "Americanized" version of his first name, but still with the umlaut over his surname.

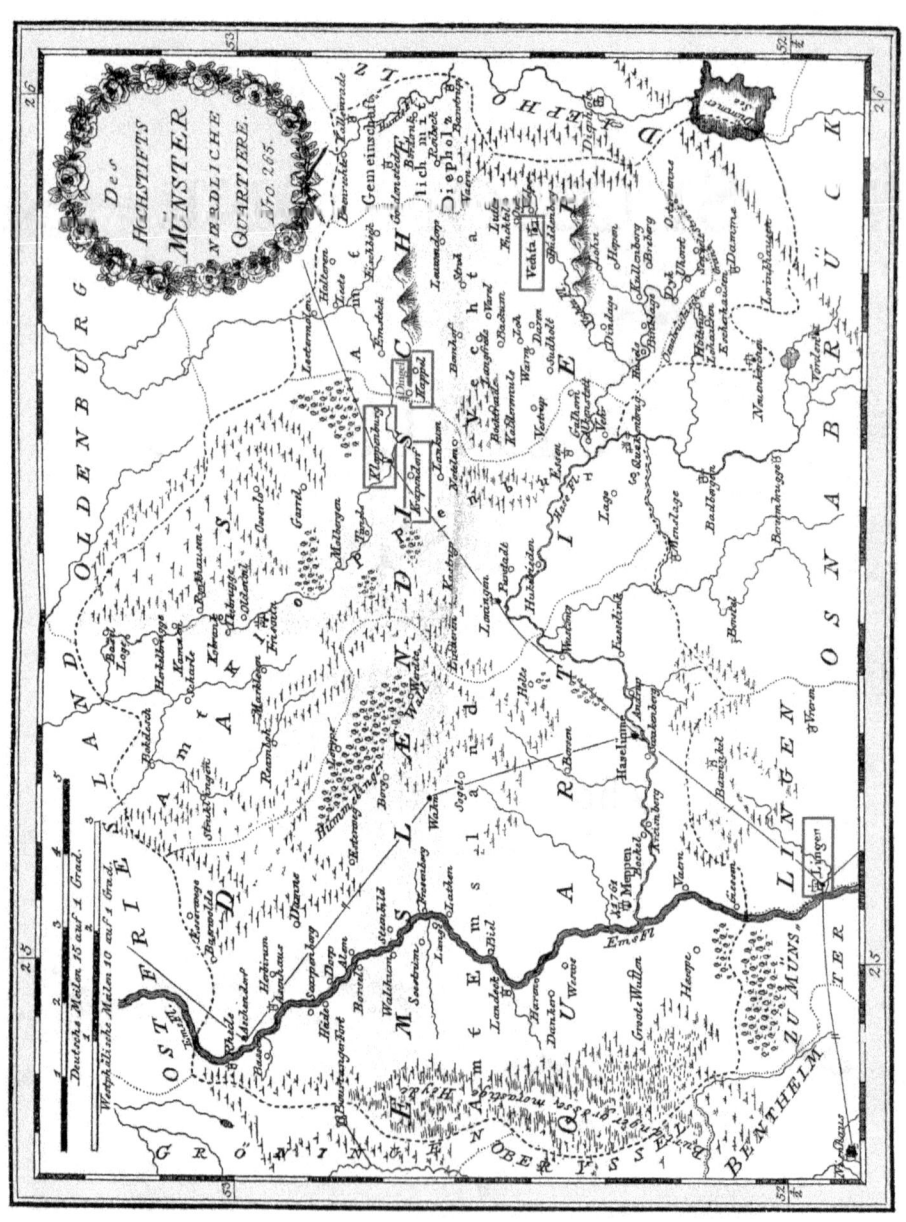

Map of Northern Germany in the time of our Hulshoff Ancestors

Showing (left to right) Lingen, Krapendorf, Kloppenburg, Kappel, and Dingel.

The History of our Hulshoff Ancestors

The Hulshoff Name and Earliest References to the Family

Family stories my mother heard when she was young suggested that the Hulshoff name may originally have been "von Huelshoff" and that they were a reasonably well-off family in Germany (with the "von" possibly suggesting some minor level of awarded nobility) but were forced by political changes there to emigrate from their homeland to the United States. I have found nothing to substantiate these stories, however. The original surname of the family in Germany was simply Hülshoff, which commonly would have been transcribed into English as either Hulshoff or Huelshoff, and there is only one instance I have seen where any United States record shows the latter spelling[10].

In English, the suffix "-hoff" means farm, which could mean that the family was originally "from" ("von" in German) "Hül's Farm." Interestingly, there is a small village about 15 kilometers west of Münster named Burg Hülshoff (literally: "city of Hül's Farm"), built around "Hül's Castle"[11] near the town of Havixbeck[12]. Based on extant evidence from the records of St. Dionysius Church[13], there were indeed Hülshoffs living around Havixbeck as early as the late sixteenth century. Although the records (or at least the microfilmed copies) are quite faded and very illegible in places, I've identified the following items from the church registers:

- Sometime in late 1590 (looks like October), the death of a Hülshoff was reported, but the name and age are illegible[14].

- On 14 September 1598, a Hülshoff male married, but most other information on the line is illegible[15].

- Sometime in 1617[16], Joannis Kramer and Elizabeth Hülshoff married. Joannis Hülshoff and Caspar Joannis (?) Hülshoff were mentioned, likely as witnesses.

---

[10] This record is for Bernard Huelshoff $^{ID\ 1662}$, who arrived 25 JUN 1866 on the SS New York at age 21, and who was living in Dubuque, Iowa in 1880 according to the United States Census. Bernard is a great-grandson of our button-maker ancestor Joannes Gerhardus Hülshoff $^{ID\ 1626}$ (see below).

[11] See a picture of one corner of the castle wall on page 15.

[12] Havixbeck today would probably be considered a suburb of Münster, and is 15 km west of that city. When you travel from Havixbeck today, you go generally east for about 6.5 miles (mostly on the K1 highway) and then north on **HülshoffStrasse** until the turn east onto the B54 into Münster.

[13] The surviving records from St. Dionysius Kirche for the period from 1590 through early 1659 can be found on LDS Microfilm 0864331, which can be ordered for viewing at a Family History Center.

[14] ibid. "Kirchenbuch Nr. 1: Taufen 1590-1600; Trauungen 1590-1600; Toten 1590-1600," p 65-L, row 13.

[15] ibid. "Kirchenbuch Nr. 1: Taufen 1590-1600; Trauungen 1590-1600; Toten 1590-1600," p 46, row 23.

[16] ibid. "Kirchenbuch Nr. 2: Taufen 1614-1639; Trauungen 1614-1619; Toten 1617-1637," page 56, row 1. This marriage was recorded on the 19th, but I wasn't able to identify the month.

- On 28 September 1651, Henricus Hülshoff, son of another Henricus, was baptized[17]. His mother's name is illegible. The younger Henricus would be barely old enough to be the father of Johannes David Hülshoff [ID 1602], our earliest confirmed Hülshoff ancestor, but I found no evidence suggesting this, and there are better candidates presented below.

- On the 25th of July in 1658, there is a very interesting entry[18], shown below:

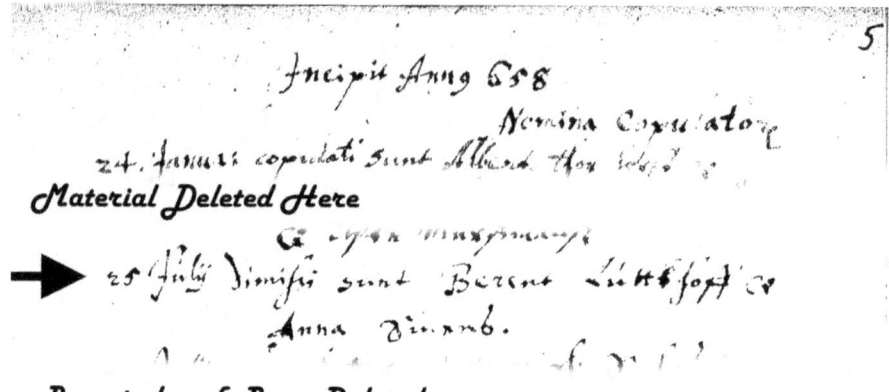

Note the entry in the marriage register "25 Julÿ Dimisis sunt Berent Hülshoff et Anna Din......[19]." This Latin entry translates to "Berent Hülshoff and Anna Din...... are dissolved," which apparently indicates an annulment, separation, or divorce – all of which were highly unusual for 1658.

- On March 11, 1659[20], Albert Hülshoff and Anna ...... baptized a son named Albert. Albert and Anna are the right age to be parents of our earliest confirmed Hülshoff ancestor, but no connection has been established.

- On 30 May 1659[21], Herman Hülshoff and Anna Astin...... baptized a child named "Caspares" or something similar. Herman and this Anna are also the right age to be parents of our earliest confirmed Hülshoff ancestor but, again, I have been unable to establish a definitive connection.

There are other entries that may be Hülshoffs as well, but the quality of the source was such that I couldn't be certain. Suggestive as all these entries may be, having been recorded in the area of Hül's Hoff, they do not conclusively

---

[17] ibid. "Kirchenbuch Nr. 3: Taufen 1641-1665," page 2, row 15.
[18] ibid. "Kirchenbuch Nr. 4: Taufen 1656-1658; Trauungen 1656-1658; Toten 1656-1658," page 5, rows 15 and 16.
[19] This is possibly "Dinaub," but I couldn't make it out. All other entries follow the form "copulati sunt" ("are joined together" e.g. the entry above); this is the only instance I found that says "dimisis sunt."
[20] ibid. "Kirchenbuch Nr. 5: Taufen 1659-; Trauungen 1659-; Toten 1659," page 6 (left side), rows 17-18.
[21] ibid. page 7 (right side), rows 3-4.

prove that our Hülshoff ancestors lived in Havixbeck during the sixteenth and seventeenth centuries, but additional circumstantial evidence of such a connection will be presented below when we discuss the oldest Hülshoff known to be in our line.

Anna Margareta Thoben – the Woman from Dingel (3 Mar 1665-)

Our earliest confirmed ancestors in the Kloppenburg area of Oldenburg in northern Germany seem to be my 6th great-grandmother Margareta Thoben $^{ID\ 1603}$ and her parents Johann Thoben $^{ID\ 1660}$ and Wibbeke Strahtmans $^{ID\ 1661}$. Margareta was born on March 3rd 1665 in the little town of Dingel. "Little" is perhaps an understatement, since the town, just northwest of Kappel[22] about a third of the way to Kloppenburg[23], consisted of only two houses at that time. The Thoben family had earlier come from Vechta[24], a town somewhat southeast of Kappel. See a map from this period reproduced on page 2. Interestingly, in all extant records I've located subsequent to her marriage (see below), Margareta is listed as "Margareta von Dingel," (i.e. "Margaret of Dingel") rather than by her given surname of Thoben.

Johannes David Hülshoff (circa 1667 - 1717)

Johannes David Hülshoff $^{ID\ 1602}$, my 6th great-grandfather, was born in about 1667, and is our earliest confirmed Hülshoff ancestor. David became a dragoner[25], which might allow us to infer a few things: he was likely not the oldest son in his family, and he was likely reasonably well educated for the period. We first find reference to him near Kappeln, where he was stationed at Gut Swede under Captain von Milckau in the latter part of the seventeenth century. Although his origins aren't known for certain, we do know that the military forces in Kappeln had been sent from the general area of Münster[26], so it seems reasonable that he *may* have come from Burg Hülshoff (i.e. von Hülshoff). If that were the case, we might also speculate that David was possibly a son of Albert or Herman Hülshoff, or even the younger Henricus Hülshoff, but there is insufficient evidence to state this one way or the other.

---

[22] Kappel is also called Cappel, or Kappeln and Cappeln depending on the source and time period.
[23] Kloppenburg is also called Cloppenburg. "C" and "K" spellings are used indiscriminately in German records of this period.
[24] My Dutch fifth cousin Sebastian Hulshoff has informed me that the Thobens are an old family whose roots can be traced back to at least 1547 in Vechta, but I haven't attempted to do this.
[25] A Dragoner was an elite, usually literate, and often reasonably well educated soldier trained to be equally competent as a foot soldier or mounted cavalryman. The Dragoners would have been the seventeenth century's equivalent of today's Special Forces.
[26] The trip from Münster to Kloppenburg today takes about an hour and a half on the A1 Highway.

On April 14th 1697, Johannes David Hülshoff [ID 1602] and Anna Margareta Thoben [ID 1603], then aged about 30 and 32 respectively, were married in Kappeln.

David and Margareta had six children, the third of whom was Johannes Henricus [ID 1606], who lived from March 12th 1704 to February 28th 1757. Henricus was the first of these to be born in Krappendorf rather than Kappeln, indicating that the family had settled there sometime between 1700 and 1704.

Children and Grandchildren of Johannes David Hülshoff & Anna Margareta Thoben

To retain a focus on our direct line, the following section provides only a brief commentary on David and Margareta's children and grandchildren.

- Joannes Otto Hülshoff [ID 1604] (born 13 Mar 1698)
- Catharina Maria Hülshoff [ID 1605] (born 6 Sep 1700)
- **Joannes Henricus Hülshoff** [ID 1606], our direct ancestor, will be discussed in more detail beginning on page 7 below.
- Frideric Godfrid Hülshoff [ID 1607] (born about 1708), married twice. With Maria Elisabeth Peltscher [ID 1611], whom he married on 10 August 1734, he had the following children:

  Theodorus Henricus Hülshoff [ID 1614] (born 6 Aug 1735)
  Christian Antonius Hülshoff [ID 1615] (born 10 Aug 1738)
  Maria Gertrudis Hülshoff [ID 1616] (born 22 Oct 1739)

  After Maria Elisabeth's death on 9 November 1739, Frideric married Anna Gesina Luers [ID 1612] (- 9 Jan 1772), who died on January 9th 1772. The entry in the St. Andreas Katholisch Kirche Kirchenbuch recording her death is shown below:.

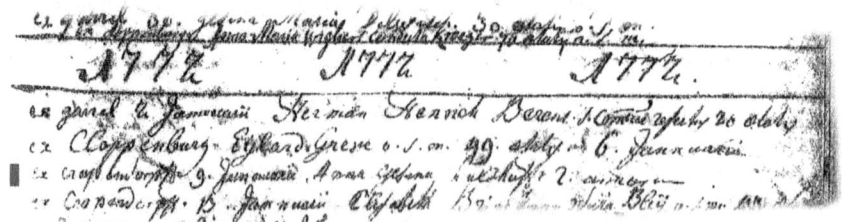

Frideric had three more children with Anna Gesina Luers:

Casparus Bernardus Hülshoff [ID 1617] (born 18 Feb 1743)
Maria Elisabeth Hülshoff [ID 1618] (31 Mar 1748 - 19 Jan 1749)
Anna Gertrudis Winanda Hülshoff [ID 1619] (20 Nov 1760 - 2 Oct 1763)

- Johan Godfrid Hülshoff [ID 1608] (born 19 Apr 1710), married Anna Gesina Thoben [ID 1613] (abt 1719 - 6 May 1791), and had four children.
  Anna Margahreta Hülshoff [ID 1620] (born 20 Jun 1742)
  Maria Gertrudis Hülshoff [ID 1621] (born 26 Oct 1745)
  Maria Christina Bernardina Hülshoff [ID 2978] (23 May 1750 - 20 Jun 1753)
  Helena Maria Hülshoff [ID 1622] (born 21 Aug 1752)
- Johan David Hülshoff [ID 1609] (born 15 Jan 1714)

The Luers and Anna Margahreta Luers (20 Jan 1710 - 20 Feb 1771)

My 5th great-grandmother Anna Margahreta Luers [ID 1610] was born in Visbeck, Germany, on January 20th 1710 to Heinrich Luers [ID 2980] and Gertrud Thoben [ID 2981] [27]. I haven't pursued any earlier history for this family. Anna Margahreta is the sister of Anna Gesina mentioned earlier.

Joannes Henricus Hülshoff (12 Mar 1704 - 28 Feb 1757)

Henricus [ID 1606] married Anna Margahreta Luers in about 1732 when he was 28 and Anna was 22. The couple had seven sons, the fourth of which was our ancestor Joannes Gerhardus Hülshoff [ID 1626] who lived from June 21st 1742 to May 14th 1820.

Most of Henricus' other direct descendants eventually migrated to the Netherlands and some of those eventually continued on to Australia[28]. His grandson Franciscus Henricus's [ID 1633] great-granddaughter Josephine Hulshoff [ID 1776], who lived from 1846 to 1930, seems to be the last of the Hülshoffs to reside in Kloppenburg.

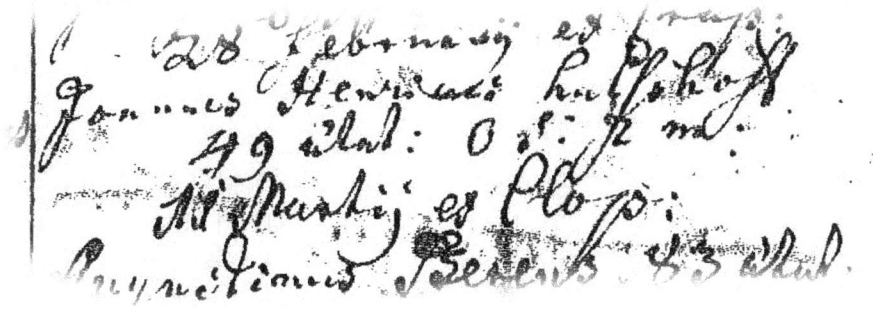

---

[27] She is presumably related to Henricus' mother, but I haven't explored the Thoben line sufficiently to say how. See footnote 22. The Luers and Thobens appear often in extant records of this period.

[28] Their descendants include the aforementioned Sebastian Hulshoff [ID 1671] of Amsterdam, and my fourth-cousin-once-removed Marcel Hulshoff [ID 2023] of Perth, Australia. I have corresponded and exchanged information with both of these distant cousins. There were already some Hulshoffs in the Netherlands as early as 1604 (there is a Hulshof [sic] birth recorded there) although it isn't clear if or how these are related.

The Kirchenbuch entry from St. Andreas Katholisch Kirche recording Joannes Henricus Hülshoff's death on February 28, 1757 is shown above. Note that Henricus' age reported here is 49 years and 2 months, which might make his birth year 1705 rather than 1704.[29]

His wife, my 5th great-grandmother Anna Margahreta, died in Crapendorf fourteen years later on the 20th of February 1771. Her death at age 60 years and 5 months, as well as that of her ten day old grandson Joanny Antonius Hülshoff [ID 1635] two days earlier, was reported in the Kirchenbuch entry seen below.

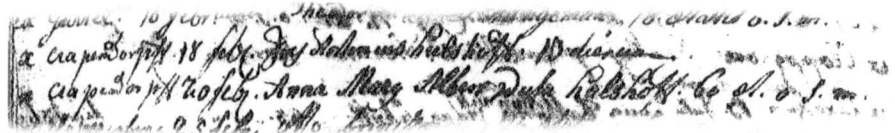

1771 entries in St. Andreas Katholisch Kirchenbuch
Report of the deaths of Anna Margahreta (Luers) Hülshoff and her grandson Joanny Antonius.

Joanny Antonius Hülshoff was the fourth child of Joannes Gerhard [I] [ID 1626] (our button-maker ancestor) and his first wife Anna Maria Macke.

Children of Joannes Henricus Hülshoff & Anna Margahreta Luers

In order to retain a focus on our direct line, the following section will provide only the names of each of Henricus and Margareta's children, since I haven't located any further information on any but their fifth child, who is our ancestor.

- Anna Marghareta Dorothea Hülshoff [ID 2979] (born 17 APR 1733)
- Johanes David Hülshoff [ID 1623] (born 7 OCT 1735)
- Joannes Henricus Hülshoff [ID 1624] (born 22 FEB 1737)
- Fridericus Godefridus Hülshoff [ID 1625] (born 2 MAY 1740)
- **Joannes Gerhardus Hülshoff** [ID 1626] (21 Jun 1742 - 14 May 1820), our direct ancestor, will be discussed in more detail beginning below.
- Eylardus Henricus Hülshoff [ID 1627] (11 MAY 1745 – 28 JAN 1799)
- Catherina Elizabeth Hülshoff [ID 2977] (born 16 DEC 1748)

---

[29] The European custom was (and is) to consider a child's age to be one year at birth ("age one" therefore, is interpreted as indicating that a child is in its "first year," rather than as having lived for at least one year, as it does in the U.S). This custom must be considered when estimating birth years from ages given in extant vital records. This particular age/birth year discrepancy is not, therefore, a significant concern. In Math terms, Europeans use ordinal age numbering, while we use cardinal numbering.

- Johannes Antonnius Hülshoff [ID 1628] (born 12 Jun 1752)
- Johannes David Hülshoff [ID 1629] (born 22 Apr 1755)

Joannes Gerhardus Hülshoff [I] – Button-Maker (21 Jun 1742 - 14 May 1820)

Joannes Gerhardus Hülshoff [ID 1626], the first of several ancestors of that name[30], listed his profession as "Knopfenmacher" ("button maker"). He married Anna Maria Macke[31] [ID 1630] (abt 1742 – June 20th 1783) in Kloppenburg on November 22nd 1763, and together they had nine children, all born in Kloppenburg, the last one on October 27th 1778. A little over a year after Anna Maria Macke's death, on October 2nd 1784, at age 42, he married his second wife Anna Maria Gertrud Kruse [ID 1631], about whom I've been unable to locate any information.

Gertrud Kruse's date of death is unknown, but must have occurred between 1820 and 1830. In January of 1820, she and her husband (who died only a few months later) appear as the sponsors of their son at his wedding to Maria Angela Klaus. This record is shown on page 12. By the time of his second marriage to our ancestor Dorothea Antoinette Janssens, however, his parents were only listed as the deceased Joannes Gerhardus Hülshoff and (incorrectly) Anna Maria Macke. The record of this second wedding can be seen on page 13.

Child of Joannes Gerhardus Hulshoff & Anna Maria Macke

The children from Gerhard's first marriage to Anna Maria Macke [ID 1630] (abt 1742 - 20 Jun 1783) are:

- Anna Marghareta Wilhemina Hülshoff [ID 1632] (11 Mar 1765 - 19 Oct 1841) married Joannes Henricus Ravensberg [ID 1644] in Cloppenburg on 15 April 1788 and had at least three children:
  Nicolaus Ravensberg [ID 1648] (born 28 Jan 1798)
  Heinricus Antonius Ravensberg [ID 1649] (born 1 Apr 1806)
  Fridericus Anton Henricus Ravensberg [ID 1650] (15 Mar 1809 - 2 Apr 1809)
- Franciscus Henricus Joseph Hülshoff [ID 1633] (3 Nov 1766 - 14 Jul 1841) married Maria Engel Carolina Quadmann [ID 1645] (born 6 Jun 1779),

---

[30] I will occasionally use the notations [I], [II], and [III] to identify these when the discussion might get confusing. There is no indication whatever that they ever used such designators themselves.

[31] My fifth cousin Sebastian Hulshoff (see footnote 27 believes this surname is Funke, not Macke, but I've included a document that mentions her (the record of her step-son Joannes Gerard's second wedding, where she is referred to as deceased) on page 13 so you can decide for yourself.

daughter of Gerardus Henricus Quadmann and Anna Maria Angela Bernardina Hellman. Henry and Maria had at least four children:

Maria Angela Hulshoff [ID 1651] (born 13 Sep 1806)

Franz Heinrich Hulshoff [ID 1652] (3 Apr 1810 - 12 Feb 1878). Franz and his wife Anna Katherina Bernardina Kuhlmann had at least seven children; the first of these, Josephine Bernadine Engeline Hulshoff [ID 1776] (30 Jul 1846 – 1930), was the last of the Hulshoffs known to live in Cloppenburg (she resided there her whole life).

Gerhardus Hulshoff [ID 1653] (born 9 May 1813)

Henricus Hulshoff [ID 1654] (born 27 Feb 1821)

- Anna Gesina Bernardina Hülshoff [ID 1634] (4 Aug 1769 - 19 Oct 1841)

- Johannes Antonius Hülshoff [ID 1635] (5 Feb 1771 - 18 Feb 1771). The report of his death appears just before the report of his Grandmother's death; see page 8.

- Anna Catherina Hülshoff [ID 1636] (born 1 Feb 1772)

- Henricus Godefridus Hülshoff [ID 1637] (23 Apr 1774 - 19 Aug 1849), married Anna Maria Husing [ID 1646], and had at least one child:

Johann Heinrich Hülshoff [ID 3246] (1808 – 1891). Johann Heinrich married Elisabeth Schrunder [ID 3247] in 1843; their third child Bernard Joseph Anton Hulshoff [ID 1662], born 5 Oct 1845, came to the United States from Lingen 25 Jun 1866 on the SS New York as "Bernard Huelshoff"[32], and listed his age as 21 when he arrived. He married in Iowa and shows up in Dubuque, Iowa in the 1880 US Census. He had at least six children.

- Johannes Henricus Hülshoff [ID 1638] (born 11 Jul 1775), married Gesina Elisabeth Lockhorn [ID 1647] in 1808 in Lingen, and had at least five children:

Joann Anton Hülshoff [ID 2068] (Dec 1810 - Dec 1810)

Heinrich Godfricus Hülshoff [ID 1656] (11 Mar 1816 - 30 Jan 1909)

Bernard Heinrich Anton Hülshoff [ID 1657] (Dec 1819 - 4 Jun 1844)

Maria Caroline Elisabeth Hülshoff [ID 1658] (born Apr 1822)

Carl Johann Hülshoff [ID 1659] (4 Jan 1825 - 1 Feb 1913)

- Anna Maria Hülshoff [ID 1639] (25 Feb 1777 - 22 Apr 1779)

- Everardus Hermanus Hülshoff [ID 1640] (27 Oct 1778 - 16 May 1787)

---

[32] See mention of Bernard Huelshoff on page 6.

Child of Joannes Gerhardus Hulshoff & Anna Maria Gertrud (Maria) Kruse

Our ancestor Joannes Gerard Hülshoff ID 665, whom I will refer to occasionally as "[II]", was the only child from his father's second marriage to Maria Kruse. He is discussed beginning on page 11 below.

The Janssens and
Dorothea Antoinette Janssens (27 Jan 1798 – 21 Jan 1878)

Twelve years after the birth of the birth of Joannes Gerardus [II] Hülshoff ID 665, on 27 Jan 1798, in Kloppenburg proper, Victor Janssens ID 2384 and his wife Anna Catherina Meyer ID 2385 had a daughter Dorothea Antonetta ID 13. Dorothea would become the oldest (but not the first) of our Hulshoff ancestors to migrate to the United States, and is the earliest ancestor buried in the Hulshoff plot at Holy Redeemer Cemetery. A segment of the Saint Andreas parish register listing her birth is shown below.

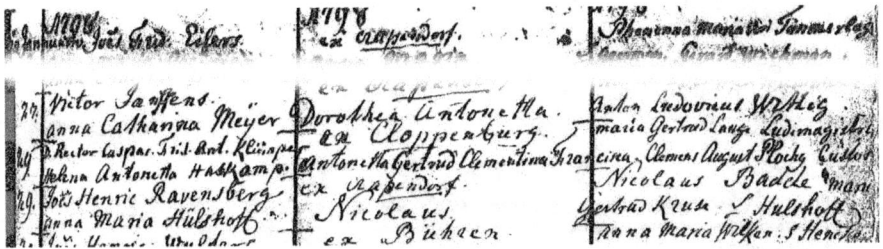

January 27, 1798 St. Andreas Kirchenbuch entry for Dorothea Antonetta Janssens.

The second entry after the Janssens birth is for the birth of Nicolaus Ravensberg ID 1648, son of "Jos. Henric Ravensberg" ID 1644 and Anna Maria (here abbreviated from Marghareta) Hülshoff ID 1632, our button-maker's oldest child and half-sister of his youngest child, our ancestor and the second Johannes Gerard ID 665.

Joannes Gerard Hulshoff [II] (18 Jan 1786 – >May 1830 / >1860)

Joannes Gerard [II] Hülshoff ID 665, was born on 18 January 1786 in the small town of Crapendorf (Krappendorf), which lies just about a mile[33] south-southwest of Kloppenburg, to Joannes Gerhardus [I] Hülshoff ID 1626 and his second wife Anna Maria Gertrud Kruse ID 1631. The record of his birth, from the parish registers of St. Andreas Catholic Church in Kloppenburg, which served the entire area, is shown below.

---

[33] A German mile at the time is not quite equivalent to our current mile, but I have been unable to determine its exact length. A Westphalen mile was another commonly used measure in the area at that time.

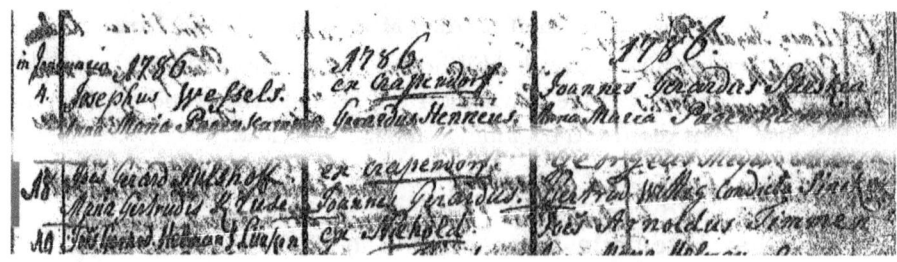

Segment of January 18, 1786 entry for the birth of "Joannes Gerardus" [ID 665]
Joannes Gerardus is listed as the son of "Joes Gerard Hülshoff" and "Anna Gertrudis Kruse"; taken from St. Andreas Katholisch Kirche Kirchenbuch.

Joannes Gerard [II] was the youngest of his father's ten children. His older half-siblings ranged in age from just under eighteen to just over five when their mother died, and the oldest wouldn't be married for another five years.

Like his father, the second Joannes Gerard married twice. On January 23rd 1820, at age 34, he married Maria Engel (a Germanic form of Angela) Klaus [ID 1641] in Kloppenburg, with whom he had at least three children.

23 January 1820 entry in St. Andreas Katholische Kirchenbuch (Cloppenburg)
The marriage of Joannes Gerard Hulshoff [ID 665] *and Maria Angela Klaus* [ID 1641]

Children of Joannes Gerard Hülshoff & Maria Angela Klaus

The record of Gerard's first marriage to Maria Angela Klaus [ID 1641] (about 1797 - 8 May 1828)[34] is shown above[35]. Their children are:

- Joannes Caspar (Caspar) Hülshoff [ID 1642] (born 21 Jun 1821). Caspar, a godson of his oldest aunt (Anna Marghareta Wilhemina Hülshoff [ID 1632]) came to the US on the ship Eutaw from Bremen to Baltimore in 1845. According to the manifest, he was heading for Cincinnati, but I have located no subsequent trace of him in the United States. as will be discussed below, there is a possibility that he either died or returned to Germany between 1845 and 1855, but this isn't certain.
- Maria Elizabeth Catharina Hülshoff [ID 2383] (born 6 May 1823)
- Joannes Henricus Hülshoff [ID 1643] (born 15 Jul 1826

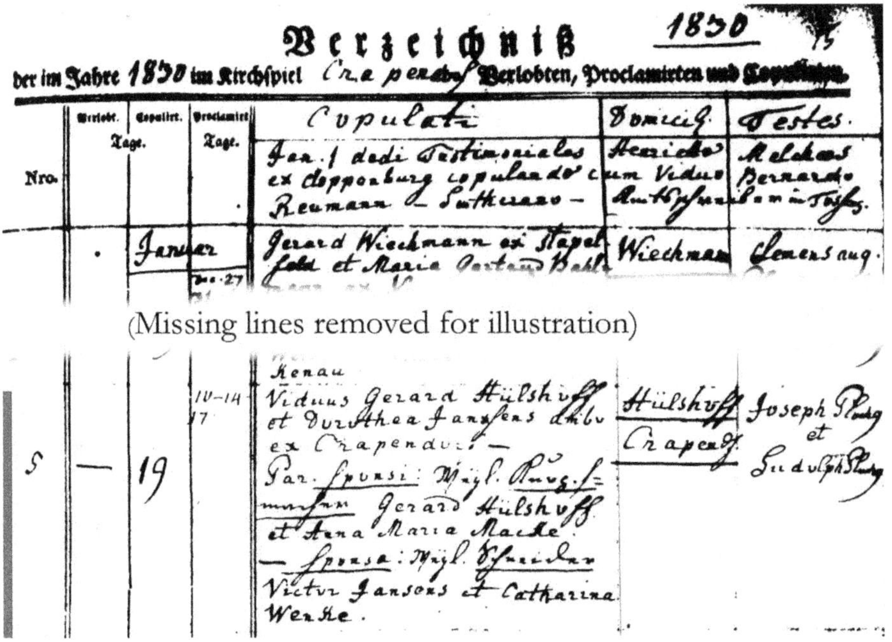

(Missing lines removed for illustration)

19 January 1830 entry in St. Andreas Katholische Kirchenbuch (Cloppenburg)
The marriage of Joannes Gerard Hulshoff [ID 665] and Dorothea Antoinetter Janssen [ID 13]

---

[34] "Maria Angela" is sometimes listed as "Maria Engel" in the extant records. Maria Engel and Maria Angela Klaus are the same person, however.

[35] The column headings "Copulati," "Domicilus," and "Testus" can be translated as "Marriages," "Residence," and "Witnesses." The three date columns are for the month, date, and the dates the marriage banns were read in the church during the weeks leading up to the marriage.

After Angela's death on 8 May 1828, my 3rd great grandfather married the aforementioned Dorothea Antoinette Jansens [ID 13] in Kloppenburg on January 19th 1830, with whom he had one child, the third Johann Gerhard [ID 12] on February 9th 1831. Their marriage record is shown above.

The columns shown on the left of the page are interpreted as follows: the number 5 indicates that this is the fifth wedding reported in 1830. The sequence of numbers "10-14-17" indicates the three dates on which their marriage banns were announced at the church services, and "Viduus" is the Latin word for Widower. At the time of this marriage, Gerard [II] was about 44 years old and Dorothea was about 32. This second of the Joannes Gerard Hülshoffs lived at least until 1860, but I've been unable to locate any record of his death.

After her husband's death, Dorothea Antoinette Janssens went to the U.S. to join her son and his family in Baltimore, where she died in January of 1876.

Child of Joannes Gerard Hülshoff & Dorothea Antoinette Janssens

Also like his father, Joannes Gerard [ID 665] had only one child with his second wife Dorothea [ID 13], which was our ancestor Johann Gerhard [III] Hulshoff [ID 12]. His story begins on page 17.

Northern Europe in the mid-nineteenth Century

As will be discussed below, Gerhard and Dorothea's son Gerhard [II] would become the first of our Hülshoff ancestors to migrate to the United States. Although it is possible that news of America may have reached him from his older half-brother Caspar, who himself had sailed to Baltimore on his way to Cincinnati earlier, there is no evidence I'm aware of that would suggest a specific reason for what had to be a significant and difficult undertaking. It therefore seems appropriate to briefly discuss the general state of the Hülshoff's homeland in the mid-nineteenth century in order to get a glimpse of what life there may have been like at the time they made the decision to leave.

The area we now know as Germany was only then entering the century during which it discovered and refined its modern identity as a group of related citizenry. With Napoleon's earlier adventures still fresh in the minds of the older generation, the threat of yet another invasion by the French in 1840 allowed a greater sense of Germanic nationalism to coalesce.

Over the next fifteen years until our Hülshoff ancestors departed, a wide area of Europe experienced aberrations in weather that significantly affected agricultural production. Although this, coupled with the increasing shifts in the political atmosphere, likely made for a stressful existence, it seems likely that our Hülshoff ancestors were more likely "pulled" to America by its promise of self-determination rather than "pushed" by conditions in Europe, since there is no evidence that they were particularly impoverished.

Banhofstrasse (Train Station Road) in Kloppenburg, late 19th century

That being said, it must be noted that travel by ship to America during this period was not something to be undertaken lightly. The document on the facing page, dated only seven years earlier than the Hülshoff family's voyage, gives an indirect but rather vivid picture of ship travel in the 19th century.

Hulshoff Origins?

Corner of the 11th century Hüls Castle in Burg Hülshoff, Havixbeck.

The inset shows an enlargement of the modern plaque identifying the structure.

See the site below for a virtual tour:
https://www.360cities.net/image/havixbeck-huelshoff-gartensalon-2000

An early "Passenger Bill of Rights" passed by the U.S. Congress in May 1848.

Elizabethe (Lizette) [Surname Unknown] (22 Jul 1829 - 19 May 1907)

According to her headstone, my 2nd great-grandmother, known as Lizette, was born on 22 July 1829 in Hannover – about seventy U.S. miles southeast of the Oldenburg/Cloppenburg area where the Hülshoff family was living at the time. I haven't been able to locate any German records that correspond to that birth date, however, so her surname and parents are so far unknown.

John Gerhardt Hülshoff [III] (9 Feb 1831 - 23 Feb 1916)

My 2nd great-grandfather, the third Johann Gerhardt [ID 12] was born in Crapendorf in 1831, the only son of his father's second wife. The witnesses shown in the extract from his birth record below are "Joann Janssens" and "Maria Anna Ravensberg (born Bleÿ)" [ID 2420] (our button maker's granddaughter-in-law, married to Nicolaus Ravensburg [ID 1648], the son of Anna Marghareta Wilhemina Hulshoff [ID 1632]). Joann Janssens seems to be Dorothea Antoinette's brother, but I can't confirm that.

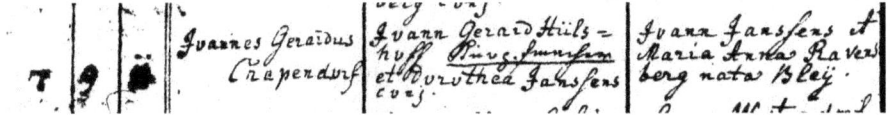

9 February 1831 entry in St. Andreas Katholische Kirchenbuch:
The birth of Johannus Gerhardus [ID 12]

Gerhardt married Lizette before they came to the United States, but I've been unable to locate any record of their marriage in the Cloppenburg area. This may or may not mean that they had already left that area, or that Gerhardt himself had relocated to the Hannover[36] area, but for now that will be left for someone else to explore.

Johann Gerhard [ID 12] (listed as "Joh. Hulshof, 25"), his wife "Lisette Hulshof, 26" [ID 10], and a daughter "Antoinette Hulshof, 1 month" [ID 1327], arrived in New Orleans, Louisiana on November 8th 1855 aboard the bark Eberhard, which originated in Bremen, Germany[37]. The end destination for Gerhard was listed as "ditto" ("St. Louis"), but his wife and daughter's were specifically listed as "Louisville."[38] As can be seen in the portions of the manifest from that ship shown below, the Hulshofs were in the section of the bark described as "between decks," a medium class designation for the time. Typical conditions aboard such ships have already been described.

---

[36] Hannover is a major city about seventy miles southeast of Cloppenburg.
[37] Bremen is the name of the overall area which encompassed the towns where the Hulshoffs lived, and is also the name of a city located on the North Sea about seventy miles northwest of where the Hulshoffs lived. Ships listed as departing from Bremen usually left from the port of Bremerhaven just north of the city of Bremen, however.
[38] This seems inexplicable, but the clerk may have lost his place on the line.

1665 – 1983

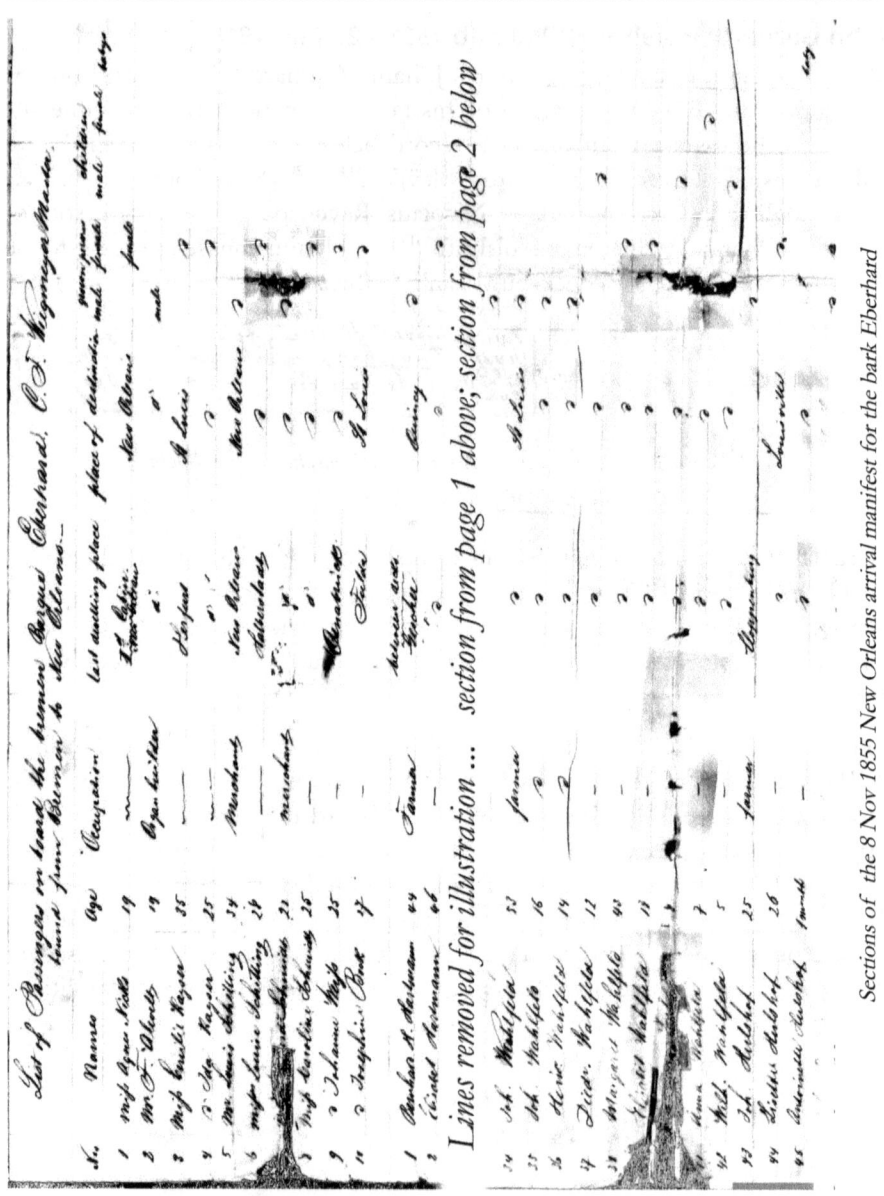

Sections of the 8 Nov 1855 New Orleans arrival manifest for the bark Eberhard

I have found nothing to suggest why they were going to Louisville or St. Louis, but that is likely the reason they chose to enter the United States at the port of New Orleans. Immigrants from northern Germany more typically traveled to an east-coast port such as Baltimore or Philadelphia unless they intended to settle in the Midwest – this possibly indicates that they may have believed Gerhard's older half-brother Caspar [ID 1642], was living there.

Regardless of what caused them to go to the east coast, their second child Henry [ID 2] was born in Baltimore, Maryland in about 1858, so the Hülshoffs apparently settled there and purchased a home soon after their arrival.

I was unable to determine the actual departure date for the Eberhard's 1855 voyage, but other records suggest that the ship's normal trips to New Orleans averaged about sixty days. Antoinette's age at arrival, given as one month, clearly implies that she was born during the voyage. On the 1860 census[39], her birthplace was listed as Louisiana, but this is likely because the birth would have had to be recorded there upon arrival. A model of the Eberhard from the Focke-Museum in Bremen is shown to the right.

1860 U.S. Census extract showing Gerhard Hulshoff's *family and* Dorie Johnson.

In addition to Antoinette and their now 2-year-old son Henry, this census shows Gerhard's family living at 2725 (unlisted street) in Baltimore, along with a woman named Dorie Johnson, aged 61. Others living with the Hulshoffs included Charles Oldenbaugh, age 18, a shoemaker's apprentice,

---

[39] National Archives Census Microfilm: Series m653, reel 464, page 70, shown above. Antoinette's name is listed here as Annette. Whether this was a nickname, a form of "Americanization," or a census taker's mistake isn't known, but the name Antoinette is common in earlier and later generations of the family.

and the Irish immigrants John and Katherine Kern[40]. Charles was likely Gerhard's apprentice, suggesting that his business was going well. This would seem to be confirmed by the entries in the "value of real estate" and "value of personal estate" columns of the census.

Earlier, on April 20th 1858, two years and five months after the Hulshoffs arrived in America, the ship Saxonia arrived in Baltimore from Bremerhaven. The image below shows a portion of the passenger manifest for that ship.

Page from the 20 April 1858 arrival manifest for the Saxonia

Here can be seen the arrival of a nine-person family named "Johnson." The interesting thing about this is that it is the only reference in extant passenger arrival records to anyone named Dorothea or Dorothy Janssens or Johnson that I was able to locate in the period from 1856 to 1876. One of the four Dorothea Johnsons listed here[41] is age 58 – an excellent match for Dorothea Janssens, although not in itself very compelling.

---

[40] These Kerns, having come from Belfast, are *apparently* unrelated to the Kern ancestors discussed in Sections II and III of this book, who came from Germany.

[41] In the order in which the Johnsons appear on the manifest, they are: Eleonore, age 33 (on previous page not shown above); Jens (male), age 9; Dorothea, age 7; S. (male), age 35 (Farmer); Dorothea, age 32 (Wife); Maria, age 9; Dorothea, age 6; and Juergen, age 3. The Dorothea in question, age 58, was listed last. Because these are listed together, it seems certain that they were part of a single family, although we can only speculate on their exact relationships.

However, ...In the 1860 census illustrated above, Dorie Johnson's relationship to the head-of-household Gerhard Hulshoff isn't specified, but several factors make it interesting to engage in a little speculation. First, she is approximately 31 years older than Gerhard[42], and also comes from Oldenburg, suggesting that, at least, she and Gerhard *may* have been acquainted in Germany. Her position as the first non-Hulshoff in the listing suggests that she may have been an older relative of either Gerhard's or Lizette's[43]. We know that Gerhard's mother, Dorothea Antoinette Janssens Hulshoff, eventually came to the United States, since she is buried with the rest of the Hulshoffs at Holy Redeemer Cemetery in Baltimore, but I have been unable to find any reference to her under the Hulshoff name in either the 1860 or 1870 U.S. Census listings.

The coincidence of Dorie Johnson's name and date of birth[44] being so similar to that of Gerhard's mother Dorothea Janssens suggests that Dorie may in fact *be* Gerhard's mother, although the fact that she is using the surname Johnson (the English variant) might be viewed as arguing against this. On the other hand, it was the custom of Europeans to list their original surnames on official records, so it could very well be her; it also would have been simpler to list herself as a Johnson if she wished to be processed with her family on arrival. If she were using her birth surname, however, we still need to locate her in the 1870 census, since, if she were here in 1860, and died here in 1876, she was likely to have been here in 1870. Unfortunately, I have been unsuccessful in locating any Dorie, Dorothy, or Dorothea with the surname Janssens, Johnson, or anything similar in the 1870 census. This seems particularly strange given that no less than four persons named Dorothea Johnson arrived on the Saxonia!

A reference to her death record, "1876/01/21 07663 CR 48,047," which I have been unable to locate, gives her name as "Dora Hulshoff," indicating that she certainly was known by a shortened form of her first name.

---

[42] And, given the European age calculations, the right age to be his mother.
[43] Household servants, boarders, and others not related to the head-of-household were supposed to be, and almost always were, identified as such in the census listings.
[44] Our ancestor Dorothea Janssens Hulshoff's date of birth is given on her tombstone as 27 Jan 1798; given Dorie Johnson's age of 61 on the 1860 census, her year of birth would be 1799 or, if she were reporting her "European-Style" age, it would be 1798. See footnote 28 on page 7 regarding ages.

American Citizenship

Family name: HÜLSHOFF
Given name or names: JOHN-GERHARD
Address: BALTIMORE, MD.
Certificate no. (or vol. and page)
Title and location of court
Country of birth or allegiance: OLDENBURG
When born (or age)
Date and port of arrival in U. S.
Date of naturalization
Names and addresses of witnesses
U. S. DEPARTMENT OF JUSTICE, Immigration and Naturalization Service. Form N-35 (Old 1-IF)
ADDITIONAL INFORMATION IN COURT RECORD
Certificate canceled (date and court)
Why canceled
Expatriated
Deceased
Other facts of record: DI. U.S.C.C. 3-2-1858 T.S. #9 Folio 37
U. S. GOVERNMENT PRINTING OFFICE 16—17302

Family name: HÜLSHOFF
Given name or names: JOHN GERHARD
Address
Certificate no. (or vol. and page)
Title and location of court
Country of birth or allegiance: OLDENBERG
When born (or age)
Date and port of arrival in U. S.
Date of naturalization
Names and addresses of witnesses
U. S. DEPARTMENT OF JUSTICE, Immigration and Naturalization Service. Form N-35 (Old 1-IF)
ADDITIONAL INFORMATION IN COURT RECORD
Certificate canceled (date and court)
Why canceled
Expatriated
Deceased
Other facts of record: D.I. U.S.D.C. BALTO. MD. 3-2-1858
U. S. GOVERNMENT PRINTING OFFICE 16—17302

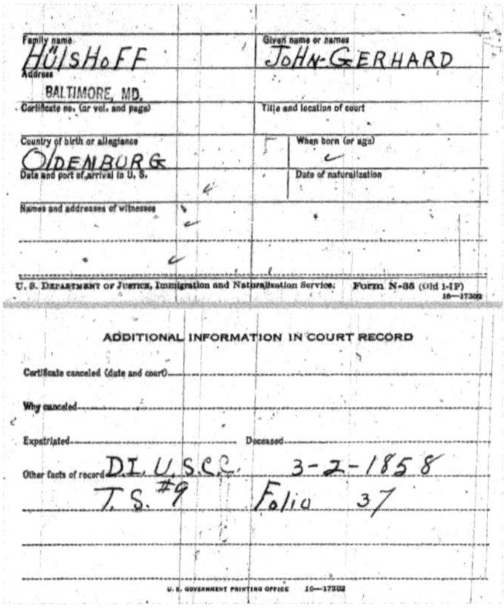

On April 25, 1865, after the Civil War, John Gerhard Hulshoff and his family became United States citizens. Note that, by the third visit, shown on the right, he had dropped the umlaut over the 'u' in his last name – symbolic, one might suppose, of his final break with Germany.

Family name: HULSHOFF
Given name or names: JOHN GERHARD
Address
Certificate no. (or vol. and page): T.S. #9 FOLIO 77
Title and location of court: U.S.C.C. BALTO, MD.
Country of birth or allegiance: OLDENBURG
When born (or age)
Date and port of arrival in U. S.
Date of naturalization: 4-25-1865
Names and addresses of witnesses: MICHAEL PISTNER
U. S. DEPARTMENT OF JUSTICE, Immigration and Naturalization Service. Form N-35 (Old 1-IF)
ADDITIONAL INFORMATION IN COURT RECORD
Certificate canceled (date and court)
Why canceled
Expatriated
Deceased
Other facts of record
U. S. GOVERNMENT PRINTING OFFICE 16—17302

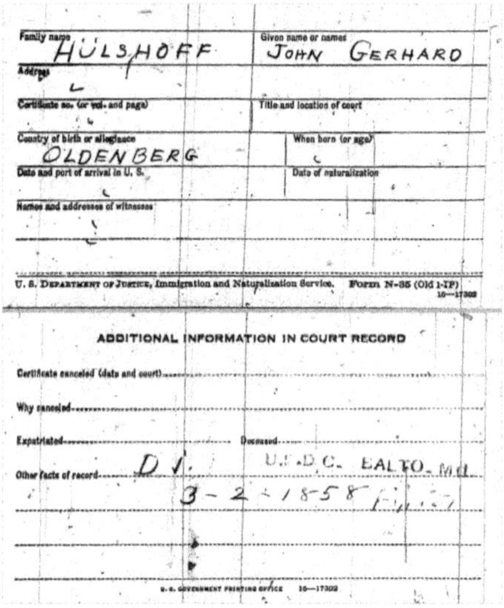

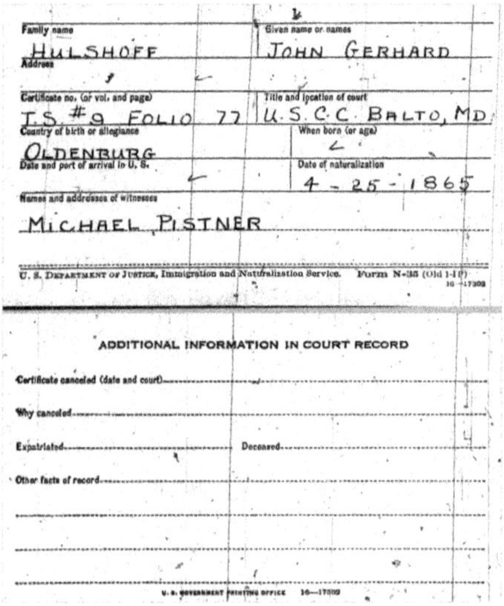

Gerhard first applied for naturalization and citizenship on March 2, 1858, just a little over two years after arriving in the country. He used the name John Gerhard Hülshoff. The three cards on this page from the Department of Immigration (U.S.C.C. T.S.#9, Folio 37) show John Gerhard Hulshoff's progression towards naturalization and citizenship. Under the immigration rules of the time, his naturalization would have covered Lizette and any children as well.

For reasons I can't determine, the 1900[45] census says that John immigrated in 1856 and had been in the United States for 44 years. The same census form reports that his wife Elizabeth immigrated in 1863 and had been in the United States for only 37 years. Interestingly, the responder wrote "N/A" (also incorrect) under the column for Naturalization.

There is nothing to suggest that Gerhard (now Gerard) served in the Civil War. As a boot-maker in Baltimore, however, one can speculate that, if he had set up shop himself by that time, business might have been brisk, since the military would have required a variety of leather products (e.g. cases, tack, etc.) as well as footwear; much of those supplies were procured in Baltimore.

By the time of the 1870 census, Gerhard (now having further Americanized his name to "George"), Lisetta (sic) and Annette were living at 445 (street name unlisted) in Baltimore, along with additional children Annie [ID 9], 9, Mary [ID 1294], 5, William [ID 1295], 3, and what appears to be "Hammond", age 8 months. See an illustration of this census page below:

1870 U.S. Census extract showing George (sic) Hulshoff's family.
(Series m593 reel 575 page 517)

The age makes it certain that this Hammond, their seventh and last child, is my great-grandfather Herman Hulshoff [ID 7], who was born on August 17th 1869. It isn't clear if "Hammond" is my misinterpretation of sloppy handwriting, the census taker's hearing or transcription mistake, or Herman's

---

[45] National Archives Census Microfilm: Series t623, reel 617, page 242. The relevant segment of this page is shown on page 31. I have also found no evidence that either John or Lizette ever returned to Europe. There is little doubt that the immigration information given in the 1900 census is incorrect.

actual given name, since I haven't been able to locate any Baltimore birth certificates or records for the period. The 1870 census does make it clear that Annette (or Antoinette [ID 1327]) and Annie [ID 9] were different children, the latter being five years younger than Annette.

Note the increase from the earlier census[46] in *Value of Real Estate* to $25,000, a substantial amount in 1870 (greater than $350,000 in 2003), likely indicating that he owned more property than just his home.

In 1870, there were two boarders, but the mysterious Dorie Johnson, who would still have been alive if she were actually Dorothea Antoinette Hulshoff, is not listed, and I have so far been unsuccessful in locating her.

Family tradition says that our immigrant ancestor Johann Gerhard Hulshoff was a "master boot maker" – a step up from the generic occupation of shoemaker recorded on the 1860 and 1870 censuses. Since the census generalized most occupations, this could very well be true, and the history of shoe making in general certainly suggests that he would not have had an apprentice or been a substantial real estate holder were he not a maker of higher-end footwear and possibly a wider variety of products. Up until about 1850, virtually all shoes were custom made, but the inventions of the Rolling Machine (1845) and Sewing Machine (1846), resulted by 1860 in the growing popularity of machine made shoes[47]. Boots and other custom leather products, however, still required a high level of manual skill. By 1864, after the Civil War, Johann Gerhard was listed in the Baltimore City Directory as a shoemaker, and remained listed for many years (see examples on pages 25 and 30.)

In January 1880, John G. Hulshoff was elected a Director of the German Fire Insurance Company of Baltimore. The only known surviving photograph of John was included in the booklet issued on the occasion of that company's 50th anniversary on March 17, 1915 and shown on page 26. John was present and was honored as the oldest living Director of the company.

---

[46] National Archives Census Microfilm: Series t623, reel 617, page 242. See illustration on page 31.

[47] These unfortunately came in only two sizes and a single width until the late 1800s, so there was a clear trade-off between having more affordable footwear and good arch support! But the handwriting was beginning to appear on the wall …

HUG — 293 — HUN

Hughes Mrs. Winifred, 126 s Castle
Hughes Winston N. plumber, 32 Block
Hughlett James, clerk, Hampden
Hughlett Martha, 399 w Fayette
Hughson Chas. L. 42 Cumberland
Hugle Julius, bookkeeper, 78 Lark
Huhn Christian, lab. Wilkens and Frederick av
Huhn Damian, butcher, 22 n Chester
Huhn Edward, boilermaker, 70 Harrison
Huhn Francis, tavern, 122 Greenmount av
Huhn Geo. huckster, 77 Johnson
Huhn Wm. P. moulder, 28 w Baltimore
Huiss Geo. lab. 34 n Spring
Huiss Mrs. Mary M. 182 n Broadway
Hulbert Mrs. Louisa, grocery, 65 McElderry
Huletz Joseph, lab. e Monument ext
Huling Chas. C. news agent, Fountain hotel
HULL, ATKINSON & CO (Wm. J. Hull, S. H. Hopkins) wholes. dry goods, 258 w Baltimore
Hull Frank C. canvasser, 44 e Chase
Hull Geo. coal and wood, 166 s Caroline, dw 101 s Ann
Hull H. P. salesman, 199 n Howard
Hull Robt. 199 n Howard
Hull Robert M. spring bed manufacturer, 88 Greenmount av, dw 44 e Chase
Hull T. B. & Co. (T. B. Hull, Chas. T. Matthews) com. merchts. 88 s Charles
Hull T. Burling, (T. E. H. & Co.) 15 Penn
Hull Wm. bookkeeper, 147 German
Hull Wm. shoemaker, 129 n Bond
Hull Wm G. V. teller Johnston Bros. & Co. 354 e Baltimore
Hull Wm. J. (H., Atkinson & Co.) 126 Lanvale
Hulle Mrs. Lizzie, 70 McElderry
Hulle Wm. drayman, 20 McElderry
Hullett David P. carpenter, 48 Brune
Hullett James, carter, 240 Franklin
Hullett John, carpenter, 240 Franklin
Hullivan Jane, porter, 331 w Baltimore
Hulman Theodore, wheelwright, 230 Central av
Hulls John, oils, paints, &c. 123 n Gay
Hulls Robt. F. painter, 97 Low
Hulse Chas. A. dyeing, 85 Mulberry and 239 s Charles
Hulse Emily, dyeing, 56 Saratoga, dw 140 s Sharp
Hulse G. T. painter, 138 n Eutaw
Hulse Henry, coachpainter, 141 s Sharp
Hulse James H. dyer, 80½ n Greene
Hulse Mrs. Mary, 50½ n Greene
Hulse Peter, lab. 26 Shakspear
Hulse Saml. oyster strainer, 5 Young
Huiseman C. builder, 195 Eastern av
Hulshoff J. Gerhard, shoemaker, 147 w Fayette
Hulsman Charlotte, mantuamkr. 245 Eastern av
Hulsman Mrs. Elizabeth, 32 n Bond
Hulsman Henry, grocery, 97 Cross
Hulsman Henry jr. machinist, 97 Cross
Hulsman Mrs. Kate, 187 Vine
Hulthaus Julius, tanner, 45 e Pratt
Hults Alfred, clerk, 143 e Lombard
Hults Alfred, clerk, 180 Lee
Hults Robert, R. H. & Co.) 119 Lee
Hults R. & Co. (Robt. Hults, Samuel A. Clickner) shoes, ne cor Calvert and Water
Hults Robert M. student, 189 Lee
Hults Wm. H. shoecutter, 189 Lee
Hultz Wm. P. cigarmaker, 431 e Eager
Huizer Fredk. dyer, 132 s Bond
Huizer Mrs. Maggie, confectionery, 132 s Bond
Hume James, fire department, 54 s Sharp

Hume Wm. driver Adams' Exp. 104 n Ann
Hume Wm. carpenter, 154 s Sharp
Humes James, fire dep't, 156 s Sharp
Humes James C. painter, 171 King
Humes Mrs. Mary, 39 Park av
Humes Wm. J. bricklayer, 336 Franklin
Hummel Anthony, barber, 953 w Baltimore
Hummel Augustus, shoemkr, 94 e Fayette
Hummel Geo. baker, 5 Biddle al
Hummel John, lab. 95 Lancaster
Hummer Geo. harness maker. 109 e Pratt
Hummer Henry, bricklayer, 9 Stockholm
Hummer Joseph, B. & O. R. R. 53 s Liberty
Humphrey O. E. sewing machines, 237 Penna av
Humphreys Andrew, lab. 10 Rupard
Humphreys Chas. 73 n Liberty
Humphreys David, clerk, American hotel
Humphreys Edw. blacksmith, 35 s Republican
Humphreys Mrs. Emma V. 357 n Broadway
Humphreys Richard, huckster, 54 Harford av
Humphreys Robt. H bookkeeper, 26 McCulloh
Humphreys Thos. fireman, 86 s Exeter
Humphreys Thos. W. jr. clerk, 234 e Fayette
Humphreys Thos. W. sr. purchasing agent fire department, 111 n Broadway
Humphrey's Wm. lab. 35 Elliott
Humphries Jas. salesman, 74 Harford av
HUMRICHOUSE, BAYLIES & CO. (C. W. Humrichouse, J. H. Baylies, W. H. Humrichouse, W. T. Baylies) wholesale grocers, 10 Commerce
Humrichouse C. W. (H., Baylies & Co.) 42 McCulloh
Humrichouse John R. police, 409 Saratoga
Humrichouse Wm. H. (H., Baylies & Co.) 42 McCulloh
Humur Geo. lab. s end of Clinton
Honckel Otto, agent, 17 Pearl
Honckel Philip, clerk, 37 n Calvert
Hundermark August, driver, 59 Greenwillow
Hundt Herman, grocery, 60 Penna av
Hundt Otto, laborer, 60 Penna av
Hunger Chas. shoemkr, 43 n Caroline
Hunger Francis, shoemkr, 142 e Madison
Hungerford James, law clerk, B. & O. R. R. 100 Barre
Hungerford W. E. clerk, 100 Barre
Hunichenn Albert S. dentist, 56 s Sharp
Hunichenn August, tobacconist, 26 n Liberty
Hunichenn Mrs. Mary, 17 Elizabeth la
Hunley B. T. M. salesman, 42 n Calvert
Hunley Wm. R. B. clerk, 42 n Calvert
Hunnigman Edward, pianomaker, 314 w Pratt
Hunt A. L. merchant, Eutaw house
Hunt Benjamin, varnisher, 37 n High
Hunt C clerk, 351 w Baltimore
Hunt Chas. E. engineer, 31 s Castle
Hunt Edw, furn., stoves, &c., 94 Hillen
Hunt Frank N. receiving teller Eutaw Savings Bank, 36 s Eutaw
Hunt Franklin B. processer, 314 Forrest
Hunt Geo. W. coachsmith, 314 Forrest
Hunt Geo. oyster packer, 237 Bank
Hunt Geo. O. blacksmith, Exeter nr Front
Hunt German H. (Poole & Hults.) 192 McCulloh
Hunt H. M. clerk, 122 w Baltimore
Hunt Henry, printer, 39 n High
Hunt Henry, 36 s Eutaw
Hunt Henry A. carpenter, 152 e Pratt
Hunt Henry, shoemaker, 152 Vine
Hunt Mrs. Ida I. periodicals, 115 s Broadway, dw 256 Gough

Ask your Grocer for Heslop's Worcestershire Sauce. W. C. Heslop & Co. manuf's, 19 s. Calvert st.

Page 293 of the 1873 Baltimore City Directory

Only known photograph of Johann Gerhardt Hulshoff, first of our Hulshoff ancestors to come to the United States.

The Hulshoff Cemetery Plot

On August 31, 1880, Johann Gerhard Hulshoff purchased one of the first lots (No. 4) in the new Saint James Catholic Cemetery[48] on Belair Road in Baltimore. This cemetery later became known as Holy Redeemer Cemetery.

The date and early deed number (4) would suggest that the plot was not purchased for a specific death, but on the occasion of the cemetery's opening. The death of his mother Dorothea had occurred more than two and a half years earlier, and family stories suggest that she was not originally buried at the current site. She was likely interred at the old St. James Church cemetery which was closed when the new Holy Redeemer) was built. It can also be assumed that Frederick and Henry (see below), both of whom seem to have died in the 1860s, were re-interred from the old St. James Cemetery as well.

Obelisk face showing John G. (Johann Gerhard) and Lizette (Elisabethe) Hulshoff in Holy Redeemer Cemetery, Baltimore, MD

Near the original Belair Road entrance, and visible from almost anywhere in the cemetery, is the large Hulshoff burial plot (Lots 111 and 112 in Section C) and family monument, one side of which is shown above. This plot holds the graves of four generations of the Hulshoff family, and several carvings on its faces provide information about the family that is not available from census records. The first is the inscription "Frederick and Henry, children of John G. & Lizette." As mentioned earlier, Henry appears on the 1860 census as a two year old, so his absence from the 1870 census suggests that he died between the 1860 and 1870 censuses. Frederick was evidently born and died between those years, since he isn't listed on either census, and we have no other record of his existence but the cemetery record showing his burial in grave BHR.C.111.2.

---

[48] See a copy of the Deed for the Hulshoff cemetery plot on the next page. Note that this is the fourth deed issued by the new cemetery.

Certificate No. 4

St. James' Catholic Cemetery

Lot No. _111 & 112_   ✝   Section _C_

THE RECTOR OF
→ ST. ✝ JAMES' ✝ ROMAN ✝ CATHOLIC ✝ CHURCH, ✝ OF ✝ BALTIMORE, ←

In Consideration of the sum of _fifty ($50.00)_ Dollars, the receipt of which is hereby acknowledged, hereby grants unto _John Gerhard Hulshoff_ of _Baltimore_ _his_ heirs and assigns the L O T, in the Cemetery of St. James' Church, situated on the Belair Road, near Gardenville, in Baltimore County, State of Maryland, distinguished on the plat of said Cemetery as Lots Nos. _111 & 112_ Section _C_, (_18 x 20_) feet), subject to such rules, regulations and charges as the Rector of the said Church may from time to time establish, and especially to the limitations and conditions hereinafter expressed and agreed to by the said _John Gerhard Hulshoff_, that is to say:

First.—The right of sepulture shall be granted only to such persons as the Rector of the said Church shall determine to be entitled to Christian burial according to the discipline of the Roman Catholic Church.

Second.—No Vault shall be dug on the said Lot; no Fence, Railing or other enclosure whatsoever, except as specified in the Rules and Regulations of the said Cemetery, shall be permitted around the said Lots Nos. _111 & 112_; nor shall any Tree or Shrub be planted therein; nor shall any Tombstones, Monuments, Headboards, Crosses or any other figures be permitted thereon, unless they be made of stone or marble, and according to a Christian design.

Third.—No sale or transfer of the aforesaid Lots Nos. _111 & 112_, Section _C_, nor of any part thereof shall be good and valid without the consent of the said Rector; and all such sales and transfers shall be made in accordance with the foregoing conditions, and interments therein shall be subject to no further charges for the ground, but only to the usual funeral fees.

In Testimony Whereof, The said Rector has hereunto subscribed his name and affixed the seal of St. James' Roman Catholic Church, of Baltimore, and the said _John Gerhard Hulshoff_ grantee _has_ hereunto subscribed _his_ name on the _thirty first_ day of _August_ 188_0_.

Rev. H. Dauenhauer, C.H.S. Rector.

John G. Hulshoff

The original of this document is in the possession of one of Johann Gerhard Hulshoff's great-granddaughters.

Because Dorothea Hulshoff's husband is not listed on the monument, it seems reasonably safe to assume that he may have died and been buried in Germany prior to her immigration into the United States, although I was unable to find a record of this. To date, I have found no categorical evidence of her arrival or even presence in the United States other than on the monument inscription; the strong possibility that she is the Dorie Johnson living with the Hulshoffs in 1860 was discussed earlier.

Obelisk face showing Dorothea Antoinette Hulshoff and her great-granddaughter Dorothy Antoinette Hulshoff at Holy Redeemer Cemetery, Baltimore, MD

The inscription reads:

DOROTHEA A. HULSHOFF
BORN IN CLOPPENBURG
GERMANY
JANUARY 27 1798
DIED JANUARY 21 1876

—

DOROTHY A. HULSHOFF
BORN FEBRUARY 9, 1906
DIED SEPTEMBER 21 1986

As with the financial information on the 1870 census, the size of this burial plot, and the size of the obelisk relative to others in the cemetery at the time (and even today), certainly indicates that Johann Gerhard had become quite well to do. All indications suggest that, even if he arrived in the United States with a higher than normal amount of money, he certainly was quite successful during his first fifteen years in this country.

1887 Baltimore City Directory, page 640, showing John G. Hulshoff and his sons

Johann Gerhard's business apparently continued to thrive throughout the remainder of the nineteenth century, and his two youngest sons Herman and William joined him in this business in the second half of the 1880s when they were in their teens. They can be seen, listed with their father, on page 640 of the 1887 Baltimore City Directory shown on the previous page.

The Baltimore City Directory of 1887 is a significant research source since, in that year, the street numbers of all buildings in Baltimore were renumbered to improve the organization of the city. The 1887 directory listed the new numbers for the first time, but also listed the old number after the address as an aid in finding buildings that did not yet have the new numbers posted.

The address "224 w Fayette 147" indicates that "224 West Fayette" was the new address assigned to Johann Gerhard Hulshoff's existing home at 147 West Fayette. The change in address from earlier years' directories does *not* indicate that they moved.

Extract from 1900 U.S. Census Series t623, reel 617, page 242
This shows the family of John G. Hulshoff, age 69, living at 109 Fulton Street in Baltimore. Only his wife Lizette, their "38"-year-old daughter Annie and a servant, Maria Justis, lived in the home by then.

By 1900, Gerhard, now known as John G. Hulshoff, lived at 109 Fulton Avenue with his wife Lizette and their daughter Annie as shown in the census extract above. Annie [ID 9] reported her birth year as 1868 rather than 1861, and her age as 38, beginning a slow age regression that is fascinating to watch over the next twenty years.

On 19 May 1907, Lizette died at age 77 and was buried in the Hulshoff plot at Holy Redeemer. Her husband Johann Gerhard continued to live at the family's home with his daughter Annie, now in reality almost forty-seven.

The 1910 census extract below shows Johann Gerhard, age 79, still living at 109 Fulton Avenue with his daughter Annie. Interestingly, his name seems to be listed as Isaac G. Hulshoff. No one I have spoken to in the family has any recollection of his using this name, nor does anyone know of any reason why he might have done so. Observe that Annie was now just 40 years old, having aged only two years since the 1900 census shown above!

Extract from 1910 U.S. Census Series t624, reel 559, page 164
This shows Isaac G. Hulshoff (Johann Gerhard Hulshoff), age 79, living at 109 Fulton Street in Baltimore with his slowly aging daughter Annie (who aged only two years since the 1900 census – see above).

Johann Gerhard Hulshoff died at age 85 on 23 February 1916, almost nine years after his wife Lizette died, more than thirty-five years after purchasing the plot at Holy Redeemer where he was buried, and slightly more than sixty years after arriving in the United States as a twenty-four year old newly married immigrant.

Children and Grandchildren of John Gerhardt & Lisette Hülshoff

In order to retain a focus on our direct line, the following section will provide only a brief commentary on each of John and Lisette's children.

- Antoinette (Annette) Hulshoff [ID 1327] (born about 1855)
- Henry Hulshoff [ID 2] (born about 1858, died before 1870)
- Annie C. Hulshoff [ID 9] (7 Nov 1860 - 12 May 1926)
- Frederick Hulshoff [ID 292] (born after 1860 - died before 1870)
- Mary Hulshoff [ID 1294] (born 1866)
- William J. Hulshoff [ID 1295] (Nov 1867 - 3 May 1928) married Catherine A. (Kate) Henneman [ID 1563] (Jan 1871 – 1943) and had one child with her:

  John Gerard Hulshoff [ID 1564] (9 Mar 1897 – 1919). This fourth John Gerard served at the base hospital at Camp Meade, MD during World War I from 27 Aug 1918 to 1 Feb 1919. Later that same year, he was drowned after being swept off a ship; he was buried at age 22 on what was supposed to have been his wedding day.

♦ **Herman R. Hulshoff** [ID 7] (17 Aug 1869 - 19 Feb 1940), our direct ancestor, will be discussed in more detail below.

The Kerchners and Mary Regina Kerchner (20 Apr 1873 - 21 Apr 1940)

Jennie [ID 8], as she was known, was a daughter and fourth child of Ferdinand Kerchner [ID 38] and Anna B. Linnenkemper [ID 39].

The history of the Kerchner and related Kern families are given at some length in two books[49] prepared by Fr. Frank Kunkel [ID 432], and reproduced in Sections Two and Three of this book, beginning on pages 64 and 144 respectively.

Jennie attended the Notre Dame Institute in Baltimore. It was during this period that she made the needlepoint shown to the right, and which is still displayed in the home of one of her youngest son Gerard's daughters.

Needlepoint made by Jennie Kerchner

---

[49] The first of these books is "John Nepomucene Kunkel and Mary Rosina Kerchner - A Short Sketch of their Lives", Rev. Frank Kunkel, SS; Nihil Obstat, 1939 (S7). Ferdinand Kerchner, Jennie's father, is one of Mary Rosina Kerchner's older brothers. The second is "John Dominic Kern and Margaret Vaeth Kern - A Family Record"; Rev. Frank Kunkel, SS; Nihil Obstat, 13 AUG 1941 (S13). Anna Maria Kern, the wife of Michael Anthony Kerchner, was Mary Rosina's mother and Jennie's Grandmother.

Herman R. Hulshoff (17 Aug 1869 - 19 Feb 1940)

Herman, the last of Gerhardt and Lizette's children, was born in Baltimore on August 17th 1869, just a few years after the end of the Civil War. As mentioned earlier, Herman joined his father as a shoemaker; this must have been when he was between the ages of 15 and 18. In the 1884 Baltimore City Directory, his father's is the only name shown as a shoemaker, but by 1887, Herman and his brother William were also listed.

It isn't known when Herman met Jennie Kerchner [ID 8], but they seem to have been married in the latter part of 1895, although I have not been able to locate a record of this. In the late nineteenth century, it had become customary for formal photographs to be taken of a bride and groom. The custom of wearing white wedding gowns, however, had not yet come into vogue. It is quite possible therefore that the pictures of Jennie and Herman below may actually be their formal wedding photos. Since neither of the originals is marked on the back, it is difficult to confirm this.

Mary Regina (Jennie) Kerchner [ID 8]
20 Apr 1873 – 21 Apr 1940

Herman R. Hulshoff [ID 7]
17 Aug 1869 – 19 Feb 1940

These are likely wedding photographs of the couple taken in late 1895.

By September 30, 1896, they had their first child (and my grandmother) Anna Gertrude (later Gonce) [ID 44], mentioned in the opening paragraph of the preface to this book. Although her great-grandmother's name was Anna

Maria Gertrud[50], that ancestor was generally known as Maria, so it is much more likely that Grandmom was named after her maternal aunt Anna Gertrude Kerchner [ID 40], Jennie's older sister, who is mentioned several times in the book "Our Gonce ancestors."

Herman, meanwhile, still a shoemaker, had set up housekeeping with Jennie and their three-year-old daughter Gertrude at 1005 East Biddle Street. By the time of the 1900 census (shown below), their household now included a new daughter Alfrieda, born on the first of May that year.

LOCATION.			NAME	RELATION.	PERSONAL DESCRIPTION.								
House Number.	Number of dwelling-house, in the order of visitation.	Number of family, in the order of visitation.	of each person whose place of abode on June 1, 1900, was in this family. Enter surname first, then the given name and middle initial, if any. Include every person living on June 1, 1900. Omit children born since June 1, 1900.	Relationship of each person to the head of the family.	Color or race.	Sex.	Date of Birth: Month.	Year.	Age at last birthday.	Whether single, married, widowed, or divorced.	Number of years married.	Mother of how many children.	Number of these children living.
	1	2	3	4	5	6	7		8	9	10	11	12
			———, William	Brother in law	W	M	July	1877	22	S			
1005	161	193	Hulshoff, Herman H	Head	W	M	Aug	1869	30	M	4		
			———, Regina	Wife	W	F	Apr	1874	26	M	4	2	2
			———, Gertrude	Daughter	W	F	Apr	1896	3	S			
			Hulshoff, Alfrieda	Daughter	W	F	May	1900	[illegible]	S			

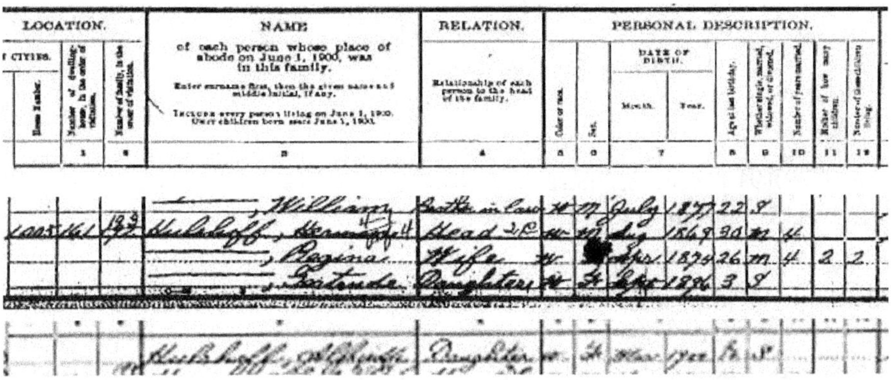

Extract from 1900 U.S. Census Series t623, reel 612, pages 45a & b showing the family of Herman H. Hulshoff, age 30, living at 1005 Biddle Street in Baltimore. Regina's year of birth is actually 1873.

Within the next six years, Herman and Jennie had two more daughters: Clara Rosalia [ID 127] (known as Rose) on 28 July 1902, and Dorothy Antoinette [ID 11] (named after her great-grandmother, but known as Dot,) on 9 February 1906.

Whether because he didn't wish to continue with his father's business, or because making custom shoes was no longer as profitable a business as it had been now that automation had progressed, Herman became a bill collector for a furniture retail store at some time during this decade. He and his growing family also moved from 1005 Biddle Street to 932 Biddle Street during the interim between the 1900 and 1910 censuses.

[50] Anna Maria Gertrud (Maria) Kruse, wife of the first Johannes Gerardus Hulshoff (the button maker).

Extract from 1910 U.S. Census Series t624, reel 556, page 165 showing the family of Herman R. Hulshoff, age 40, living at 932 Biddle Street in Baltimore with his wife Regina and their first four children.

On the 1910 census, illustrated above, Herman R., Regina, Gertrude, Alfrieda, Rosalie and Dorothy A. were living at 932 East Biddle Street.

On May 24, 1911, Jennie gave birth to triplets, which she and Herman named Herman [ID 4], Margaret Regina [ID 5] and Mary Agnes [ID 67]. Herman died during birth[51] and, when they were about 10 months old, the remaining two girls developed whooping cough. On April 5, 1912, Regina died, but Agnes recovered. Ironically, "Aunt Ag" grew up to become a chain smoker and acquired the raspy voice typical of many older people with this habit.

When Gerard was just three and a half years old, his oldest sister Gertrude became the first of Herman and Jennie's children to marry. She and her husband Charles married on 8 January 1919[52], immediately upon his return from World War I, and before he had fully recovered from his wounds. Perhaps because Charles was kept in the army until his rehabilitation was completed, he and Gertrude initially set up household by renting space at 930 East Biddle, next door to Herman and Jennie.

Charles Gonce and Gertrude Hulshoff in about 1917

---

[51] Fr. Kunkel, on page Forty-two of his book "John Nepomucene Kunkel and Mary Rosina Kerchner - A Short Sketch of their Lives," lists Gerard as the male of the triplets who died, but that is incorrect. Gerard wasn't born until four years later. See page 114 in Section II of this book.

[52] For the quite interesting story of the circumstances surrounding their marriage in New York's St. Patrick's Cathedral, see the book "Our Gonce Ancestors."

Extract from 1920 U.S. Census Series t625, reel 662, page 147 showing the family of Herman I. Hulshoff, age 50, living at 932 Biddle Street in Baltimore with his wife Regina M. and five remaining children. Alfrieda had died and Gertrude married since 1910.

At the time of the 1920 Census, Herman I. (sic), Regina, Rosalie, Dorothy A., Agnes, and Gerard were living at 932 East Biddle Street, but Gertrude and her new husband Charles had already moved to 918 Chase Street[53]. Recall that on the 1910 census, Herman's father had used the name Isaac; whether the middle initial "I" that Herman used in 1920 is a coincidence is an interesting question, since the "I" could simply be very sloppy penmanship on the part of the census taker. Note that Herman is recorded with three different initials in the four twentieth century censuses in which he appears.

Herman gave each of his daughters a diamond ring as an eighteenth birthday gift. The receipt for his daughter (my Grandmother) Gertrude's ring, shown on page 50, shows a payment of $56.00 in 1915 – an amount that in 2003 would have been slightly over $1,000.00. Since his last surviving daughter to receive a ring (Agnes) celebrated her eighteenth birthday in May of 1929, it isn't known if the tradition would have continued into the great depression.

At some time during the late 1920s[54], Herman, Jennie, and their children moved into a new house at 602 Springhill Terrace[55]. The settlement document for that purchase, shown on the following page, indicates that the price of the home was $5250, with most of the settlement amount coming from a loan.

---

[53] National Archives Census Microfilm: Series t625, reel 662, page 162. See illustration in the Gonce Biography.

[54] There is no date on the document, but Gerard still appeared in the Saint James School yearbook in 1925, and their daughter Gertrude and her husband Charles bought a house down the street (613 Springfield Avenue) in about 1927, so the move likely occurred around that time.

[55] Later known as Springfield Avenue.

MEMORANDUM OF SETTLEMENT

HARRY A. KOHLERMAN
ATTORNEY-AT-LAW
BALTIMORE, MARYLAND

Sale made by Albert T. Lemkuhl and Florence H. Lemkuhl, his wife
of ~~Mortgage Loan~~
to Herman B. Hulshoff and Regina M. Hulshoff, his wife
Property 602 Springhill Terrace .... Adjustment made to ....

CREDIT TO SELLER OR MORTGAGOR

Amount of purchase price (~~mortgage loan~~)	5250	00
19.... Taxes paid in advance..........months..........days		
19.... Water rent paid in advance..........months..........days		
Interest on purchase money..........months..........days		
House rent..........months..........days		
Accruing ground rent..........months..........days		
Fire Insurance..........Acknowledgements		
Total Credit to Seller	5250	00

ALLOWED BY SELLER

Cash paid on account	100	00		
19...... taxes				
19...... taxes (Current Year)....2..months..16..days	22	42		
19...... water rent				
19...... water rent (Current Year)..2..months..16..days	4	16		
Ground rent—6 months ended..........interest				
Ground rent (Current period)....1..months..........days	6	66		
House rent..........months..........days				
War Stamp				
Mortgages and interest thereon				
TOTAL ALLOWANCES			133	24
BALANCE DUE	133	24	5116	76

COST OF TRANSFER

Attorney, for Title Examination	35	00
Recording (....Indexes....Lots)..1..Deeds....~~Mortgages~~	3	25
Notary Fees		60
President Fees		
Committee fee..........Entrance fee..........Book		
Certificate of Liens		
Judgment Search		
½ War Stamp on Deed..........~~on bond~~..........~~Mortgage note~~	1	50
	2	75
TOTAL	43	10

RETAINED TO PAY
Insurance, $..........For..........Years
Taxes for 19
Ground Rent, 6 months ended
Accrued Ground Rent, Returned to the Building Association to be credited on the expense account
Returned to Building Asso. to credit dues account
Alley paving liens
Week's payment in the Building Association
Check to Mortgagor

	43	10	43	10
Total Due			5159	86
Loan by			5159	86
Balance				
Paid by purchaser				

WEEKLY PAYMENTS
Dues ....
Interest..........   Meets................., between 7.30 and 9 P. M.
Expenses..........
Total..........   At..................

Settlement Papers for Herman and Jennie Hulshoff's purchase of their new home at 602 Springhill Terrace (later known as Springfield Avenue). Aunt Dot (Dorothy Hulshoff) continued to live in this house until the mid-1970s.

Hulshoff Children and Grandchildren taken in Spring (Easter, April 8?) 1928.

The picture above shows Jennie and Herman Hulshoff with their children and grandchildren, probably on Easter of 1928. On the top row, from left to right are Dot [ID 11] at about age 22, Ag [ID 67] at about age 17, Rose [ID 127] at about age 26, Jennie [ID 8] at about age 55, Herman [ID 7] at about age 59, and Jerry [ID 3] at about age 13.

On the bottom row, again from left to right, are their grandchildren Charles [ID 243] at about age 5, George [ID 245] at about age 1½ with only his head showing, Jean [ID 248] at about age 7, and Ro [ID 242] at about age 8. These are their daughter Gertrude's children, suggesting that Gertrude herself likely took the picture.

The Stock Market Crash

The stock market crash of September 1929 apparently had a significant impact on Herman and Jennie's financial state, although they did retain ownership of their house on Springfield Avenue. According to some of his grandchildren[56], Herman later had a reputation of being "tight with a dollar", although Jennie was said to have managed to come up with whatever was needed. If, like many reasonably well off homeowners of the time, Herman had been investing in the stock market (heavily recommended in the heady days of the 1920s), the crash could certainly have resulted in significant losses. Unlike many, however, the Hulshoffs retained their home and household possessions, and Herman remained employed.

PLACE OF ABODE			NAME	RELATION	HOME DATA				PERSONAL DESCRIPTION					EDUCATION
602	3	3	Hulshoff Herman R.	Head	O	6500	R		M	W	60	M	25	No	yes
			Regina M.	Wife H					F	W	56	M	21	No	yes
			Dorothy	Daughter					F	W	24	S		No	yes
			Agnes	Daughter					F	W	18	S		yes	yes
			Gerard H.	Son					M	W	14	S		yes	yes

Extract from 1930 U.S. Census Series t626, reel 0869, page 134a showing the Hulshoff family, now living at 602 Springfield Avenue. Rosalie had since married Frank Easter and moved out.

The 1930 Census segment above shows Herman R. (still an installment loan collector at age 60 – the column for occupation isn't shown above), his wife Regina M., and their children Dorothy A., Agnes, and Gerard H. still living at 602 Springfield Avenue. Note that the value of the home at 602 Springfield Avenue is shown as $6,500 in 1930 – probably indicating a strong appreciation in the few years before the stock market crash. It would later decline and, by the mid-1930s, be less than the purchase price.

---

[56] None of whom, in fairness, could have known him very well before the 1929 crash. Giving gifts of diamond rings to each of his daughters doesn't seem consistent with such a reputation.

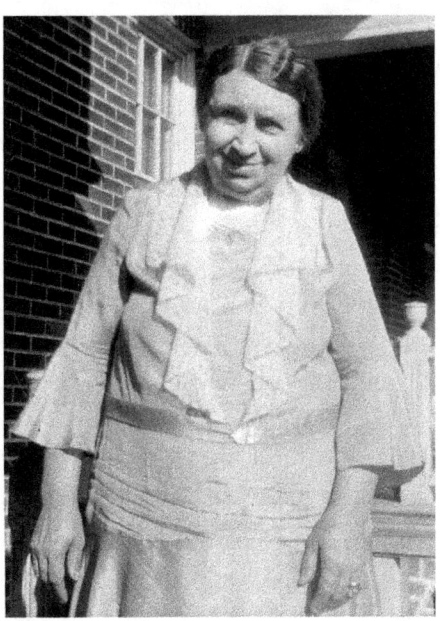

Herman Hulshoff in the back yard of 602 Springfield Avenue – probably late 1930s.

Jennie Hulshoff on the front porch of 602 Springfield Avenue – probably late 1930s.

Some time in 1939, Jennie suffered a serious stroke and was confined to her bed. It is said that Herman sat by her bedside almost constantly, although she was apparently uncommunicative.

Herman died on 19 February 1940, and Jennie passed away shortly afterward on 21 April 1940. Both were buried, of course, in the family lot at Holy Redeemer Cemetery.

On their deaths, the house at 602 Springfield Avenue passed to their oldest unmarried child Dorothy, who lived there until the 1970s, when her age, combined with the deteriorating conditions in that area of Baltimore, forced her to relocate to a small apartment. I stayed in a spare bedroom at Aunt Dot's Springfield Avenue house quite often in the late 1960s when I traveled back in the summer from New York to visit my friends in Baltimore.

OBITUARIES

Mrs. Mary Regina Hulshoff

After an illness of eleven months which she bore with great fortitude, Mrs. Regina Hulshoff died on April 21, a day after her sixty-seventh birthday.

She was a faithful member of the Blessed Virgin Sodality. Her death followed that of her husband who died on February 19.

A Solemn Requiem High Mass was celebrated at the Church of the Blessed Sacrament by the Rev. William Jameson, with the Rev. Arthur Slade as deacon, and the Rev. Thaddeus Skryznski, subdeacon.

Present in the sanctuary were the Rev. James O'Connell, the Rev. Francis W. Kunkel, S. S., and the Rev. George Hopkins.

Two of Mrs. Hulshoff's grandchildren, Charles and George Gonce, assisted on the altar. Burial was in Holy Redeemer Cemetery.

Mrs. Hulshoff is survived by five children: Mrs. Gertrude Gonce, Mrs. Frank Easter, Misses Dorothy and Agnes Hulshoff, and Gerard Hulshoff, six grandchildren, a sister and a brother.

Children and grandchildren of Herman Hulshoff & Mary Regina (Jennie) Kerchner

- **Anna Gertrude Hulshoff** ID 44 (30 Sep 1896 - 18 Jul 1983), our direct ancestor, married Charles R. Gonce, and is discussed below beginning on page 49 and in more detail in the book "Our Gonce Ancestors."
- Alfrieda Hulshoff ID 6 (1 May 1900 - 25 Nov 1910) is discussed on page 43 below.
- Clara Rosalia (Rose) Hulshoff ID 127 (28 Jul 1902 - 21 Sep 1989) is discussed on page 43 below.
- Dorothy Antoinette Hulshoff ID 11 (9 Feb 1906 - 21 Sep 1986). There is more about Aunt Dot on page 45.
- Mary Agnes (Ag) Hulshoff ID 67 (24 May 1911 [*Triplet*] - 1 Oct 1984) married William Hausman ID 66 (16 Dec 1906 - 15 Jun 1991); Aunt Ag and Uncle Bill had no children. See page 47 for more about Agnes.
- Herman Hulshoff ID 4 (24 May 1911 [*Triplet*] - 24 May 1911)
- Margaret Regina Hulshoff ID 5 (24 May 1911 [*Triplet*] - 5 Apr 1912)
- Gerard Herman Hulshoff ID 3 (1 Jul 1915 - 21 Aug 1993); Uncle Jerry is discussed beginning on page 48.

More Details about Herman and Jennie's Children

The children of Herman and Jennie Hulshoff who survived into adulthood are shown to the left outside of my grandmother Gertrude's house at 613 Springfield Avenue. There are no notations on the original photograph to indicate the date or occasion, but Uncle Jerry's uniform suggests a date between his enlistment in 1942 and 1945.

The picture of (left to right) Rose, Ag, Jerry, Dot and Gert, as they were known, was obviously taken in the fall (leaves on the ground, some folks in coats, some not), so it may have been Thanksgiving.

Some discussion of each of Herman and Jennie's children follows.

Alfrieda Hulshoff

Insomuch as a mother can have favorites, Herman and Jennie's second child Alfrieda ^{ID 6} was apparently a favorite of her mother's, but she was also her older sister Gertrude's constant companion and friend as well. Alfrieda is shown with her younger sister Rose to the left.

Rose and Alfrieda Hulshoff circa 1906

In the early part of the 1910 school year, when she was 10 years old, Alfrieda lent her collapsible drinking cup (such tin cups were popular with kids at the time) to a friend at school who had diphtheria[57] and she thus contracted the disease herself. Although her friend recovered, Alfrieda died on the 25th of November – which happened to be Thanksgiving that year. Jennie, who was in the early stages of pregnancy at the time, was so deeply affected by Alfrieda's death that she and Herman never again celebrated Thanksgiving in their household.

Clara Rosalia (Rose) Hulshoff

Herman and Jennie's third child – the second to survive to adulthood – was always known as Rose ^{ID 127}. There is a picture of her as a child with her sister Alfreida above and another on page 39.

Rose married Frank M. Easter ^{ID 126} (about 1903 - 13 Sep 1970), with whom she lived in Philadelphia. Aunt Rose is shown with Uncle Frank in the photograph to the right, taken some time in the early 1960s.

Uncle Frank died on 13 Sep 1970 and Aunt Rose died at age 87 on 21 September 1989.

---

[57] In addition to secreting potentially lethal toxins, the diphtheria bacilli form an exudate on the mucous membranes that can eventually block air passages and cause asphyxiation. Alfrieda's specific cause of death isn't known.

The couple's two children were Donald and Mary, who are discussed below.

Cathy and Donald Easter

Aunt Rose and Uncle Frank's first child, Donald [ID 130] was born on December 2, 1922. Due to a genetic abnormality, he was quite tall, in particular contrast to his Aunt Dot (see page 45), who was quite short.

Donald married Cathy Donnelly [ID 131] and they had three children: Richard [ID 450], Donna [ID 451], and Robert [ID 452], all of whom married and had children of their own. Donald and Cathy Easter moved to Havre de Grace, Maryland after their retirement. Donald Easter died 26 July 2002 at the University of Maryland Hospital, and is buried at Harford Memorial Gardens in Aberdeen, Maryland. Cathy passed away on October 12, 2015 at the age of 88, and was interred with her husband in Aberdeen.

Mary Easter

Mary Easter [ID 132], born in 1927, became a nurse and career military officer, rising to the rank of Navy Commander. "Aunt Mary" served on the Navy hospital ship Repose off the coast of Vietnam during that conflict. The name "Mary Easter" was enough to fascinate me as a young boy[58], but "Aunt Mary" herself was fascinating as well.

When she visited us during leave, she took me downtown (an adventure for me in the early 1950s), and brought gifts from far off exotic places. I still have the metal toy car she brought me from Japan, and the brass lamps she brought back for my parents are currently in my living room.

"Aunt Mary" and I came close to meeting again while we were both stationed in Southeast Asia during the Vietnam conflict, but our planned reunion in

---

[58] Well, the natural order of things was to have a "Merry Christmas" and a "Happy Easter," right?

Bangkok, Thailand fell through when her leave was canceled abruptly due to an upsurge in military activity that required the services of the Repose.

The Hospital Ship Repose

After her retirement from the service, Mary lived in the Navy town of Concord, New Hampshire. Mary died on September 25th 2004 in Concord and is buried at Newport Memorial Park in Middletown, Rhode Island.

Frank and Rose Easter also took in and raised two brothers named Wasser after their mother died, although these were never formally adopted.

Dorothy Antoinette (Dot) Hulshoff

Herman and Jennie's third surviving child Dorothy [ID 11], known to all of us as "Aunt Dot," was named after her great-grandmother Dorothea Antoinette Janssens Hulshoff. She is also shown on page 39.

Possibly due to her slightly premature birth, Aunt Dot was quite short. Compare her height to that of her siblings in the group picture on page 42. The comparison is more dramatic in the picture shown on page 46.

Although all the Hulshoffs were accomplished cooks, Aunt Dot's cooking was always a step above. This was supposedly the reason that Fr. Jameson[59] began visiting the Hulshoff home regularly after his assignment to Blessed Sacrament Church across the street in the 1930s. Older members of the family report that Aunt Dot's father Herman

---

[59] Fr. Jameson is the priest who officiated at Jennie Hulshoff's funeral and later officiated at the wedding of my parents Rosalie Gonce (Anna Gertrude's daughter) and Cornelius Oberle in October of 1941.

particularly frowned on this, perhaps sensing that Fr. Jameson's interests were not confined solely to Aunt Dot's culinary skills. Even after his reassignment to the southwest in the early 1950s, Fr. Jameson would often visit Aunt Dot during his trips back to Baltimore.

As mentioned earlier, Aunt Dot inherited her parents' house after Herman's death in 1940. She also inherited most of the furniture and other artifacts in the home. Perhaps reflecting the quality of Jennie's taste, many of these items, including furniture and lamps, are still in use in our family. One of the more historically interesting of these was a needlepoint that her mother Jennie made while a student at Notre Dame Institute; now framed and in the possession of her oldest niece, it is shown on page 33.

Aunt Dot loved to travel; the left of the pictures on the next page was taken before a trip she made to Italy in the 1950s. After her retirement, Aunt Dot's picture was taken with her younger brother Jerry when he wasn't attempting to minimize the differences in their heights for the camera (right picture).

Aunt Dot passed away on September 21st 1986 at age 80, and is buried in the Hulshoff plot at Holy Redeemer Cemetery. Her inscription is on the on same face of the Hulshoff monument as that of her namesake and great-grandmother Dorothea Antoinette Janssens Hulshoff, and can be seen in the picture on page 29.

Aunt Dot with her siblings before leaving for Italy

Aunt Dot and Uncle Jerry after her retirement

Mary Agnes (Ag) Hulshoff

Agnes [ID 67], born 24 May 1911, was the fourth of Herman and Jennie's surviving children, and the only one of the triplets to survive.

She married William Hausman [ID 66] (16 Dec 1906 - 15 Jun 1991), the son of John Henry Hausman [ID 119] and Annie E. Cross [ID 120]; Aunt Ag and Uncle Bill had no children.

Aunt Ag and Uncle Bill[60], shown to the left on the day of their wedding, were certified "characters", both of whom chain-smoked, and could have been prototypes for a classic TV sitcom's bickering but loving family. Aunt Ag was the craftsperson of the Hulshoff family, and many of her crocheted blankets are still in use by the family.

Ag and Bill Hausman on their wedding day.

Before I left for Thailand in September 1967, Uncle Bill, who worked at Bethlehem Steel's Sparrows Point plant, had lost one of his fingers in a work accident.

When I returned seven years later, we paid a visit to Aunt Ag and Uncle Bill. When he brought his hand out to shake mine, I grasped it and he gave a laugh – "Yeah, I lost some more," he said. Aunt Ag seemed slightly embarrassed by how nonplussed he acted about this, but Uncle Bill seemed to wear this as a badge of honor.

Aunt Ag died on 1 October 1984. Uncle Bill died less than seven years later on 15 June 1991. Both are buried in Holy Redeemer Cemetery in Lot 254 of the St. Martin section, at almost the opposite end of the cemetery from the Hulshoff plot.

---

[60] She was actually my Mother's Aunt, but my generation of cousins all called them Aunt Ag and Uncle Bill.

Gerard Herman Hulshoff

Herman and Jennie's eighth and last child was Gerard [ID 3] (shown on the left[61]), who was born on the first of July in 1915. He was the only surviving male child, and the last male Hulshoff from his immigrant grandfather Johann Gerhard's line. A picture of him as a child is shown on page 39.

A 1924-1925 yearbook for Saint James' Parish school in Baltimore lists Gerard, then in the fourth grade, as a bugler in the school's Fife, Drum and Bugle Corps[62]. Although this is the only extant documentation I'm aware of, all of Herman and Jennie's children are thought to have attended Saint James parochial grammar school on Aisquith Street.

Gerard Hulshoff – circa 1930

Seven months after the Japanese attack on Pearl Harbor, on 7 July 1942, Uncle Jerry enlisted in the Army; at the time of his enlistment, his height was listed as 74" (6 feet, 2 inches) and his weight as 219 lbs. By the time he entered the service, he was already dating Helen Polianski (b.30 Sep 1916), shown below during her 1943 visits to see him at Camp Meade.

---

[61] It is interesting to compare this picture to that of his father Herman on page 34.
[62] Interestingly, so was Joseph Oberle, later a Redemptorist missionary, and older brother of Fr. Jerry Oberle, both cousins of my father's.

Helen Polianski (later Hulshoff) in about 1943 at Camp Meade, Maryland

Gerard and Helen were married on June 28, 1943, at Blessed Sacrament Church. They had three daughters, all of whom married and had children themselves.

Uncle Jerry died while seated on a living room chair in his apartment on 21 August 1993, some years after he and Aunt Helen had separated. Like his ancestors, he too is buried in the Hulshoff plot at Holy Redeemer Cemetery.

Aunt Helen passed away 22 January 2007 at her daughter Barbara's home in Towson, Maryland. As far as I am aware, with Uncle Jerry's three daughters all married, there are no more Hulshoffs living in the Baltimore area.

The Gonces and Charles R. Gonce (16 May 1896 - 25 Jun 1936)

My grandfather Charles Richard Gonce [ID 43] was the son of William Henry Gonce [ID 32] and Alice Elizabeth Clautice [ID 33], and was descended from Justice [ID 2577] and Magdalen Gonce [ID 2858], who first came to pre-Revolutionary America in the mid-eighteenth century.

The history of the Gonce family is given in my book[63] "Our Gonce Ancestors," and so will not be covered here.

Anna Gertrude Hulshoff (30 Sep 1896 - 18 Jul 1983)

My grandmother Anna Gertrude Hulshoff [ID 44], born on Wednesday September 30, 1896, was the first of eight children of Herman [ID 7] and Jennie

---

[63] ISBN 978-1-61600-253-4.

(Mary Regina) Kerchner Hulshoff [ID 8]. Grandmom was known as "Gert" by her family.

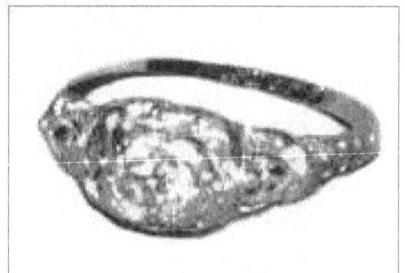

Ring given to Agnes by her father on her 18th Birthday in May 1929

On Gertrude's eighteenth birthday, 30 September 1914, Herman presented her with a diamond ring, a tradition that he followed with each of his daughters when they reached that milestone. Many years later, Grandmom lost the diamond from the ring while she was on the roof of St. Mary's Seminary at Roland Park in Baltimore. Several older members of the family recall this incident, but I haven't yet heard anyone who was able to suggest how she came to be on the roof in the first place. Her sister Agnes' ring, passed on her death to her goddaughter, is shown here.

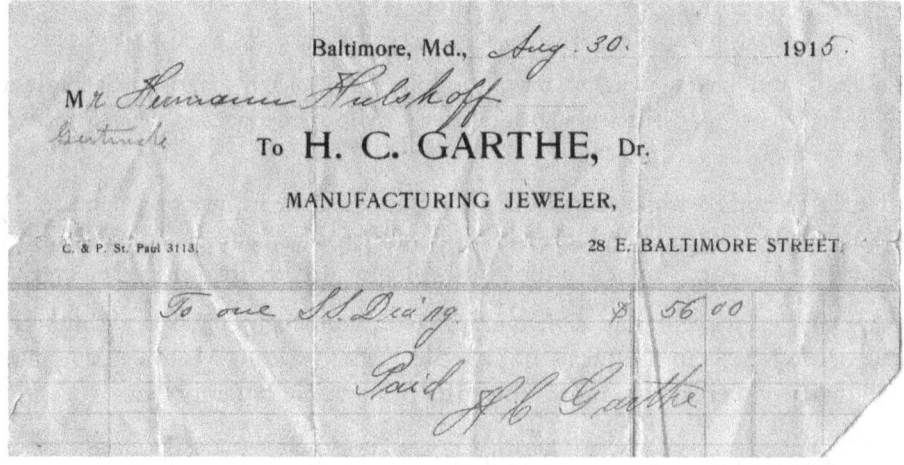

Receipt for my Grandmother Anna Gertrude Hulshoff Gonce's 18th birthday gift from her father Herman.

The receipt for my Grandmother Gertrude's ring, passed down through the Hulshoff family, and currently in my possession[64], shows the price paid to H.C. Garthe Jewelers in Baltimore by Herman Hulshoff was $56, an amount that in 2003 would be worth $1,018.48 according to the Consumer Price Index[65]. Her sister Agnes' ring is still in our family, but no appraisal has been

---

[64] The receipt was given to me by one of Gerard Hulshoff's daughters.

[65] The source for this figure is the on-line inflation calculator at http://eh.net/hmit/compare/. Using various other indexes on the site gives differing results, but CPI seemed to be the most appropriate for a ring. The ring was paid off in 1915.

done. It is interesting that Agnes' eighteenth birthday (perhaps luckily for her) occurred earlier in the same year as the 1929 stock market crash that triggered the lengthy depression.

My Grandmother Anna Gertrude Hulshoff [ID 44], Herman and Jennie's first child, married Charles R. Gonce and had four children. Their history, as mentioned earlier, is given in a separate document.

As with her brother Jerry and their father Herman, there is a strong resemblance between their mother Jennie in old age (e.g. the picture on page 41) and her daughter Gertrude (my grandmother) shown on the next page.

A. Gertrude Gonce, 86
Managed Arundel ice cream plant

A mass of Christian burial was to be held for A. Gertrude Gonce today at the Stella Maris Chapel, 2300 Dulaney Valley Road.

Mrs. Gonce died Monday at the Stella Maris Nursing Home after an extended illness. She was 86.

A native of Baltimore, she was a graduate of the St. James Commercial Institute.

She married Charles R. Gonce in 1920. He died in 1936.

She was employed for more than 40 years as a manager for the Arundel Ice Cream Co.

A longtime member of the Blessed Sacrament parish, she was active in the Sodality and all the women's activities at the church.

Mrs. Gonce is survived by two daughters, Rosalie G. Oberle, of Huntington, Conn., and M. Regina Iglehart, of Bel Air; two sons, Charles R. Gonce, of Bel Air, and George J. Gonce, of Pasadena; three sisters, Rosalie Easter, of Philadelphia, Dorothy Hulshoff, of Towson, and Agnes Hausman, of Govens; a brother, Gerard Hulshoff, of Govens; and by 16 grandchildren and 19 great-grandchildren.

Burial was to be in Most Holy Redeemer Cemetery.

GONCE 20e
On July 18, 1983, A. GERTRUDE (nee Hulshoff), beloved wife of the late Charles R. Gonce, dear mother of Rosalie G. Oberle, M. Regina Iglehart, Charles R. Gonce and George J. Gonce, dear sister of Rosalie Easter, Dorothy Hulshoff, Agnes Hausman and Gerard Hulshoff. Also survived by 16 grandchildren and 19 great-grandchildren.

Friends may call at the Gonce Home, 4001 Ritchie highway on Tuesday and Wednesday from 3 to 5 and 7 to 9 P.M. Visitation at Stella Maris Chapel, Dulaney Valley road on Thursday from 10 to 10:30 A.M. at which time a Mass of Christian burial will be celebrated. Interment in Holy Redeemer Cemetery.

Note that her funeral and burial were handled by her youngest son George's funeral home.

Obituaries for my grandmother Anna Gertrude Hulshoff Gonce

1665 – 1983

Herman and Jennie's children Gerard, Gertrude, Dorothy and Agnes (late 1950s or early 1960s).

The picture above shows Uncle Jerry (Gerard), Gert (Anna Gertrude, my grandmother), Aunt Dot (Dorothy Antoinette), and Aunt Ag (Agnes), taken possibly in the mid-to-late 1950s or even early 1960s. The turkey on the table suggests this was a holiday get-together – possibly Thanksgiving. I don't recognize the location for certain, but I don't believe it was any of their houses.[66]

---

[66] My guess is that this picture was taken in the home of Gertrude's son, my Uncle Charles Gonce.

Descendants of Joannes David Hulshoff

The table below lists eight generations of the family of Joannes David and Anna Margareta Hulshoff. The number preceding each line identifies the generation, and the number at the end of each line is the person's identification number in my genealogical database which is used to reference documents and other material relating to that person. The "a" number preceding the identification number is the Ahnentafel Number showing my direct line to Joannes David Hulshoff.

> A Note about Ahnentafel Numbers ...
>
> *The Ahnentafel (literally, "Ancestor Table) numbering scheme was developed by German genealogists to permit easy identification of particular ancestors in an ancestry tree relative to the person creating the tree. Essentially, the person creating the tree (in this case, me) would be assigned the arbitrary number a1. My father would then be number a2 (my number 1 multiplied by 2), and my mother would be number a3 (my father's number plus 1).*
>
> *My paternal grandparents would be a4 (2 x 2) and a5 (4 + 1), and my maternal grandparents would be a6 (3 x 2) and a7 (6 + 1) and so forth. My four great-grandparents would be 8 & 9, 10 & 11, 12 & 13, and 14 & 15. Anyone's father can be found by doubling his or her Ahnentafel number and adding 1 to that to obtain their mother's number.*

Modern day entrance bridge to Gut Swede near Kappeln
Johannes David Hülshoff's posting as a Dragoner, where he met Anna Margareta.

1. Joannes David HULSHOFF (b.1667;d.1717)..a448 id 1602
++ spouse: Anna Margareta THOBEN (b.1665;m.1697)......................a449 id 1603
...2. Joannes Otto HULSHOFF (b.1698)..id 1604
...2. Catharina Maria HULSHOFF (b.1700)..id 1605
...2. Joannes Henricus HULSHOFF (b.1704;d.1757)..........................a224 id 1606
...++ spouse: Anna Margahreta LUERS (b.1700;d.1771)....................a225 id 1610
......3. Anna Marghareta Dorothea HULSHOFF (b.1733)........................id 2979
......3. Johanes David HULSHOFF (b.1735)...id 1623
......3. Joannes Henricus HULSHOFF (b.1737)..id 1624
......3. Fridericus Godefridus HULSHOFF (b.1740)..................................id 1625
......3. Joannes Gerhardus HULSHOFF (b.1742;d.1820).....................a112 id 1626
......++ spouse: Anna Maria Gertrud KRUSE (m.1784;d.1820)...........a113 id 1631
.........4. Joannes Gerard HULSHOFF (b.1786)....................................a56 id 665
.........++ spouse: Dorothea Antoin. JANSSENS (b.1798;m.1830;d.1878) a57 id 13
............5. John Gerhart HULSHOFF (b.1831;d.1916)..........................a28 id 12
............++ spouse: Elisabethe UNKF[67] (b.1829;d.1907)..................a29 id 10
...............6. Antoinette HULSHOFF (b.1855)...id 1327
...............6. Henry HULSHOFF (b.1858)..id 2
...............6. Annie C. HULSHOFF (b.1860;d.1926).....................................id 9
...............6. Frederick HULSHOFF (b.1860;d.1870)................................id 292
...............6. Mary HULSHOFF (b.1866)..id 1294
...............6. William J. HULSHOFF (b.1867;d.1928).............................id 1295
...............++ spouse: Catherine A. HENNEMAN (b.1871;d.1943)....................id 1563
..................7. John Gerard HULSHOFF (b.1897;d.1919)......................id 1564
...............6. Herman R. HULSHOFF (b.1869;d.1940).........................a14 id 7
...............++ spouse: Mary Regina KERCHNER (b.1873;d.1940)..............a15 id 8
..................7. Anna Gertrude HULSHOFF (b.1896;d.1983)..................a7 id 44
..................++ spouse: Charles Richard GONCE (b.1896;m.1919;d.1936) a6 id 43
.....................8. Rosalie Gertrude GONCE (b.1919)...........................a3 id 242
.....................++ spouse: Cornelius F. OBERLE (b.1917;m.1941;d.2004) a2 id 196
.....................8. Mary Regina GONCE (b.1921)....................................id 248
.....................++ spouse: Henry Otis COOPER (m.[Div];d.1975)...............id 247
.....................++ spouse: Robert Doug. IGLEHART (b.1911;m.1955;d.1996)..id 249
.....................8. Charles Richard GONCE (b.1923;d.2007)....................id 243
.....................++ spouse: Dorothy M. DUNN (b.1923;m.1944;d.2007)............id 244
.....................8. George Joseph GONCE (b.1927)................................id 245

---

[67] The designations UNKF and UNKM represent "Unknown Female" and "Unknown Male" respectively, and are used in cases where I have not been able to determine the actual name.

..................++ spouse: Marguerite MORTILLARO (b.1924;m.1945)..............id 246
..................7. Alfrieda HULSHOFF (b.1900;d.1910)..id 6
..................7. Clara Rosalia HULSHOFF (b.1902;d.1989)..id 127
..................++ spouse: Frank M. EASTER (b.1903;d.1970)....................................id 126
....................8. Donald EASTER (b.1922;d.2002)..id 130
..................++ spouse: Catherine DONNELLY (m.1948)..................................id 131
....................8. Mary EASTER (b.1927;d.2004)..id 132
..................7. Dorothy Antoinette HULSHOFF (b.1906;d.1986)......................id 11
..................7. Herman HULSHOFF (b.1911;d.1911)..id 4
..................7. Margaret Regina HULSHOFF (b.1911;d.1912)..........................id 5
..................7. Mary Agnes HULSHOFF (b.1911;d.1984)..................................id 67
..................++ spouse: Charles William HAUSMAN (b.1906;d.1991)..................id 66
..................7. Gerard Herman HULSHOFF (b.1915;d.1993)..........................id 3
..................++ spouse: Helen POLIANSKI (b.1919;d.2007)..............................id 129
..........++ spouse: Maria Angela KLAUS (b.1797;m.1820;d.1828)........................id 1641
............5. Joannes Caspar HULSHOFF (b.1821)..id 1642
............5. Maria Elizabeth Catharina HULSHOFF (b.1823)................................id 2383
............5. Joannes Henricus HULSHOFF (b.1826)..id 1643
......++ spouse: Anna Maria MACKE (b.1742;m.1763;d.1783)................................id 1630
........4. Anna Margahreta Wilhemina HULSHOFF (b.1765;d.1841)................id 1632
........++ spouse: Joannes Henricus RAVENSBERG (m.1788)................................id 1644
............5. Nicolaus RAVENSBERG (b.1798)..id 1648
............++ spouse: Maria Anna BLEY..id 2420
................6. Henricus Josephus RAVENSBERG (b.1823)................................id 2421
................6. Gerardus Augustus RAVENSBERG (b.1825)................................id 2422
................6. Franciscus Nicolaus RAVENSBERG (b.1828)................................id 2423
................6. Maria Anna RAVENSBERG (b.1830)................................id 2424
................6. Josephus Stephanus RAVENSBERG (b.1832)................................id 2425
................6. Johannes Gerardus Augustus RAVENSBERG (b.1835)..................id 2426
................6. Maria Elisabeth Bernardina RAVENSBERG (b.1837)......................id 2427
................6. Anna Elisabeth RAVENSBERG (b.1838)................................id 2428
................6. Bernard Wilhelm Ferdinand RAVENSBERG (b.1842)..................id 2429
................6. Margaretha Elise Antonie RAVENSBERG (b.1846)........................id 2430
............5. Heinricus Antonius RAVENSBERG (b.1806)................................id 1649
............5. Fridericus Anton Henricus RAVENSBERG (b.1809;d.1809)..............id 1650
........4. Franciscus Henricus Joseph HULSHOFF (b.1766;d.1841)......................id 1633
........++ spouse: Maria Engel Carolina QUADMANN (b.1779;m.1803)..........id 1645
............5. Maria Angela HULSHOFF (b.1806)................................id 1651

............5. Franz Heinrich HULSHOFF (b.1810;d.1878)...id 1652
............++ spouse: Anna Katharina KUHLMANN (b.1822;m.1845;d.1885)...id 1655
...............6. Josephine Bernadine Engeline HULSHOFF (b.1846;d.1930).........id 1776
...............6. Johanne Franz HULSHOFF (b.1848)..id 1731
...............6. Johanna Bernadine Catharina HULSHOFF (b.1851)......................id 2007
...............6. Engelina Franzisca HULSHOFF (b.1853)......................................id 2008
...............6. Franz Heinrich Anton HULSHOFF (b.1856)..................................id 1732
...............6. Bernard Friederich HULSHOFF (b.1859;d.1869)...........................id 2009
...............6. Heinrich Joseph HULSHOFF (b.1862;d.1949)...............................id 1663
...............++ spouse: Francisca Maria CORSTJENS (b.1874;m.1942;d.1955)..id 2067
...............++ spouse: Johanna Antoinette THIJSSEN (b.1872;m.1927;d.1942) id 2066
...............++ spouse: Hermina Theo Jo THIJSSEN (b.1875;m.1898;d.1927)...id 1664
..................7. Bernardine Anne Catharina Th HULSHOFF (b.1899;d.1946)....id 1995
..................++ spouse: Lambert KLEYHEEG (b.1900).......................................id 2035
.....................8. Frieder KLEYHEEG (b.1926)...id 2036
.....................8. Dieter KLEYHEEG (b.1927)...id 2037
..................7. Johannes Petrus Joseph HULSHOFF (b.1901;d.1954).................id 1665
..................++ spouse: Ellen Mary WELTER (b.1906;m.1940;d.1998).............id 1667
.....................8. Henri Charles Ignace HULSHOFF (b.1941)..............................id 2050
.....................++ spouse: Josephine Maria DE WOLF (b.1939).........................id 2052
.....................8. Louise Antoinette HULSHOFF (b.1945)....................................id 2051
.....................++ spouse: Wobbe Piet VAN DER WOUDE (b.1939;m.1969). id 2055
.....................8. Maarten Johannes HULSHOFF (b.1947)...................................id 1669
.....................++ spouse: Ingrid den HOLLANDER (b.1946;m.1972)...............id 1670
..................++ spouse: Elisabeth MENDEL (b.1903;m.1925;d.1927)...............id 1666
.....................8. Dorien HULSHOFF (b.1926)..id 2038
.....................++ spouse: Willie Eugene Marie Clem KRUL (b.1928;m.1955)..id 2040
.....................8. Therese HULSHOFF (b.1927)..id 2039
.....................++ spouse: Johan Henri Conelis DE VALK (b.1923;m.1954)....id 2041
..................7. Franz Heinrich HULSHOFF (b.1902;d.1962)................................id 1996
..................++ spouse: Catharina Johan VAN DIEREN BYVOET (b.1911). .id 2069
..................7. Hermanus Johannas Joseph HULSHOFF (b.1903;d.1904)..........id 1997
..................7. Maria Josephina Bernhardina HULSHOFF (b.1905;d.1964)........id 1998
..................++ spouse: Friedrich Th. KLEYHEEG (b.1902;m.1926;d.1978)...id 2070
.....................8. Therese KLEYHEEG (b.1927)..id 2125
..................++ spouse: Hendrick C DEN DAAS (b.1920;m.1952;d.1988)....id 2088
.....................8. Josef KLEYHEEG (b.1929;d.1973)...id 2126
..................++ spouse: Elisabeth SACK (b.1933;m.1955;d.1974)....................id 2172

................8. Elisabeth KLEYHEEG (b.1931;d.1995)..id 2127
................++ spouse: Hendrick VAN WEES (b.1930;m.1973)....................id 2189
................8. Frederich KLEYHEEG (b.1933)...id 2128
................++ spouse: Mary VAN HARTEN (b.1932;m.1960;d.1997).........id 2178
................8. Hans KLEYHEEG (b.1936;d.1937)...id 2129
................8. Petrus Johannes KLEYHEEG (b.1938)....................................id 2130
................++ spouse: Wilhelmina Adri VAN ROSSUM (b.1939;m.1961)...id 2180
................8. Johannes Joseph KLEYHEEG (b.1945).................................id 2131
................++ spouse: Wilma KOMMER..id 2156
................++ spouse: Marian VISSER (b.1968)..id 2191
................8. Frederica Adriana KLEYHEEG (b.1949)...............................id 2132
................++ spouse: Willem PONDMAN (b.1944;m.1969)......................id 2169
................7. Josefine Enceline Bernardine HULSHOFF (b.1906;d.2001)........id 1999
................++ spouse: Henri Josef SASBURG...id 2173
................8. Victor SASBURG (b.1945)..id 2174
................7. Hermina Theodora Johanna HULSHOFF (b.1907;d.2001).........id 2000
................++ spouse: Johannes Nicolaas VAN 'T SPIJKER (b.1909;d.1995) id 2182
................8. Peter Take VAN 'T SPIJKER (b.1940;d.2000)........................id 2184
................++ spouse: Anneke UNKF...id 2118
................8. Babs Theorade Anne VAN 'T SPIJKER (b.1943)...................id 2183
................++ spouse: Jacob DE KONING...id 2080
................8. Jan Paul VAN 'T SPIJKER (b.1944).......................................id 2185
................7. Antoinette Johanna Maria HULSHOFF (b.1909;d.1975)............id 2001
................++ spouse: Henri Theodor BRORING (b.1906;m.1941;d.1993)...id 2075
................8. Johanna Gerarda Gesina Maria BRORING (b.1945)................id 2076
................++ spouse: Bernardus Johannes Marie GEISE (b.1943;m.1970) id 2094
................8. Rudolf Henri Gemma BRORING (b.1947).............................id 2077
................++ spouse: Ria Regina Antonia VAN DER MEYS (b.1954).......id 2176
................7. Johanna Maria Antoinette HULSHOFF (b.1912;d.1913)............id 2002
................7. Heinrich Josef HULSHOFF (b.1914;d.1971)..............................id 2003
................++ spouse: Lucia Brigitta VAN BOXEL (b.1916).......................id 2175
................8. Ellen Petronelle Theodora HULSHOFF (b.1939)......................id 2115
................++ spouse: Robert Jan MARGADANT (b.1937;m.1962)............id 2160
................8. Ilja Maria Jose HULSHOFF (b.1944).......................................id 2116
................++ spouse: Maarten Ronald DEN OUTER (b.1942;m.1967)......id 2089
................7. Infant HULSHOFF (b.1915;d.1915)...id 2117
................7. Antonius Joseph Maria HULSHOFF (b.1916;d.1998)..................id 2004
................++ spouse: Elisabeth Magda GROENENDYK (b.1924;m.1944)..id 2018

................8. Catharina Magdalena Maria HULSHOFF (b.1944)....................id 2019
....................++ spouse: Denis John CHERRY , MD (b.1943).........................id 2059
................8. Magdalean Maria HULSHOFF (b.1946).................................id 2020
....................++ spouse: Elmo Jay NEWMAN (b.1945;d.1996).....................id 2165
................8. Antonius Johannes Maria HULSHOFF (b.1947)....................id 2021
....................++ spouse: Rhonda Margaret FISHER (b.1956)......................id 2093
................8. Eleanora Maria HULSHOFF (b.1948)..................................id 2022
....................++ spouse: Jack Gustaf ANDERSON (b.1946;m.1973)..............id 2071
................8. Marcellinus Maria HULSHOFF (b.1948)..............................id 2023
....................++ spouse: Pamela Lillian BALL (b.1952;m.1980[Div])...............id 2030
................8. Francesca Maria HULSHOFF (b.1952)................................id 2024
....................++ spouse: Noel STEPHEN (b.1947;m.1972)........................id 2063
....................++ spouse: Gill Morgan KNOWLES (b.1938).............................id 2155
................8. Vincent Maria HULSHOFF (b.1958)....................................id 2025
................8. Robert Maria HULSHOFF (b.1959).....................................id 2026
................8. Phillip Maria HULSHOFF (b.1959)......................................id 2027
............7. Elisabeth Frederika Theodora HULSHOFF (b.1917;d.1956)......id 2005
................++ spouse: Antonius Hubertus Josephus HOUBIERS (b.1915)....id 2102
................8. Johanna Maria Hubertine Elisabeth HOUBIERS (b.1943)........id 2103
....................++ spouse: Petrus Johannes Maria MAAS (b.1940;m.1969)........id 2157
................8. Josephine Hubertine Elisabeth HOUBIERS (b.1946)...............id 2104
....................++ spouse: Onno Benj Nietard KLAZINGA (b.1946;m.1971)..id 2122
................8. Jean Hubert HOUBIERS (b.1948)..id 2105
....................++ spouse: Johanna Maria Don VAN HEEL (b.1964;m.1996)...id 2179
....................++ spouse: Marleen Godefrida DEBEURME (b.1949;m.1973). id 2087
................8. Lucie Marie Elisabeth HOUBIERS (b.1951)..............................id 2106
....................++ spouse: Paulus Antonius JANSEN (b.1947;m.1971)..............id 2119
................8. Elisabeth Wilhelmina Marie HOUBIERS (b.1954)....................id 2107
....................++ spouse: Tzachy GROSS (b.1949).......................................id 2098
................8. Francien Maria Elisabeth HOUBIERS (b.1956).........................id 2108
....................++ spouse: Cornelius WILLEMSTEIN (b.1951).......................id 2192
............7. Johanna Maria Antoinette HULSHOFF (b.1920;d.1996).............id 2006
..........5. Gerhardus HULSHOFF (b.1813)...id 1653
..........5. Henricus HULSHOFF (b.1821)..id 1654
........4. Anna Gesina Bernardina HULSHOFF (b.1769;d.1841).........................id 1634
........4. Johannes Antonius HULSHOFF (b.1771;d.1771).............................id 1635
........4. Anna Catherina HULSHOFF (b.1772)...id 1636
........4. Henricus Godefridus HULSHOFF (b.1774;d.1849).........................id 1637

..........++ spouse: Anna Maria HUSING..id 1646
............5. Johann Heinrich HULSHOFF (b.1808;d.1891)....................................id 3246
............++ spouse: Elisabeth SCHRUNDER (m.1843).......................................id 3247
..............6. Heinrich Gottfried HULSHOFF...id 3248
..............6. Anna HULSHOFF..id 3249
..............6. Bernard Joseph Anton HULSHOFF (b.1845)..................................id 1662
..............++ spouse: Bertha HOFBAUER (b.1853)..id 2750
..................7. Ellen HULSHOFF (b.1874)..id 2751
..................7. Julia HULSHOFF (b.1876)...id 2752
..................7. Leo HULSHOFF..id 3254
..................7. Carl HULSHOFF (b.1880)...id 2753
..................7. Alfons HULSHOFF..id 3255
..................7. Thekla HULSHOFF...id 3256
..............6. Arnold HULSHOFF (b.1850;d.1915)..id 3250
..............++ spouse: Pauline HUTER (m.1874)..id 3251
..................7. Christine HULSHOFF (b.1879;d.1936).....................................id 3258
..................++ spouse: Friedrich WESTPHAL (m.1907)..................................id 3257
......................8. Wolfgang WESTPHAL...id 3265
..................7. Martha HULSHOFF (b.1881)...id 3259
..................7. Hedwig HULSHOFF (b.1884)..id 3260
..................7. Heinrich HULSHOFF (b.1885;d.1887)......................................id 3261
..................7. Walter HULSHOFF (b.1888)..id 3262
..................++ spouse: Margarete OBERLANDER...id 3263
......................8. Leonore HULSHOFF..id 3266
..............6. Marie HULSHOFF (b.1854;d.1931)...id 3253
..............++ spouse: Ludwig DERCKEN (m.1892)...id 3252
..................7. Martha DERCKEN (b.1892)..id 3264
..........4. Johannes Henricus HULSHOFF (b.1775)...id 1638
..........++ spouse: Gesina Elisabeth LOCKHORN (m.1808)................................id 1647
............5. Joann Anton HULSHOFF (b.1810;d.1810).......................................id 2068
............5. Heinrich Godfricus HULSHOFF (b.1816;d.1909).............................id 1656
............5. Bernard Heinrich Anton HULSHOFF (b.1819;d.1844).....................id 1657
............5. Maria Caroline Elisabeth HULSHOFF (b.1822)................................id 1658
............5. Carl Johann HULSHOFF (b.1825;d.1913)..id 1659
..........4. Anna Maria HULSHOFF (b.1777;d.1779)..id 1639
..........4. Everardus Hermanus HULSHOFF (b.1778;d.1787)..............................id 1640
......3. Eylardus Henricus HULSHOFF (b.1745;d.1799).......................................id 1627
......3. Catherina Elizabeth HULSHOFF (b.1748)..id 2977

......3. Johannes Antonnius HULSHOFF (b.1752)..id 1628
......3. Johannes David HULSHOFF (b.1755)..id 1629
...2. Frideric Godfrid HULSHOFF (b.1708)...id 1607
...++ spouse: Anna Gesina LUERS (m.1741;d.1772)..id 1612
......3. Casparus Bernardus HULSHOFF (b.1743)..id 1617
......3. Maria Elisabeth HULSHOFF (b.1748;d.1749)...id 1618
......3. Anna Gertrudis Winanda HULSHOFF (b.1760;d.1763)...........................id 1619
...++ spouse: Maria Elisabeth PELTSCHER (m.1734;d.1739)..............................id 1611
......3. Theodorus Henricus HULSHOFF (b.1735)..id 1614
......3. Christian Antonius HULSHOFF (b.1738)...id 1615
......3. Maria Gertrudis HULSHOFF (b.1739)...id 1616
...2. Johan Godfrid HULSHOFF (b.1710)..id 1608
...++ spouse: Anna Gesina THOLEN (b.1719;d.1791)..id 1613
......3. Anna Margahreta HULSHOFF (b.1742)...id 1620
......3. Maria Gertrudis HULSHOFF (b.1745)...id 1621
......3. Maria Christina Bernardina HULSHOFF (b.1750;d.1753).........................id 2978
......3. Helena Maria HULSHOFF (b.1752)...id 1622
...2. Johan David HULSHOFF (b.1714)..id 1609

None of the ninth (of which I am a part), tenth, eleventh and twelfth generations of American Hulshoffs have been listed for privacy reasons, and it should be noted that a few of those in the eighth generation listed here are still alive.

Section Two

—

Our Kerchner Ancestors

This section consists primarily of a reproduction of the 1939 self-published manuscript "John Nepomucene Kunkel and his wife Mary Rosina Kerchner – A Short Sketch of their Lives," by Rev. Frank Kunkel, SS. It provides a history of the Kerchner line beginning with Johannes Michael Kerchner, born on 15 September 1709, through the birth of my Mother Rosalie Gonce Oberle in December of 1919.

Original Manuscript prepared by Fr. Frank Kunkel; 21 November 1939 Introduction, Errata, and Index prepared by Frank Oberle for this book.

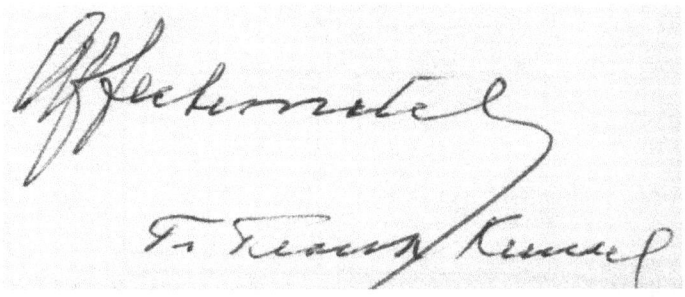

Signature of Fr. Kunkel from a January 31, 1951 letter to Rosalie (Gonce) Oberle

Five Generations of Kerchners from Johannes Michael to Ferdinand

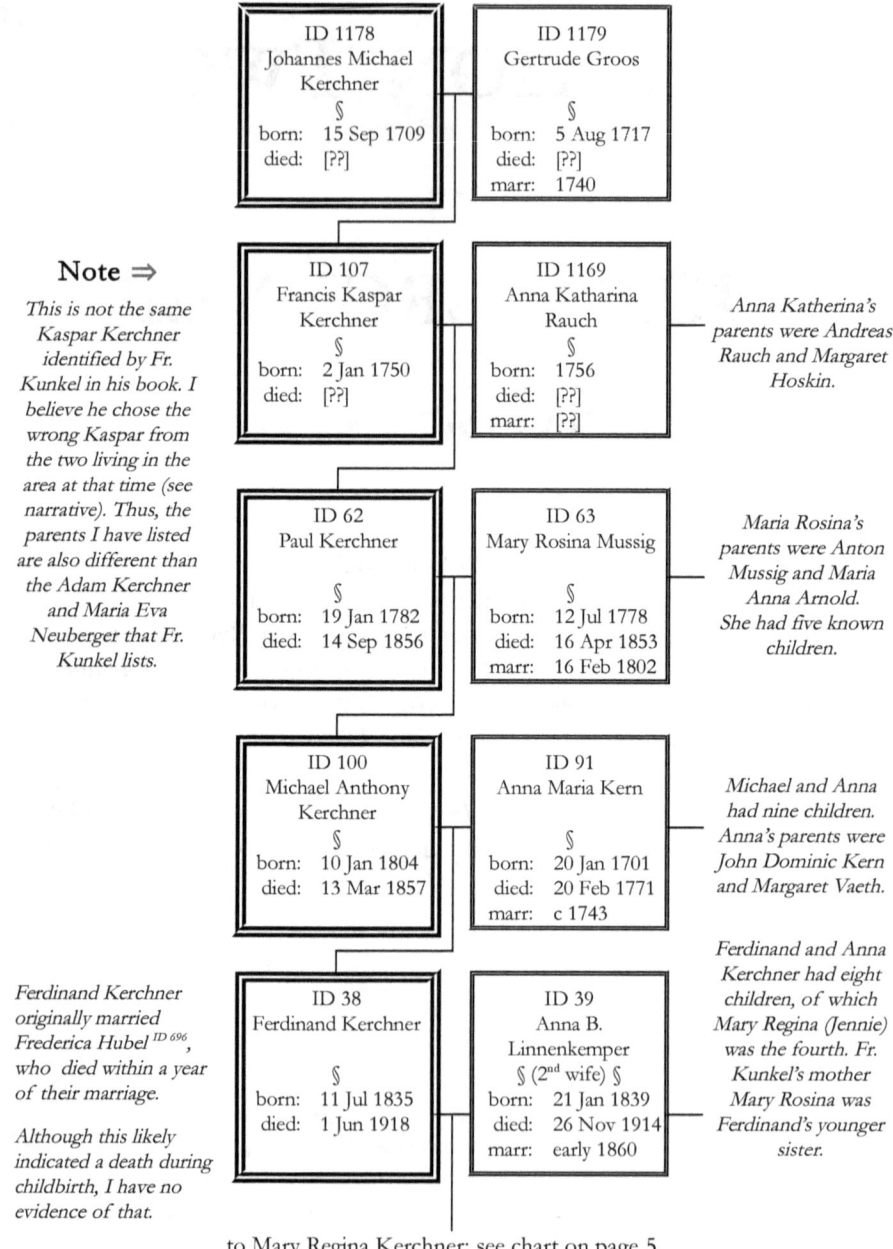

Note ⇒

This is not the same Kaspar Kerchner identified by Fr. Kunkel in his book. I believe he chose the wrong Kaspar from the two living in the area at that time (see narrative). Thus, the parents I have listed are also different than the Adam Kerchner and Maria Eva Neuberger that Fr. Kunkel lists.

Ferdinand Kerchner originally married Frederica Hubel [ID 696], who died within a year of their marriage.

Although this likely indicated a death during childbirth, I have no evidence of that.

to Mary Regina Kerchner: see chart on page 5.

About Father Frank Kunkel

Fr. Frank was a close friend of my mother's family from before she was born. As mentioned in the preface, he recruited my mother to assist him in typing of his genealogical manuscripts.

His obituary from 1951, reproduced on the left, gives a summary of his life, although misspelling the name of his mother.

The last sentence refers to his remaining "active until his death."

FRIDAY, JUNE 22, 1951

Pontifical Requiem Sung For Fr. Kunkel

Was Oldest Member Of Society Of St. Sulpice In U. S.

A Pontifical Requiem Mass for the Rev. Francis William Kunkel, S.S., oldest member of the Society of St. Sulpice in the United States, was offered Tuesday at St. Mary's Seminary, Roland Park, by Archbishop Francis P. Keough.

Father Kunkel died last Friday at St. Agnes' Hospital. He would have been 81 on July 9. Burial was in the cemetery at St. Charles College.

The Very Rev. Lloyd T. McDonald, S.S., provincial of the Sulpicians in the United States, was assistant priest at the Requiem Mass. Deacons of honor were the Very Rev. Lyman A. Fenn, S.S., superior of St. John's Seminary, Detroit, Mich., and the Rev. Edward A. Cerny, S.S., of St. Mary's.

Fr. Bazinet, Preacher

Deacon of the Mass was the Rev. Nicholas Kunkel, S.J., nephew of the deceased. Subdeacon was the Rev. Joseph McCourt, pastor of St. Margaret's, Bel Air.

The Rev. John L. Bazinet, S.S., preached the sermon.

Masters of ceremonies were the Rev. Raymond B. Meyer, S.S., of St. Mary's, and the Rev. Cornelius M. Cuyler, S.S., of St. Charles. Minor officers were Sulpician priests.

Bishop John J. McNamara, Auxiliary of Washington, said the prayers at the grave.

Music for the Mass was sung by the choir of St. Mary's, Paca street, under the direction of the Rev. Eugene A. Walsh, S.S.

Pallbearers

The Mass was attended by many lay friends of the deceased, 170 priests, and 9 Monsignori.

Pallbearers were the Revs. William O'Shea, John Galvin, John Sullivan, Francis Connerton, Edward Hogan, and Edward Atzert. Father Kunkel was the seventh of twelve children. He is survived by one brother, Joseph A. Kunkel, of 216 East Lake avenue. The deceased, a native of Balti-

Father Kunkel

more, was the oldest living alumnus of Calvert Hall College.

Father Kunkel was born July 9, 1870, the son of John Nepomucene Kunkel and Mary Rosina Kirchner. His early education was received at Holy Cross school and St. Joseph's Academy. He received his college education at St. Charles College, Ellicott City, Md. He studied philosophy at St. Mary's Seminary, Paca street, and theology at St. Mary's and St. Sulpice, Issy-les-Moulineaux near Paris.

Father Kunkel was ordained in Paris June 4, 1898, by Cardinal Richard, Archbishop of Paris. Upon his return to this country, he taught at St. Charles College, St. Patrick's Seminary, Menlo Park, Calif., and St. Joseph's College, Mountain View, Calif.

In 1930, he was recalled to Baltimore to be treasurer of the new St. Mary's Seminary. Father Kunkel held this post until 1937 when he became professor of German and French. He remained active until his death.

Dies In Britain At 69

London (NC) — Mother of 26

One of these activities was serving as the chaplain for St. Elizabeth's Home, an orphanage very near my childhood home. Thus, he visited fairly often when he was in the area. Because he died when I was quite young, I barely remember him so can't offer any further anecdotal information.

The Kerchner and Kunkel Families

"John Nepomucene Kunkel & Mary Rosina Kerchner – A Short Sketch of their Lives"

On 21 November 1939, shortly before World War II began, Fr. Frank Kunkel finalized his manuscript titled "John Nepomucene Kunkel and Mary Rosina Kerchner – A Short History of their Lives." Fr. Frank had been researching his genealogy for many years and, while attending school in Europe in the late nineteenth century, took that opportunity to travel to some of his ancestors' hometowns and collect records of their lives.

While only his Kerchner-side (maternal) ancestry is relevant to my own lineage, his material is reproduced in its entirety to preserve its character. Father Kunkel's mother Mary Rosina was the younger sister of our own ancestor, my 2nd great grandfather Ferdinand Kerchner [ID 38]. See "Section Two – Our Kerchner Ancestors" on page 3 in the preface of this book for background on the relevance of this material to our family.

The Kerchner Name

"Kerchner" and "Kirchner" are believed by onomastics[68] experts to be variants of the same surname, both of which can be found in German as well as American records. So far as I have been able to determine, however, our ancestors themselves consistently used the spelling "Kerchner" as far back as the eighteenth century.

Other spellings, which all appear to mean the same thing, include "Kärchner," and "Kaerrichner." All of these names are generally thought to have originally meant a person who worked at or lived at the church – what we would likely today call a sexton. Somewhere a little further back than I have been able to go, there was probably someone named (for example) "Johann der Kerchner," or "Johann the Sexton," from whom the family eventually took its surname.

Errata

Although I have been able to validate the information in Fr. Kunkel's books in the portions where we share common ancestry, there are a few additional facts and some errors that should be mentioned.

---

[68] See, for example, German-English Genealogical Dictionary by Ernest Thode, German-American Names by George F. Jones, the Dictionary of German Names by Hans Bahlow - 1993 English language edition, and the Pennsylvania-German Dictionary by Marcus Bachman Lambert, M.A.

In the listing of his maternal ancestry on page Thirty-eight[69] of the book in this section (reproduced on page 110 of this book), Fr. Kunkel shows the Kerchner line going back to Paul Kerchner (19 Jan 1782-14 Sep 1856) and Rosina Müssig (12 Jul 1778-16 Apr 1855). In a chart on page 35 of his subsequent book (reproduced on page 183 in the section three of this book) however, he provides names for two earlier generations. I believe some of the information related to the earliest of these is incorrect, however, but that will be discussed in the commentary for that book.

The most significant factual error in "John Nepomucene Kunkel & Mary Rosina Kerchner – A Short Sketch of their Lives" that relates to our Hulshoff and Kerchner ancestry, however, is on page Forty-two (page 114 in this reproduction). There he identifies Gerard Hulshoff [ID 3] as one of the triplets born to Herman Hulshoff [ID 7] and Herman's wife Mary Regina Kerchner [ID 8]. Fr. Kunkel apparently confused Gerard, a later son who was born in July of 1915, with Herman Hulshoff [ID 4], the triplet who died.

The other errors in this book appear for the most part to be typographical errors and/or internal inconsistencies, for example:

- On page Thirty-four he gives the wedding year for Harry Kunkel and Elizabeth Frosch as 1895, while on page Thirty-six it is given as 1897.
- On page Forty-one, Helen Kerchner's husband's name is given as Wich, but it appears to have actually been Wicks.

Supplemental Information

Fr. Kunkel's grandfather, and my 3rd great grandfather, Michael Anthony Kerchner [ID 100] was the first of our Kerchner ancestors known to have come to the United States. On page Eleven of Fr. Kunkel's first manuscript (see page 83), he mentions this immigration of his mother's parents and their two sons Francis William (Billie) [ID 54] and Frederick Augustus [ID 57] from Freudenberg, a town in Baden, Germany.

On page 18 of the Kern history reproduced in the next section (seen on page 166 of this book), Fr. Kunkel further discusses the migration. There, he says "The original passport (still preserved) tells us they left Germany with their 2 young sons, Francis William, aged 3 years and Fred Augustus, 1 year old. ... They set sail from the port of Bremen for Philadelphia, June 29, 1832, and on landing three months later took up their residence in Philadelphia."

---

[69] The page numbers are given as they appear in Fr. Kunkel's manuscripts – thus some are written out (as he did in his first book) and some given as numbers.

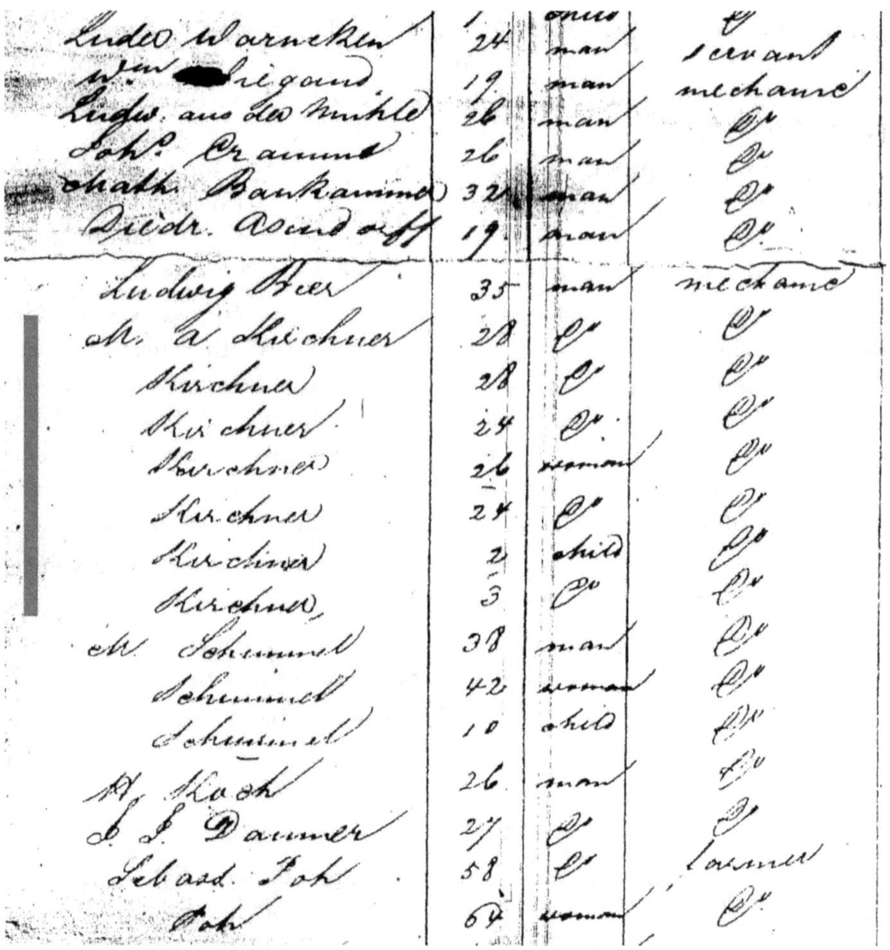

REPRODUCTION OF FR. KUNKEL'S MANUSCRIPT

We now know that the family, recorded as "Kirchner" on the list of arriving passengers[70], left from Bremen[71] on the Adler Eagle, and arrived in Philadelphia on 5 September 1832. See page 16 for an Act of Congress issued in May of 1948, which will provide a glimpse into the conditions on board many of the passenger ships in the middle of the nineteenth century.

A section of the passenger manifest[72] for the Eagle, which is shown below, has the lines showing "M. A. Kerchner" and his family indicated by a dark

---

[70] Spellings, particularly for names like Kerchner, generally mean little, since the names on the manifests were written by a third party as they were heard.

[71] The same port discussed in footnote 38 on page 17. In this case, however, since they originated in Baden, the Kerchner family had a considerably longer trek to Bremerhaven than the Hulshoff family did twenty-three years later. Baden, in western Germany, borders Alsace, France.

[72] Likely not available to Father Frank at the time he did the bulk of his research in the late nineteenth and early twentieth centuries.

bar on the left side, suggesting that there were actually seven members of the family traveling together – and leaving us with an interesting mystery.

Since it seems safe to assume that all the "Kirchners" listed here are related to us, it also seems appropriate to speculate as to whom they might be. Given that all we have to work with is gender and age, a reasonable approach would seem to be to first match the names we know, such as Michael Anthony himself, and his wife and two sons, to the genders and ages given in the document. We might then make an educated guess as to which other members of their family made the voyage with them.

The following table will match the manifest listings to what we know of the Kerchner family members and guess at their identities:

Adler Eagle Manifest			Implied YOB	My Conclusions as to the identities of the persons listed
Name	Age	Sex		
M.A. Kirchner	28	Man	1804	Michael Anthony [ID 100], b.10 Jan 1804, d.13 Mar 1857
Kirchner	28	Man	1804	I can find no Kerchner male matching this age criteria.
Kirchner	24	Man	1808	Matches the age of Michael Anthony's younger brother John David Kerchner [ID 48], b.1808, d. ~1838, but cannot be him (see text). Probably not Joseph Anthony Kern [ID 22] either.
Kirchner	26	Woman	1806	Anna Maria Kern (Michael Anthony's wife) [ID 91], b.21 Jan 1806, d.5 May 1879
Kirchner	24	Woman	1808	Year of birth matches Susanna Kern [ID 21], b.9 Aug 1807, d.19 Jan 1896, and younger sister of Anna Maria. Might also be spouse of either unidentified male listed above.
Kirchner	2	Child	1831	Frederick Augustus [ID 57], b.13 Jan 1831, d.31 Dec 1898; Michael Anthony's second son.
Kirchner	3	Child	1829	Francis William [ID 54], b.29 Jan 1829, d.2 Apr 1910; Michael Anthony's first son.

The information given for the first, fourth, sixth and seventh names match Michael Anthony and his family, so the identification of these seems certain.

I have been unable to identify any member of the Kerchner family that matches the second entry, however. This male appears to be the same age as Michael, so it isn't likely any of his brothers.

For the 24 year-old male listed third, John David Kerchner [ID 48] (13 Jan 1808 - about 1838), Michael Anthony's next younger brother, who is known to have traveled to the United States[73], would seem to be a good match, but this doesn't appear possible. On page 54 of Fr. Kunkel's second manuscript, shown on page 202 of this book, he translates and transcribes a letter written by David Kerchner to Michael Anthony and addressed "Dear Brother." This letter was in response to his receipt of a letter from Michael confirming that his brother and family had safely arrived in Philadelphia.

Joseph Anthony Kern [ID 22] (6 Oct 1809-10 May 1848) might match the criteria of "24 year-old male," but the same letter also contained a section written by Dominic Kern [ID 58] (4 Dec 1811 - 16 Aug 1871), the younger brother of Michael Anthony's wife Anna Maria Kern (the fourth name on the manifest). Dominic suggests that "Jos. Anthony" is still in Hamburg. Therefore, the third name on the list remains unidentified as well.

Regarding the fifth name on the list – identifying the 24 year-old woman as the wife of one of the men listed on the second or third lines has to be considered a possibility, but I suspect that this female is actually Michael Anthony's sister-in-law. The section of the letter written by Dominic Kern also says, in part, "I should also like to know why Susanna did not write us along with your letter."

This clearly implies that Susanna, whoever she was, traveled with Michael's party to America. Anna Maria's younger sister (and Dominic's older sister) is named Susanna [ID 21] (9 Aug 1807 - 19 Jan 1896), and is the right age to be the female listed in the fifth line. We know that she traveled to Philadelphia, since she married Emil Ulysse Hugenin [ID 20] there in 1833, and it is unlikely that she would have made the cross-Atlantic trip alone. Emil (Sep 1810-25 Sep 1880), a watchmaker from Locle, Switzerland, came to Philadelphia in about 1830, and so could not have been either of the unidentified males above.

That she is listed under the surname "Kirchner" rather than Kern would not have been unusual at the time, since those traveling together generally all went under a single surname to insure that they remained together as a family.

Although Fr. Kunkel adequately discusses the last name on the manifest, Francis William Kerchner [ID 54], it seems appropriate to draw some specific attention to him simply because of his direct connection to a significant event in American history.

---

[73] Fr. Kunkel states on page Thirty-eight of his first manuscript (see page 110) that John David died in Wilmington, Delaware, so I haven't included any other documentation of this.

Several of the Kerchners served in the Civil War[74], mostly on the Confederate side. The most interesting of these was our ancestor Ferdinand's oldest brother Francis William, known as Billie[75] Kerchner, who served under Colonel (and later Confederate General) Robert E. Lee, and took part in the raid against John Brown's forces at Harpers Ferry. If the stories related by Fr. Kunkel on page 20 of Fr. Kunkel's second manuscript (page 168 of this book) are true, Lee presented "Colonel Billy" with John Brown's personal rifle (or at least the one he was using) and powder flask.

Other references to then Lieutenant Kerchner's activities during the raid[76] on Harpers Ferry can be found on page Twenty-one of Fr. Kunkel's first manuscript (see page 93 below).

Mary Lewis [ID 780] Coakley's book[77] of stories about her side of the family adds a few tales as well.

Ferdinand Kerchner and his Hulshoff Grandchildren; Spring 1915

From Left to Right:

Top Row: my grandmother Anna Gertrude, almost 19 years old; my great-great-grandfather Ferdinand; Ferdinand's brother Adolph.

Clara Rosalia (Rose), almost 13 and Dorothy Antoinette (Dot), almost 9.

Ferdinand's wife Anna had died the previous November and Adolph's wife died years earlier.

Agnes, the surviving triplet who was then about 4, isn't shown.

Note the double exposure on left edge of the photograph!

---

[74] Although neither of our direct ancestors Michael Anthony or his son Ferdinand Kerchner did.
[75] "Uncle Billie" is the Francis William Kerchner [ID 54] from above. He was the oldest of Michael Anthony's sons, born 29 January 1829.
[76] Web sites and history books abound with details of this event; one example is
http://www.wvculture.org/hiStory/jbexhibit/shepherdstownregraid.html
[77] "Family Flashbacks – A Book About my Family - For my Family"; Mary Lewis Coakley; self-published by Mary Lewis Coakley based on her own recollections. (S9). Mary, born in 1907 and a granddaughter of Frederick Augustus Kerchner, is my second cousin twice-removed. She and my grandmother's sister Rose Hulshoff Easter corresponded regularly and remained close friends until their respective deaths.

Holy Redeemer Cemetery

Holy Redeemer Cemetery; Section V, Lot 70

In front of the headstone of my grandparents Charles [ID 43] and Anna Gertrude (Hulshoff) Gonce [ID 44] at Holy Redeemer Cemetery in Baltimore are four headstones of the Kerchners. From left to right, these are Francis William [ID 54] (1829-1910, known as "Colonel Billie"), whom came to the U.S. as a child (see above), my 2nd great-grandfather Ferdinand [ID 38] (1835-1918), his wife Anna Linnenkemper [ID 39] (1839-1914), and their unmarried daughter Anna Gertrude [ID 40] (1865-1950). Except for Adrian, who died in infancy, our ancestor Ferdinand was the first of the Kerchners to be born in the United States. Anna Gertrude, known as "Aunt Annie," lived with my Grandmother Gonce (her niece) for some years after my grandfather died[78].

A reproduction of Fr. Kunkel's original manuscript begins on the next page, and is followed by a new index to permit cross-referencing between Fr. Kunkel's book and my various genealogical documents.

---

[78] See my book "Our Gonce Ancestors".

JOHN N. KUNKEL
1831-1910

MARY R. KUNKEL
1839-1906

[*Reverse Side of Cover is blank*]

John Nepomucene Kunkel

and his wife

Mary Rosina Kerchner

A Short Sketch of their Lives

1839 :-: **1939**

Nihil obstat:—
  M. F. DINNEEN, *S.S., D.D., censor deputatus.*
  Balto., Md., Nov. 21, 1939.

"How great is the dignity of chaste wedlock, Venerable Brethren, may be judged best from this that Christ Our Lord, Son of the Eternal Father, having assumed the nature of fallen man, not only, with his loving desire of compassing the redemption of our race, ordained it in an especial manner as the principle and foundation of domestic society and therefore of all human intercourse, but also raised it to the rank of a truly and great sacrament of the New Law, restored it to the original purity of its divine institution, and accordingly entrusted all its discipline and care His spouse the Church."

Encyclical of Pius XI on "Christian Marriage."

JOHN N. KUNKEL
(1831-1910)

John Nepomuck Kunkel, (1831-1910)

✠

THIS short sketch of a loving and devoted Christian father, I wish to pass on to his grandchildren and to future generations, as a precious heritage and an inspiring example.

Father was born in the village of Gailbach, near Aschaffenburg, in Bavaria in the year 1831. When he had reached the age of 24, owing to the disturbed conditions then prevailing, not only in Germany but throughout Europe, he decided to come to America, and accordingly in 1855 set sail for Philadelphia, where three of his brothers were then living. He remained there but a short time, when he came to Baltimore, his future home. He almost immediately secured employment as a Wheelwright at the corner of Pennsylvania Ave. and McMechen St. We next find him employed at the corner of Pierce St. and Chatsworth St. (now Myrtle Ave.). About the year 1862, he entered into partnership with Angelina Vaeth in the Blacksmith and Wheelwright Business, on the West side of Hanover St. between Hamburg and Cross Sts. Finally, in 1864, he started in business for himself at No. 8 Lee St. near the water front, where the building of the Monumental Wagon Works is still to be seen (1939).

In the development of this business and in the rearing of a large family, his slender resources were oftentimes severely taxed; but his firm faith in Divine Providence coupled with his sterling integrity and capacity for business enabled him successfully to meet every difficulty. As the Wagon business progressed, he bought adjoining property, erected new buildings and installed modern machinery, so that he had eventually one of the best equipped wagon factories in the South. After 42 years spent in building up and developing the plant, and upon the death of my dear mother, he decided to retire from business. Accordingly in 1906, he left the entire management of the factory in the capable hands of my eldest brother, Frederick J. Kunkel. With him were soon associated two brothers, John, who took over the Painting Department and Nicholas, who became the Engineer.

For 20 years more the business continued to expand and meet the demands of the changing conditions of the times. The Monumental Patent Coal Wagons were eventually converted into auto trucks, and the firm assumed the Baltimore agency of the Goodyear Rubber Tires. This new business grew rapidly and within a short period, there were agencies in Norfolk, Va. and Bel Air, Md. Before many years the horse-driven vehicle had to yield to the auto and the Wagon Factory, in 1926, after an existence of more than 60 years, went out of business. There still remains, however, the agency for the Goodyear Rubber Co. and Automobile Accessories, conducted by John N. Kunkel, a grandson, in Bel Air, Md.

As a business man, my father had acquired so great a reputation for honesty and integrity, that the name of Kunkel on a vehicle, was a sure guarantee for good workmanship and honest material. As evidence of this statement, some of the Monumental Patent Coal Wagons were still operating in Baltimore in 1936, 10 years after the closing of the factory. Among the patrons of the Wagon Co. were the Baltimore Fire, Health and

Page Five

BIRTHPLACE OF JOHN N. KUNKEL
GAILBACH, BAVARIA

Police Departments as well as some of the leading wholesale and retail firms of the city, state and surrounding territory. The employees also looked up to their 'boss' with respect and affection, for he was not only just, but uniformly kind to all those with whom he had any dealings. One might have gotten a glimpse of this when a new job was turned out. As most of the men were either Germans by birth or of German descent they were treated to a keg of Beer. On such occasions the 'boss' mingled good naturedly among his men and shared in their simple pleasure.

But while father was beyond question, a successful business man, that which we most admire in him, was the example he gave of a model Christian father and husband. What sacrifices did he not make to give his children the benefits of a Christian and Catholic education. And what we learned in church or school was safeguarded and enhanced in the atmosphere of a really Catholic home. Every week day he was to be seen in St. Joseph's Church at the 6.00 o'clock mass. With him also went every child of school age. On Sundays, as a member of Holy Cross Parish, he was present at all the services. Regularly, once a month, he went to Confession and Holy Communion with the Archconfraternity of the Holy Family. Prayers before and after meals, morning and night prayers including the rosary, were always said in common. As for night prayers, if any of the older children were to go out, prayers were said before leaving and an admonition given as to the time when all were to be under the parental roof. In the earlier days we all knew the Morning and Evening Prayers in German. And how really beautiful were those rhymed prayers.

"O Gott Du hast in dieser Nacht,
So väterlich bei mir gewacht,"
"Bevor ich mich zur Ruhe leg,
Ich Händ und Herz zu Got erheb!"

Occasionally, after lessons were learned, there were refreshments and no one was denied his sip of Beer. Then came the singing of religious hymns in which both father and mother joined most heartily. At Christmas time we never failed to have our 'Crib' with its setting and we gathered round the Babe of Bethlehem and sang——

"Jesu Kindlein, komm zu mir,
Mach ein gutes Kind aus mir,
Mein Herz ist klein,
Darf Niemand 'nein,
Als Du, mein Liebes Jesulein."

Father's deep religious convictions were often expressed in charity of a practical kind. Not only did he provide for his own numerous family, (there were 12 children), but I can recall the names of 4 or 5 others who, for a longer or shorter period, became members of the household. The demands for a cup of coffee and a bite to eat, were rather frequent so near the water front, and no one was ever turned away. Is it surprising that out of such a family, there should have come a priest and a nun?

Let us not conclude, therefore, because father was so devoted to religion, that he failed to make reasonable allowance for legitimate recreation and amusement. At regular intervals we had our enjoyable family gatherings, our outings to the seashore, and we also shared in the parish Picnics and Excursions. Within the family circle father enjoyed a friendly game of cards and a glass of beer, and none of the children got the impression that any of these pleasures, indulged in with moderation, was in the least wrong or harmful. From this we may gather, that while father was a man of duty and discipline, he knew well the old motto 'all work and no play makes Jack a dull boy'. He therefore made due allowance for rest and pleasure. When we had studied our lessons under parental supervision and attended to our chores, seasonable pleasure was never barred from the Kunkel home.

Of the family gatherings there were two that stand out prominently in my memory. The first took place Sept. 23, 1881. It was a double celebration; for while father had just reached the half-century mark, my oldest brother Fred attained his majority, on the very same day. The home at No. 16 Lee St. was crowded with uncles, aunts and cousins, besides many other friends of the family. The Silver Wedding Anniversary which occurred on Thanksgiving Day, 1884 was even more memorable for the number of guests. Not only relatives from Baltimore and Washington were there; but they came also from Philadelphia, Wilmington, N.C., and from St. Louis. The many handsome pieces of silverware presented to my happy parents on this occasion, testified to the esteem and affection in which they were held by their friends and relatives. In keeping with the pious sentiments of my parents, there was a special mass at Holy Cross Church at which all the members of the family assisted and received Holy Communion.

After the death of our dear mother (Feb. 3, 1906), father's health began to fail. On this account it was thought that a home in the suburbs would not only be beneficial to his health and help to prolong his life, but would also serve as a distraction from his grief. A home was accordingly purchased in Hamilton (No. 8 White Ave.). Our expectations were not, however, realized, and in the fall of 1909 he was obliged to undergo a serious and painful operation. Although he returned from the hospital after the operation, and the doctors gave us some faint hope of his recovery, his condition became so alarming towards the end of April following, that both myself and Sister Johanetta were summoned to his bedside. A few days after our arrival, father rallied somewhat, and the doctor declared there was no longer any immediate danger. Both Sister Johanetta and myself, at father's request then returned to our respective posts of duty. But the angel of death had not withdrawn for long, and 2 months later we received the sad news of our dear father's death, June 29, 1910. During the 8 months that intervened between the operation and his death, he was hardly ever free from severe pain; but he bore all with Christian resignation and fortitude, uttering throughout the day pious ejaculations and acts of submission to God's holy will. During this long illness Father Manley, the pastor of St. Dominic's, was most attentive in his priestly ministrations, and when the end came on Wednesday, June 29th, administered the last sacraments and imparted the blessing for the dying, in the presence of most of the members of the family. The funeral took place on the following Saturday, when a Solemn High Mass of Requiem was celebrated at St. Dominic's Church. The Mass was well attended by the clergy conspicuous among whom was Cardinal Gibbons and a large number of Sulpician Fathers. When the funeral, on the way to the cemetery, passed by Holy Cross, the pastor, Rev. Father Damer, had the church bells tolled, as a tribute to one of his former most faithful parishioners.

If you, dear reader, claim relationship with this good father, treasure his memory as a precious inheritance, follow his example, and transmit his beloved name in benediction to future generations.

Page Eight

From the Baltimore Sun—June 30, 1910

Mr. John N. Kunkel Dead

Well-Know Wagon Builder Expires At Home, Hamilton

PROMINENT IN CHARITY WORK

One Of His Sons Is A Sulpician Priest, While A Daughter Is A Nun In Chicago.

Mr. John N. Kunkel, 78 years old, president of the Kunkel Wagon Company, died at his home on White Avenue, Hamilton, yesterday morning from a complication of diseases.

Mr. Kunkel was born in Gailbach, Bavaria, Germany, 78 years ago. His father was a weaver and farmer. His mother was also a native of the same place. On the death of her husband Mrs. Kunkel came to America.

At the age of 14 Mr. Kunkel began a four years' apprenticeship in the wheelwright's trade in his native town, and obtained work at his chosen occupation. In March, 1855, he embarked for America. From New York he went to Philadelphia, joining his three brothers there. One year later he came to Baltimore, where he secured work at his trade. Later he started in business for himself at McMechen street and Pennsylvania avenue, but after a short time removed to Chatsworth and Pierce Streets, and later opened a shop at Hanover and Cross Streets. In November, 1864, he removed to the present location, 37 East Lee Street, where he erected a three-story building. The building has since been greatly enlarged.

In 1884 Mr. Kunkel invented and patented the Monumental coal discharger, built in such a manner that it can be raised and tilted. These are now manufactured at the plant. In politics he was a pronounced adherent to Democratic principles. As a member of Holy Cross Catholic Church he always took and active part in the work of the church and the various societies connected with it.

He was a member of the Catholic Benevolent Legion, treasurer of St. Vincent de Paul Society, and a member of the Young Catholic Friend Society.

He was married in November, 1859, to Mary Rosina Kerchner, of Wilmington, a daughter of Aton Kerchner, a prominent business man of that city. After a trip to Europe in 1906 she died after a long illness in February, 1906.

Mr. Kunkel is survived by six sons—Messrs. Frederick J., John A., Nicholas A., William F., Joseph A. and Rev. Francis F. Kunkel, of St. Patrick's Seminary, California—and three daughters—Mrs. Mary T. Ward, of Philadelphia; Sister Margaret Kunkel, of Chicago, and Miss Mary R. Kunkel.

Page Nine

From The Baltimore Sun—July 3, 1910

Funeral of Mr. John N. Kunkel

The funeral of Mr. John N. Kunkel took place yesterday morning at 9 o'clock from St. Dominic's Catholic Church, Hamilton, where a solemn requiem mass was celebrated. Rev. Charles Damer, pastor of Holy Cross Church, South Baltimore, was the celebrant; Rev. F. X. McKenny, president of St. Charles' College, was the deacon, and Mr. John N. Kunkel, a grandson of the deceased and a student at St. Mary's Seminary, was the subdeacon. The master of ceremonies was Mr. Frank Swift, and the censer-bearer was Mr. Jerome Dignan, both seminarians.

The other clergymen present were Rev. J. M. Haug, of St. Charles' College; Rev. Andrew Levatois and Rev. Leo Besnard, of St. Mary's Seminary; Rev. A. Gamp, of St. Anthony's Church, Gardenville, and Rev. Richard McCarthy, of St. Joseph Seminary. Messrs. Charles Roach and John Collins, seminarians of St. Mary's Seminary; Mr. Charles J. Kunkel, a student for the priesthood at St. Charles' College, and Mr. Francis Kunkel, grandsons of the deceased, were also in the sanctuary.

The eulogy was delivered by Rev. J. B. Manley, pastor of St. Dominic's Church. Special music was rendered by friends of the two sons of Mr. Kunkel, one of whom is the organist of St. Dominic's Church, and the other had been for many years before his death four years ago, organist of St. Patrick's Church, under the direction of Prof. Alphonse Schenuit. The pallbearers were Messrs. Charles F., Ferdinand, John J., and Harry A. Kerchner, Charles Lewis, Robert Norman, Adolph Neubeck and Frank Hessler, all nephews of Mr. Kunkel. The honorary pallbearers were selected from the delegation present from Father Kolping Council, No. 64, Catholic Benevolent Legion, of Holy Cross Church.

Four of the Sisters of Christian Charity from Holy Cross School, the same order of which Sister Johanetta, a daughter of Mr. Kunkel, is a member, and stationed in Chicago, were at the church. Regrets were received from Rev. Francis W. Kunkel, of St. Patrick's Seminary, California, that distance prevented him from being present at his father's funeral. A handsome floral design was sent as a tribute from the Carriage and Wagon Manufacturers' Association, of Baltimore. Interment was made in Holy Cross Cemetery, Brooklyn, Anne Arundel county. The funeral car Dolores and an extra car was used. As the car traversed Holy Cross parish the bell on that church was tolled and parishioners lined the sidewalks as a tribute of respect.

At the grave appropriate remarks were made by Father Damer in the German language, who spoke of the prominent part Mr. Kunkel had taken in his congregation during the many years he had lived in the parish, and of the charitable work he had accomplished.

The following acted as Honorary pallbearers: Messrs. S. F. Janney, M.P. Elder, H. W. White, R. M. White, Thomas Craddock, and Arthur Hall.

Page Ten

Mary Rosina (Kerchner) Kunkel
(1839-1906)

✠

THE PARENTS of Mary Rosina Kerchner were Michael Kerchner and Anna Maria Kern. Born in Wilmington, Delaware, August 9, 1839, my mother was baptised in the venerable little church of St. Joseph, the parish church of Dupont's Mills, on the banks of the Brandywine. In a recent inquiry for the records of her baptism, I learned that the records of that particular period had been accidentally destroyed by fire. When grandmother Kerchner, whose name was also Rosina, heard of the birth of her little namesake, she thus expressed herself in a letter to Rosina's father: "May God bless your little daughter, who bears my own name. I am happy that my name and memory are being perpetuated in America." The blessing of her grandmother seems to have borne fruit a hundredfold in little Rosina.

When her parents came to this country from Freudenberg, Duchy of Baden, in 1833, they brought with them two sons, William aged 3, and Frederick aged 1 year. They went direct to Philadelphia, and made their residence on Fourth St., near the "Cock and Lion" Hotel. Six years later they moved to Wilmington, Del., remained there for three years, and after a short period went to Cambridge, Md., where Caroline, one of Rosina's younger sisters was born. They were finally located in Baltimore at 67 Hillen St. The nearest church at this time was the present St. Vincent's Church, on Front St. Here, in 1846, when mother was 7 years old, the Sisters of Charity opened a school for girls, and it was probably here that mother received her elementary education. That she attended St. Vincent's Church I know from an incident she relates of her childhood days. One Sunday morning during the children's mass at this church, the children cried out with one voice: "Oh! Father————" Unfortunately I do not remember the name of the parish priest who had died but a short time before. Sometime later she attended St. Alphonsus School, on Saratoga St. which was then taught by the Sisters of Notre Dame. Shortly after making her First Holy Communion at St. Alphonsus, Mary Rosina being the oldest of the girls, was kept at home in order to assist her mother, in the management of the household. Though she was thus deprived of the advantages of a High School education, she assisted the younger children in the preparation of their lessons, always preserved a taste for good reading, and was both gentle and refined in her manner.

In sharing the duties of the household, she was fitting herself in a thoroughly practical manner for her future station in life. At the age of 20, Nov. 24, 1859, she was happily married at St. Alphonsus Church, by Rev. Geo. Ruland, C.SS.R. The marriage was witnessed by Peter and Margaret Kunkel, my father's eldest brother and his wife. My parents took up their residence on the corner of Pierce St. and Chatsworth St. (now Myrtle Ave.) It was here that my oldest brother Frederick was born. What were the labors and anxieties of those early years, when father had

Page Eleven

MARY ROSINA KUNKEL
(1839-1906)

not yet mastered the intricacies of the English language and was only beginning to establish himself in business, only a devoted wife and mother of a large family can appreciate. She was a real helpmate, and by her thrift and household economy, enabled father to develop his business and to meet his ever increasing obligations. In the care of her growing family she was indefatigable. By her sewing and mending, by her industry in putting up home fruits and vegetables for winter use, she merits to be called in the words of Scripture: "A valiant woman...one who ate not the bread of idleness...and her children rose up to bless her." What an inspiration for the girls of such a household, to be brought up in this school of domestic science, under so capable and devoted a teacher.

Notwithstanding her many duties, she assisted at daily mass when it was possible. The morning paper was scanned for a Requiem Mass and her marketing was done in the neighborhood where she could hear Mass. She invariably took one of the children not yet of school age and thus instilled into their tender hearts a love for God's house and the Holy Sacrifice of the Mass. She lived her religion in her home, and seasoned all her labors with prayer. As the children grew older and she was able to absent herself from household duties, she would visit the sick and by her charitable services bring comfort to the unfortunate. With what loving devotion have I seen her at the bedside of the sick, reciting the prayers for the dying, and whispering in their ears the sweet names of Jesus, Mary and Joseph, urging them when possible to repeat with her these and other pious ejaculations. To the sick in their last hour she was truly a ministering angel.

She was also a tireless and efficient church-worker. And that, not only for her own parish church, but also for St. James Home for Boys, St. Joseph's Technical School and for the Christian Brothers when they were planning the present Calvert Hall, at the corner of Cathedral and Mulberry Sts. But all these activties in a mother of 12 children, gradually undermined her health, which was never at any time robust. After she had suffered from one or two minor strokes of paralysis, it was decided that she and father would take a trip to Europe, in the hope that it would help to restore her health. Accordingly in the month of July, 1905, they embarked from Baltimore for Hamburg. It was father's first return to his Vaterland and mother's first trip across the ocean. Little did they anticipate what sorrow was in store for them, as they prepared themselves for this long journey. On the morning after their arrival in Germany, just as they were entering the Capuchin Church in Aschaffenberg to hear Mass she was fatally stricken. It was fully two months before they were able to undertake their return journey and then with serious misgivings whether she would be able to stand the ocean voyage. We can imagine what a sore trial this must have been for my father, then in his 76th year. That both father and mother accepted this visitation of Divine Providence in a Christian spirit and bowed submissively to the Divine Will, there can be no doubt.

At the end of October they were again in Baltimore, when mother was brought from the steamer to the home on Hanover St. and placed in bed from which she was never again to rise. For 3 months, Sisters of Bon Secours tenderly cared for her day and night until she was called to her eternal reward. On the morning of Feb. 3, 1906, fortified by the rites of the church she so ardently loved and of which she was a shining example, surrounded by her sorrowing husband and children, she gently slept in the Lord.

Page Thirteen

THE HOME OF FRANZ MAI IN 1926
FREUDENBERG, BADEN
Birthplace of the Kerchner Family

During that long period of physical pain, she was likewise tortured by the thought of her utter helplessness. She who had throughout the years been to her husband a constant helpmate, his devoted partner in every duty, toil and burden, can now but lie still and suffer him to bear the burden alone. Instead of sharing his burden, she is now only an added burden. But the true husband falters not in his love; rather is he the more solicitous to comfort the ever faithful spouse, and his love grows deeper and more tender, because rooted and founded in divine charity. The devoted husband finds even sweeter joy in serving her in her pain and anguish, than in being served by her.

A Requiem High Mass was sung in Holy Cross Church on Tuesday, Feb. 5th by Father Damer, the pastor. Testifying to the esteem in which she was held, His Eminence Cardinal Gibbons together with a large number of clergy were present in the sanctuary, and the body of the church was well filled with relatives and friends. Very Rev. E. R. Dyer, S.S. of St. Mary's Seminary and Rev. Father Haug, S.S., an esteemed friend of the family, accompanied the remains to Holy Cross Cemetery.

This brief notice of my dear mother, very sketchy at best, is intended to be read in conjunction with that of my father. The one is necessarily a complement of the other, for those two great Catholic hearts beat as one. They cooperated in all the concerns of the family, in the Christian education and religious training of the children, in the family prayers, gatherings, and home amusements; in the religious and charitable activities of their church, in making this Christian home a sanctuary of peace, joy and contentment. This good father and mother have thus bequeathed to their children a memory worthy of being transmitted from generation to generation.

Letter of Miss Mary Kunkel advising Father Kunkel of the illness of his mother.

Dear Father Frank:—   Dec. 29, 1905

I should first of all have carried out my intention of wishing you a Happy New Year, strengthened by an abundance of graces and blessings. Let us ask God each day to help us to bear our burdens, so that they may prove true blessings in the end. We certainly have in the year nearly closed been brought nearer to God. In our distress we turned to God, for aid and received it. Our prayers were not unheard. Our dear mother whose prayer was that she might live to spend this joyous season with us, seemed to improve each day during the past week. She sleeps well, meets her friends cheerfully, plans an outing with them, and tells of the good times she had when out with them.

She tells also with much animation of your visit to her on last Tuesday, 3 weeks ago. One week before she told us that Father Frank would come to see her. After the reception of the sacraments on that morning when I was bringing in her tray for breakfast, she told me of her great pleasure in seeing you....

Mary Regina

N.B. I really did not come to see her. But she prayed that I would come, and in her great desire to see me she seemed to do so when Joseph my youngest brother entered the room. **Note of F. K.**
Letter of Miss Mary R. Kunkel to Father Kunkel after the death of mother.

Page Fifteen

Reproduction of Fr. Kunkel's Manuscript

My dear Father Frank:—

At last an opportunity presents itself to write to you, my dear bereaved brother. How can I sufficiently thank you for all the services rendered us during Ma's illness by your precious functions at God's holy altar and by your fatherly solicitude for us all. Would that I were able to express my appreciation and gratitude as I ought. But my heart is still so full of sorrow and the recollections of Ma's sufferings, witnessed since October 26, that I can hardly shape my thoughts. My mind is on her every moment of the day, and when I awake at night. The greatest consolation for us, however, is that we had her at home with all the care human hands could, to help her bear up under her agony. The final sinking spell occurred on the night of Jan. 22nd when she lapsed into unconsciousness. During these periods which lasted from 24 to 48 hours, no word but prayer escaped from her lips. The ejaculations of Jesus, Mary and Joseph, acts of Faith, Hope, Charity and Contrition, the Confiteor and prayers to St. Barbara were frequently said by her. Tuesday the Feast of St. Francis de Sales, was Ma's last communion day. Little did we think she could live through the night. That afternoon all were gathered at her bedside. It seemed the end had come. Yet she rallied and on Thursday, after a similar attack, I wrote to you, to Sister Johannetta and to Sister Teresa (Mrs. Ward). Sister Teresa came at 11:00 o'clock that night and Aunt Catherine the following afternoon. Ma recognized both after some time. Father Dirkes was called and gave the final absolution, and said the prayers for the dying. Then he asked Ma if she had any request to make. She asked only that she might receive Holy Communion once more. When she was asked if anything worried her, she replied: "No, Father". He then spoke to her about being resigned to God's will, and when he left her she seemed very calm and happy. She never appeared to have any fear of death. Pa and I were debating weeks before whether we should tell her of her condition. But Sister Regina (of Bon Secours) was in attendance and we left it to her to tell her at the proper time. "If only we were as well prepared" she replied. "Mrs. Kunkel is always praying. She is certainly a good woman." When she had callers she received them cheerfully, and everyone was surprised to see how well she looked, not realising how much she was suffering. On Thursday, the evening before the Purification of B.V.M., we had just finished the Rosary; at her bedside were Fred and Kate, Nicholas and Bettie, Teresa, Sister Regina, Mame (Will's wife), Aunt Catherine, Aunt Kate, and brother Joseph, who was the nearest to Ma. Opening her eyes, she smiled and turning to Joseph said: "Oh 'Father Frank' You here?" "I'm feeling fairly well. I'm so sorry I can't wait on you. I'm feeling so tired". After a few moments she turned to me: "Mary, you know what Father Frank likes, get a nice chicken, etc." She wanted to say more but her strength failed. I sat up till 11:30 with Bettie and Sister Regina, who was to spend the night with her. The next morning after Sister Regina returned from Mass, she gave Ma Holy Water, as she was conscious, and spoke a little until the Angelus rang, when she blessed herself and answered the prayers. Then I left her with Teresa and went to get breakfast. She was conscious only at intervals during the day, and spoke very little, as she was very weak. I remained with her until nearly midnight when Sister Regina urged me to take some rest, promising to call me, if necessary. About 2:00 o'clock I heard Betty praying aloud and also Ma's labored breathing. I dressed hurriedly and saw that Ma was sinking. She was lying quietly with her eyes

Page Sixteen

closed,...After the prayers for a happy death, we started the Rosary and finished it all but the last 3 Hail Mary's, when Ma suddenly opened her eyes gave 2 or 3 gasps and all was over at 2 min. past 5:00 (Feb. 3, 1906).

Feb. 18, 1906   Mary Regina

Letter of Very Rev. E. R. Dyer, S.S. to Father Kunkel.

Feb. 5, 1906

Dear Father Frank:—

    My heart is full of sorrow on returning from the funeral of your venerated, sainted mother. If this is so hard in what is human and natural, it is beautiful and consoling for him that loves God and is truly devoted to Him. Your mother during her life and your father now, so illuminated by faith, understand and appreciate this. What must be your mother's realization of it now?...My eldest sister is sick unto death, in one of its most dreaded forms—cancer. I was in Washington spending a few days with her when I saw the notice of your mother's death and later got a dispatch from Joe. I came over last night and with Fathers Boyer, Cheneau and Haug attended the Mass. Father Haug and I accompanied Father Dirkes to the cemetery. I shall try soon to go and see your family. It was my intention all along to pay them another visit, and how I regret that I could not again see your mother alive. I said Mass for her this morning and will do so again tomorrow and the next day and remember her habitually after that.

                                                                                   E. R. Dyer

Letter of Rev. J. M. Haug, S.S.

My dear Father Frank:—   Feb. 7, 1906

    We were not quite through our Oral Examinations when John came with the sad news of your mother's death. I expected to see her at least once more alive, but it was not to be. I went to Baltimore Sunday the 4th, inst. and paid your good folks a visit in the afternoon. All the rooms were crowded. Pious persons recited the Rosary at the side of your mother's remains. How edifying is such a sight. The good people taught by their faith think first and last of the immortal soul. Very Rev. Father Dyer, and Fathers Boyer, and Cheneau and myself went with Father Dirkes to the Cemetery. We were astonished at the large, neatly kept place of rest of Holy Cross Parish. All honor to them. Your good folks of course feel the loss of your dear mother. But they must have been consoled at seeing so many show their grief and pray for her soul. His Eminence Cardinal Gibbons, who was about to go to the bedside of his sister-in-law, in New Orleans, assisted at the Mass. Good Father Dyer feels it keenly that you could not be there. He must have written to you, but we must leave Providence take its course. Your good father was especially admirable in this respect. You know Father Dyer weeks ago left the decision to him. May God bless him for this additional sacrifice. Your good mother believed that she saw you, and was consoled as if she had really seen you. It was her and your good father's conviction that they might have fared much worse in Europe. God was indeed good to you all in sparing your good mother's Life, until she could give it up in peace amid her own. Let us pray daily for your dear departed mother. May we all die like your pious mother.

                                                                                   J. M. Haug

Page Seventeen

REPRODUCTION OF FR. KUNKEL'S MANUSCRIPT

From 'The Catholic Mirror' Baltimore, Feb. 10, 1906

Funeral of Mrs. Kunkel

Her Life Spent in Charitable Work. Cardinal and Clergy Present.

THE FUNERAL of Mrs. John N. Kunkel took place Monday, February 5, at Holy Cross Church, where a solemn high mass of requiem was sung for the repose of her soul at which numerous relatives and friends assisted. Rev. Charles Damer, pastor of Holy Cross, was celebrant. Rev Henry Dirkes, assistant of the same parish, who during the long illness of Mrs. Kunkel so faithfully ministered unto her the consolations of religion, was deacon, and Rev. Leo Otterbein, sub-deacon. Rev. Leonard J. Ripple acted as master of ceremonies, assisted by Rev. Andrew Mihm. His Eminence Cardinal Gibbons paid a high tribute to the memory of the deceased by honoring the bereaved with his presence. He was attended by Rev. Dr. Dyer, of St. Mary's Seminary and Rev. George Wolf, of Philadelphia, Pa., a cousin of Mrs. Kunkel.

Others of the clergy present were: Rev. Fathers Boyer and Cheneau, of St. Mary's Seminary; Rev. Joseph M. Haug, of St. Charles' College, and Rev. Michael Ryan, of St. Patrick's Church, this city. Mr. John N. Kunkel, a grandchild and at present a student at St. Charles' College, was also present in the sanctuary.

The choir of Holy Cross Church, augmented by that of St. Patrick's, at which Mr. Wm. F. Kunkel, son of the deceased is organist, rendered in a very becoming manner an appropriate musical program.

After the mass numerous relatives and friends, including Rev. Dr. Dyer, Rev. Joseph M. Haug and Rev. Henry Dirkes, accompanied the corpse to Holy Cross Cemetery, Brooklyn.

Mrs. Mary Rosina Kunkel, nee Kerchner, the deceased, was born in Wilmington, Del., August 9, 1839, but at an early age removed to Baltimore, where in 1859 she became the wife of Mr. John N. Kunkel, at present president of the Kunkel Wagon Co. A woman of strong character and of the purest morals, she endeared herself to all with whom it was her lot to come in contact. Soon she became the nucleus of many friends in Baltimore. In view of this fact and of Mrs. Kunkel's love for charitable work, the pastors of parishes and the superiors of institutions, requested her on frequent occasions to take an active part in affairs of charity. With what success her enterprises met, is too well known to need repetition. Only a few months before her death she was stricken for the third time with paralysis, and although then sixty-five years of age, she was actively engaged in this charitable work.

Mr. John N. Kunkel, husband of the deceased, being a native of Germany, desiring to visit Europe, Mrs. Kunkel accompanied him on his trip in July. The trip over was an exceptionally beautiful one and the joy of the happy couple unbounded when they set foot on the Fatherland. August 9, the birthday of the deceased, they having the day previous, gone to confession, were on their way to church with the in-

Page Eighteen

tention of receiving holy communion, when to the indescribable grief of Mr. Kunkel, his wife, stricken with the dire disease of paralysis, lay unconscious at his feet. The last rites of the church were immediately tendered her, after which she was removed to a hospital, and thence to the Kneipp Water Cure Establishment in Ashaffenburg, Germany, in which institution, during two months she made such slow progress, that Mr. Kunkel, fearing she might end her days in a foreign land, away from home and children decided to return to Baltimore, where they arrived October 26, 1905. Since that time Mrs. Kunkel had been confined to her bed, suffering intense pain, but an example of patience and submission to the will of God.

Mr. and Mrs. Kunkel had lived happily together for forty-six years. Mr. John N. Kunkel and nine children survive the deceased, of whom two are religious. Rev. F. W. Kunkel, S. S., California, and Sister Johannetta, Order of Christian Charity, Chicago, Ill. The other children are Fred. J., Mary R., and John A. Kunkel, Mrs. P. J. Ward, Wm. F. and Joseph A. Kunkel.

The pallbearers were all nephews of the deceased: Charles F. Kerchner, Harry A. Kerchner, Ferd. J. Kerchner, John J. Kerchner, Frank A. Hessler, Andrew J. Frosch, Chas. E. Lewis and Herman Hulshoff.

Out of town relatives present were Rev. George J. Wolf, Mr. and Mrs. P. J. Ward, Miss Teresa Kunkel, Mr. and Mrs. Caspar Kunkel, Mrs. Margaret Kunkel Mr. and Mrs. Andrew J. Frosch, Mrs. Emma Raeyling, Mr. Caspar Schreck, Miss Gertie Schreck, all of Philadelphia.

Page Nineteen

COL. F. W. KERCHNER
Brother of Mrs. John N. Kunkel

Baltimore Sun, Nov. 1908.

Col. F. W. Kerchner Ill

Confederate Veteran Suffering From Partial Paralysis

CARDINAL GIBBONS VISITS HIM

The Two Have Been Friends Since They Lived In North Carolina Many Years Ago.

COL. FRANCIS W. KERCHNER, a personal friend of Cardinal Gibbons and formerly one of the most influential men in North Carolina, is critically ill at his home, White Avenue, Hamilton.

He has been suffering from partial paralysis since October, 1908. The Cardinal has made several visits to him.

Colonel Kerchner was born in Germany in 1829 and came to Baltimore when two years old. He started in business when a young man and at the outbreak of the Civil War had one of the largest custom shoemaking establishments in the city. He was a lieutenant in the Independent Grays, Maryland National Guard, at the time of John Brown's raid in 1859 and took an active part in the capture of Brown and his band. His company secured Brown's papers and supplies. Some of the contents of the papers were published in **The Sun** when the troops returned to Baltimore before the Federal Government took charge of them.

When the war broke out Colonel Kerchner is said to have been the last militia officer in Baltimore to surrender to Gen. B. F. Butler. During the war he was a blockade runner, carrying letters and packages between the Confederate troops and sympathizers in Baltimore. His brother, Mr. Ferdinand Kerchner, now in the service of the Colonial Trust Company, often delivered the letters in the city for him and had narrow escapes from detection. Once he came near delivering a letter to a Federal officer which was intended for a Confederate sympathizer. The fright he received then caused him to give up the work of private letter carrier for the Colonel.

After the war Colonel Kerchner went to Wilmington, N. C., and engaged in the wholesale grocery business. He was successful and soon his was the largest firm in the State. He took an active part in State politics, and while not running for office himself, the election of Congressmen and others was credited to his influence and activity. About 15 years ago his establishment was destroyed by fire and he never recovered his former affluence. Later he came back to Baltimore to live and has spent his last years in this city.

When Cardinal Gibbons became vicar apostolic of North Carolina he was often entertained by Colonel Kerchner, who was then living in Wilmington. The warm personal friendship formed then between them has never been broken.

The year of the Colonel's return to the city his wife, who was Miss Lydia C. Hatch before her marriage, died and was buried here. He has no children.

Colonel Kerchner has been a reader of **The Sun** since 1843, and takes pride in the fact that he has rarely missed an issue during the entire 67 years. He has two brothers living, Messrs. Ferdinand and Adolphus Kerchner, and one sister, Mrs. Catherine Neubeck, of Washington.

Page Twenty-one

With regard to the mention of "Brown's papers" in the third paragraph of this page, see the document reproduced on page 117.

Col. F. W. Kerchner Dead

Well-Known Confederate Veteran Succumbs To Paralysis.

INTIMATE FRIEND OF CARDINAL

Baltimore Sun, September 3, 1910

Often Entertained Him When They Lived In North Carolina—Blockade Runner In War.

COL FRANCIS W. KERCHNER, at one time an influential man in North Carolina and a personal friend of Cardinal Gibbons, died at his home, 8 White Avenue, Hamilton, early yesterday morning from paralysis. He suffered the attack in October, 1908, and on last Thursday the muscles of his throat became affected. He was attended by Dr. George C. E. Vogler, of Hamilton.

Born in Germany in 1829, Colonel Kerchner came to Baltimore when young. He became the proprietor of one of the largest custom shoemaking establishments in this city prior to the outbreak of the Civil War. He was lieutenant in the Independent Grays, Maryland National Guard, at the time of John Brown's raid in 1859, and took an active part in the capture of Brown and his band. His company secured Brown's papers and supplies. Some of the contents of the papers were published in **The Sun** when the troops returned to Baltimore before the documents were delivered to the Federal Government.

When the Civil War broke out Colonel Kerchner is said to have been the last militia officer in Baltimore to surrender to Gen. B. F. Butler. During the war he was a blockade runner, carrying letters and packages between the Confederate troops and the sympathizers in Baltimore. His brother, Mr. Ferdinand, Kerchner, now in the service of the Colonial Trust Company, often delivered the letters in this city for him and had narrow escapes from detection.

After the war Colonel Kerchner went to Wilmington, N. C. and engaged in the wholesale grocery business. He was successful. He took an active part in State politics. About 15 years ago his establishment was destroyed by fire. Later he returned to Baltimore.

When Cardinal Gibbons became vicar apostolic of North Carolina he was often entertained by Colonel Kerchner, who was then living in Wilmington. Their personal friendship was never broken.

The year of Colonel Kerchner's return to Baltimore his wife, who was Miss Lydia C. Hatch before her marriage, died. He had no children.

Colonel Kerchner had been a reader of **The Sun** since 1843, and took pride in the fact that he rarely missed an issue. He is survived by two brothers, Messrs. Ferdinand and Adolphus Kerchner, and one sister, Mrs. Catherine Neubeck, of Washington. He also leaves a number of nieces and nephews. Among them are Rev. Francis W. Kunkel, procurator at St. Patrick's Seminary, Menlo Park, Cal., and Sister Johannette, of the Sisters of Charity in Chicago, who was Miss Margaret Kunkel.

The funeral will take place at 8:30 o'clock tomorrow morning from his home. A solemn high mass of requiem will be celebrated at St. Dom-

Page Twenty-two

inic's Catholic Church at 9 o'clock. Burial will be in Bonnie Brae Cemetery.

Rev. Dr. W. A. Fletcher will probably officiate. The same pallbearers who bore Colonel Kerchner's wife to the grave will be his. They are Messrs. Adolph and Francis Neubeck, Ferdinand, John, Harry and Charles Kerchner, Frederick Kunkel and Charles E. Lewis.

The honorary pallbearers will be Messrs. James R. Wheeler, Louis W. Hopkins, Judge Charles W. Heuisler and Frederick W. Glantz.

Col. F. W. Kerchner

The funeral of Col. F. W. Kerchner, who died Friday at his home, 8 White Avenue, Hamilton, from paralysis, took place yesterday morning from his home. A solemn requiem high mass was celebrated at St. Dominic's Catholic Church at 9 o'clock. Burial was in Bonnie Brae Cemetery.

The celebrant was Rev. J. B. Manley, Rev. C. F. Thomas, of St. Ann's, deacon, and Mr. John N. Kunkel, a nephew of Colonel Kerchner and a student in St. Mary's Seminary, subdeacon. Another nephew, Mr. Charles Kunkel, a student for the priesthood at St. Charles' College took part in the sanctuary. Rev. Joseph M. Haug, of St. Charles' College; Rev. James Donahue, of St. Patrick's; Rev. A. Gamp, Rev. Charles A. Trinkhaus, Rev. Michael J. Riordan and Rev. Theodore Meade attended.

The mass was sung under the direction of Mr. Joseph Kunkel, the organist of the church. At the offertory Mr. F. X. Hale sang the baritone solo, "Domine ne in Furare". After the elevation "O Christe Salvator" was sung by Messrs. Thomas F. McNulty, Hale, E. J. Thomas and J. E. Farrell. Following the mass the choir sang "Nearer, My God, to Thee."

The pallbearers were Messrs. Adolph and Francis Nuebeck, Ferdinand, John, Harry and Charles Kerchner, Frederick Kunkel and Charles E. Lewis. The honorary pallbearers were Messrs. James R. Wheeler, Louis W. Hopkins, Judge Charles W. Heuisler and Frederick W. Glantz. Rev. Dr. W. A. Fletcher delivered the eulogy.

Morning Star, Wilmington, N. C.—Date Unknown

Messrs. Editors:—Through the campaign just fought, mention has been made of the acts of noble and brave men; and while all has done so well, it seems to me, that there is one man of whom mention should be made whose person and purse have been at the service of the great party whose principles are so dear to him. Night and day he has been found doing battle for the cause, always leading, **never** faltering. That man is F. W. Kerchner, and the thanks and gratitude of this whole community are due him. As Chairman of the Township Executive Committee, his cool, calm and solid advice, given to the Ward Clubs the night before election, should be appreciated alike by friend and foe. His manly counseling the night before our grand jubilee, was that of a true patriot and a true son of this, his adopted State. His persevering efforts, his sober judgment, his wise counseling marks him as a man well fitted for a leader under any and all circumstances. Our discipline and success as a party and our good order as a city, are due **strongly** to the leadership of the man whom we have all been proud to follow—**F. W. Kerchner.**

Yours in justice,

First Ward

Page Twenty-three

JOHN N. KUNKEL, JR.

The Catholic Review, Nov. 24, 1939.

Grandson of John N. Kunkel, Sr. Delivers Address for the laity, Speaks Fealty and Devotion of the Laity

John N. Kunkel Extends Felicitations On Their Behalf To Archbishop

PARENTS ARE INDEBTED FOR CATHOLIC SCHOOLS

Children Feel Perfectly At Home In Presence Of His Excellency

By JOHN N. KUNKEL
President of the Batimore Archdiocesan Holy Name Union

(The following address of felicitation to Archbishop Curley on behalf of the laity of the Archdiocese of Baltimore and the newly-erected Archdiocese of Washington was delivered by Mr. Kunkel at the dinner at Saint Mary's Seminary Thursday, Nov. 23, 1939.)

BELOVED Archbishop, on this your jubilee day, which we have awaited in joyous anticipation, we pour out to you from the recesses of our souls, our sincere and heartfelt felicitations on this, the observance of the silver anniversary of your episcopacy.

His People Rejoice

We are happily reminded of the signal honor but recently bestowed upon you by His Holiness, Pius XII. We therefore desire to rejoice with Your Excellency on your elevation as Archbishop of the Premier See of the United States and also as Archbishop of the See in which is situated the capital of our great nation.

We salute you as head of the oldest archdiocese in the United States and as Archbishop-Designate of the youngest archdiocese in the world.

Surely we have much to be thankful for on this day set aside for expression of gratitude to God, the Lord and Giver of all good things. We thank Him for having so ordained in His infinite wisdom and goodness that Archbishop Curley should have come into our midst eighteen years ago and spend the best years of his life as our faithful shepherd and Archbishop.

Time and again during these eighteen years we have observed him as the kind and gentle father, especially when he came among our children on their Confirmation day or when he addressed our Holy Name Juniors.

Children Like Him

The dignity of his robes at first may have awed the little ones, but his patience, loving disposition and gentle perseverance soon won the children over, and their timidity gave way to positive confidence.

We have recognized at other times in our Archbishop the dauntless, intrepid defender of the Holy Father, of our Catholic Faith, and the avowed enemy of the "isms" of today. Never has he hesitated to speak

Page Twenty-five

his mind and speak it freely. Always has he stood free from fear of men. He fears only the Lord and Master of us all. He fears alone to offend Him Whom he was born to serve.

May we not say that he foresaw the evils that today are engulfing the world foreign to ours, that he outguessed the autocrats and despots who are paying such strict attention to their youth; who are training them not alone in the science in modern warfare, but are poisoning their young minds and corrupting their tender hearts in an effort to wean them away from God and righteousness?

Danger At Home

He has only too well realized that those evils are not confined to foreign shores, but exist in our own country, in our own State, yes, in our own metropolitan areas of Baltimore and Washington.

Your Excellency, we recall distinctly one of your first utterances when you became our Archbishop and it was that you would concern yourself definitely, and make it your first order of business, to see that schools were built and properly manned to give our children the great blessings and advantages of a parochial school education.

"A school for every parish," became the goal of your ambitions; keep our children under the everwatchful eye of good Sisters and Brothers was the one thought uppermost in your mind; we must hold our youth together; throw about them the armor of Jesus, rally to the defense of the true religion and true patriotism; teach them to place Divine interest above human interest, have them show respect for properly constituted authority as being derived from the Supreme Authority of God. Archbishop Curley, as always, heartily subscribed to the Catholic idea in that man is composed of body, mind and soul. All three must be educated.

His People Are Grateful

Beloved Archbishop, we are grateful to you for the energy and zeal and devotion shown in the furtherance of your zeal and desire for the education of our children. The schools in our two Archdioceses today are second to none in national usefulness and effectiveness. The grand results of your labors are much in evidence. Our schools will abide as permanent reminders of our great Archbishop. "Si Monumentum Requiris, Circumspice."

Beloved Archbishop, may our gratitude be expressed to you on this your day of jubilation in the thousands of Holy Communions of your faithful people in which you have been so well remembered, in the fervent supplications of young and old beseeching the good God to grant you long life, sound health and happiness for many more years of useful service. Ours is the realizations of how much we need you.

Long Life To Him

May your integrity of purpose, your high courage, your willingness to serve, your thought for the welfare of others, your love of the finer things of life, may all these be woven like threads of gold into the warp and woof of the history of our two Archdioceses.

God bless Your Excellency!
God save our Archbishop!
"Ad Multos Annos!"

Page Twenty-six

MR. AND MRS. JOHN N. KUNKEL
WITH THEIR ELDEST SON, FREDERICK, TAKEN IN 1862.

BAPTISMAL RECORD

                                        Kleinwallstadt, 24 Febr. 37.
Sehr geehrter Herr Kunkel!

Ihr Grossvater, Johann Adam Kunkel, stammt aus einer sehr kinderreichen Familie. Sein Vater, Georg Kunkel, Bauer in Rossbach war zweimal verheiratet und hatte zusammen 12 Kinder.

Aus 1. Ehe mit Katharina geb. Schreck stammen:

1. Barbara geb. 24 Sept. 1795
2. Johann Adam geb. 3. Sept. 1800
    (Father of John N. Kunkel)
3. Nikolaus Lorenz geb. 9. August 1805
4. Johann Nikolaus geb. 18. Okt. 1807+1807
5. Johann Nikolaus geb. 27. Juli 1810
6. Johann Nepomuk geb. 19. Febr. 1812.

Aus 2. Ehe, mit Apollonia geb. Englert stammen:

7. Peter Anton geb. 3. Nov. 1815
8. Jakob Johann geb. 24. Okt. 1818
9. Margaretha geb. 11. Febr. 1821
10. Rosalie Susanne geb. 9. Jan. 1824
11. Wilhelmine geb. 25. Nov. 1827
12. Maria Agnes geb. 19. Jan. 1831+1836.

Ihre Vettern: Pius Kunkel und Aloys Schmitt sind nicht mehr am Leben.

Ihren Scheck über 4 M. habe ich erhalten. Besten Dank!

Mit den besten Wünschen verbleibe ich

                            Ihr ergebener
                                S. Spangenberger Pfr.

Page Twenty-eight

ANCESTORS AND LINEAL DESCENDENTS OF JOHN N. KUNKEL

I. GEORGE KUNKEL and CATHARINE SCHRECK (Parents of Adam Kunkel)
II. ADAM KUNKEL, b. Rossbach, Bavaria, Sept. 3, 1800.
ANNA MARIA CHRIST (his wife), b. Gailbach, Bavaria, June 24, 1801.
d. Philadelphia, Pa., July 27, 1887.

Parents of A. M. Christ-Henry Christ and Marg. Koerbel

Children of Adam Kunkel and Anna Maria Christ:—

III. NICHOLAS ....b. Mar. 23, 1823   d.
     PETER ....b. Apr. 9, 1825   d. Oct. 23, 1883   Mar. Marg. Hoffman
     GENEVIEVE .....b. 1827   d. 1827
     EVA ....b. Feb. 24, 1829   d. Aug. 31, 1894   Mar. John Schreck
     JOHN NEP. ......b. Sept. 23, 1831   d. June 29, 1910   Mar. Mary R. Kerchner
     GEORGE ....b. Nov. 19, 1833   d. Oct. 13, 1888   Mar. Mary Amberg
         After death Adam, A. M. Christ married his brother Nicholas
         Nich. Kunkel, b. Oct. 18, 1807, d. Aug. 23, 1908 (Phila.)
     ALOIS ....b. Apr. 22, 1840   d. Jan. 4, 1844
     CASPER   b. Jan. 18, 1842   d. May 21, 1929   Mar. Marg. Benkler

IV. Children of John N. Kunkel and Mary R. Kunkel nee Kerchner, Married Nov. 24, 1859
     1. Frederick .....b. Sept. 23, 1860   Mar. Cath. Bush
     2. Joseph A. (1) ..b. July 12, 1862   d. infant
     3. Mary Regina ..b. Sept. 6, 1863   d. Feb. 14, 1915   Single
     4. Mich. A. ......b. July 10, 1865   d. infant
     5. John Alph. ....b. Aug. 5, 1866   d. May 30, 1935   Mar. Anna Vaeth
     6. Nich. A. ......b. June 17, 1868   d. Dec. 12, 1935   Mar. Barb. Schneider
     7. Francis F. ....b. July 9, 1870   Ord. Priest
     8. Teresa M. ....b. Aug. 14, 1872   d. Feb. 8, 1932   Mar. Peter J. Ward
     9. Marg. Dor. ...b. Dec. 1, 1874   Sister Christ. Charity
    10. Joseph A. (2) ..b. May 27, 1876   d. June 6, 1882
    11. Wm. Francis ..b. Dec. 4, 1878   d. Jan. 10, 1907   Mar. Mary Becker
    12. Joseph A. (3) ..b. Dec. 10, 1882   Mar. Dora Becker
    13. Teresa (Purzer).b. Aug. 27, 1880   Mar. Jos. Brennan

JOHN N. KUNKEL and MARY R. KERCHNER
(1831-1910)   (1839-1906)

IV. Gen.	V. Gen.	VI. Gen.	VII. Gen.
1. Fred. J. Cath. Bush	1. John N. Dora Bilz	1. Catherine Adolph Pons	1. Barbara Kath.
		2. Helen J. Carvel Archer	1. John Carvel 2. Dorothea Lee
		3. Gerard	
	2. Catherine Chas. Miller		
	3. Charles Evelyne Kraus	1. Charllotte	
	4. Lydia Sr. Philomena		
	5. Regina d. infant		
	6. Francis W. Dor. Heinicke	1. Fred. J.	
2. Joseph (1) d. infant			
3. M. Regina	Single		
4. Michael d. infant			
5. John Alph. Anna Vaeth	1. Anna		
	2. Mary		
	3. Francis 1st. wife—Marg. von Gestal 2nd. wife—Mary Willenburg		
	4. Teresa F. Thim	1. Bernadette 2. Margaret 3. Regina 4. Dorothy 5. Catherine 6. Francis 7. Charles 8. Richard 9. Eliz. Patricia	

Page Twenty-nine

LINEAL DESCENDENTS OF MR. JOHN N. KUNKEL

IV. Gen.	V. Gen.		VI. Gen.
	5. {	James Marg. Hubbard	1. Joseph 2. Margaret
	6. {	William Mary Bond	1. William
	7. Agnes		
6. Nicholas Barb. Schneider.. 7. Francis F. 8. Teresa Peter J. Ward	1. {	Francis Mary Bellis Ord. Priest	1. Gertrude
	1. Rose Marie b. 1898 d. 1914		
	2. Francis J.		
	3. {	Jeannette Thos. Cunaugh	1. Philip 2. Rose 3. Regina 4. Thomas 5. Peter
	4. John J.		
	5. {	Joseph A. Eliz. Smith	1. Joseph A. 2. Mary Ellen
	6. {	Regina Geo. Wist	1. George 2. Paul 3. Rose 4. Jean
	7. Peter J.		
	8. Edward		
9. Marg. Dorothy	Sister of Christ. Charity		
10. Joseph A. (2)	d. 1882—aged 6		
11. William F. Mary Becker	1. {	Joseph A. Angela Hooper	1. Joan 2. Joseph A.
12. Joseph A. (3) Dora Becker	1. Genevieve		Sister of Notre Dame
	2. {	Dorothy C. E. Jackson	1. Charles E. 2. Joseph N. Jesuit
	3. Nicholas		
	4. Marie		
	5. Anne		
	6. Irene		
	7. Joseph		
	8. Francis		
	9. Teresa		
13. Teresa Purzer Joseph Brennan			

FRED KUNKEL b. Sept. 23, 1890 married CATH. BUSCH b. Sept. 30, 1865 d. Sept. 1, 1934.
Married, May 5, 1885   Parents: Henry Busch and Lydia Kummel

```
V. Generation       Children—                              Married—
   John N., Jr. .....b. Sept. 12, 1888                     Dora Bilz, June 19, 1912
   Denis F. .........b. Apr. 15, 1891    d. May 7, 1891
   Joseph ...........b. Sept. 27, 1892   d. Apr. 27, 1892
   John H. ..........b. Sept. 16, 1894   d. Dec. 2, 1894
   Mary Cath. .......b. Nov. 10, 1894    (Adopted)          Chas. Miller
   Chas. John .......b. Nov. 4, 1896                        Evelyne Kraus, Aug. 1, 1936
   Mary Lydia .......b. Aug. 30, 1899                       Sister of Good Shepherd
                                                            Prof. Oct. 12, 1928
   Mary Regina ......b. June 23, 1901    d. Nov. 29, 1902
   Francis W. .......b. Apr. 24, 1906                       Dorothy Heinicke, July 8, 1933.

   JOHN ALPH. .......b. Aug. 5, 1866     d. May 30, 1935    Anna Vaeth, Aug. 5, 1890
                                                            b. Jan. 19, 1865 d. Oct. 4, 1905
   Children—
   Anna M. ..........b. May 5, 1891
   Mary E. ..........b. Sept. 5, 1892
   Francis Ferd. ....b. Sept. 29, 1894                      Marg. von Gestal d. May 22,
                                                            Mary Willenburg
   Teresa ...........b. Sept. 7, 1896                       Francis Thim Oct. 9, 1923
   James ............b. Sept. 9, 1898                       Marg. Hubbard May 12, 1931
   William ..........b. Feb. 18, 1901                       Mary Bond
   Agnes ............b. Jan. 31, 1903
```

Page Thirty

LINEAL DESCENDENTS OF MR. JOHN N. KUNKEL

NICH. ALOYS. ...b. June 17, 1868   d. Dec. 12, 1935   Mar. Barb. Schneider July, 4 1893
Children—
Francis ....b. July 23, 1894   Mar. Mary Beilis, May 15, 1916 b. Oct. 31, 1891
   Gertrude, b. Feb. 11, 1917

TERESA M. ......b. Aug. 14, 1872   Mar. Peter J. Ward, May 5, 1897. b. Aug. 10, 1872
   Marriage—May 5, 1897

Rose Marie ......b. Feb. 8, 1898   d. Apr. 2, 1914
Francis J. ....b. Jan. 26, 1899
Johannetta M. ...,b. Mar. 4, 1900   Mar. Thos. J. Cavanagh d. Aug. 30, 1938

John J. ....b. Mar. 30, 1902
Joseph Anth. ......b. July 9, 1903
Regina M. ....b. Oct. 31, 1904   Mar. George Wist
Peter J. ....b. Mar. 3, 1909
Edward ....b. Apr. 24, 1911
WILLIAM F. .....b. Dec. 4, 1878   d. Jan. 10, 1907   Mar. Mary Teresa Becker b. Oct. 9, 1879—Parents— Jno. Becker & Josephine Sellmayer
   Married—Thanksgiving 1903

Marie ....b. Sept. 19, 1904
Joseph ....b. July 17, 1906   Mar. Angela Hooper
JOSEPH A. ......b. Dec. 10, 1882   Mar. Dora Becker, b. Apr. 25, 1882
   Sister to Mary Teresa Becker
   Marriage—July 4, 1907

Genevieve ....b. Jan. 3, 1910   Sister of Notre Dame Aug. 8, 1935
Dorothy ....b. July, 10, 1912   Mar. Charles E. Jackson— Parents—Chas. Elmer & Alma M. Childress.
   Soc. of Jesus, Aug. 15, 1932

Nicholas ....b. Jan. 17, 1914
Marie ....b. Aug. 14, 1915
Anne ....b. Dec. 9, 1917
Irene ....b. Dec. 1, 1919
Joseph ....b. May 19, 1921
Francis ....b. Jan. 31, 1924
Teresa ....b. Sept. 26, 1926

VI. Generation—Children of Fred. J. Kunkel and Kath. K. nee Busch
   Mar. Dora Bilz, Parents—Joseph Bilz & Barb. Beyer

1. John N. Kunkel, Jr.   Marriage—June 19, 1912
   Children—1. Catherine .b. Nov. 26, 1914   mar. Adolph Pons
      Child—Barbara
      2. Helen ...b. Sept. 12, 1915   mar. J. Carvel Archer
      Child.—1. J. Carvel ...b. Jan. 26, 1938
      2. Dorothea Lee.b. Jan. 27, 1939
      3. Gerard ...b. Jan. 24, 1925
2. Catherine ....b. Nov. 10, 1894   Mar. Charles Miller
3. Charles ....b. Nov. 4, 1896   Mar. Eveloyne Kraus, Aug. 1, 1936
   Child—Charlotte
4. M. Lydia ....b. Aug. 30, 1899   Sister of Good Shepherd, Sister Philomena
5. Francis W. ....b. Apr. 24, 1906   Mar. Dorothy Heinicke, July 8, 1933
   Child—Fred. J.

VI. Generation—Children of John A. Kunkel and Anna Vaeth
   FRANCIS F. .....b. Sept. 29, 1894   mar. 1st wife—Marg. von Gestal, d. 1922
   2nd wife—Mary Willenburg
   TERESA ....b. Sept. 7, 1896   mar. Francis Thim, Oct. 9, 1923. b. Apr. 7, 1891. Son of Frank P. Thim and Cath. Rudel.
   Children—
1. Bernadette ....b. May. 20, 1925
2. Margaret ....b. Aug. 27, 1926
3. Regina ....b. Feb. 3, 1928
4. Dorothy ....b. Apr. 2, 1930
5. Catherine ....b. Mar. 20, 1932
6. Francis ....b. Mar. 3, 1934
7. Charles ....b. Mar. 9, 1936
8. Richard ....b. Dec. 14, 1938
9. Elizabeth Patricia ..b. Feb. 5, 1940

Page Thirty-one

FOUR GENERATIONS OF KUNKELS
(1940)

Above—Mrs. Chas. Miller, Mrs. Chas. J. Kunkel, Fred. J. Kunkel, Rev. F. W. Kunkel, Francis W. Kunkel, Gerard Kunkel, John N. Kunkel, Mrs. Francis W. Kunkel, Mrs. John N. Kunkel.
Below—Mrs. Adolph Pons, Mrs. J. Carvel Archer, J. Carvel Archer, Jr., Charlotte Kunkel, Dorothy Lee Archer, Barbara Katharine Pons.

LINEAL DESCENDENTS OF MR. JOHN N. KUNKEL

JAMES ....b. Sept. 9, 1898   mar. Marg. Hubbard, May 12, 1931.
b. Nov. 22, 1900
Children—
Joseph ....b. Mar. 1, 1934
Marg. M. ....b. Jan. 30, 1936
WILLIAM ....b. Feb. 18, 1901   mar. Mary Bond, June 15, 1926
Children
William ....b. Dec. 19, 1927

VI. Generation—Children of TERESA M. KUNKEL and PETER J. WARD

JEANNETTE .....b. Mar. 4, 1900   mar. Thos. Cavanaugh, b. Apr. 6, 1893
d. Aug. 30, 1938
Parents—Philip and Cath. Cavanaugh
Mar. Apr. 15, 1920

Children—
Philip ....b. Feb. 15, 1921
Rose ....b. Feb. 24, 1924
Regina ....b. July 18, 1926
Thomas ....b. Oct. 29, 1927
Peter ....b. Mar. 27, 1930

JOSEPH J. ....b. Mar. 30, 1902   mar. Eliz. Smith, b. Nov. 26, 1905
Parents—George and Cecelia Hammel
mar. June 4, 1929
Children—
Joseph A. ....b. Feb. 26, 1931
Mary Ellen ....b. Aug. 6, 1934

REGINA ....b. Oct. 31, 1904   mar. George Wist
Parents—Michael and Teresa Schleicher
mar. Aug. 2, 1927

George J. ....b. Apr. 21, 1928
Paul G. ....b. July 25, 1929
Rose M. ....b. Dec. 27, 1930
Jean ....b. Dec. 9, 1937

Children of WILLIAM F. KUNKEL and MARY BECKER

JOSEPH A. ....b. July 17, 1906   mar. Angela Hooper, b. Jan. 22, 1908
Parents—Timothy Hooper and Mary Weidenham
mar. Aug. 10, 1929

Joan ....b. Mar. 11, 1931
Jay ....b. Oct. 16, 1932

Children of JOSEPH A. KUNKEL and DORA BECKER

DOROTHY ....b. July 20, 1912   mar. Chas. Jackson
Parents—Chas. E. Jackson and Alma M. Childress

Charles E. ....b. Oct. 1, 1935
Joseph Nicholas ..b. Dec. 7, 1939

TAUFBESCHEINIGUNG
Name— Johan Adam Kunkel
Vater—George Kunkel
Mutter—Katharina geb. Schreck
Geboren u. getauft 3 Sept., 1800 zu Rossbach
    Kath. Pfarramt Kleiwallstadt 21 Juni, 1936
       L. Spangenberger, Pfarrer.
Name—Anna Maria Christ
*Vater—Heinrich Christ
Mutter—Margaretha geb. Koerbel
Geboren u. getauft 24 Juni, 1801, zu Gailbach
    Kath. Pfarramt zu U.Lb. Frau
      Aschaffenburg 21 Mai, 1936
      Liebenstein, Kpl.
*Parents of Heinrich Christ
    John Geo. Christ and Marg. Emmerich
      Children—Catherine, b. 1782
          John Henry, b. 1784
          Paul, b. 1790

Page Thirty-three

COLLATERAL DESCENDENTS OF JOHN N. KUNKEL

ADAM KUNKEL (1st Husband), b. Rossbach, Sept 3, 1800, d. Jan. 4, 1837

NICH. KUNKEL (2nd Husband), b. July 27, 1810, d. Phila., July 3, 1887

ANNA MARIA CHRIST, b. Gailbach, June 24, 1801, d. Phila., July 3, 1887.

Children—1st Marriage—III Generation

1. NICHOLAS ...... b. May, 23, 1823 — came to America about 1866, died 1 year later at his son George's
2. PETER .... b. Apr. 9, 1825 — d. Oct. 22, 1883 — mar. Marg. Hoffman, Phila.
3. GENEVIEVE .... b. Feb. 25, 1827 — d. Mar. 13, 1827
4. EVA .... b. Feb. 24, 1829 — d. Aug. 31, 1894 — mar. John Schreck, Phila.
5. JOHN N. .... b. Sept. 23, 1831 — d. June 29, 1910 — mar. Mary R. Kerchner
6. GEORGE .... b. Nov. 19, 1833 — d. Oct. 18, 1888 — mar. Mary Amberg, Phila.

after the death of ADAM, A. M. CHRIST mar. NICH. brother of Adam

7. ALOIS .... b. Apr. 22, 1840 — d. Jan. 4, 1844
8. KASPER .... b. Jan. 18, 1842 — mar. Marg. Benkler, d. Jan. 2, 1919

PETER KUNKEL (1825-1883)—MARG. HOFFMAN (1830-1916)

Children   IV Generation

1. JOHN N. .... b. Oct. 29, 1855 — d. Oct. 23, 1938 — mar. Sallie Casey, d. May 27, 1912
2. SEBASTIAN ..... b. Aug. 1, 1858 — d. Oct. 18 1924 — mar. Ottillie Linder
3. HARRY .... b. Jan. 11, 1862 — mar. Elizabeth Frosch, Nov. 26 1893
4. MARY ANNE .... b. Jan. 24, 1864 — mar. Andrew Frosch
5. EMMA .... b. Aug. 25, 1868 — d. July 14, 1913 — mar. Joseph Raeyling
6. GEO. PETER .... b. Oct. 19, 1870 — d. July 30, 1870

EVA KUNKEL, b. Feb. 24, 1829, d. Aug. 31, 1894—mar. JOHN S. SCHRECK, b. 1826, d. Mar. 1, 1875

Children—
CASPER .... b. Oct. 13, 1859
GERTRUDE ..... b. Mar. 17, 1862 — d. Dec. 18, 1910
NICHOLAS ..... b. Jan. 8, 1866 — d. Oct. 25, 1893

1. JOHN N. (1855-1938) married SALLIE CASEY (1852-1912)

Katharine ..... b. May 13, 1875 — mar. Oct. 12, 1899, Dominic Olivieri, b. Mar. 30, 1868. Son—John P. b. April, 1892

Margaret ...... b. May 22, 1878 — Mar. J. Kerper Propert, 1913. Children Frank, b. 1915. John Oliver and Kerper Geo.—twins, b. 1917.

Page Thirty-four

Top Row—Eliz. Raeyling, Harry K., Mary and And. Frosch, Jos. Raeyling, Sebast. K.
Mid. Row—Marg. K., Mary K., Mrs. Ward and Rose M. Mrs. Harry K. and John, Marg. Propert, Sallie K., Katie Oliver, Tillie K.
Bot. Row—Wm. K. (Seb's son), Harry F., Mame (Seb's D.), John (Seb's son), John Oliver, Joe K., Teresa Purzer, Margaret (Mrs. Bruckheiser)

COLLATERAL DESCENDENTS OF JOHN N. KUNKEL
PETER KUNKEL AND MARG. HOFFMANN

2. SEBASTIAN (1858-1924) married (OTTILLIE LINDER 1858-   )

   1. Mary E. .....b. Feb. 26, 1885

   2. Harry F. ...b. Nov. 8, 1886   d. 1887

   3. Edward H. ..b. May 13, 1888   d. Aug. 3, 1888

   4. William A. ..b. June 6, 1889   mar. Marg. Mayer, Aug. 11, 1914, d. Dec. 22, 1917. Mar. Mary Claughsey, Aug. 31, 1920.
      Children—
      Dorothy Mary .....b. Aug. 23, 1921
      Wm. A. ....b. Jan 19, 1930

   5. Marg. E. ....b. Dec. 9, 1890   Mar. Wm. Bruckheiser, June 9, 1914. Son—Wm. A., b. Feb. 5, 1917.

   6. John H. ....b. April 13, 1893   Mar. Evelyn M. Bowen, June 16, 1917

   7. Florence E. .b. Aug. 30, 1895   Mar. Jos. M. Adam, Nov. 24, 1921.
      Children—
      Florence M. ....b. Oct. 10, 1922
      Marg. Evelyn .....b. June 6, 1924
      Ruth B. ....b. Feb. 26, 1926
      Jos. M. ....b. Aug. 6, 1931

   8. Joseph G. ...b. Jan. 19, 1897   Mar. Lillian B. Welsh, June 28, 1922.
      Children—
      Joseph M. ....b. Sept. 24, 1923
      Mary T. ....b. Aug. 6, 1925
      Regina A. ....b. May 23, 1927
      Loretta ....b. Nov. 10, 1928
      Dolores E. ....b. May 10, 1930
      Jno. Jos. M. ....b. Nov. 16, 1931
      Mercedes Jos. .....b. Mar. 19, 1933

   9. Henry Edw. .b. Dec. 26, 1898   Mar. Anna C. Diegel, Aug. 22, 1923.
      Children—
      Anna ....b. Apr. 24, 1925
      Henry E. ....b. Jan. 14, 1927
      Charles ....b. Sept. 4, 1932
      Eugene ....b. Apr. 11, 1935
      Jos. Richard ...... b. Feb. 13, 1937

   10. Francis S. ..b. Oct. 24, 1902   Mar. Florence M. Scheihing, Sept. 24, 1930.

   11. Regina O. ...b. July, 1904   d. 1905

3. CASPER HERMAN (Harry) KUNKEL (1862-   ) and ELIZABETH FROSCH (1867-   ) Mar. Nov. 26, 1897.

   1. John H. ....b. Oct. 10, 1897   d. Dec. 10, 1913
   2. Andrew C. ..b. May 5, 1899   Mar. Loretto Maloney.   Child—Elizabeth C., b. July 7, 1935.

4. MARY A. KUNKEL (1864-   ) and ANDREW FROSCH (1863-1940) Mar. Sept. 22, 1884

   1. Harry ....b. Dec. 21, 1885   Mar. Jennie Barr, b. 1887.
      1. Maria (1909) mar. Wm. Porter (1896)
      Children—
      Mary Anne ....b. 1932
      Joan ....b. 1933
      William ....b. 1936
      2. Harry, Jr. (1913) mar. Magdalen Lang (1918)
      3. Ava Sarah (1914)
      4. Andrew (1918)
      5. Jane (1920)
      6. Margaret (1922)

   2. Mary E. ......b. Nov. 22, 1890   Mar. Albert Murphy, Sept. 9, 1913. Daughter—Mary E., b. Aug. 12, 1914. Mar. Julius Foldes, M.D.

5. EMMA KUNKEL (1868-1913) and JOSEPH RAEYLING

6. GEO. PETER . b. Oct. 19, 1870   d. July 30, 1872

4. EVA KUNKEL (1829-1894) and JOHN SCHRECK (1826-1875)
   Children—
     1. Casper ....b. Oct. 13, 1859   Mar. Emma Seitz, b. 1872.
     Children—
     Gertrude ....b. May 2, 1914
     John A. ....b. Aug. 13, 1916
     2. Gertrude ....b. Mar. 17, 1862   d. Dec. 18, 1910
     3. Nicholas ....b. Jan. 8, 1866   d. Oct. 25, 1893

Page Thirty-six

COLLATERAL DESCENDANTS OF JOHN N. KUNKEL

5. JOHN NEPOMUCK KUNKEL (1831-1910) and MARY ROSINA KERCHNER (1839-1906)
   Children—
   1. Fred. J. ....b. Sept. 23, 1860   Mar. Catherine Busch (1865-1934)
   2. Joseph A. ......b. July 12, 1862   d. same day
   3. Mary Regina ..b. Sept. 6, 1863   d. Feb. 14, 1915 Single
   4. Mich. A. ....b. July 10, 1865   d. Aug. 31, 1865
   5. Jno. Alph. .....b. Aug. 5, 1866   Mar. Anna Vaeth (1865-1905)
                     d. May 30, 1935
   6. Nich. A. ....b. June 17, 1868   Mar. Barb. Schneider
                     d. Dec. 12, 1935
   7. Francis F. ....b. July 9, 1870   Ord. Priest, June 4, 189
   8. Teresa M. .....b. Aug. 14, 1872   Mar. Peter J. Ward
                     d. Feb. 8, 1932   (1872-   )
   9. Marg. Dorothy .b. Dec. 1, 1874   Sister Johannetta
                                           Prof. Aug. 12, 1896
   10. Jos. Anth. ......b. May 27, 1876   d. June 6, 1882
   11. Wm. Francis ..b. Dec. 4, 1878   Mar. Mary Becker,
                     d. Jan. 10, 1907   b. 1879
   12. Joseph A. .....b. Dec. 10, 1882   Mar. Dora E. Becker, 1882
   13. Teresa Purzur .b. Aug. 27, 1880   Mar. Jos. Brennan
                     (adopted)

6. GEORGE KUNKEL (1833-1888) and MARY AMBERG (1841-1900)
   Children—
   1. Frances A. .....b. Nov. 3, 1865   Mar. Chas. Albert
      Children—
        1. Chas. G. ....b. Mar. 20, 1891
        2. Florence ....b. May 17, 1892
        3. Edward, J. ....b. Feb. 28, 1894
        4. Anna T. ....b. Feb. 25, 1895
        5. Marie A. ....b. June 27, 1896
        6. Frances C. ....b. Nov. 5, 1897
        7. Raymond ....b. Oct. 26, 1899
        8. Adelle E. ....b. Oct. 28, 19""
        9. Frank A. ....b. July 9, 19""
        10. Gerard A. ....b. Oct. 23, 1903
   2. Anna T. ....b. Dec. 4, 1868   Single
   3. John G. ....b. 1874   died infant
   4. Mary C. ....b. Jan. 2, 1876   Single
      George ....b. 1877   d. 1878

7. CASPER EMMANUEL KUNKEL (1842-1929) and MARG. BENKLER (1850-1919)
   Children—
   1. Anna Marie 1873-1882
   2. Fred. 1875-1920
   3. Emma 1876-1887
   4. George 1877-1878
   5. Mary Genevieve .b. Apr. 20, 1879
         Mar. Wm. Vincent (1864-1935). Son—Wm. H.
         Jr., b. Sept. 25, 1907. Mar. Marg. M. Carlron on Aug. 7, 1937.
         Child—William H. Vincent, Jr., b. Aug. 14, 1938.
   6. Herman 1881-1882
   7. Frances G. .....b. Sept. 28, 1882
         Mar. Chas. A. Born, b. Aug. 7, 1881.
         Daughter—Dorothy, Mar. Wm Muller.
         Children—Wm. C., b. Dec. 3, 1932.
                   Dorothy, Sept. 20, 1935.
   8. Marg. C. ....b. Mar. 5, 1884
         Mar. Aug. Koenig, b. 1879.
         Daughter—Lucille, b. Oct. 4, 1909. Mar John
         B. Scheuhing on Oct. 8, 1938.
         Child—Sarah Ann, b. Nov. 2, 1939.
   9. Anne Cecile ....b. Dec. 3, 1889   Mar. Edward Hartman
      Children—
        1. Marg. Elizabeth, b. July 1, 1914, mar.
           William Coulter on July 1st, 1939.
        2. Edward John ..b. Mar. 8, 1925

Page Thirty-seven

PATERNAL GRANDPARENTS OF MARY R. KERCHNER

From The Parish Records, Freudenberg, Baden, Germany
Oct. 16, 1936—Otto Zaehringer

PAUL KERCHNER
Born—Jan. 19, 1782
Died—Sept. 14, 1856

ROSINA MUSSIG
Born—July 12, 1778
Died—April 16, 1855
Married February 16, 1802
Children—
1. Michael A. .....b. Jan. 10, 1804 Died Mar. 13, 1857
2. John David ....b. Jan. 13, 1808 (Died Wilmington, Del., 1838?)
3. Mary Marg. ....b. Aug. 24, 1812 Mar. James Mai, Feb. 5, 1834
              d. Sept. 1, 1857
4. John Paul ....b. Mar. 29, 1817
              d. Apr. 7, 1817
5. Anna ....b. Jan. 13, 1822 Mar. Leonard Mai (brother of James)
              d. July 8, 1872   June 18, 1844.

MICHAEL A. KERCHNER (1807-1849) and ANNA MARIA KERN (1806-1870)

Children—
1. Francis Wm. ..b. Jan. 20, 1829   Mar. Lydia C. Hatch   b. 1857
              d. Apr. 2, 1910   d. 1894
2. Fred. Aug. ....b. Jan. 13, 1831   Mar. Marg. Cath. Burger   b. ....
              d. Dec. 31, 1898   d. 1902
3. Adrian ....b. 1834, d. infant
4. Ferdinand ....b. July 11, 1835   Mar. Frederica Hubel
              d. June 2, 1918   Mar. Anna Linnenkemper   d. 1914
5. Adolph ....b. June 1, 1837   Mar. Mary Hubel
              d. Dec. 31, 1913
6. M. Rosina ....b. Aug. 9, 1839   Mar. John N. Kunkel   b. 1831
              d. Feb. 3, 1906   d. 1910
7. Catherine ....b. Nov. 21, 1841   Mar. Henry Neubeck   b. 1841
              d. Nov. 11, 1924 1924   d. 1916
8. Caroline .....b. Dec. 22, 1843   Mar. Mich. Hessler   d. 1910
              d. 1898
9. Josephine ....b. 1847
              d. 1855

MATERNAL GRANDPARENTS OF MARY ROSINA KERCHNER

Parish Records, Freudenberg, Baden, Germany
August 17, 1836, Hormuth, Pastor

John Dom. Kern born Feb. 12, 1781. (died Mar. 29, 1826)
Margaret Vaeth, his 1st wife born Feb. 24, 1780. (died Nov. 16, 1820)
Marriage was blessed by the Church, Apr. 30, 1805.
Children:—
1. Anna Maria ....b. Jan. 21, 1806   d. Balto., Mar. 5, 1870—Mar. M. A. Kerchner.
2. Susanna ....b. Aug. 9, 1807   d. St. Louis, Jan. 19, 1896—Mar. Emil U. Hugunin.
3. Jos. Anth. ....b. Oct. 6, 1809   d. May 10, 1848—Letter No. 27, Brother-in-law, Fautter.
4. Dominic ....b. Dec. 4, 1811   d. Aug. 16, 1871—Mar. Regina Kettinger, 1834.
5. Vitus ....b. June 14, 1814   d. in infancy
6. Matthew ....b. Sept. 12, 1816 d. Mar. 1893
7. David ....b. Dec. 30, 1818
8. Dorothy ....b. Oct. 11, 1820   d. Balto., Feb. 11, 1903—Mar. Val. Ruppert.

Second Marriage
John Dom. Kern married Susanna Ziegler—Feb. 21, 1821.
9. Ehrhardt ....b. Jan. 8, 1822
10. Mary Josepha .....b. Mar. 23, 1824   Mar. Jos. Mich. Meck.
                                         Rev. Jos. A. Meck, son of this last Marriage was Teacher in the Gymnasium and Prison Chaplain, in Mannheim, Germany in 1897, when F.W.K. visited him.

Page Thirty-eight

PATERNAL GRANDPARENTS OF MARY ROSINA KERCHNER

From the Parish Records of Freudenberg, (Baden) Oct. 16, 1930,
by the Parish Priest Otto Zaehringer

PAUL KERCHNER
Born Jan. 19 1782
Died Sept. 14, 1856

ROSINA MUSSIG
Born July 12, 1778
Died April 16, 1855
Married Feb. 16, 1802

Children:—
1. Michael Anthony ....b. Jan. 10, 1804   d. Mar. 13, 1857
2. John David ....b. Jan. 13 1808   (Died in Wilmington, Del. 1838)
3. Mary Margaret ......b. Aug. 24, 1812   Mar. James Mai, Feb. 5, 1834
                            d. Sept. 1, 1857
4. John Paul ....b. Mar. 29, 1817   d. April 7, 1817
5. Anna ....b. Jan. 13, 1822   Mar. Leonard, brother of James Mai, June 18,
                            d. July 8, 1872   1844

Margaret Kerchner (sister of Michael Anthony K.)
Married James Mai, 1834

Children

Louis	Edward	Regina	Joseph	Barbara	Ignatius	Mary
August		Rose	Elizabeth	Emma	James	Anthony
Emma		Anna	Rudolph	Katherine	Katherine	Bertha
Charles		Mary	Teresa	Mary	Joseph	Joseph
Eugene		Ida	Frederick	Edward	Lina	
		Helen		Clara		
		Bertha		Lawrence		
				Joseph		

Anna Kerchner (sister of Michael A. K.)
Married Leonard Mai, 1844

Children

| Francis | Teresa | Herman | Rose | Anna | Emma | Matilda |
	Adolf	Brand				
Adolph	Anna*	Matilda	Louis	Herman		
Teresa	Otto-1932	Anna	Anna	Rose		
Otto**	Emma	Frank-1935	Matilda			
August***		Mary	Charles			
Herman****		Emma	Richard			
			Otto			
			Anthony			

    *Anna Brand became Franciscan Sister, Glen Riddle, Pa., Sister Adelheima, O. F. M. Purcell, Okla. Emma Brand, also entered convent and died in Westfalen.
    **Otto Mai has a Bakery in Freudenberg.
    ***August was a teacher in Donaueschingen, died in 1930 and was buried at home.
    ****Herman was Principal of a School in Voelkersbach, in 1926, later in 1930 in Pforzheim, according to Rev. Otto Zaehringer, Pastor of Freudenberg, 1930.
    The above list was given Rev. F. W. Kunkel on his visit to Freudenberg.
                                            —Sept. 1897

Thirty-nine

See page 189 for an index to the numbers in this photograph. The index was apparently left out of this document.

COLLATERAL DESCENDENTS OF MARY ROSINA KERCHNER

MICHAEL ANTHONY KERCHNER, b. Jan. 10, 1807, Freudenberg, d. July 11, 1849, Baltimore.
ANNA MARIA KERN, b. Jan. 21, 1806, Freudenberg, d. May 5, 1870, Baltimore.
Married Feb. 12, 1828.
Children—

1. FRANCIS WM. .....b. Jan. 29, 1829 Mar. Lydia C. Kerchner nee Hatch
   d. Apr. 2, 1910 b. Jan. '37, d. June 21, 1894
2. FRED. AUGUSTUS .d Jan. 13, 1831 Mar. Cath. Burger, d. Oct. 17, 1912.
   d. Dec. 31, 1898
3. ADRIAN ....b. 1833
   d. 1834
4. FERDINAND ......b. July 11, 1835 Mar. Frederica Hubel 1st wife—Anna Linnenkemper, d. Nov. 26, 1914.
   d. June 2, 1918
5. ADOLPH ....b. June 1, 1837 Mar. Mary Hubel
   d. 1915
6. M. ROSINA ....b. Aug. 9, 1839 Mar. John N. Kunkel
   d. Feb. 3, 1906
7. CATHERINE ......b. Nov. 21, 1841 Mar. Henry Neubeck
   d. 1924
8. CAROLINE ....b. Dec. 22, 1843 Mar. Mich. Hessler
9. JOSEPHINE ....b. 1847
   d. 1855

II. Frederick A. Kerchner (1831-1898) and Anna Catherine Burger (1831-1912)

1. Catherine Dorothy (1855-1910) mar. John E. Hoover (d. June 21, 1927)
   Children:—
   (a) Frederick ...d. R.R. accident
   (b) Ella Rose ..Mar. John McDonald
       Child—Rose Agnes
   (c) Francis ....Mar. May Stafford, d. 1918
       Mar. Marg. Eleanor Fischer
       Child.—1. Catherine mar Henry E. Tiepermann, Jr.
       2. Francis
       3. Elizabeth
       4. John
       5. Jerome
       6. Margaret
   (d) Catherine ..Mar. Henry Curlander
       Child.—1. Henry
       2. Carroll
   (e) Joseph .....Mar. Bertha Wilhelm
       Child.—1. Helen
       2. Virginia
   (f) Helen ......Mar. Henry Wich
       Child.—1. Carl
       2. Mary Lucille
   (g) Mary ......Mar. Robert Hoy
       Child.—1. Robert
       2. Dorothy

2. Francis William (1857-1926) mar. Flora Letta (1896)
   d. Auto accident, Feb. 15, 1926.

3. Charles Frederick mar. Mary McGowan (1887)
   d. July 15, 1937
   Child.—(a) Pauline mar. Julius O. Knight
       Child.—1. Lyle mar. Helen L. Imbach
           Child.—1. R o b e r t Lyle, e. Jan. 12, 1940.
       2. Mary mar. John O'Mara
           Child.—1. John Paul
           2. Mary Jean
       3. Julius
   (b) Charles mar. Helen Blair
       Child.—1. Blair
   (c) Mary, d. infant
   (d) Beatrice Sister Aloysius, Sister of Mercy

4. Henry Adolph (1861-   ) mar. Isabelle Forman
   Child.—1. Helen mar. Fred. Essary
       Child.—1. Annabelle
       2. Margaret
   2. Hilda mar. Walter Heger
       Child.—1. Caroline
   3. Isabelle mar. Bennet Croswell
       Child.—1. Harry

Page Forty-one

COLLATERAL DESCENDENTS OF MARY ROSINA KERCHNER

Children of Fred. A. Kerchner and Catherine Burger

5. Ella Anastasia (1864-   ) mar. Oct. 26, 1886 Robert Charles Norman (d. Apr. 9, 1937)
   Children:—
   (a) John Hugh .. mar. Julia Bowie Tisdale
     Child.—1. Julia Waring mar. Donald Francis Krick, Lieut., U.S.N.
        2. John H., Jr.
        3. Ella mar. Wm. Dean Roberson, Lieut. U.S.M.C.
        4. Robert
        5. Katherine
   (b) Ella M. J. ...
   (c) Marg. Cath. ..
   (d) Rose Teresa ..
   (e) Robert C., Jr. .mar. Winifred Halberstadt
   (f) Oswald Byrne. d. Feb. 8, 1920
   (g) Mary Dor. ...

6. Rosina Athalia (1871-   ) mar Charles Edward Lewis (d. Jan. 21, 1927)
   (a) Katherine ....mar. Paul McDonnell
     Child.—1. Paul, d. infant
        2. M. Katherine, Dec. 30, 1921
        3. Chas. Lewis, Feb. 9, 1924
        4. Rosina, Feb. 24, 1927
        5. James Edw., Dec. 24, 1928
        6. Francis Virginia, Jan. 28, 1930
        7. Dorothy Irene, Jan. 12, 1932
        8. Bernadine, Nov. 4, 1936
   (b) Rosina ....Carmelite—Sister Regina of Jesus
     (1900-)
   (c) Mary Bertha .mar. Henry Abella, d. 1937
     (1907-)
     Child.—1. Henry Chas., b. Dec. 5, 1928, d. Feb. 23, 1928.
        2. Joseph, b. Apr. 24, 1930
     mar. Wm. Drummond Coakley, Dec. 25, 1939
   (d) Charles F. ...b. Dec. 22, 1909 d. Auto accident, Nov. 10, 1925

III ADRIAN died in infancy

IV. FERDINAND, b. July 11, 1835,   1st Wife—Frederica Hubel—no issue
    d. June, 1918   2nd wife—Anna Linnenkemper
                                      b. Jan. 21, 1839, d. Nov. 26, 1914

  1. Mary Cath., b. June 10, 1861   Mar. John Zang
     d. Jan. 3, 1925
                                     1. Anna M., b. Feb. 2, 1883
                                     2. Margaret, b. July 3, 1884
                                     3. Catharine, b. Mar. 10, 1886
                                     4. M. Clara, b. Jan. 13, 1888
                                     5. M. Regina, b. Feb. 9, 1890
                                     6. M. Teresa, b. May 12, 1892
                                     7. M. Gertrude, b. June 28, 1894
                                     8. Mabel Genev., b. Mar. 8, 1896
                                     9. Jno. Gerard, b. Feb. 4, 1898
                                     10. William, b. Aug. 2, 1901
                                     11. M. Beatrice, b. April 19, 1904

  2. Anna, b. Nov. 6, 1865   Single

  3. M. Regina, b. Apr. 20, 1873   Mar. Herman Hulshoff
                                     1. Anna Gert., b. Sept. 30, 1896. Mar. Charles Gonce
                                     2. M. Alfrida, b. Mar. 1, 1900
                                     3. M. Rosalia, b. July 28, 1902
                                     4. Dorothy Antoinette, b. Feb. 9, 1906
                                     5. M. Agnes
                                         Gerard   } b. May 24, 1911
                                         Regina

  4. Ferd. Jno., b. June 15, 1875   Mar. Mary Mullaly
     d. May 3, 1925
                                     1. Wm. Ferd.
                                     2. Francis
                                     3. Jas. Albert
                                     4. Kathleen
                                     5. Jno. Norbert

Page Forty-two

Note that in line IV.3.5, the middle triplet was named Herman; he died at birth. Regina's last son Gerard was born in July of 1915. See "Errata" on page 64.

COLLATERAL DESCENDENTS OF MARY ROSINA KERCHNER

5. John J., b. Dec. 11, 1877 — Mar. Caroline Fisher
   1. M. Loretta
   2. M. Lucille. Mar. Jos. F. Fritzges
      Children:—1. Mary Joe
                2. Jane Frances
   3. Geo. W.
   4. John A.

6. William F., b. June 6, 1881 — Single
   d. June 19, 1922

7. Mary Teresa, b. Oct. 15, 1883
   d. July 2, 1885

V. ADOLPH .... b. June 1, 1837 — Mar. Mary Hubel
                d. Dec. 31, 1915   no children

VI. MARY ROSINA ... b. Aug. 9, 1839 — Mar. John N. Kunkel
                  d. Feb. 3, 1906   b. 1831, d. 1910
   1. Frederick   Mar. Catherine Busch—1865-1934
     (1860-   )   Children:—John N.—1888
                            Denis—1891
                            Joseph—1892
                            John H. 1894
                            M. Cath.—adopted
                            Chas. J.—1896
                            M. Lydia—1899
                            M. Regina—1901
                            Francis—1906

   2. Jos. Anthony (1) — died an infant

   3. Mary Regina — 1863-1915 unmarried

   4. Mich. Anth. — died an infant

   5. John Alph. — Mar. Anna Vaeth 1865-1905
     (1866-1935)   Children:—Anna M.—1891
                             Mary E.—1892
                           Francis F.—1894
                           Teresa—1896
                           James—1898
                           William—1901
                           Agnes—1903

   6. Nicholas A. — Mar. Barbara Schneider, d. 1933
     (1868-1935)   Child:—Francis, 1894

   7. Francis Ferd. — ord. June 4, 1898
     (1870-   )

   8. Teresa — Mar. Peter J. Ward, 1872-
     (1872-1932)   Children:—Rose Marie—1898
                             Francis—1899
                           Jeannette—1900
                           John J.—1902
                           Joseph A.—1903
                           Regina M.—1904
                           Peter J.—1909
                           Edward—1911

   9. Marg. Dorothy — Sister of Chr. Charity—1896
     (1874-   )

   10. Jos. Anth. (3) — b. 1876, d. 1882

   11. Wm. Francis — Mar. Mary Becker, b. 1879
     (1878-1907)   Children:—Marie—1904
                           Joseph—1906

Page Forty-three

COLLATERAL DESCENDENTS OF MARY ROSINA KERCHNER

Children of Mary Rosina and John N. Kunkel

12. Joseph Anth.   Mar. Dora E. Becker
    (1882-   )   1882-
    Children:—Genevieve—1910—Sister Notre Dame
    Dorothy—1912—Mar. Chas. E. Jackson, Jr.
    Nicholas—1914—Jesuit
    Marie—1915
    Anne—1917
    Irene—1919
    Joseph—1921
    Francis—1924
    Teresa—1926

13. Theresa Purzer   Mar. Jos. Brennan
    (adopted 1889-   ).

7. CATHERINE KERCHNER and Henry Neubeck 1841-1916

    Adolph   Mar. Ella G. Ballenger
    (1874-1931)   1889
    Children:—Cath. Barbara—1907
    Francis G.—1908
    Mary Estelle—1910—Mar. Wm. Newton Landis, Sept. 29, 1939
    Ella Rose—1911
    Gertrude Emily—1913—Mar. M. Kibler

    Francis L.   Mar. Mary D. Curran
                     1875-1933
    Children:—John H.—1909—Mar. Marg. Nemmers. Child.—1. Margaret
    Cath. A.—1911
    Mary A.—1914
    Francis L.—1916

8. CAROLINE KERCHNER and Michael Hessler
   1846-1898, b. Cambridge, Md.   -1910

    John Wm.
    1869-1931
    Anna Eva, b. 1871   d.
    Frank A.   Mar. Tillie Werner
    1873-   Children:—Minnie C. (Krespach)—1890
    Geo. F.—1900
    Madeline (Bonhoff)—1905
    Josephine (Ritter)—1913

9. JOSEPHINE KERCHNER, b. 1847, d. 1855

Page Forty-four

*** END OF FR. KUNKEL'S KUNKEL-KERCHNER MANUSCRIPT ***

John Brown's Papers from Harpers Ferry

The document below relates to the papers taken from John Brown after his capture at Harpers Ferry, which was mentioned on page Error: Reference source not found above.

---

84   CALENDAR OF STATE PAPERS.

W. P. SMITH, M. OF D. B. & O. R. R., TO A. HUNTER, ESQ'R.

1859. October 25, Baltimore.

At the request of Gov'r Wise, of Virginia, President Garrett, of this Company, has directed me to receive and send to you for use in prosecution of the Rioters, taken at Harper's Ferry, such letters and other papers as could be found in this city bearing upon the case. I enclose herewith three letters obtained from the "Clipper" newspaper office, which are all they say they have, viz., a letter (without signature), dated at Akron, May 25, '59; a letter dated Philadelphia, June 6, '59, addressed to Alonzo G. Bradley by R. T. Steif, Jr.; and another dated at Hallowell, April 28th, '58, addressed to "My dear Brother," and signed "Lizzie." Upon enquiry at the offices of the "American," "Exchange," and "Sun" newspapers, I was informed that they did not have any letters or papers bearing upon the case, and that those they published were borrowed from the office of the "Clipper."

We have secured for a few days for you, the use of the following named papers from Mr. F. W. Kerchner, a Lieut. of one of our Militia Companies. These papers were taken from Brown's house by Mr. K., and he gives us the use of them only on condition that they will be safely returned to him, which we have promised, and which, we hope, you will enable us to faithfully carry out by returning them to this office as soon as you may have finished with them. It may be proper to state that these papers were secured together by Mr. Kerchner with a view to their preservation.

They are as follows:

Four pages of the life of "Old Brown."
A printed circular, "The duty of the Soldier No. 1."
Letter signed "O. S." to "Brother and Sister," dated at Chambersburg.
Receipt from Chas. Blair to Jno. Brown for $150—on ac.
Letter to J. H. Kagi, dated Aug. 16th, 1858.
Letter to Jno. Brown from Gerrit Smith, June 8th, '59.
Receipt to E. A. Adams from Orwin Phelps, for $7.
A printed Blank Officer's Commission.
A Letter from A. Wettler, dated Moneka, K. T., March 29, '59.
Letter to J. Brown from J. R. Giddings, May 26th, 1859.
Receipt to J. Brown, from W. and L. E. Ensley for one compass, June 7, '59.
Letter to Brown from Fred. Douglass.
Letter to Brown from Charles Blair.

Your particular attention to the preservation and safe return to me of the above enumerated papers will much oblige,

Yours, &c.

From "Calendar of Virginia State Papers and Other Manuscripts from January 1, 1836 to April 15, 1869 Preserved in the Capitol at Richmond." Volume XI, Richmond, 1893. Harvard College Library Call Number 12861.15 (U.S. 18315.10)

Disposition of John Brown's papers recovered by Lt Francis William Kerchner at Harpers Ferry

This Sharp's rifle, captured during the raid at Harper's Ferry, was presented to then Lt. Francis W. Kerchner by then Colonel Robert. E. Lee.

The rifle is currently in the possession of one of my first cousin's sons; the photos were made by his wife.

The top image shows the inscription placed on the rifle for it's presentation, and reads:

Captured by The Independent Greys at The insurrection at Harper's Ferry, Oct 18th 1859 Lt. F.W. Kerchner

The lower image shows the serial number of the rifle.

SHARPS PATENT 15502 1848

Details of John Brown's Sharps Rifle presented to Lt. Kerchner

Retired Col. Francis W. Kerchner holding the Sharps Rifle at an early twentieth century reunion of the Independent Greys. - Photographed from the original mounted, framed portrait by the relative referenced above.

ID Number Cross-Reference

This is *not* an index to all the names in this document, but rather a reference to persons who are mentioned in my other books and manuscripts. Using the ID numbers from my genealogy database, references to those persons in Fr. Kunkel's book "John Nepocene Kunkel and his wife Mary Rosina Kerchner – A Short Sketch of their Lives" can be more easily located.

The page number given is that of Fr. Kunkel's book, and the reference type indicates whether the name appears in a table or chart, the narrative, or an obituary – or whether there is a photograph of the person.

ID#	Page	Ref Type	Surname	Given Name
4	42	Table	Hulshoff	Herman {M}
5	42	Table	Hulshoff	Margaret Regina (Regina) {F}
6	42	Table	Hulshoff	Alfrieda {F}
7	42	Table	Hulshoff	Herman R. {M}
8	42	Table	Kerchner [m=Hulshoff]	Mary Regina (Jennie) {F}
11	42	Table	Hulshoff	Dorothy Antoinette (Dot) {F}
14	33	Trans	Christ	Johann Georg {M}
15	33	Trans	Emmerich [m=Christ]	Margaretha {F}
16	33	Trans	Christ	Catherine {F}
17	29	Table	Christ	Johann Heinrich (Henry) {M}
17	33	Trans	Christ	Johann Heinrich (Henry) {M}
17	33	Trans	Christ	Johann Heinrich (Henry) {M}
17	33	Trans	Christ	Johann Heinrich (Henry) {M}
18	29	Table	Koerbel [m=Christ]	Margaretha (Margaret) {F}
18	33	Trans	Koerbel [m=Christ]	Margaretha (Margaret) {F}
19	33	Trans	Christ	Paul {M}
20	38	Table	Hugunin	Emil U. {M}
21	38	Table	Kern [m=Hugunin]	Susanna {F}
22	38	Table	Kern	Joseph Anthony {M}
37	43	Table	Kerchner	Francis William {M}
38	38	Table	Kerchner	Ferdinand {M}
38	41	Table	Kerchner	Ferdinand {M}
38	42	Table	Kerchner	Ferdinand {M}
39	38	Table	Linnenkemper [m=Kerchner]	Anna B. {F}
39	41	Table	Linnenkemper [m=Kerchner]	Anna B. {F}
39	42	Table	Linnenkemper [m=Kerchner]	Anna B. {F}
40	42	Table	Kerchner	Anna Gertrude {F}
44	42	Table	Hulshoff [m=Gonce]	Anna Gertrude {F}
48	38	Table	Kerchner	John David {M}
48	39	Table	Kerchner	John David {M}
49	38	Table	Mai	James {M}

Reproduction of Fr. Kunkel's Manuscript

ID#	Page	Ref Type	Surname	Given Name
49	39	Table	Mai	James {M}
49	39	Table	Mai	James {M}
50	38	Table	Kerchner [m=Mai]	Mary Margaret (Margaret) {F}
50	39	Table	Kerchner [m=Mai]	Mary Margaret (Margaret) {F}
50	39	Table	Kerchner [m=Mai]	Mary Margaret (Margaret) {F}
51	38	Table	Kerchner	John Paul {M}
51	39	Table	Kerchner	John Paul {M}
52	38	Table	Mai	Leonard {M}
52	39	Table	Mai	Leonard {M}
52	39	Table	Mai	Leonard {M}
53	38	Table	Kerchner [m=Mai]	Anna {F}
53	39	Table	Kerchner [m=Mai]	Anna {F}
53	39	Table	Kerchner [m=Mai]	Anna {F}
54	20	Photo	Kerchner	Francis William (Colonel Billy) {M}
54	21	Narrative	Kerchner	Francis William (Colonel Billy) {M}
54	22	Obituary	Kerchner	Francis William (Colonel Billy) {M}
54	38	Table	Kerchner	Francis William (Colonel Billy) {M}
54	41	Table	Kerchner	Francis William (Colonel Billy) {M}
55	38	Table	Hatch [m=Kerchner]	Lydia C. (Cass) {F}
55	41	Table	Hatch [m=Kerchner]	Lydia C. (Cass) {F}
57	38	Table	Kerchner	Frederick Augustus {M}
57	41	Table	Kerchner	Frederick Augustus {M}
57	41	Table	Kerchner	Frederick Augustus {M}
58	38	Table	Kern	Dominic {M}
59	38	Table	Kettinger [m=Kern]	Regina {F}
67	42	Table	Hulshoff [m=Hausman]	Mary Agnes (Ag) {F}
71	38	Table	Kern	Vitus {M}
72	38	Table	Kern	Matthew {M}
73	38	Table	Kern	David {M}
74	38	Table	Rupert	Valentine (Val) {M}
75	38	Table	Kern [m=Rupert]	Dorothy {F}
76	38	Table	Kern	Earhardt {M}
77	38	Table	Meck	Joseph Michael {M}
78	38	Table	Kern [m=Meck]	Mary Josepha {F}
79	38	Table	Meck	Rev. Joseph A. {M}
82	38	Table	Kerchner	Paul {M}
82	39	Table	Kerchner	Paul {M}
83	38	Table	Mussig [m=Kerchner]	Maria Rosina (Mary) {F}
83	39	Table	Mussig [m=Kerchner]	Maria Rosina (Mary) {F}
84	38	Table	Kern	John Dominic {M}
85	38	Table	Vaeth [m=Kern]	Margaret {F}
86	38	Table	Ziegler [m=Kern]	Suzanna {F}

ID#	Page	Ref Type	Surname	Given Name
91	38	Table	Kern [m=Kerchner]	Anna Maria {F}
91	41	Table	Kern [m=Kerchner]	Anna Maria {F}
92	38	Table	Kerchner	Adrian {M}
92	41	Table	Kerchner	Adrian {M}
92	42	Table	Kerchner	Adrian {M}
93	38	Table	Kerchner	Adolph {M}
93	41	Table	Kerchner	Adolph {M}
93	43	Table	Kerchner	Adolph {M}
94	38	Table	Hubel [m=Kerchner]	Mary {F}
94	41	Table	Hubel [m=Kerchner]	Mary {F}
94	43	Table	Hubel [m=Kerchner]	Mary {F}
95	38	Table	Kerchner [m=Neubeck]	Catherine {F}
95	41	Table	Kerchner [m=Neubeck]	Catherine {F}
95	44	Table	Kerchner [m=Neubeck]	Catherine {F}
96	38	Table	Neubeck	Henry {M}
96	41	Table	Neubeck	Henry {M}
96	44	Table	Neubeck	Henry {M}
97	38	Table	Kerchner	Josephine {F}
97	41	Table	Kerchner	Josephine {F}
97	44	Table	Kerchner	Josephine {F}
100	38	Table	Kerchner	Michael Anthony {M}
100	39	Table	Kerchner	Michael Anthony {M}
100	41	Table	Kerchner	Michael Anthony {M}
102	38	Table	Kerchner [m=Hessler]	Caroline {F}
102	41	Table	Kerchner [m=Hessler]	Caroline {F}
102	44	Table	Kerchner [m=Hessler]	Caroline {F}
108	43	Table	Kerchner	John Joseph {M}
109	42	Table	Kerchner	Ferdinand John {M}
110	42	Table	Mullahy [m=Kerchner]	Mary {F}
115	11	Narrative	Kerchner [m=Kunkel]	Mary Rosina {F}
115	12	Photo	Kerchner [m=Kunkel]	Mary Rosina {F}
115	13	Narrative	Kerchner [m=Kunkel]	Mary Rosina {F}
115	15	Narrative	Kerchner [m=Kunkel]	Mary Rosina {F}
115	18	Obituary	Kerchner [m=Kunkel]	Mary Rosina {F}
115	27	Photo	Kerchner [m=Kunkel]	Mary Rosina {F}
115	29	Table	Kerchner [m=Kunkel]	Mary Rosina {F}
115	29	Table	Kerchner [m=Kunkel]	Mary Rosina {F}
115	34	Table	Kerchner [m=Kunkel]	Mary Rosina {F}
115	37	Table	Kerchner [m=Kunkel]	Mary Rosina {F}
115	38	Table	Kerchner [m=Kunkel]	Mary Rosina {F}
115	41	Table	Kerchner [m=Kunkel]	Mary Rosina {F}
115	43	Table	Kerchner [m=Kunkel]	Mary Rosina {F}

Reproduction of Fr. Kunkel's Manuscript

ID#	Page	Ref Type	Surname	Given Name
115	44	Table	Kerchner [m=Kunkel]	Mary Rosina {F}
127	42	Table	Hulshoff [m=Easter]	Clara Rosalia (Rose) {F}
128	38	Table	Hessler	Michael {M}
128	41	Table	Hessler	Michael {M}
128	44	Table	Hessler	Michael {M}
134	42	Table	Zang [m=Horgan]	Mabel Genevieve {F}
135	42	Table	Zang	M. Beatrice {F}
232	29	Table	Amberg [m=Kunkel]	Mary {F}
232	34	Table	Amberg [m=Kunkel]	Mary {F}
232	37	Table	Amberg [m=Kunkel]	Mary {F}
274	28	Referral	Englert [m=Kunkel]	Apollonia {F}
275	28	Baptism	Kunkel	Barbara {F}
332	28	Baptism	Kunkel	Nikolaus Lorenz {M}
333	28	Baptism	Kunkel	Johann Nikolaus {M}
334	28	Baptism	Kunkel	Johann Nepomuk {M}
335	28	Baptism	Kunkel	Peter Anton {M}
336	28	Baptism	Kunkel	Jakob Johann {M}
337	28	Baptism	Kunkel	Margaretha {F}
338	28	Baptism	Kunkel	Rosalie Susanne {F}
339	28	Baptism	Kunkel	Wilhelmine {F}
392	28	Baptism	Kunkel	Maria Agnes {F}
419	29	Table	Hoffman [m=Kunkel]	Margaret {F}
419	34	Table	Hoffman [m=Kunkel]	Margaret {F}
419	34	Table	Hoffman [m=Kunkel]	Margaret {F}
420	30	Table	Busch	Henry {M}
421	30	Table	Kummel [m=Busch]	Lydia {F}
422	29	Table	Busch [m=Kunkel]	Catherine {F}
422	29	Table	Busch [m=Kunkel]	Catherine {F}
422	30	Table	Busch [m=Kunkel]	Catherine {F}
422	31	Table	Busch [m=Kunkel]	Catherine {F}
422	37	Table	Busch [m=Kunkel]	Catherine {F}
422	43	Table	Busch [m=Kunkel]	Catherine {F}
423	29	Table	Kunkel	Joseph A. I {M}
423	29	Table	Kunkel	Joseph A. I {M}
423	31	Table	Kunkel	Joseph A. I {M}
423	37	Table	Kunkel	Joseph A. I {M}
423	43	Table	Kunkel	Joseph A. I {M}
424	29	Table	Kunkel	Joseph A. II {M}
424	30	Table	Kunkel	Joseph A. II {M}
424	43	Table	Kunkel	Joseph A. II {M}
425	29	Table	Kunkel	Joseph A. III {M}
425	30	Table	Kunkel	Joseph A. III {M}

ID#	Page	Ref Type	Surname	Given Name
425	33	Table	Kunkel	Joseph A. III {M}
425	43	Table	Kunkel	Joseph A. III {M}
426	29	Table	Kunkel	Mary Regina {F}
426	29	Table	Kunkel	Mary Regina {F}
426	31	Table	Kunkel	Mary Regina {F}
426	32	Photo	Kunkel	Mary Regina {F}
426	37	Table	Kunkel	Mary Regina {F}
426	43	Table	Kunkel	Mary Regina {F}
426	44	Table	Kunkel	Mary Regina {F}
427	29	Table	Kunkel	Michael Anthony {M}
427	29	Table	Kunkel	Michael Anthony {M}
427	37	Table	Kunkel	Michael Anthony {M}
427	43	Table	Kunkel	Michael Anthony {M}
428	29	Table	Kunkel	John Alphonse {M}
428	29	Table	Kunkel	John Alphonse {M}
428	30	Table	Kunkel	John Alphonse {M}
428	37	Table	Kunkel	John Alphonse {M}
428	43	Table	Kunkel	John Alphonse {M}
429	29	Table	Vaeth [m=Kunkel]	Anna {F}
429	29	Table	Vaeth [m=Kunkel]	Anna {F}
429	30	Table	Vaeth [m=Kunkel]	Anna {F}
429	37	Table	Vaeth [m=Kunkel]	Anna {F}
429	43	Table	Vaeth [m=Kunkel]	Anna {F}
430	29	Table	Kunkel	Nicholas Aloysius {M}
430	30	Table	Kunkel	Nicholas Aloysius {M}
430	30	Table	Kunkel	Nicholas Aloysius {M}
430	37	Table	Kunkel	Nicholas Aloysius {M}
430	43	Table	Kunkel	Nicholas Aloysius {M}
431	29	Table	Schneider [m=Kunkel]	Barbara {F}
431	30	Table	Schneider [m=Kunkel]	Barbara {F}
431	31	Table	Schneider [m=Kunkel]	Barbara {F}
431	37	Table	Schneider [m=Kunkel]	Barbara {F}
431	43	Table	Schneider [m=Kunkel]	Barbara {F}
432	29	Table	Kunkel	Francis Ferdinand (Fr. Frank) {M}
432	30	Table	Kunkel	Francis Ferdinand (Fr. Frank) {M}
432	32	Photo	Kunkel	Francis Ferdinand (Fr. Frank) {M}
432	37	Table	Kunkel	Francis Ferdinand (Fr. Frank) {M}
432	43	Table	Kunkel	Francis Ferdinand (Fr. Frank) {M}
433	29	Table	Ward	Peter J. {M}
433	30	Table	Ward	Peter J. {M}
433	31	Table	Ward	Peter J. {M}
433	37	Table	Ward	Peter J. {M}

Reproduction of Fr. Kunkel's Manuscript

ID#	Page	Ref Type	Surname	Given Name
433	43	Table	Ward	Peter J. {M}
434	29	Table	Kunkel [m=Ward]	Teresa M. {F}
434	30	Table	Kunkel [m=Ward]	Teresa M. {F}
434	31	Table	Kunkel [m=Ward]	Teresa M. {F}
434	37	Table	Kunkel [m=Ward]	Teresa M. {F}
434	43	Table	Kunkel [m=Ward]	Teresa M. {F}
435	29	Table	Kunkel	William Francis {M}
435	30	Table	Kunkel	William Francis {M}
435	31	Table	Kunkel	William Francis {M}
435	33	Table	Kunkel	William Francis {M}
435	37	Table	Kunkel	William Francis {M}
435	43	Table	Kunkel	William Francis {M}
436	29	Table	Brennan	Joseph {M}
436	30	Table	Brennan	Joseph {M}
436	37	Table	Brennan	Joseph {M}
436	44	Table	Brennan	Joseph {M}
437	29	Table	Kunkel [m=Brennan]	Teresa Purzer {F}
437	30	Table	Kunkel [m=Brennan]	Teresa Purzer {F}
437	37	Table	Kunkel [m=Brennan]	Teresa Purzer {F}
437	44	Table	Kunkel [m=Brennan]	Teresa Purzer {F}
438	30	Table	Kunkel	Francis {M}
438	31	Table	Kunkel	Francis {M}
438	43	Table	Kunkel	Francis {M}
439	30	Table	Bellis [m=Kunkel]	Mary {F}
439	31	Table	Bellis [m=Kunkel]	Mary {F}
440	31	Table	Bilz	Joseph {M}
441	31	Table	Beyer [m=Bilz]	Barbara {F}
442	29	Table	Bilz [m=Kunkel]	Dora {F}
442	30	Table	Bilz [m=Kunkel]	Dora {F}
442	31	Table	Bilz [m=Kunkel]	Dora {F}
442	32	Photo	Bilz [m=Kunkel]	Dora {F}
443	24	Photo	Kunkel	John Nepomuk {M}
443	29	Table	Kunkel	John Nepomuk {M}
443	30	Table	Kunkel	John Nepomuk {M}
443	31	Table	Kunkel	John Nepomuk {M}
443	32	Photo	Kunkel	John Nepomuk {M}
443	43	Table	Kunkel	John Nepomuk {M}
444	30	Table	Kunkel	Denis F. {M}
444	43	Table	Kunkel	Denis F. {M}
445	30	Table	Kunkel	Joseph {M}
445	43	Table	Kunkel	Joseph {M}
446	30	Table	Kunkel	John H. {M}

ID#	Page	Ref Type	Surname	Given Name
446	43	Table	Kunkel	John H. {M}
447	29	Table	Miller	Charles {M}
447	30	Table	Miller	Charles {M}
447	31	Table	Miller	Charles {M}
448	29	Table	Kunkel [m=Miller]	Mary Catherine (Catherine) {F}
448	30	Table	Kunkel [m=Miller]	Mary Catherine (Catherine) {F}
448	31	Table	Kunkel [m=Miller]	Mary Catherine (Catherine) {F}
448	32	Photo	Kunkel [m=Miller]	Mary Catherine (Catherine) {F}
448	43	Table	Kunkel [m=Miller]	Mary Catherine (Catherine) {F}
449	29	Table	Kunkel	Charles John {M}
449	30	Table	Kunkel	Charles John {M}
449	31	Table	Kunkel	Charles John {M}
449	43	Table	Kunkel	Charles John {M}
453	29	Table	Kraus [m=Kunkel]	Evelyne {F}
453	30	Table	Kraus [m=Kunkel]	Evelyne {F}
453	31	Table	Kraus [m=Kunkel]	Evelyne {F}
453	32	Photo	Kraus [m=Kunkel]	Evelyne {F}
454	29	Table	Kunkel	Mary Lydia {F}
454	30	Table	Kunkel	Mary Lydia {F}
454	31	Table	Kunkel	Mary Lydia {F}
454	43	Table	Kunkel	Mary Lydia {F}
455	33	Table	Wist	George {M}
456	29	Table	Kunkel	Mary Regina (Regina) {F}
456	30	Table	Kunkel	Mary Regina (Regina) {F}
456	43	Table	Kunkel	Mary Regina (Regina) {F}
457	29	Table	Kunkel	Francis W. (Frank) {M}
457	30	Table	Kunkel	Francis W. (Frank) {M}
457	31	Table	Kunkel	Francis W. (Frank) {M}
457	32	Photo	Kunkel	Francis W. (Frank) {M}
457	43	Table	Kunkel	Francis W. (Frank) {M}
458	29	Table	Heinicke [m=Kunkel]	Dorothy {F}
458	30	Table	Heinicke [m=Kunkel]	Dorothy {F}
458	31	Table	Heinicke [m=Kunkel]	Dorothy {F}
458	32	Photo	Heinicke [m=Kunkel]	Dorothy {F}
459	29	Table	Kunkel	Charlotte {F}
459	31	Table	Kunkel	Charlotte {F}
459	32	Photo	Kunkel	Charlotte {F}
460	29	Table	Kunkel	Frederick J. (Fred) {M}
460	31	Table	Kunkel	Frederick J. (Fred) {M}
461	29	Table	Pons	Adolph {M}
461	31	Table	Pons	Adolph {M}
462	29	Table	Kunkel [m=Pons]	Catherine {F}

Reproduction of Fr. Kunkel's Manuscript

ID#	Page	Ref Type	Surname	Given Name
462	31	Table	Kunkel [m=Pons]	Catherine {F}
463	29	Table	Archer	J. Carvel {M}
463	31	Table	Archer	J. Carvel {M}
464	29	Table	Kunkel [m=Archer]	Helen {F}
464	31	Table	Kunkel [m=Archer]	Helen {F}
464	32	Photo	Kunkel [m=Archer]	Helen {F}
465	29	Table	Kunkel	Gerard {M}
465	31	Table	Kunkel	Gerard {M}
465	32	Photo	Kunkel	Gerard {M}
467	31	Table	Thim	Frank P. {M}
468	31	Table	Rudel [m=Thim]	Catherine {F}
469	29	Table	Kunkel	Anna M. {F}
469	30	Table	Kunkel	Anna M. {F}
469	43	Table	Kunkel	Anna M. {F}
470	29	Table	Kunkel	Mary E. {F}
470	30	Table	Kunkel	Mary E. {F}
470	43	Table	Kunkel	Mary E. {F}
471	29	Table	Kunkel	Francis Ferdinand {M}
471	30	Table	Kunkel	Francis Ferdinand {M}
471	31	Table	Kunkel	Francis Ferdinand {M}
471	43	Table	Kunkel	Francis Ferdinand {M}
472	29	Table	von Gestal [m=Kunkel]	Margaret {F}
472	30	Table	von Gestal [m=Kunkel]	Margaret {F}
472	31	Table	von Gestal [m=Kunkel]	Margaret {F}
473	29	Table	Willenburg [m=Kunkel]	Mary {F}
473	30	Table	Willenburg [m=Kunkel]	Mary {F}
473	31	Table	Willenburg [m=Kunkel]	Mary {F}
474	29	Table	Thim	Francis (Frank) {M}
474	30	Table	Thim	Francis (Frank) {M}
474	31	Table	Thim	Francis (Frank) {M}
475	30	Table	Kunkel [m=Thim]	Teresa {F}
475	31	Table	Kunkel [m=Thim]	Teresa {F}
475	43	Table	Kunkel [m=Thim]	Teresa {F}
476	30	Table	Kunkel	James {M}
476	30	Table	Kunkel	James {M}
476	33	Table	Kunkel	James {M}
476	43	Table	Kunkel	James {M}
477	30	Table	Hubbard [m=Kunkel]	Margaret {F}
477	30	Table	Hubbard [m=Kunkel]	Margaret {F}
477	33	Table	Hubbard [m=Kunkel]	Margaret {F}
478	30	Table	Kunkel	William {M}
478	30	Table	Kunkel	William {M}

ID#	Page	Ref Type	Surname	Given Name
478	33	Table	Kunkel	William {M}
478	43	Table	Kunkel	William {M}
479	30	Table	Bond [m=Kunkel]	Mary {F}
479	30	Table	Bond [m=Kunkel]	Mary {F}
479	33	Table	Bond [m=Kunkel]	Mary {F}
480	30	Table	Kunkel	Agnes {F}
480	30	Table	Kunkel	Agnes {F}
480	43	Table	Kunkel	Agnes {F}
481	29	Table	Thim	Bernadette {F}
481	31	Table	Thim	Bernadette {F}
482	29	Table	Thim	Margaret {F}
482	31	Table	Thim	Margaret {F}
483	29	Table	Thim	Regina {F}
483	31	Table	Thim	Regina {F}
484	29	Table	Thim	Dorothy {F}
484	31	Table	Thim	Dorothy {F}
485	29	Table	Thim	Catherine {F}
485	31	Table	Thim	Catherine {F}
486	29	Table	Thim	Francis {M}
486	31	Table	Thim	Francis {M}
487	29	Table	Thim	Charles {M}
487	31	Table	Thim	Charles {M}
488	29	Table	Thim	Richard {M}
488	31	Table	Thim	Richard {M}
489	29	Table	Thim	Elizabeth Patricia {F}
489	31	Table	Thim	Elizabeth Patricia {F}
490	33	Table	Kunkel	Joseph {M}
491	33	Table	Kunkel	Margaret {F}
492	33	Table	Kunkel	William {M}
493	30	Table	Ward	Rose Marie {F}
493	31	Table	Ward	Rose Marie {F}
493	43	Table	Ward	Rose Marie {F}
494	30	Table	Ward	Francis J. {M}
494	31	Table	Ward	Francis J. {M}
494	43	Table	Ward	Francis J. {M}
495	30	Table	Ward [m=Cavanaugh]	Johanetta M. (Jeanette) {F}
495	31	Table	Ward [m=Cavanaugh]	Johanetta M. (Jeanette) {F}
495	33	Table	Ward [m=Cavanaugh]	Johanetta M. (Jeanette) {F}
495	43	Table	Ward [m=Cavanaugh]	Johanetta M. (Jeanette) {F}
496	30	Table	Ward	John J. {M}
496	31	Table	Ward	John J. {M}
496	43	Table	Ward	John J. {M}

ID#	Page	Ref Type	Surname	Given Name
497	30	Table	Ward	Joseph Anthony {M}
497	31	Table	Ward	Joseph Anthony {M}
497	33	Table	Ward	Joseph Anthony {M}
497	43	Table	Ward	Joseph Anthony {M}
498	30	Table	Ward [m=Wist]	Regina M. {F}
498	31	Table	Ward [m=Wist]	Regina M. {F}
498	33	Table	Ward [m=Wist]	Regina M. {F}
498	43	Table	Ward [m=Wist]	Regina M. {F}
499	30	Table	Cavanaugh	Thomas J. {M}
499	31	Table	Cavanaugh	Thomas J. {M}
499	33	Table	Cavanaugh	Thomas J. {M}
500	28	Referral	Kunkel	George {M}
500	29	Table	Kunkel	George {M}
500	33	Trans	Kunkel	George {M}
501	29	Table	Pons [m=Archer]	Barbara Katherine {F}
501	31	Table	Pons [m=Archer]	Barbara Katherine {F}
501	32	Photo	Pons [m=Archer]	Barbara Katherine {F}
502	28	Baptism	Kunkel	Johann Adam (Adam) {M}
502	28	Referral	Kunkel	Johann Adam (Adam) {M}
502	29	Table	Kunkel	Johann Adam (Adam) {M}
502	29	Table	Kunkel	Johann Adam (Adam) {M}
502	33	Trans	Kunkel	Johann Adam (Adam) {M}
502	34	Table	Kunkel	Johann Adam (Adam) {M}
503	29	Table	Christ [m=Kunkel]	Anna Marie {F}
503	29	Table	Christ [m=Kunkel]	Anna Marie {F}
503	33	Trans	Christ [m=Kunkel]	Anna Marie {F}
503	34	Table	Christ [m=Kunkel]	Anna Marie {F}
504	29	Table	Kunkel	Nicholas {M}
504	34	Table	Kunkel	Nicholas {M}
505	29	Table	Kunkel	Peter {M}
505	34	Table	Kunkel	Peter {M}
505	34	Table	Kunkel	Peter {M}
506	29	Table	Kunkel	Genevieve {F}
506	34	Table	Kunkel	Genevieve {F}
507	4	Photo	Kunkel	Johann Nepomuk {M}
507	5	Narrative	Kunkel	Johann Nepomuk {M}
507	7	Narrative	Kunkel	Johann Nepomuk {M}
507	8	Narrative	Kunkel	Johann Nepomuk {M}
507	9	Obituary	Kunkel	Johann Nepomuk {M}
507	27	Photo	Kunkel	Johann Nepomuk {M}
507	29	Table	Kunkel	Johann Nepomuk {M}
507	29	Table	Kunkel	Johann Nepomuk {M}

ID#	Page	Ref Type	Surname	Given Name
507	34	Table	Kunkel	Johann Nepomuk {M}
507	37	Table	Kunkel	Johann Nepomuk {M}
507	38	Table	Kunkel	Johann Nepomuk {M}
507	41	Table	Kunkel	Johann Nepomuk {M}
507	43	Table	Kunkel	Johann Nepomuk {M}
507	44	Table	Kunkel	Johann Nepomuk {M}
508	29	Table	Kunkel	George {M}
508	34	Table	Kunkel	George {M}
508	37	Table	Kunkel	George {M}
509	28	Baptism	Kunkel	Johann Nikolaus (Nicholas) {M}
509	34	Table	Kunkel	Johann Nikolaus (Nicholas) {M}
510	29	Table	Kunkel	Alois {M}
510	34	Table	Kunkel	Alois {M}
511	29	Table	Kunkel	Casper Emmanuel {M}
511	34	Table	Kunkel	Casper Emmanuel {M}
511	37	Table	Kunkel	Casper Emmanuel {M}
512	29	Table	Benkler [m=Kunkel]	Marg {F}
512	34	Table	Benkler [m=Kunkel]	Marg {F}
512	37	Table	Benkler [m=Kunkel]	Marg {F}
513	29	Table	Kunkel [m=Schreck]	Eva {F}
513	34	Table	Kunkel [m=Schreck]	Eva {F}
513	34	Table	Kunkel [m=Schreck]	Eva {F}
513	36	Table	Kunkel [m=Schreck]	Eva {F}
514	29	Table	Schreck	John {M}
514	34	Table	Schreck	John {M}
514	34	Table	Schreck	John {M}
514	36	Table	Schreck	John {M}
515	34	Table	Schreck	Caspar {M}
515	36	Table	Schreck	Caspar {M}
516	34	Table	Schreck	Gertrude {F}
516	36	Table	Schreck	Gertrude {F}
517	28	Referral	Schreck [m=Kunkel]	Katharina {F}
517	29	Table	Schreck [m=Kunkel]	Katharina {F}
517	33	Trans	Schreck [m=Kunkel]	Katharina {F}
533	30	Table	Ward	Peter J. {M}
533	31	Table	Ward	Peter J. {M}
533	43	Table	Ward	Peter J. {M}
534	30	Table	Ward	Edward {M}
534	31	Table	Ward	Edward {M}
534	43	Table	Ward	Edward {M}
561	42	Table	Zang [m=Metz]	Margaret (Maggie) {F}
564	29	Table	Kunkel	Margaret Dorothy {F}

REPRODUCTION OF FR. KUNKEL'S MANUSCRIPT

ID#	Page	Ref Type	Surname	Given Name
564	30	Table	Kunkel	Margaret Dorothy {F}
564	37	Table	Kunkel	Margaret Dorothy {F}
564	43	Table	Kunkel	Margaret Dorothy {F}
565	42	Table	Kerchner [m=Zang]	Mary Catherine {F}
566	42	Table	Zang	Anna M. {F}
567	42	Table	Zang	Mollie {F}
568	42	Table	Zang	Mindy {F}
569	42	Table	Zang	Catherine (Kate) {F}
570	42	Table	Zang	M. Therese {F}
571	42	Table	Zang	M. Gertrude {F}
572	42	Table	Zang	John Gerard {M}
573	42	Table	Zang	?Male? {M}
585	29	Table	Becker [m=Kunkel]	Mary Teresa {F}
585	30	Table	Becker [m=Kunkel]	Mary Teresa {F}
585	31	Table	Becker [m=Kunkel]	Mary Teresa {F}
585	31	Table	Becker [m=Kunkel]	Mary Teresa {F}
585	33	Table	Becker [m=Kunkel]	Mary Teresa {F}
585	37	Table	Becker [m=Kunkel]	Mary Teresa {F}
585	43	Table	Becker [m=Kunkel]	Mary Teresa {F}
586	29	Table	Becker [m=Kunkel]	Dorathy Eva (Dora) {F}
586	30	Table	Becker [m=Kunkel]	Dorathy Eva (Dora) {F}
586	31	Table	Becker [m=Kunkel]	Dorathy Eva (Dora) {F}
586	33	Table	Becker [m=Kunkel]	Dorathy Eva (Dora) {F}
586	37	Table	Becker [m=Kunkel]	Dorathy Eva (Dora) {F}
586	44	Table	Becker [m=Kunkel]	Dorathy Eva (Dora) {F}
587	31	Table	Jackson	Charles Elmer {M}
587	33	Table	Jackson	Charles Elmer {M}
589	31	Table	Childress [m=Jackson]	Alma M. {F}
589	33	Table	Childress [m=Jackson]	Alma M. {F}
595	31	Table	Kunkel	Marie (Mary) {F}
595	43	Table	Kunkel	Marie (Mary) {F}
596	30	Table	Kunkel	Joseph A. {M}
596	31	Table	Kunkel	Joseph A. {M}
596	33	Table	Kunkel	Joseph A. {M}
596	43	Table	Kunkel	Joseph A. {M}
597	30	Table	Kunkel	Genevieve {F}
597	31	Table	Kunkel	Genevieve {F}
597	44	Table	Kunkel	Genevieve {F}
598	30	Table	Jackson	Charles E. {M}
598	31	Table	Jackson	Charles E. {M}
598	33	Table	Jackson	Charles E. {M}
598	44	Table	Jackson	Charles E. {M}

ID#	Page	Ref Type	Surname	Given Name
602	30	Table	Kunkel [m=Jackson]	Dorothy {F}
602	31	Table	Kunkel [m=Jackson]	Dorothy {F}
602	33	Table	Kunkel [m=Jackson]	Dorothy {F}
602	44	Table	Kunkel [m=Jackson]	Dorothy {F}
603	30	Table	Kunkel	Nicholas {M}
603	31	Table	Kunkel	Nicholas {M}
603	44	Table	Kunkel	Nicholas {M}
604	30	Table	Kunkel	Marie {F}
604	31	Table	Kunkel	Marie {F}
604	44	Table	Kunkel	Marie {F}
605	30	Table	Kunkel	Anne {F}
605	31	Table	Kunkel	Anne {F}
605	44	Table	Kunkel	Anne {F}
606	30	Table	Kunkel	Irene {F}
606	31	Table	Kunkel	Irene {F}
606	44	Table	Kunkel	Irene {F}
607	30	Table	Kunkel	Joseph {M}
607	31	Table	Kunkel	Joseph {M}
607	44	Table	Kunkel	Joseph {M}
608	30	Table	Kunkel	Francis {M}
608	31	Table	Kunkel	Francis {M}
608	44	Table	Kunkel	Francis {M}
609	30	Table	Kunkel	Teresa {F}
609	31	Table	Kunkel	Teresa {F}
609	44	Table	Kunkel	Teresa {F}
622	29	Table	Archer	John Carvel {M}
622	31	Table	Archer	John Carvel {M}
622	32	Photo	Archer	John Carvel {M}
639	38	Table	Burger [m=Kerchner]	Anna Catherine (Catherine) {F}
639	41	Table	Burger [m=Kerchner]	Anna Catherine (Catherine) {F}
639	41	Table	Burger [m=Kerchner]	Anna Catherine (Catherine) {F}
651	44	Table	Neubeck	Francis L. {M}
696	38	Table	Hubel [m=Kerchner]	Frederica {F}
696	41	Table	Hubel [m=Kerchner]	Frederica {F}
696	42	Table	Hubel [m=Kerchner]	Frederica {F}
703	29	Table	Archer	Dorothea Lee {F}
703	31	Table	Archer	Dorothea Lee {F}
703	32	Photo	Archer	Dorothea Lee {F}
708	43	Table	Oberle	Seraphin {M}
709	42	Table	Zang	William Alphonse {M}
710	43	Table	Kerchner	Mary Teresa {F}
711	42	Table	Neubeck	Adolph {M}

REPRODUCTION OF FR. KUNKEL'S MANUSCRIPT

ID#	Page	Ref Type	Surname	Given Name
711	44	Table	Neubeck	Adolph {M}
712	42	Table	Kerchner	Francis C. {M}
713	42	Table	Kerchner	James Albert {M}
714	42	Table	Kerchner	Kathleen {F}
715	42	Table	Kerchner	John Norbert {M}
716	43	Table	Kerchner	M. Loretta {F}
717	43	Table	Kerchner [m=Fritzges]	M. Lucille {F}
718	43	Table	Kerchner	George W. {M}
719	43	Table	Ballenger [m=Neubeck]	Ella G. {F}
719	44	Table	Ballenger [m=Neubeck]	Ella G. {F}
720	43	Table	Fritzges	Joseph F. {M}
721	43	Table	Fritzges	Mary Joe {F}
722	43	Table	Fritzges	Jane Frances {F}
723	44	Table	Curran [m=Neubeck]	Mary D. {F}
724	44	Table	Neubeck	Catherine Barbara {F}
725	44	Table	Neubeck	Francis G. {M}
726	44	Table	Neubeck [m=Landis]	Mary Estelle {F}
727	44	Table	Neubeck	Ella Rose {F}
728	44	Table	Neubeck [m=Kibler]	Gertrude Emily {F}
729	44	Table	Neubeck	John H. {M}
730	44	Table	Neubeck	Catherine A. {F}
731	44	Table	Neubeck	Mary A. {F}
732	44	Table	Neubeck	Francis L. {M}
733	44	Table	Landis	William Newton {M}
734	44	Table	Kibler	M. {M}
735	44	Table	Nemmers [m=Neubeck]	Margaret {F}
736	44	Table	Neubeck	Margaret {F}
737	44	Table	Hessler	John William {M}
738	44	Table	Hessler	Anna Eva {F}
739	44	Table	Hessler	Frank A. {M}
740	44	Table	Werner [m=Hessler]	Tillie {F}
741	44	Table	Hessler [m=Krespach]	Minnie C. {F}
742	44	Table	Hessler	George F. {M}
743	44	Table	Hessler [m=Bonhoff]	Madeline {F}
744	44	Table	Hessler [m=Ritter]	Josephine {F}
745	44	Table	Krespach	?Male? {M}
746	44	Table	Bonhoff	?Male? {M}
747	44	Table	Ritter	?Male? {M}
748	41	Table	Kerchner [m=Hoover]	Catherine Dorothy {F}
748	41	Table	Kerchner [m=Hoover]	Catherine Dorothy {F}
749	41	Table	Kerchner	Francis William (Will) {M}
750	41	Table	Kerchner	Charles Frederick (Charlie) {M}

ID#	Page	Ref Type	Surname	Given Name
751	41	Table	Kerchner	Henry Adolph (Harry) {M}
752	42	Table	Kerchner [m=Norman]	Ella Anastasia {F}
753	42	Table	Kerchner [m=Lewis]	Rosina Athalia (Rose) {F}
754	41	Table	Hoover	John E. {M}
755	41	Table	Latta [m=Kerchner]	Flora {F}
756	41	Table	McGowan [m=Kerchner]	Mary (Mame) {F}
757	41	Table	Forman [m=Kerchner]	Isabelle {F}
758	42	Table	Norman	Robert Charles {M}
759	42	Table	Lewis	Charles Edward (Buck) {M}
760	41	Table	Hoover	Frederick {M}
761	41	Table	Hoover [m=McDonald]	Ella Rose {F}
762	41	Table	Hoover	Francis {M}
763	41	Table	Hoover [m=Curlander]	Katherine {F}
764	41	Table	Hoover	Joseph {M}
765	41	Table	Hoover [m=Wicks]	Helen {F}
766	41	Table	Hoover [m=Hoy]	Mary {F}
767	41	Table	Kerchner [m=Knight]	Pauline {F}
768	41	Table	Kerchner	Charles {M}
769	41	Table	Kerchner	Mary {F}
770	41	Table	Kerchner	Beatrice Crawford {F}
771	42	Table	Norman	John Hugh {M}
772	42	Table	Norman	Ella M. J. {F}
773	42	Table	Norman	Margaret Catherine {F}
774	42	Table	Norman	Rose Teresa {F}
775	42	Table	Norman	Robert Charles {M}
776	42	Table	Norman	Oswald Byrne {M}
777	42	Table	Norman	Mary Dorothy (Dorothy) {F}
778	42	Table	Lewis [m=McDonnell]	Katherine ("K") {F}
779	42	Table	Lewis	Rosina {F}
780	42	Table	Lewis [m=Coakley]	Mary Bertha (Mary) {F}
781	42	Table	Lewis	Charles F. {M}
782	27	Photo	Kunkel	Frederick J. (Fred) {M}
782	29	Table	Kunkel	Frederick J. (Fred) {M}
782	30	Table	Kunkel	Frederick J. (Fred) {M}
782	32	Photo	Kunkel	Frederick J. (Fred) {M}
782	37	Table	Kunkel	Frederick J. (Fred) {M}
783	30	Table	Kunkel	Gertrude {F}
791	41	Table	Knight	Julius O. (Jude) {M}
792	41	Table	Blair [m=Kerchner]	Helen {F}
793	41	Table	Knight	Lyle {M}
794	41	Table	Knight [m=O'Mara]	Mary {F}
795	41	Table	Knight	Julius {M}

ID#	Page	Ref Type	Surname	Given Name
796	41	Table	Kerchner	Blair {M}
797	41	Table	Knight	Robert Lyle {M}
798	41	Table	Imbach [m=Knight]	Helen L. {F}
799	41	Table	O'Mara	John {M}
800	41	Table	O'Mara	John Paul {M}
801	41	Table	O'Mara	Mary Jean {F}
802	42	Table	Tisdale [m=Norman]	Julia Bowie {F}
804	42	Table	Norman [m=Crick]	Julia Waring {F}
805	42	Table	Norman	John H. {M}
806	42	Table	Norman [m=Roberson]	Ella {F}
807	42	Table	Norman	Robert {M}
808	42	Table	Norman	Katherine {F}
809	42	Table	Crick	Donald Francis {M}
810	42	Table	Roberson	William Dean {M}
811	42	Table	McDonnell	Paul {M}
812	42	Table	Abella	Henry {M}
813	42	Table	Coakley	William Drummond {M}
814	42	Table	Abella	Henry Charles {M}
815	42	Table	Abella	Joseph {M}
816	42	Table	McDonnell	Paul {M}
817	42	Table	McDonnell	Mary Katherine {F}
818	42	Table	McDonnell	Charles Lewis (Lewis) {M}
819	42	Table	McDonnell [m=Carter]	Rosina Lewis {F}
820	42	Table	McDonnell	James Edward {M}
821	42	Table	McDonnell	Frances Virginia {F}
822	42	Table	McDonnell	Dorothy Irene {F}
823	42	Table	McDonnell	Bernadine {F}
824	39	Table	Mai	Louis {M}
825	39	Table	Mai	Edward {M}
826	39	Table	Mai	Regina {F}
827	39	Table	Mai	Joseph {M}
828	39	Table	Mai	Barbara {F}
829	39	Table	Mai	Ignatius {M}
830	39	Table	Mai	Mary {F}
831	39	Table	Mai	Francis {M}
832	39	Table	Mai [m=Brand]	Teresa {F}
833	39	Table	Mai	Herman {M}
834	39	Table	Mai	Rose {F}
835	39	Table	Mai	Anna {F}
836	39	Table	Mai	Emma {F}
837	39	Table	Mai	Matilda {F}
838	33	Table	Cavanaugh	Philip {M}

ID#	Page	Ref Type	Surname	Given Name
839	33	Table	UnkF [m=Cavanaugh]	Catherine {F}
840	33	Table	Smith [m=Ward]	Elizabeth {F}
841	33	Table	Wist	Michael {M}
842	33	Table	Schleicher [m=Wist]	Teresa {F}
843	33	Table	Smith	George {M}
844	33	Table	Hammel [m=Smith]	Cecelia {F}
845	30	Table	Cavanaugh	Philip {M}
845	33	Table	Cavanaugh	Philip {M}
846	30	Table	Cavanaugh	Rose {F}
846	33	Table	Cavanaugh	Rose {F}
847	30	Table	Cavanaugh	Regina {F}
847	33	Table	Cavanaugh	Regina {F}
848	30	Table	Cavanaugh	Thomas {M}
848	33	Table	Cavanaugh	Thomas {M}
849	30	Table	Cavanaugh	Peter {M}
849	33	Table	Cavanaugh	Peter {M}
850	30	Table	Ward	Joseph A. {M}
850	33	Table	Ward	Joseph A. {M}
851	30	Table	Ward	Mary Ellen {F}
851	33	Table	Ward	Mary Ellen {F}
852	30	Table	Wist	George J. {M}
852	33	Table	Wist	George J. {M}
853	30	Table	Wist	Paul G. {M}
853	33	Table	Wist	Paul G. {M}
854	30	Table	Wist	Rose M. {F}
854	33	Table	Wist	Rose M. {F}
855	30	Table	Wist	Jean {F}
855	33	Table	Wist	Jean {F}
856	30	Table	Hooper	Timothy {M}
856	33	Table	Hooper	Timothy {M}
857	30	Table	Weldenham [m=Hooper]	Mary {F}
857	33	Table	Weldenham [m=Hooper]	Mary {F}
858	30	Table	Hooper [m=Kunkel]	Angela {F}
858	33	Table	Hooper [m=Kunkel]	Angela {F}
859	30	Table	Kunkel	Joan {F}
859	33	Table	Kunkel	Joan {F}
860	30	Table	Kunkel	Joseph A. (Jay) {F}
860	33	Table	Kunkel	Joseph A. (Jay) {F}
861	30	Table	Jackson	Charles E. {M}
861	33	Table	Jackson	Charles E. {M}
862	30	Table	Jackson	Joseph Nicholas {M}
862	33	Table	Jackson	Joseph Nicholas {M}

Reproduction of Fr. Kunkel's Manuscript

ID#	Page	Ref Type	Surname	Given Name
863	34	Table	Kunkel	John N. {M}
864	34	Table	Kunkel	Sebastian {M}
864	36	Table	Kunkel	Sebastian {M}
865	34	Table	Kunkel	Caspar Herman (Harry) {M}
865	36	Table	Kunkel	Caspar Herman (Harry) {M}
866	34	Table	Kunkel [m=Frosch]	Mary Anne {F}
866	36	Table	Kunkel [m=Frosch]	Mary Anne {F}
867	34	Table	Kunkel [m=Raeyling]	Emma {F}
867	36	Table	Kunkel [m=Raeyling]	Emma {F}
868	34	Table	Kunkel	George Peter {M}
868	36	Table	Kunkel	George Peter {M}
869	34	Table	Casey [m=Kunkel]	Sallie {F}
870	34	Table	Linder [m=Kunkel]	Ottillie {F}
870	36	Table	Linder [m=Kunkel]	Ottillie {F}
871	34	Table	Frosch [m=Kunkel]	Elizabeth {F}
871	36	Table	Frosch [m=Kunkel]	Elizabeth {F}
872	34	Table	Frosch	Andrew {M}
872	36	Table	Frosch	Andrew {M}
873	34	Table	Raeyling	Joseph {M}
873	36	Table	Raeyling	Joseph {M}
874	34	Table	Schreck	Nicholas {M}
874	36	Table	Schreck	Nicholas {M}
909	39	Table	Mai	August {M}
910	39	Table	Mai	Teresa {F}
911	39	Table	Mai	Charles {M}
912	39	Table	Mai	Eugene {M}
913	39	Table	UnkF [m=Mai]	?Female? {F}
914	39	Table	UnkM	?Male? {M}
915	39	Table	UnkF	Rose {F}
916	39	Table	UnkF	Anna {F}
917	39	Table	UnkF	Mary {F}
918	39	Table	UnkF	Ida {F}
919	39	Table	UnkF	Helen {F}
920	39	Table	UnkF	Bertha {F}
921	39	Table	UnkF [m=Mai]	?Female? {F}
922	39	Table	Mai	Elizabeth {F}
923	39	Table	Mai	Rudolph {M}
924	39	Table	Mai	Teresa {F}
925	39	Table	Mai	Frederick {M}
926	39	Table	UnkM	?Male? {M}
927	39	Table	UnkF	Emma {F}
928	39	Table	UnkF	Katherine {F}

ID#	Page	Ref Type	Surname	Given Name
929	39	Table	UnkF	Mary {F}
930	39	Table	UnkM	Edward {M}
931	39	Table	UnkF	Clara {F}
932	39	Table	UnkM	Lawrence {M}
933	39	Table	UnkM	Joseph {M}
934	39	Table	UnkF [m=Mai]	?Female? {F}
935	39	Table	Mai	James {M}
936	39	Table	Mai	Catherine {F}
937	39	Table	Mai	Joseph {M}
938	39	Table	Mai	Lina {F}
939	39	Table	UnkM	?Male? {M}
940	39	Table	UnkM	Anthony {M}
941	39	Table	UnkF	Bertha {F}
942	39	Table	UnkM	Joseph {M}
943	39	Table	UnkF [m=Mai]	?Female? {F}
944	39	Table	Brand	Adolf {M}
945	39	Table	UnkF [m=Mai]	?Female? {F}
946	39	Table	UnkM	?Male? {M}
947	39	Table	UnkM	?Male? {M}
948	39	Table	Mai	Adolph {M}
949	39	Table	Mai	Teresa {F}
950	39	Table	Mai	Otto {M}
951	39	Table	Mai	August {M}
952	39	Table	Mai	Herman {M}
953	39	Table	Brand	Anna {F}
954	39	Table	Brand	Otto {M}
955	39	Table	Brand	Emma {F}
956	39	Table	Mai	Matilda {F}
957	39	Table	Mai	Anna {F}
958	39	Table	Mai	Frank {M}
959	39	Table	Mai	Mary {F}
960	39	Table	Mai	Emma {F}
961	39	Table	UnkM	Louis {M}
962	39	Table	UnkF	Anna {F}
963	39	Table	UnkF	Matilda {F}
964	39	Table	UnkM	Charles {M}
965	39	Table	UnkM	Richard {M}
966	39	Table	UnkM	Otto {M}
967	39	Table	UnkM	Anthony {M}
968	39	Table	UnkM	Herman {M}
969	39	Table	UnkF	Rose {F}
970	41	Table	Kerchner [m=Essary]	Helen {F}

Reproduction of Fr. Kunkel's Manuscript

ID#	Page	Ref Type	Surname	Given Name
971	41	Table	Essary	J. Frederick {M}
972	41	Table	Essary	Annabelle {F}
973	41	Table	Essary	Margaret {F}
974	41	Table	Kerchner [m=Heger]	Hilda {F}
975	41	Table	Heger	Walter {M}
976	41	Table	Heger	Caroline {F}
977	41	Table	Kerchner [m=Croswell]	Isabelle {F}
978	41	Table	Croswell	Bennet {M}
979	41	Table	Croswell	Harry {M}
980	34	Table	Kunkel [m=Olivieri]	Katherine {F}
981	34	Table	Kunkel [m=Propert]	Margaret {F}
982	34	Table	Olivieri	Dominic {M}
983	34	Table	Olivieri	John P. {M}
984	34	Table	Propert	J. Kerper {M}
985	34	Table	Propert	Frank {M}
986	34	Table	Propert	John Oliver {M}
987	34	Table	Propert	Kerper George {M}
988	36	Table	Kunkel	Mary E. {F}
989	36	Table	Kunkel	Harry F. {M}
990	36	Table	Kunkel	Edward H. {M}
991	36	Table	Kunkel	William A. {M}
992	36	Table	Kunkel [m=Bruckheiser]	Margaret E. {F}
993	36	Table	Kunkel	John H. {M}
994	36	Table	Kunkel [m=Adam]	Florence E. {F}
995	36	Table	Kunkel	Joseph G. {M}
996	36	Table	Kunkel	Henry Edward {M}
997	36	Table	Kunkel	Francis S. {M}
998	36	Table	Kunkel	Regina O. {F}
999	36	Table	Kunkel	John H. {M}
1000	36	Table	Kunkel	Andrew C. {M}
1001	36	Table	Frosch	Harry {M}
1002	36	Table	Frosch [m=Murphy]	Mary E. {F}
1003	36	Table	Mayer [m=Kunkel]	Margaret {F}
1004	36	Table	Claughsey [m=Kunkel]	Mary {F}
1005	36	Table	Bruckheiser	William {M}
1006	36	Table	Bowen [m=Kunkel]	Evelyn M. {F}
1007	36	Table	Adam	Joseph M. {M}
1008	36	Table	Welsh [m=Kunkel]	Lillian B. {F}
1009	36	Table	Diegel [m=Kunkel]	Anna C. {F}
1010	36	Table	Scheihing [m=Kunkel]	Florence M. {F}
1011	36	Table	Maloney [m=Kunkel]	Loretto {F}
1012	36	Table	Barr [m=Frosch]	Jennie {F}

ID#	Page	Ref Type	Surname	Given Name
1013	36	Table	Murphy	Albert {M}
1014	36	Table	Kunkel	Dorothy Mary {F}
1015	36	Table	Kunkel	William A. {M}
1016	36	Table	Bruckheiser	William A. {M}
1017	36	Table	Adam	Florence M. {F}
1018	36	Table	Adam	Margaret Evelyn {F}
1019	36	Table	Adam	Ruth B. {F}
1020	36	Table	Adam	Joseph M. {M}
1021	36	Table	Kunkel	Joseph M. {M}
1022	36	Table	Kunkel	Mary T. {F}
1023	36	Table	Kunkel	Regina A. {F}
1024	36	Table	Kunkel	Loretta {F}
1025	36	Table	Kunkel	Dolores E. {F}
1026	36	Table	Kunkel	John Joseph M. {M}
1027	36	Table	Kunkel	Mercedes Jos. {F}
1028	36	Table	Kunkel	Anna {F}
1029	36	Table	Kunkel	Henry E. {M}
1030	36	Table	Kunkel	Charles {M}
1031	36	Table	Kunkel	Eugene {M}
1032	36	Table	Kunkel	Joseph Richard {M}
1033	36	Table	Kunkel	Elizabeth C. {F}
1034	36	Table	Frosch [m=Porter]	Maria {F}
1035	36	Table	Frosch	Harry {M}
1036	36	Table	Frosch	Ava Sarah {F}
1037	36	Table	Frosch	Andrew {M}
1038	36	Table	Frosch	Jane {F}
1039	36	Table	Frosch	Margaret {F}
1040	36	Table	Porter	William {M}
1041	36	Table	Porter	Mary Anne {F}
1042	36	Table	Porter	Joan {F}
1043	36	Table	Porter	William {M}
1044	36	Table	Lang [m=Frosch]	Magdalen {F}
1045	36	Table	Murphy [m=Foldes]	Mary E. {F}
1046	36	Table	Foldes	Julius {M}
1047	36	Table	Seitz [m=Schreck]	Emma {F}
1048	36	Table	Schreck	Gertrude {F}
1049	36	Table	Schreck	John A. {M}
1050	37	Table	Kunkel [m=Albert]	Frances A. {F}
1051	37	Table	Kunkel	Anna T. {F}
1052	37	Table	Kunkel	John G. {M}
1053	37	Table	Kunkel	Mary C. {F}
1054	37	Table	Kunkel	George {M}

Reproduction of Fr. Kunkel's Manuscript

ID#	Page	Ref Type	Surname	Given Name
1055	37	Table	Albert	Charles {M}
1056	37	Table	Albert	Charles G. {M}
1057	37	Table	Albert	Florence M. {F}
1058	37	Table	Albert	Edward J. {M}
1059	37	Table	Albert	Anna T. {F}
1060	37	Table	Albert	Marie A. {F}
1061	37	Table	Albert	Frances C. {F}
1062	37	Table	Albert	Raymond {M}
1063	37	Table	Albert	Adelle E. {F}
1064	37	Table	Albert	Frank A. {M}
1065	37	Table	Albert	Gerard A. {M}
1066	37	Table	Kunkel	Anna Marie {F}
1067	37	Table	Kunkel	Frederick {M}
1068	37	Table	Kunkel	Emma {F}
1069	37	Table	Kunkel	George {M}
1070	37	Table	Kunkel [m=Vincent]	Mary Genevieve {F}
1071	37	Table	Kunkel	Herman {M}
1072	37	Table	Kunkel [m=Born]	Frances G. {F}
1073	37	Table	Kunkel [m=Koenig]	Margaret C. {F}
1074	37	Table	Kunkel [m=Hartman]	Anne Cecile {F}
1075	37	Table	Vincent	William {M}
1076	37	Table	Born	Charles A. {M}
1077	37	Table	Koenig	August {M}
1078	37	Table	Hartman	Edward {M}
1079	37	Table	Vincent	William H. {M}
1080	37	Table	Carlson [m=Vincent]	Margaret M. {F}
1081	37	Table	Vincent	William H. {M}
1082	37	Table	Born [m=Muller]	Dorothy {F}
1083	37	Table	Muller	William {M}
1084	37	Table	Muller	William C. {M}
1085	37	Table	Muller	Dorothy {F}
1086	37	Table	Koenig [m=Scheuhing]	Lucille {F}
1087	37	Table	Scheuhing	John B. {M}
1088	37	Table	Scheuhing	Sarah Ann {F}
1089	37	Table	Hartman [m=Coulter]	Margaret Elizabeth {F}
1090	37	Table	Hartman	Edward John {M}
1091	37	Table	Coulter	William {M}
1266	41	Table	Stafford [m=Hoover]	May {F}
1267	41	Table	Hoover [m=Tiepermann]	Catherine {F}
1268	41	Table	Hoover	Francis {M}
1269	41	Table	Hoover	Elizabeth {F}
1270	41	Table	Hoover	John {M}

ID#	Page	Ref Type	Surname	Given Name
1271	41	Table	Hoover	Jerome {M}
1272	41	Table	Hoover	Margaret {F}
1273	41	Table	Tiepermann	Henry E. {M}
1274	41	Table	Curlander	Henry {M}
1275	41	Table	Curlander	Carroll {M}
1276	41	Table	Wilhelm [m=Hoover]	Bertha {F}
1277	41	Table	Hoover	Helen {F}
1278	41	Table	Hoover	Virginia {F}
1279	41	Table	Wicks	Carl {M}
1280	41	Table	Wicks	Mary Lucille {F}
1281	41	Table	Hoy	Robert {M}
1282	41	Table	Hoy	Robert {M}
1283	41	Table	Hoy	Dorothy {F}
1284	41	Table	McDonald	John {M}
1285	41	Table	McDonald	Rose Agnes {F}

SECTION THREE

—

OUR KERN ANCESTORS

This section is primarily a reproduction of the 1941 self-published manuscript "The Descendants of Dominic Kern and his wife Margaret Vaeth," by Rev. Frank Kunkel, SS. It provides a history of the Kern line beginning with John Dominic Kern, born 12 February 1781, through the early twentieth century; this document also includes much information about the Kerchner family discussed in the previous section.

Original Manuscript prepared by Fr. Frank Kunkel;
15 August 1941

Introduction and Errata prepared by Frank Oberle

The Kern Family

"Descendants of (John) Dominic Kern and his wife Margaret Vaeth"

The second of Fr. Frank Kunkel's genealogy manuscripts was completed in August of 1941, just a few months before the Japanese invasion of Pearl Harbor that precipitated the formal entry of the United States into World War II.

The Kern Name

The word kern, which is the root of the English word "kernel," means simply the "core" or, by extension, "pit," "crux," "nucleus," and the like. Unlike the root for the name "Kerchner," it doesn't provide any insight into the history of the family or suggest a possible early occupation for one of our ancestors.

Errata

The only significant error[79] in this second of Fr. Kunkel's books appears in the Kunkel-Kerchner Family Tree provided on page 35 (reproduced to the right and on page 183).

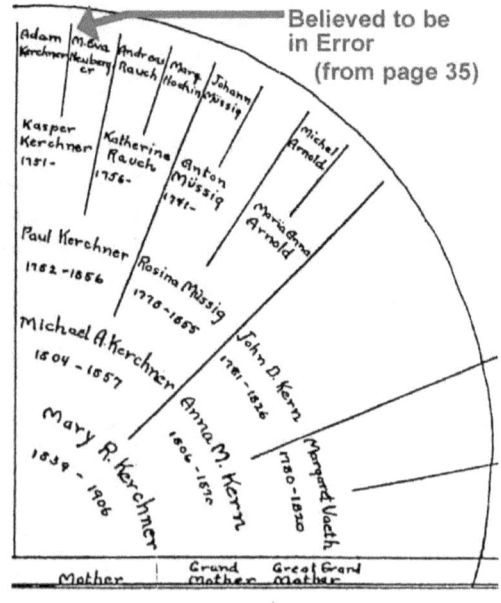

On the maternal side of this chart, I believe that Fr. Kunkel was mistaken in his identification of Kaspar Kerchner's parents, whom he shows as Adam Kerchner and Maria Eva Neuberger.

My belief is that Kaspar Kerchner's parents are actually Johannes Michael Kerchner [ID 1178] and Gertrude Groos [ID 1179]. A possible source of confusion was likely that there are references to two Caspar Kerchners in the records for that period, each of which had a son named Paul. It isn't clear whether or not these Kerchners were all related although, given the size of the town, that certainly seems likely.

---

[79] I should repeat once again that I only attempted to verify facts related to my own ancestral line.

Fr. Kunkel's Interesting Omission

On page 13 of his book (reproduced here on page 162), there is a reference to "104. William F. Kerchner (1898-). Probably because the book had to pass muster with Catholic Church laws of the time, Fr. Kunkel neglected to mention that William Ferdinand Kerchner [ID 113] married Margaret Bernice Charles [ID 114] (16 Nov 1904 - 13 May 1966) in 1930. Because Margaret was a non-catholic, the marriage was not recognized by the church. This third Ferdinand[80], the first of which is also our own family's ancestor, was the nephew of my great-grandmother Regina (Jennie [ID 8]) Kerchner Hulshoff.

A reproduction of Fr. Kunkel's original manuscript of "The Descendants of (John) Dominic Kern and his wife Margaret Vaeth" begins on the next page.

---

[80] Our ancestor Ferdinand Kerchner [ID 38] (11 Jul 1835 - 1 Jun 1918) was the first of these. The second was his son, Ferdinand John Kerchner [ID 109] (1875 – 1925), who was the younger brother of our ancestor Mary Regina (Jennie) Kerchner [ID 8]. William Ferdinand Kerchner, Sr [ID 113] (29 Dec 1898 – 1960) was the oldest son of Ferdinand John, and also had a son named Ferdinand.

OUR KERN ANCESTORS

JOHN DOMINIC KERN and MARGARET VAETH KERN
1781-1826   1780-1829

IN
SPES MESSIS   SEMINE
KERN

A FAMILY RECORD WITH THE NAMES OF MORE THAN
ONE THOUSAND DESCENDENTS

[*Reverse Side of Cover Page is blank*]

The Descendents

of

Dominic Kern

and his wife

Margaret Vaeth

1780   1841

REPRODUCTION OF FR. KUNKEL'S MANUSCRIPT

Foreword

It was in the summer of 1897, when I was a seminarian at St. Sulpice, Paris, that I visited Germany, for the first time. As I had not particularly prepared myself for this visit, I found, on reaching Freudenberg, the ancestral village of the Kerns, that I had neither a list of relatives nor a letter of identification. As it was just about noon when I arrived in the village by the Mail Stage, I went direct to the Village Inn, the 'Gasthaus zur Traube,' and there let it be known that I was an American looking up his cousins among the Kerns and the Kerchners. After lunch I called on the Herr Pfarrer, the village pastor, and to give you an idea how quickly the news of my arrival had spread, I was at the rectory but a short time, when a little girl came with the photo referred to above. It was the picture of Anna Maria (Kern) Kerchner and her 2 little sons, Billy and Fred taken just before they left for America, in 1832. **

Before long I was introduced to all the cousins near and remote, and from that time, September 1897, began my interest in the Kern Family Tree. I did not then realize the many difficulties I would encounter. For besides establishing the relationship of those who never left Germany, I learned that those who had come to this country a century ago were scattered from New York to California, and many of the latter, even of the same generation, were utterly unknown to one another. However, by dint of writing and of travelling, and by the kind cooperation on the part of many, I have been able to bring to light many hitherto unknown cousins. Without their assistance, I would not have been able to locate the many relatives resident in 10 different states and the District of Columbia and this record of the Kern Family could not have been published. I wish to express to them my sincere thanks for their invaluable assistance.

It is my hope that through this little publication, the many cousins as yet unknown to one another may be drawn closer together and by personal contact throw further light on the Kern family and their numerous descendants. (There are 1041 names in the record.)

Accompanying this genealogy of the Kerns is a series of letters written for the most part to my grandfather, Michael Anthony Kerchner, by his mother and extending over a period of 20 years from 1832 to 1855. They have a peculiar charm, not being intended for publication, and are the sincere outpourings of a mother's heart in her solicitude and love for her children, separated from her by the vast expanse of the Atlantic Ocean. They likewise give evidence of her sound judgment and her deeply religious spirit. The letters, most of which were written over a century ago, came into my possession and I am happy to be able to transmit the English translation to posterity. I believe that my readers will be interested in reading these simple and sincere expressions of a mother's love.

F. W. KUNKEL, S.S.
August 15, 1941

** This photo of Anna, Billy and Fred doesn't seem to appear in the document, and I haven't been able to locate it.

TABLE OF CONTENTS

Anna Maria Kern, descendents of ....Pp.   4- 47

Letters of Grandmother Rosina Mussig Kerchner..................Pp. 48- 75

Susanna Kern, descendents of ....Pp. 76- 91

Dominic Kern, descendents of ....Pp. 92-123

Matthew, descendents of ....Pp. 124-126

Dorothy Kern, descendents of ....Pp. 127-133

'Unclaimed Millions' ....Pp. 134-136

Erhard and Mary Kern, descendents of ....Pp. 137

Nihil Obstat:
 EDWARD A. CERNY, S.S., S.T.D.
 St. Mary's Seminary
 Baltimore, Md.
 Aug. 13, 1941

Imprimatur:
 ✠ MICHAEL J. CURLEY,
 Archbishop of Baltimore and Washington
 Aug. 15, 1941

"God in His infinite mercy and goodness, at the very beginning of Christianity, gave to the world a model of a divinely constituted family, in which all may find a perfect example of domestic society,—a model of virtue and sanctity. That family consisted of Christ, Our Savior, Mary, His Virgin Mother and Joseph His holy foster-father. Fathers will find in Joseph an exemplar of an ever vigilant, paternal provider; mothers may look to the most holy Mother of God as a beautiful example of affection, modesty, submission and perfect fidelity; children have in the child Jesus, an example of love and obedience to be admired, cherished and imitated." Encyclical of His Holiness, Pope Leo XIII, published June 14, 1892.

"O Lord Jesus Christ, Who when Thou wast subject to Mary and Joseph didst sanctify the home life with ineffable virtues: grant that by their joint assistance, we may profit by the example of Thy Holy Family and become partakers of their eternal happiness."

Collect taken from the Mass for the *Feast of the Holy Family.*

Dedication

To Jesus, Mary and Joseph, the Holy Family, I dedicate this modest brochure, praying that the present generation and the generations to come may see in Joseph, a devoted husband and father, as well as a faithful provider; in Mary, the Mother of God, a loving spouse and the gentlest of mothers; in Jesus, the Divine Child, the model of an obedient reverent and affectionate child.

Descendents of Dominic Kern and Margaret Vaeth (1st Mar.) 1780-1820
(1781-1826)   Susanna Ziegler (2nd Mar.)

First Generation
KERN

2. Anna Maria ......(1806-1870)
3. Susanna ....(1807-1896)
4. Joseph Anthony ...(1809-1848)
5. Dominic ....(1811-1871)
6. Vitus ....(1814- died infant)
7. Matthew ....(1816-1893)
8. David ....(1818-
9. Dorothy ....(1820-1903)

Second Marriage
10. Erhard ....(1822-1887)
11. Mary Josepha ....(1824-1902)

361 Descendents

223 Living Descendents

Descendents of
ANNA MARIA KERN and MICHAEL A. KERCHNER

I. Generation	II. Generation	Birth-Death
1. Anna Maria Kern (1806-1870)	KERCHNER	
2. Michael A. Kerchner (1807-1849)	3. Francis Wm.	1829-1910
	4. Fred. Augustine	1831-1898
	5. Adrian	1834- d. Infant
	6. Ferdinand	1835-1918
	7. Adolph	1837-1915
	8. Mary Rosina	1839-1906
	9. Catherine	1841-1924
	10. Caroline	1843-1898
	11. Josephine	1847-1855

II. Generation	III. Generation	
3. Francis Wm. Kerchner (1829-1910)		
12. Lydia Cath. Hatch (1834-1894)		
4. Fred. Augustine Kerchner (1831-1898)	KERCHNER	
	14. Mary Catherine	1855-1910
13. Anna Catherine Berger (1831-1912)	15. Francis Wm.	1857-1926
	16. Charles Fred.	1859-1937
	17. Henry Adolph	1861-
	18. Ella Anastasia	1864-
	19. Rosina Athalia	1871
6. Ferdinand Kerchner (1835-1918)	KERCHNER	
	21. Mary Cath.	1861-1925
20. Anna Linnenkemper (1839-1914)	22. Anna	1865-
	23. M. Regina	1873-1940
	24. Ferd. John	1875-1925
	25. John J.	1877-
	26. William F.	1881-1922
7. Adolph Kerchner (1837-1915)	27. M. Teresa	d. Infant
28. Mary Hubel		
	KUNKEL	
8. Mary Rosina Kerchner (1839-1906)	30. Fred John	1860-
	31. Joseph A. (1)	1861-
29. John Nep. Kunkel (1831-1910)	32. Mary Regina	1863-1915
	33. Michael A.	1865-d. Infant
	34. John Alphons.	1866-1935
	35. Nicholas A.	1868-1933
	36. Francis Ferd.	1870- Ord. Priest 1898
	37. Teresa M.	1872-1932
	38. Marg. Dorothy	1874- Sister Christ. Charity, 8-18-94
	39. Joseph A. (2)	1876-1882
	40. William F.	1878-1907
	41. Joseph A. (3)	1882-
	42. Teresa Purzer	1889-
9. Catherine Kerchner (1841-1924)	NEUBECK	
43. Henry Neubeck (1841-1916)	44. Adolph	1874-1931
	45. Francis L.	1877-
10. Caroline Kerchner (1843-1898)	HESSLER	
	47. John Wm.	1869-1931
46. Michael Hessler (1841-1910)	48. Anna Eva	1871-
	49. Frank A.	1873-
	50. Ferdinand	1875- d. 40

III. Generation	IV. Generation	Birth Death
	HOOVER	
11. Mary Catherine Kerchner (1866-1910)		
51. John M. Hoover (1875-1927)	52. Frederick	1880-
	53. Ella Rose	1882-
	54. Francis A.	1884-
	55. Katherine	1886-
	56. Joseph	1889-
	57. Helen	1891-
	58. Mary	1893-
15. Francis Wm. Kerchner* (1857-1926)		
59. Florence Latta (1866-)		
	KERCHNER	
16. Chas. Fred. Kerchner (1859-1937)	61. Pauline	1890-
60. Mary McGowan (1867-)	62. Charles	1891-
	63. Mary	1893- d. Infant
	64. Beatrice	1896- Sister Beatrice, R.S.M.
	KERCHNER	
17. Henry Adolph Kerchner (1861-)	66. Helen	1890-
65. Isabelle Forman (1862-1926)	67. Hilda	1893-
	68. Isabelle	1894-
	NORMAN	
18. Ella Anastasia Kerchner (1864-)	70. John Hugh	
69. Robt. Chas. Norman** (1858-1937)	71. Ella Mary Jos.	
	72. Marg. Catherine	
	73. Rose Teresa	
	74. Robert C., Jr.	
	75. Oswald Byrne	
	76. M. Dorothy	
	LEWIS	
19. Rosina A. Kerchner (1871-)	78. Katherine	1898-
77. Chas. Edw. Lewis*** (1870-1927)	79. Rosina	1900-
	80. Mary Bertha	1907-
	81. Charles F.	1909-1925
	ZANG	
21. M. Catherine Kerchner (1801-1925)	83. Anna M.	1882-
82. John Zang (1878-1910)	84. Margaret	1884-
	85. Catherine	1884-
	86. M. Clara	1888-
	87. M. Regina	1890-1892
	88. M. Teresa	1892-
	89. M. Gertrude	1894-
	90. Mabel Genevieve	1895-
	91. John Gerard	1896-
	92. William Alph.	1902-
	93. M. Beatrice	1904-
	HULSHOFF	
23. M. Regina Kerchner (1873-1940)	95. Anna Gertruda	1896-
94. Herman Hulshoff (1856-1940)	96. M. Alfrida	1899-
	97. M. Rosalia	1902-
	98. Dorothy A.	1906-
	99. M. Agnes	1911-
	100. Herman	1911- d. Infant
	101. Regina	1911- d. Infant
	102. Gerard	1914-

** ROBERT CHARLES NORMAN (No. 69)
(New York Bureau, Baltimore Sun, April 9, 1937)

Robert Chas. Norman, importer of broom corn and former President of the Seaboard Broom Co. of Petersburg, Va., died today at his home, 404 Riverside Drive.

Mr. Norman, born in Baltimore, was the son of the late Capt. John Norman and Margaret Byrne Norman, and was educated at Calvert Hall College. While a young man he joined the Atlantic Southwestern Broom Co., Baltimore, and later became vice-president of this concern. In his business as importer, Mr. Norman travelled extensively abroad.

Surviving are his wife, the former Ella Kerchner of Baltimore, five children and five grandchildren.

* FRANCIS WM. KERCHNER (No. 15)
(San Francisco, The Examiner, Feb. 16, 1926)

In Sonora, California, Feb. 15, 1926, Francis William Kerchner, beloved husband of Flora Latta Kerchner, and loving brother of Mrs. Rose Kerchner Lewis of San Francisco, Mrs. Ella Kerchner Norman of New York City, Charles F. and Harry C. Kerchner of Baltimore, Md., aged 68 years. Lately a member of Berkeley Lodge, B.P.O.E.

*** CHARLES EDWARD LEWIS (No. 77)
(San Francisco, The Examiner, Jan. 22, 1927)

In this city, Jan. 21, 1927, Charles Edward Lewis, beloved husband of Rose Kerchner Lewis, father of Mrs. Paul McDonald, of Memphis, Tenn.; Sister Mary Regina of Jesus, D.C.U., Carmelite Convent, Alhambra, Calif., Miss Mary Bertha Lewis and the late Chas. Fred. Lewis, a native of Baltimore, Md. A member of the Holy Name Society, St. Edward's Church and San Francisco Council No. 615.

III. Generation	IV. Generation	Birth Death
24. Ferd. John Kerchner (1875-1925)	KERCHNER	
103. Mary Mullahy (1880-1923)	104. William F.	1898-
	105. Jas. Albert	1900-1931
	106. Francis Pat.	1903-
	107. Kathleen Anne	1905-
	108. John Norbert	1914-
25. John J. Kerchner (1877-	KERCHNER	
109. Caroline Fisher (1877-1935)	110. M. Loretta	1911-
	111. M. Lucille	1918-
	112. George W.	1920-
	113. John A.	1922-
30. Fred. Jno. Kunkel (1860-	KUNKEL	
114. Catherine Busch (1865-1934)	115. John N., Jr.	1887-
	116. Denis	1891- d. Infant
	117. Joseph	1892- d. Infant
	118. John H.	1894- d. Infant
	119. M. Catherine (adopted)	1894-
	120. Charles J.	1896-
	121. M. Lydia	1899- Sr. Philomena of Good Shepherd
	122. M. Regina	d. Infant
	123. Francis W.	1900-
34. John Alph. Kunkel (1866-1935)	KUNKEL	
124. Anna Vaeth (1865-1905)	125. Anna M.	1891-
	126. Mary E.	1892-
	127. Francis F.	1894-
	128. Teresa M.	1896
	129. James	1898-
	130. William	1901-
	131. Agnes	1903-
35. Nich. A. Kunkel (1868-1935)	KUNKEL	
132. Barbara Schneider (1870-1933)	133. Francis	1894-
35. Teresa M. Kunkel (1872-1932)	WARD	
134. Peter J. Ward* (1872-	135. Rose Marie	1898-1914
	136. Francis J.	1899-
	137. Johannetta M.	1900-
	138. John J.	1902-
	139. Joseph A.	1903-
	140. Regina M.	1904-
	141. Peter J., Jr.	1909-
	142. Edward	1911-
40. William F. Kunkel (1878-1907)	KUNKEL	
143. Mary T. Becker (1879-	144. Marie	1901
	145. Joseph	1906-
41. Joseph A. Kunkel (1882-	KUNKEL	
146. Dora Eva Becker (1882-	147. Genevieve Louise Sr. M. Nicholas, S.S.N.D.	1911- 1912
	148. Dorothy Margaret	
	149. Nicholas Aloysius	1914-
	150. Marie Josephine	1915-
	151. Anne Mary	1917-
	152. Irene Barbara	1919
	153. Joseph Anthony	1921
	154. Francis Xavier	1924-
	155. Theresa Maureen	1928

*Mr. Peter J. Ward (native of Philadelphia) was employed in the Stetson Hat Factory for upward of 25 years. In 1897 he married Teresa M. Kunkel, daughter of John N. and Mary R. Kunkel, and moved to Baltimore. For many years he conducted a successful Hat Business on Baltimore St.

III. Generation	IV. Generation	Birth	Death
42. Teresa Purzer	PURZER		
(1889-			
150. Joseph Brennan	157. Joseph	1922-	
(1887-	158. Alice	1925-	
	159. Jeannette	1927-	
	NEUBECK		
44. Adolph Neubeck			
(1874-1931)			
160. Ella Ballenger	161. Catherine	1907-	
(1875-	162. Francis G.	1908-	
	163. Mary Estelle	1910-	
	164. Ella R.	1911-	
	165. Gertrude E.	1913-	
45. Francis L. Neubeck	NEUBECK		
(1877-			
166. Mary D. Curran	167. John H.	1909-	
(1875-1933)	168. Catherine A.	1911-	
	169. Mary A.	1914-	
	170. Francis L.	1916-	
	HESSLER		
49. Frank A. Hessler			
(1873-			
171. Ottillie Werner	172. Minnie	1896-	
(1878-1934)	173. George F.	1900-	
	174. Madeleine	1902-	
	175. Josephine	1911-	

IV. Generation	V. Generation		
53. Ella Rose Hoover	McDONALD		
(1882-			
176. John McDonald	177. Rose Agnes		
54. Francis Hoover	HOOVER		
(1884-	179. Catherine	1915-	
178. May Stafford—1st. Mar.	180. Francis	1917-	
(1886-1918)	181. Elizabeth	1919-	
182. Marg. E. Fischer—2nd Mar.	183. John R.	1922-	
(1887-	184. Bernard J.	1925-	
	CURLANDER		
55. Catherine Hoover			
(1887-	186. Henry		
185. Henry Curlander	187. Carroll		
	HOOVER		
56. Joseph Hoover			
(1889-	189. Helen		
188. Bertha Wilhelm	190. Virginia		
	HOOVER		
57. Helen Hoover			
(1891-	192. Carl		
191. Henry Wich	193. Mary Lucille		
	HOY		
58. Mary Hoover			
(1893-	195. Robert		
194. Robert Hoy	196. Dorothy		
	KNIGHT		
61. Pauline Kerchner			
(1890-	198. C. Lyle	1911-	
197. Julius O. Knight	199. Mary	1913-	
(1887-	200. Julius	1915-	
62. Charles F. Kerchner	KERCHNER		
(1891-			
201. Helen Blair	202. Blair		

11

IV. Generation	V. Generation	Birth-Death
66. Helen Kerchner (1880)	ESSARY	
203. J. Fred. Essary (1881)	204. Annabel	1911-
	205. Ruth	1915-
	206. Elene	1922-
	HEYER	
67. Hilda Kerchner (1880-1940)		
207. Walter Heyer	208. Carolyn Forman	
	CROSWELL	
68. Isabel Kerchner (1884-)		
209. Bennel Croswell	210. Harry B.	
	NORMAN	
70. John H. Norman	212. Julia Waring	
211. Julia H. Tisdale	213. John H., Jr.	
	214. Ella	
	215. Robert	
	216. Katherine	
74. Robert C. Norman		
217. Winifred Halberstadt		
78. Katherine Lewis (1898-)	McDONNELL	
218. Paul McDonnell (1897-)	219. Paul	d. infant
	220. M. Katherine	1921-
	221. Chas. Lewis	1924-
	222. Rosina	1927-
	223. James Edward	1928-
	224. Frances Virginia	1930-
	225. Dorothy Irene	1932-
	226. Bernardine	1936-
	ABELLA	
80. Mary Bertha Lewis (1907-)		
227. Henry Abella —1st Mar. (1906-1937)	228. Henry	d. infant
	229. Joseph	1930-
230. Wm. Drummond Coakley		
	METZ	
84. Margaret Zang (1884-)		
231. Joseph Metz, D.D.S. (1882-)	232. Mary	1907-
	233. Gertrude	1910-
	234. Joseph, Jr., D.D.S.	1913-
85. Catherine Zang (1884-)	PREIS	
235. F. William Preis (1884-)	236. John Gerard	1907-
86. M. Clara Zang (1886-)		
237. Chas. L. Weddell		
88. M. Teresa Zang (1892-)		
238. J. Miles Byrne		
89. M. Gertrude Zang (1894-)	MALLOY	
239. Francis X. Malloy	240. Anne Teresa	1989-
	241. Mary Frances	1894-
	242. Michael James	1939-
90. Mabel Genev. Zang (1896-)	HORGAN	
243. Edward Horgan	244. Mariam Ruth	1917-
	245. Janet Helen	1922-
	246. Dorothy M.	1929-
	247. Donald E.	1932-

IV. Generation	V. Generation	Birth-Death
	ZANG	
92. William Alph. Zang (1900-		
248. Marie Logue (1901-	249. Jeanne M.	1923-
	250. Mary Louise	1928-
	251. William F.	1933-
	GONCE	
96. Anna Gertrude Hulshoff (1899-		
252. Chas. Rich. Gonce (1896-1956)	253. Rosalie	1920-
	254. Regina	1921-
	256. Chas. Rich., Jr.	1924-
	257. Jos. George	1927-
97. M. Rosalie Hulshoff (1911-		
258. William Hausmann		
104. William F. Kerchner (1898-		
259. Frances Lippy—1st Mar. Margaret Charles—2nd Mar.		
	KERCHNER	
106. Francis Pat. Kerchner (1903-		
260. Catherine Wilke	261. Richard	1927-
107. Kathleen A. Kerchner (1905-		
262. Albert Beck (1898-		
	FRITZGES	
111. M. Lucille Kerchner (1913-		
263. Joseph F. Fritzges (1913-	264. Mary Joe	1937-
	265. Jane Frances	1938-
	361. Caroline Ann	1943-
	KERCHNER	
112. George W. Kerchner (1920- Violet Schunemann	358. Mary Lucille	1940-
	KUNKEL	
115. John N. Kunkel, Jr. (1888-	267. Catherine	1914-
266. Dora Dilz (1888-	268. Helen	1915-
	269. Gerard	1925-
119. M. Catherine Kunkel (1894-		
270. Charles Miller		
120. Charles J. Kunkel (1894-		
271. Evelyn Kraus (1896-	272. Charlotte Anne	1937-
	KUNKEL	
123. Francis W. Kunkel (1900-		
273. Dorothy Heinicke (1900-	274. Frederick J.	1937-
	359. John Francis	1941-
127. Francis F. Kunkel (1894-		
275. Margaret von Gestel—1st Mar.		
276. Marie Willenburg—2nd Mar.		

13

REPRODUCTION OF FR. KUNKEL'S MANUSCRIPT

IV. Generation	V. Generation	Birth-Death
	THIM	
128. Teresa M. Kunkel (1896-		
277. Frank Thim (1891-	278. Bernadette	1926-
	279. Margaret	1928
	280. Regina	1929-
	281. Dorothy	1930-
	282. Catherine	1932-
	283. Francis W.	1934-
	284. Charles	1936-
	285. Rich. J.	1938-
	286. Elizabeth P.	1940-
	KUNKEL	
129. James Kunkel (1898-		
287. Margaret Hubbard (1900-	288. Joseph	1934-
	289. Margaret M.	1936-
	KUNKEL	
130. William Kunkel (1901-		
290. Mary Bond (1902-	291. William	1927-
	KUNKEL	
133. Francis Kunkel (1894-		
292. Mary Bellis (1891-	293. Gertrude	1917-
	CAVANAUGH	
137. Jeannette Ward (1900-		
294. Thomas Cavanaugh (1893-1938)	295. Philip	1921-
	296. Rose	1924-
	297. Regina	1926-
	298. Thomas	1927-
	299. Peter	1930-
	WARD	
139. Joseph A. Ward (1903-		
300. Elizabeth Smith (1905-	301. Joseph A., Jr.	1931-
	302. Mary Ellen	1934-
	WIST	
140. Regina Ward (1904-		
303. George Wist (1903-	304. George J.	1928-
	305. Paul G.	1929-
	306. Rose Marie	1930-
	307. Jeanne	1937-
	KUNKEL	
145. Joseph Kunkel (1906-		
308. Angela Hooper (1908-	309. Joan	1931-
	310. Jay	1932-
	JACKSON	
148. Dorothy M. Kunkel (1912-		
311. Chas. Elmer Jackson (1912-	312. Charles E., Jr.	1935-
	313. Joseph Nicholas	1939-
	NEUBECK	
162. Francis G. Neubeck (1908-		
314. M. Marg. Madden (1910-	315. Mary A. Patricia	1930-
	316. Francis Greg.	1932-
	317. Teresa	1933-
	LANDIS	
163. Mary Estelle Neubeck (1910-		
318. Wm. Newton Landis	319. Mary Marg.	1940

IV. Generation	V. Generation	Birth-Death
165. Gertrude E. Neubeck (1913-		
320. Joseph Kibler (1909-		
167. John H. Neubeck (1909-		
321. Margaret Nemmers (1914-	322. Mary Marg.	1939-
	KRESPACH	
172. Minnie Hessler (1889-	324. Carolyn	1920-
323. Victor W. Krespach	325. Madelyn	1925-
	HESSLER	
173. George F. Hessler (1900-	327. Audrey O.	1933-
326. Lillian Butterhoff (1901-	328. Lillian M.	1935-
	329. George F., Jr.	1937-
	BONHOFF	
174. Madeleine Hessler (1902-	331. Francis H.	1927-
330. Henry M. Bonhoff	332. Henry M., Jr.	1934-
	RITTER	
175. Josephine Hessler (1911-		
333. Michael J. Ritter		
335. Robt. Kerner—2nd Mar.	334. Joan	1933-
	KERNER	
	336. Robt., Jr.	1940-
179. Catherine Hoover (1915-		
337. Harry Tieperman		
	KNIGHT	
198. C. Lyle Knight (1911-		
338. Helen M. Imbach	339. Robert L.	1940-
	O'MARA	
199. Mary Knight (1913-	341. John P.	1936-
340. John O'Mara	342. Mary J.	1938-
	343. Gerald K.	1940-
	ANSELL	
204. Annabel Essary (1911-		
344. Samuel T. Ansell	345. Helen Essary	1940-
231. Mary Metz (1907-		
346. Geo. Abel Morris		
232. Gertrude Metz (1910-		
348. Edward Cain		
	METZ	
233. Jos. F. Metz, Jr., D.D.S. (1913-		
349. Bernardette Drummond	362. Bernadette M.	1941-
V. Generation	VI. Generation	
236. John Gerard Preis (1907-		
350. Helen Morningstar		
	COOPER	
254. Regina Gonce (1921-		
351. Henry Otis Cooper	360. Mary Regina	1941-

15

V. Generation	VI. Generation	Birth-Death
	PONS	
267. Catherine Kunkel		
(1914-	353. Barbara	1937-
352. Adolph Pons, II	354. Adolph, III	1940-
	ARCHER	
268. Helen Kunkel		
(1915-	356. J. Carvel, Jr.	1938-
353. John Carvel Archer	357. Dorothea Lee	1939-
	Elizabeth Reid	1941-

16

ANNA MARIA KERN

17

ANNA MARIA KERN

Anna Maria Kern, born in 1806, was the first of the Freudenberg Kerns to come to America. She was married to Michael Anthony Kerchner, in Freudenberg, Baden and we have on hand the Marriage Contract, a 4-page document, making provision of their material possessions, and signed at Wertheim, May 15, 1828. There has come into our possession, also, in an excellent state of preservation, the "Wanderbuch" of Michael Kerchner, containing an account of his travels as a journeyman shoemaker and the names of the Master Shoemakers by whom he was employed. For this was in those days a necessary procedure, before a man could practice his trade, and grandfather, having complied with these conditions became a Master Shoemaker, before coming to America.

But conditions at that time were so unfavorable in Germany while, on the other hand, the reports of the wonderful opportunities in America for young people were so roseate, that my grandparents were induced to fold their tents in Freudenberg and try their fortune in this land of opportunity. The original passport (still preserved) tells us they left Germany with their 2 young sons, Francis William, aged 3 years and Fred Augustus, 1 year old. The document states that as a guarantee against their landing in America as paupers, the father was provided with 400 Gulden, and the mother with 200 Gulden while there was a provision of 100 Gulden for each of the children. They set sail from the port of Bremen for Philadelphia, June 29, 1832, and on landing 3 months later took up their residence in Philadelphia at the Cock and Lion Hotel, on 4th St. just north of Market St.

Michael Kerchner lost little time in applying for citizenship and his naturalization papers in our possession state that he first appeared before the Court, in Philadelphia October 9, 1834, and 3 years from that date was declared a citizen of the United States. But he was evidently not satisfied that Philadelphia was the best place for his business, and in 1839 we find the family in Wilmington, Delaware, where my mother, Mary Rosina was born, August 9, 1839. On the following Sunday she was baptized at the celebrated little St. Joseph's Church, at Dupont's Mills, on the banks of the Brandywine. But grandfather Kerchner was a restless man, as we learn from the letters of his mother, and so we find him later in Delaware City, Delaware, and in 1843, in Cambridge, Md. where Caroline was born. In 1844 they established themselves permanently in Baltimore, where grandfather was able to maintain the family in reasonable comfort, by the practice of his trade.

Grandfather died in 1857 and grandmother in 1870, the latter just 2 months before my birth, so that I did not see either of my grandparents. We have a picture of grandmother Kerchner with her 2 young sons, taken in Germany just before they left for America.

No. 3. Francis William Kerchner (1829-1910). I have already devoted considerable attention to this distinguished member of our family, (see the KUNKEL-KERCHNER ALBUM), who was the eldest son of Anna Maria Kern Kerchner. I feel, however, that because of his remarkable character, he has undoubtedly reflected great honor on the Kern family, and is therefore entitled to more than a passing notice. Although he enjoyed none of the educational advantages of the present generation he was endowed with a natural intelligence and he profited by every op-

18

COL. F. W. KERCHNER
Brother of Mrs. John N. Kunkel

portunity to cultivate and develop his inborn genius. I have in my possession page after page of foolscap filled with passages which he copied from the Bible in order to improve his knowledge of English. There can be no doubt that this practice was of great assistance to him. For he was a ready and convincing public speaker as well as a brilliant conversationalist and entertainer, and achieved a real success in business, in politics and in society.

Before the Civil War he conducted a Shoe Store on Fayette St. near Liberty St. and at a later period on Baltimore St. in the former Carrollton Hotel. He enjoyed the patronage of many of the most prominent business and professional men of the city. At the same time he was a Lieutenant of the Independent Grays, a branch of the Maryland National Guard. He served as aide-de-camp to Gen. Robert E. Lee when John Brown was captured at Harper's Ferry in 1859. In appreciation of his distinguished services on this occasion, he was presented by Gen. Lee with the rifle and powder flask that had belonged to John Brown. During the Civil War he was a blockade runner for the Confederates and undertook many a hazardous journey in carrying military dispatches between the North and the South.

After the Civil War he settled in Wilmington, N.C. and there became the friend and confidant of the late Card. Gibbons, when the latter was Vicar-Apostolic of North Carolina. Rarely did any prominent ecclesiastic visit Bishop Gibbons, who was not at the same time hospitably entertained at the home of Col. and Mrs. Kerchner on Front St. Though he never sought public office he was a keen politician and was looked up to by members of the Democratic party. He was for a long period President of the Chamber of Commerce of Wilmington, and a portrait of the Colonel now adorns its walls. He was the proprietor of a Wholesale Grocery and Hardware business and proved himself a successful merchant. When, however, he lost his wife in 1904, he never fully recovered from the shock. He closed his residence in Wilmington and up to the time of his death lived at our home in Hamilton. During this period he was always a welcome guest at the Cardinal's residence and in his last illness was comforted by visits from His Eminence. He died in 1910 in his eighty first year and was buried from St. Dominic's Church, Hamilton. At the Requiem High Mass which was sung by the Pastor, Rev. J. B. Manley, the late Msgr. Thomas was deacon, Rev. Dr. Wm. A. Fletcher, Rector of the Cathedral, preached the funeral sermon, while His Eminence Card. Gibbons and a considerable number of the clergy were present in the sanctuary.

No. 12. Lydia Catherine Hatch was happily married to William F. Kerchner (No. 3). Perhaps, some extracts from letters received by Col. Kerchner on the occasion of her death in 1894, will give us a better estimate of her remarkable character than any words of my own. I here quote from some of the numerous letters of condolence sent to the bureaved husband.

"I was much shocked at the news of your dear wife's death which I learned from his Eminence, Card. Gibbons. My heartfelt sympathy and sentiments of condolence to you, who were ever a faithful and loving husband to her. Your dear wife was one of my most esteemed friends and revered for her sterling qualities of mind and heart. I had the satisfaction of receiving her profession of faith and of admitting her into the Church. Her long sufferings borne with so much patience, and resignation to the will of God prepared her to enter that

20

kingdom of Christ, purchased by the Cross."
Rev. Mark S. Gross.

"We regret to chronicle the death of that noble Christian woman, Mrs. Lydia Catherine Kerchner, wife of our esteemed citizen, Col. F. W. Kerchner...The deceased lady was a devout Catholic and was a woman of gracious Christian character, bearing her long suffering with Christian resignation. She was a large-hearted, charitable and benevolent person, and it was her greatest pleasure to do good without the world's knowing it. Many will grieve at her death and not only will she be mourned by her devoted husband, friends and relatives, but by numbers of those whose wants and cares she has relieved and soothed in her quiet and unostentatious way. Indeed she was greatly beloved by all who knew her and the deepest sympathy is felt for her bereaved husband in this hour of disconsolation".
Wilmington Morning Star, June 21, 1894

"Her many noble deeds of charity made her name loved throughout the Cape Fear section of the state."
Charleston, (S.C.) News, June 23, 1894

"Mrs. Kerchner was the daughter of the late Nathaniel Hatch and the niece of Samuel T. Hatch, of Baltimore. Her husband left Baltimore during the civil war and joined the Confederate navy. After the war he entered business in Wilmington, N. C. When Card. Gibbons was Bishop of North Carolina, he made Mrs. Kerchner's residence his home."
The Baltimore Sun, June 22, 1894

"Card. Gibbons called yesterday at the residence of Fred A. Kerchner, 930 Harlem Ave., to view the remains of Mrs. Lydia C. Kerchner, the wife of F. W. Kerchner...His Eminence spoke in touching terms of the deceased and with the assistance of the Rev. N. W. Caughey, recited the prayers for the dead".
The Baltimore Evening Sun, June 22, 1894

"A patient and long sufferer, she had been bearing her affliction with most commendable Christian fortitude, always so kind and thoughtful of others."
James and Henrietta Smith,
Haymount, Fayetteville, N. C.

"I have just learned of the death of your wife and hasten to tender my sincere sympathy to you. Would that I could say something that would tend to mitigate your sorrow."
Edward Chambers Smith,
Law Offices, Raleigh, N.C., June, 1894.

"Illness has prevented me from writing to condole with you in the sad loss of your sainted wife. Mr. Nolan and I were filled with sincere sorrow when the news reached us. For we both revered Mrs. Kerchner as a truly good woman, one of God's elect, whose example was a just tribute to the Catholic faith that animated all her actions."
Columbia, S. C., July 20, 1894
Mr. and Mrs. N. Nolan

"I was distressed to read in the newspaper this morning of your irreparable loss."
Raleigh, N. C., June 23, 1894
John W. Hinsdale

Mr. Fred A. Kerchner
(1831-1898)

Mrs. Fred A. Kerchner
née Anna Catherine Berger
(1831-1912)

22

"It was with deep regret that we learned through the mortuary card sent us, of the death of your estimable wife. . .May our dear Lord sustain and comfort you. . .Expressing anew the sympathy of our community. We have offered our prayers for her eternal repose."

Ursuline Convent, Columbia, S.C.
Madame Ignatia

No. 4. Frederick Augusthic Kerchner (1831-1898)

Uncle Fred was but one year old, when, in June 1832, he and his brother William, just 2 years older, left Freudenberg, in the company of his parents and set sail for America. The family lived for a short period in Philadelphia. But Grandfather Kerchner was in search of a more suitable place for the practice of his special trade of "Shoes to Order". From Philadelphia he went to Wilmington and then to Delaware City in Delaware, passed along the Eastern Shore of Maryland from Oxford to Cambridge, and finally settled in Baltimore about the year 1844.

This frequent change of residence did not permit his children to pursue a regular course of studies. William and Fred had not therefore the advantages of an education, so universally enjoyed by the youth of our day. They had, however, acquired by their limited travels an experience and a wisdom, which coupled with their native talent, enabled them to achieve a creditable success in life, the success of self-made men, so greatly admired in pioneer days.

As a young man Mr. Kerchner was a carrier for the 'Baltimore Sun' (We might mention, here, that one of his granddaughters is married to Mr. J. Fred Essary, the distinguished Washington correspondent of the *Sun*). He was for a time Superintendent of the Western Public Cemetery and in later years held an honorable position with the Baltimore Board of Health.

With his silvery gray hair and his merry laugh, he was conspicuous in a group. At the family gatherings which took place at regular intervals in the homes of the Kerchners and Kunkels, he was unquestionably the life of the party. He was a good singer, and sang equally well in German and English, was familiar with church hymns as well as the popular folk songs of the day and by his enthusiasm induced both young and old to join in, so that the party at times reached almost to the proportions of a German Saenger-Fest. Occasionally the merriment continued until the last street car had passed, and all were compelled to trudge their weary way home, afoot; for the hack of those days was rather expensive for so many individuals and the Taxicab was as yet unknown.

Alas, such family gatherings, such inexpensive and inoffensive convivialities, have almost passed into oblivion. Could we but revive 'the good old days' when uncles and aunts and cousins were more closely united, shared one another's joys and sorrows, and were bound together by a bond of mutual comfort and helpfulness.

A few months after my ordination to the priesthood, I found myself at the death-bed of this good uncle. My mother was also there and by common consent was permitted to perform the offices of a ministering angel for her dying brother, whispering into his ear pious ejaculations in German and English, while the grief stricken wife with her sons and daughters, as a truly Catholic family, knelt around the bed of their departing husband and father, repeating the Rosary again and again, until the end which occurred on the last day of the year 1898.

23

CHARLES FRANCIS LEWIS
(age 16 years)
son of Charles E. and Rose Kerchner Lewis, killed in a fall from
bicycle, San Francisco, Nov. 10, 1925. Grandson of
Mr. and Mrs. Fred A. Kerchner.

ANNA (Linnenkemper) KERCHNER and FERDINAND KERCHNER
(1839-1914)   (1835-1918)

The following references are taken from the Baltimore City Directory:
1868-69 Shoemaker and Newspaper carrier, 14 Green St
1860   Newspaper carrier, 20 Josephine St.
1864-65 Newspaper carrier, 18 Chatsworth St.
1866-80 Dry Goods, 60 So. Republican St.
1881-85 Health Department, 930 Harlem Ave.
1886   Superintendent Western Public Cemetery.

No. 6-20.Ferdinand Kerchner (1835-1918) and Anna Linnenkemper (1830-1914).

Ferdinand Kerchner was the third oldest son of Michael Kerchner and Anna Maria Kern and the first of their children to be born in America. On the death of Frederica Hubel, his first wife, he married Anna Linnenkemper. If happy marriages are made in heaven, then this marriage was the result of divine intervention. There were 7 children as the fruits of this happy union and they lived to celebrate their Golden Wedding, an account of which is given below. Their home was conspicuous as a house of hospitality if Dorothy Day permit us to use the term, for they were shining examples of genuine kindness and warm-hearted hospitality. How often did I and a group of seminarians from St. Mary's Seminary enjoy their hospitality. They loved and revered the priest, and through their long wedded life were members of St. James Parish and closely identified with its activities. From this church of the Redemptorist Fathers, their mortal remains were blessed and consigned to their last resting place in Holy Redeemer Cemetery.

Golden Wedding of Mr. and Mrs. Ferdinand Kerchner
(The Baltimore 'Sun' June, 1909)

At St. James Catholic Church at 8:30 o'clock yesterday morning, Mr. and Mrs. Ferdinand Kerchner of 920 N. Central Ave., celebrated the golden anniversary of their wedding by renewing their marriage promises in the presence of their six children, 16 grandchildren and 3 great grandchildren. A nuptial mass was celebrated by Rev. F. X. Baden, assistant pastor of the church. Mrs. Catherine Ancher who acted as bridesmaid at the wedding was present. Two of their sons Messrs. J. Ferdinand and John J. Kerchner and Messrs. John Zang and Herman Hulshoff, sons-in-law of Mr. and Mrs. Kerchner acted as ushers. At the Offertory Miss Pauline Knight, a niece, sang Gounod's Ave Maria.

Yesterday was also the twenty-eighth anniversary of the wedding of their daughter Mrs. John Zang. After the Mass breakfast was served at the home of Mr. and Mrs. Kerchner. Many handsome presents were received from friends and relatives and from a nephew Rev. Frank Kunkel of California. Cardinal Gibbons sent a note of congratulation.

During the day Mr. and Mrs. Kerchner received a number of their friends. In the evening there was a reception in which more than 300 persons were in attendance. Mr. Kerchner was born in Philadelphia and came to Baltimore when quite young. Miss Anna B. Linnenkemper was born in Germany but arrived in Baltimore as a child. They were married in St. Alphonsus Church. Mr. Kerchner was the senior member of the firm of Kerchner and O'Malley, dealers in leather goods, and retired from business about 10 years ago. Their children are Messrs. J. Ferdinand, John J. and Francis W. Kerchner, Mrs. John Zang, Mrs. Herman Hulshoff and Miss Anna Kerchner. Mr. Francis W. Kerchner is assistant secretary to the Governor, at Zamboango, Mindanao, Philippine Is."

25

MRS. HENRY NEUBECK (1841-1924)
MR. AND MRS. ADOLPH NEUBECK, SON AND DAUGHTER-IN-LAW
FRANCIS NEUBECK, GRANDSON

DEATH COMES SUDDENLY TO MRS. MARY C. ZANG

She Was Ardent Member Of St. James' Parish, Northeast Baltimore.

Oldest Daughter of Fred. Kerchner

Mrs. Mary C. Zang, who was found dead in bed at her home, 100 Somerset street, was a devout Catholic woman, who was always prepared to die. She heard Mass every day she was well and was a frequent Communient.

Mrs. Zang lived in Saint James' parish all her life, within the very shadow of the church. She was a member of the various ladies' sodalities and societies of the church and was interested in many worthy causes. She made suits for the orphans and in other ways showed her interest in them.

She was known to many Redemptorist priests throughout the province and had many friends among the secular priests of the Archdiocese. A Mass for the repose of her soul was celebrated on Tuesday by the Rev. Joseph Meier, C.SS.R., of Saint James' Church. The Revs. Carl F. Hess and Michael J. Cuddy of Saint John the Evangelist Church; the Rev. Thaddeus Shkzynski of the Immaculate Conception Church, Washington, and Mr. John Cyz of Saint Mary's Seminary, were present in the sanctuary.

Mrs. Zang was the wife of the late John C. Zang. She is survived by eight daughters, four of whom are trained nurses. The daughters are, the Misses Annie M., Gertrude and Mary Zang; Mrs. Joseph F. Metz, Mrs. W. F. Pries, Mrs. S. A. Weddel of California; Mrs. Myles E. Byrne and Mrs. Edward F. Horgan; a son, William Zang; two sisters, Miss Annie Kerchner and Mrs. Herman Hulshoff and two brothers, John and Ferdinand Zang.

The six pallbears where: John and Joseph Schneider, Ferdinand and Frank Kerchner, Charles Gonce and Frank Neubeck of Washington.

No. 7. Adolph Kerchner married Mary Hubel, who died shortly after marriage. Adolph was like his father a shoemaker, but with the outbreak of the Civil War joined the Confederate army. After the war he lived mostly at the Kunkel home and we boys often took delight in donning his gray Confederate uniform with its gold tassled epaulettes.

Nos. 9-34. Catherine Kerchner (1841-1924) and Henry Neubeck (1841-1916)

Catherine Kerchner married Henry Neubeck of Meadville, Pa. In their early married life, the Neubecks lived in Ellicott City, Md. where Mr. Neubeck practiced his trade of expert locksmith. The family later moved to Washington, where Mr. Neubeck owing to his exceptional ability as a locksmith was often called upon to adjust some of the complicated locks in the buildings of the national government. His son, Francis L. Neubeck has for a great many years successfully practiced law in the nation's capitol.

Reproduction of Fr. Kunkel's Manuscript

MR. AND MRS. JOHN N. KUNKEL
WITH ELDEST SON FRED J.

John Nepomuck Kunkel, (1831-1910)
✠

THIS short sketch of a loving and devoted Christian father, I wish to pass on to his grandchildren and to future generations, as a precious heritage and an inspiring example.

Father was born in the village of Gailbach, near Aschaffenburg, in Bavaria in the year 1831. When he had reached the age of 24, owing to the disturbed conditions then prevailing, not only in Germany but throughout Europe, he decided to come to America, and accordingly in 1855 set sail for Philadelphia, where three of his brothers were then living. He remained there but a short time, when he came to Baltimore, his future home. He almost immediately secured employment as a Wheelwright at the corner of Pennsylvania Ave. and McMechen St. We next find him employed at the corner of Pierce St. and Chatsworth St. (now Myrtle Ave.). About the year 1862, he entered into partnership with Angelina Vaeth in the Blacksmith and Wheelwright Business, on the West side of Hanover St. between Hamburg and Cross Sts. Finally, in 1864, he started in business for himself at No. 8 Lee St. near the water front, where the building of the Monumental Wagon Works is still to be seen (1939).

In the development of this business and in the rearing of a large family, his slender resources were oftentimes severely taxed; but his firm faith in Divine Providence coupled with his sterling integrity and capacity for business enabled him successfully to meet every difficulty. As the Wagon business progressed, he bought adjoining property, erected new buildings and installed modern machinery, so that he had eventually one of the best equipped wagon factories in the South. After 42 years spent in building up and developing the plant, and upon the death of my dear mother, he decided to retire from business. Accordingly in 1906, he left the entire management of the factory in the capable hands of my eldest brother, Frederick J. Kunkel. With him were soon associated two brothers, John, who took over the Painting Department and Nicholas, who became the Engineer.

For 20 years more the business continued to expand and meet the demands of the changing conditions of the times. The Monumental Patent Coal Wagons were eventually converted into auto trucks, and the firm assumed the Baltimore agency of the Goodyear Rubber Tires. This new business grew rapidly and within a short period, there were agencies in Norfolk, Va. and Bel Air, Md. Before many years the horse-driven vehicle had to yield to the auto and the Wagon Factory, in 1926, after an existence of more than 60 years, went out of business. There still remains, however, the agency for the Goodyear Rubber Co. and Automobile Accessories, conducted by John N. Kunkel, a grandson, in Bel Air, Md.

As a business man, my father had acquired so great a reputation for honesty and integrity, that the name of Kunkel on a vehicle, was a sure guarantee for good workmanship and honest material. As evidence of this statement, some of the Monumental Patent Coal Wagons were still operating in Baltimore in 1936, 10 years after the closing of the factory. Among the patrons of the Wagon Co. were the Baltimore Fire, Health and

Police Departments as well as some of the leading wholesale and retail firms of the city, state and surrounding territory. The employees also looked up to their 'boss' with respect and affection, for he was not only just, but uniformly kind to all those with whom he had any dealings. One might have gotten a glimpse of this when a new job was turned out. As most of the men were either Germans by birth or of German descent they were treated to a keg of Beer. On such occasions the 'boss' mingled good naturedly among his men and shared in their simple pleasure.

But while father was beyond question, a successful business man, that which we most admire in him, was the example he gave of a model Christian father and husband. What sacrifices did he not make to give his children the benefits of a Christian and Catholic education. And what we learned in church or school was safeguarded and enhanced in the atmosphere of a really Catholic home. Every week day he was to be seen in St. Joseph's Church at the 6.00 o'clock mass. With him also went every child of school age. On Sundays, as a member of Holy Cross Parish, he was present at all the services. Regularly, once a month, he went to Confession and Holy Communion with the Archconfraternity of the Holy Family. Prayers before and after meals, morning and night prayers including the rosary, were always said in common. As for night prayers, if any of the older children were to go out, prayers were said before leaving and an admonition given as to the time when all were to be under the parental roof. In the earlier days we all knew the Morning and Evening Prayers in German. And how really beautiful were those rhymed prayers.

"O Gott Du hast in dieser Nacht,
So väterlich bei mir gewacht,"
"Bevor ich mich zur Ruhe leg,
Ich Händ und Herz Got erheb!"

Occasionally, after lessons were learned, there were refreshments and no one was denied his sip of Beer. Then came the singing of religious hymns in which both father and mother joined most heartily. At Christmas time we never failed to have our 'Crib' with its setting and we gathered round the Babe of Bethlehem and sang—

"Jesu Kindlein, komm zu mir,
Mach ein gutes Kind aus mir,
Mein Herz ist klein,
Darf Niemand 'nein,
Als Du, mein Liebes Jesulein,"

Father's deep religious convictions were often expressed in charity of a practical kind. Not only did he provide for his own numerous family, (there were 12 children), but I can recall the names of 4 or 5 others who, for a longer or shorter period, became members of the household. The demands for a cup of coffee and a bite to eat, were rather frequent, so near the water front, and no one was ever turned away. Is it surprising that out of such a family, there should have come a priest and a nun?

Let us not conclude, therefore, because father was so devoted to religion, that he failed to make reasonable allowance for legitimate recreation and amusement. At regular intervals we had our enjoyable family gatherings, our outings to the seashore, and we also shared in the parish Picnics and Excursions. Within the family circle father enjoyed a friendly game of cards and a glass of beer, and none of the children got the impression that any of these pleasures, indulged in with modera-

30

tion, was in the least wrong or harmful. From this we may gather, that while father was a man of duty and discipline, he knew well the old motto 'all work and no play makes Jack a dull boy'. He therefore made due allowance for rest and pleasure. When we had studied our lessons under parental supervision and attended to our chores, seasonable pleasures were never barred from the Kunkel home.

Of the family gatherings there were two that stand out prominently in my memory. The first took place Sept. 23, 1881. It was a double celebration; for while father had just reached the half-century mark, my oldest brother Fred attained his majority, on the very same day. The home at No. 16 Lee St. was crowded with uncles, aunts and cousins, besides many other friends of the family. The Silver Wedding Anniversary which occurred on Thanksgiving Day, 1884 was even more memorable for the number of guests. Not only relatives from Baltimore and Washington were there; but they came also from Philadelphia, Wilmington, N.C., and from St. Louis. The many handsome pieces of silverware presented to my happy parents on this occasion, testified to the esteem and affection in which they were held by their friends and relatives. In keeping with the pious sentiments of my parents, there was a special mass at Holy Cross Church at which all the members of the family assisted and received Holy Communion.

After the death of our dear mother (Feb. 3, 1906), father's health began to fail. On this acount it was thought that a home in the suburbs would not only be beneficial to his health and help to prolong his life, but would also serve as a distraction from his grief. A home was accordingly purchased in Hamilton (No. 8 White Ave.). Our expectations were not, however realized, and in the fall of 1909 he was obliged to undergo a serious and painful operation. Although he returned from the hospital after the operation, and the doctors gave us some faint hope of his recovery, his condition became so alarming towards the end of April following, that both myself and Sister Johanetta were summoned to his bedside. A few days after our arrival, father rallied somewhat, and the doctor declared there was no longer any immediate danger. Both Sister Johanetta and myself, at father's request then returned to our respective posts of duty. But the angel of death had not withdrawn for long, and 2 months later we received the sad news of our dear father's death, June 29, 1910. During the 8 months that intervened between the operation and his death, he was hardly ever free from severe pain; but he bore all with Christian resignation and fortitude, uttering throughout the day pious ejaculations and acts of submission to God's holy will. During this long illness Father Manley, the pastor of St. Dominic's, was most attentive in his priestly ministrations, and when the end came on Wednesday, June 29th, administered the last sacraments and imparted the blessing for the dying, in the presence of most of the members of the family. The funeral took place on the following Saturday, when a Solemn High Mass of Requiem was celebrated at St. Dominic's Church. The Mass was well attended by the clergy conspicuous among whom was Cardinal Gibbons and a large number of Sulpician Fathers. When the funeral, on the way to the cemetery, passed by Holy Cross, the pastor, Rev. Father Danner, had the church bells tolled, as a tribute to one of his former most faithful parishioners.

If you, dear reader, claim relationship with this good father, treasure his memory as a precious inheritance, follow his example, and transmit his beloved name in benediction to future generations.

31

BIRTHPLACE OF JOHN N. KUNKEL
GAILBACH, BAVARIA

From the Baltimore Sun—June 30, 1910

Mr. John N. Kunkel Dead

Well-Known Wagon Builder Expires At Home, Hamilton

PROMINENT IN CHARITY WORK

One Of His Sons Is A Sulpician Priest, While A Daughter Is A Nun In Chicago.

Mr. John N. Kunkel, 78 years old, president of the Kunkel Wagon Company, died at his home on White Avenue, Hamilton, yesterday morning from a complication of diseases.

Mr. Kunkel was born in Gailbach, Bavaria, Germany, 78 years ago. His father was a weaver and farmer. His mother was also a native of the same place. On the death of her husband Mrs. Kunkel came to America.

At the age of 14 Mr. Kunkel began a four years' apprenticeship in the wheelwright's trade in his native town, and obtained work at his chosen occupation. In March, 1855, he embarked for America. From New York he went to Philadelphia, joining his three brothers there. One year later he came to Baltimore, where he secured work at his trade. Later he started in business for himself at McMechen street and Pennsylvania avenue, but after a short time removed to Chatsworth and Pierce Streets, and later opened a shop at Hanover and Cross Streets. In November, 1864, he removed to the present location, 37 East Lee Street, where he erected a three-story building. The building has since been greatly enlarged.

In 1884 Mr. Kunkel invented and patented the Monumental coal discharger, built in such a manner that it can be raised and tilted. These are now manufactured at the plant. In politics he was a pronounced adherent to Democratic principles. As a member of Holy Cross Catholic Church he always took an active part in the work of the church and the various societies connected with it.

He was a member of the Catholic Benevolent Legion, treasurer of St. Vincent de Paul Society, and a member of the Young Catholic Friend Society.

He was married in November, 1859, to Mary Rosina Kerchner, of Wilmington, a daughter of Aton Kerchner, a prominent business man of that city. After a trip to Europe in 1906 she died after a long illness in February, 1906.

Mr. Kunkel is survived by six sons—Messrs. Frederick J., John A., Nicholas A., William F., Joseph A. and Rev. Francis F. Kunkel, of St. Patrick's Seminary, California—and three daughters—Mrs. Mary T. Ward, of Philadelphia; Sister Margaret Kunkel, of Chicago, and Miss Mary R. Kunkel.

Monumental Wagon Works

OUR KERN ANCESTORS

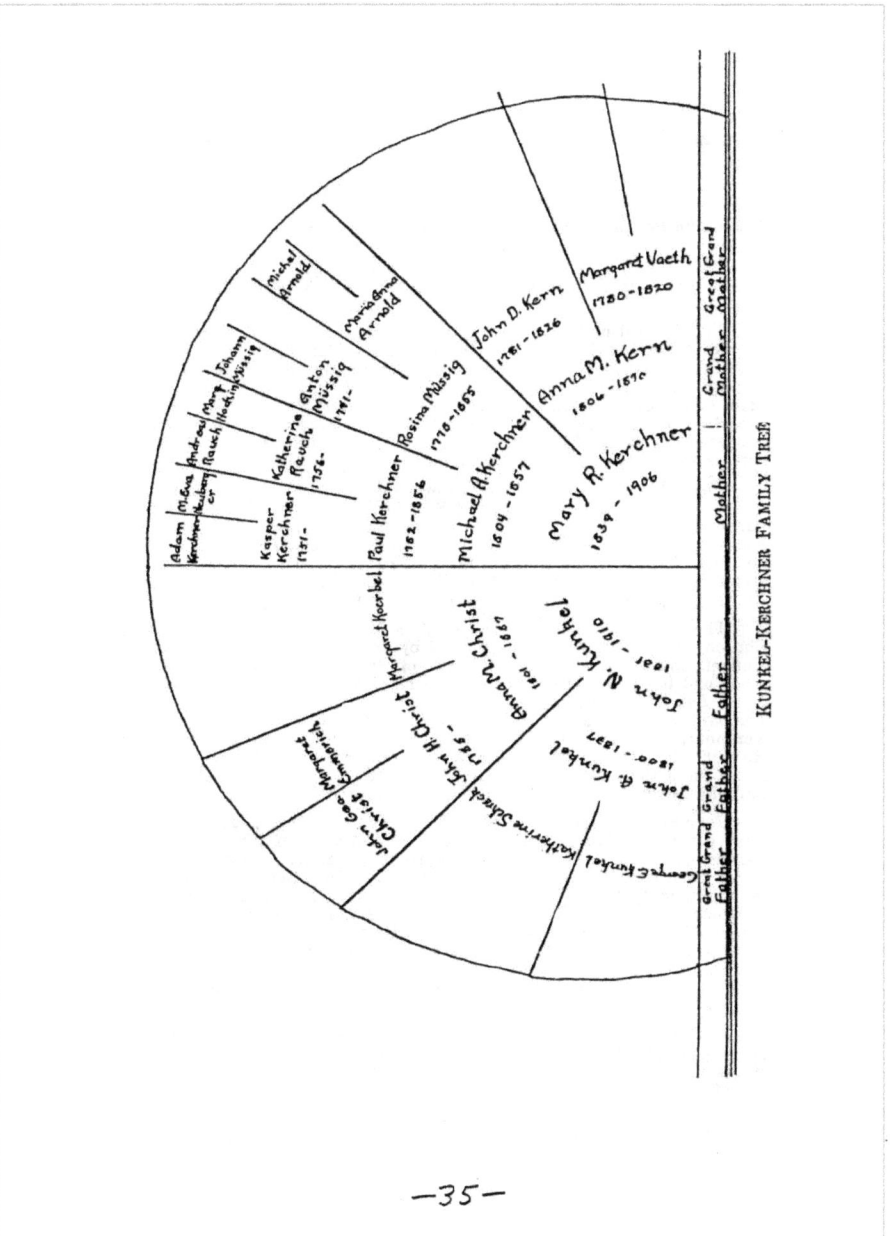

KUNKEL-KERCHNER FAMILY TREE

—35—

Note: see Errata on page 64 for a comment on a suspected error in this chart.

From The Baltimore Sun—July 3, 1910

Funeral of Mr. John N. Kunkel

The funeral of Mr. John N. Kunkel took place yesterday morning at 9 o'clock from St. Dominic's Catholic Church, Hamilton, where a solemn requiem mass was celebrated. Rev. Charles Damer, pastor of Holy Cross Church, South Baltimore, was the celebrant; Rev. F. X. McKenny, president of St. Charles' College, was the deacon, and Mr. John N. Kunkel, a grandson of the deceased and a student at St. Mary's Seminary, was the subdeacon. The master of ceremonies was Mr. Frank Swift, and the censer-bearer was Mr. Jerome Dignan, both seminarians.

The other clergymen present were Rev. J. M. Haug, of St. Charles' College; Rev. Andrew Levatois and Rev. Leo Besnard, of St. Mary's Seminary; Rev. A. Gamp, of St. Anthony's Church, Gardenville, and Rev. Richard McCarthy, of St. Joseph Seminary. Messrs. Charles Roach and John Collins, seminarians of St. Mary's Seminary; Mr. Charles J. Kunkel, a student for the priesthood at St. Charles' College, and Mr. Francis Kunkel, grandsons of the deceased, were also in the sanctuary.

The eulogy was delivered by Rev. J. B. Manley, pastor of St. Dominic's Church. Special music was rendered by friends of the two sons of Mr. Kunkel, one of whom is the organist of St. Dominic's Church, and the other had been for many years before his death four years ago, organist of St. Patrick's Church, under the direction of Prof. Alphonse Schenuit. The pallbearers were Messrs. Charles F., Ferdinand, John J., and Harry A. Kerchner, Charles Lewis, Robert Norman, Adolph Neubeck and Frank Hessler, all nephews of Mr. Kunkel. The honorary pallbearers were selected from the delegation present from Father Kolping Council, No. 64, Catholic Benevolent Legion, of Holy Cross Church.

Four of the Sisters of Christian Charity from Holy Cross School, the same order of which Sister Johanetta, a daughter of Mr. Kunkel, is a member, and stationed in Chicago, were at the church. Regrets were received from Rev. Francis W. Kunkel, of St. Patrick's Seminary, California, that distance prevented him from being present at his father's funeral. A handsome floral design was sent as a tribute from the Carriage and Wagon Manufacturers' Association, of Baltimore. Interment was made in Holy Cross Cemetery, Brooklyn, Anne Arundel county. The funeral car Dolores and an extra car was used. As the car traversed Holy Cross parish the bell on that church was tolled and parishioners lined the sidewalks as a tribute of respect.

At the grave appropriate remarks were made by Father Damer in the German language, who spoke of the prominent part Mr. Kunkel had taken in his congregation during the many years he had lived in the parish, and of the charitable work he had accomplished.

The following acted as Honorary pallbearers: Messrs. S. F. Janney, M. P. Elder, H. W. White, R. M. White, Thomas Craddock, and Arthur Hall.

36

Mary Rosina (Kerchner) Kunkel
(1839-1906)
✠

THE PARENTS of Mary Rosina Kerchner were Michael Kerchner and Anna Maria Kern. Born in Wilmington, Delaware, August 9, 1839, my mother was baptised in the venerable little church of St. Joseph, the parish church of Dupont's Mills, on the banks of the Brandywine. In a recent inquiry for the records of her baptism, I learned that the records of that particular period had been accidentally destroyed by fire. When grandmother Kerchner, whose name was also Rosina, heard of the birth of her little namesake, she thus expressed herself in a letter to Rosina's father: "May God bless your little daughter, who bears my own name. I am happy that my name and memory are being perpetuated in America." The blessing of her grandmother seems to have borne fruit a hundredfold in little Rosina.

When her parents came to this country from Freudenberg, Duchy of Baden, in 1833, they brought with them two sons, William aged 3, and Frederick aged 1 year. They went direct to Philadelphia, and made their residence on Fourth St., near the "Cock and Lion" Hotel. Six year later they moved to Wilmington, Del., remained there for three yars, and after a short period went to Cambridge, Md., where Caroline, one of Rosina's younger sisters was born. They were finally located in Baltimore at 67 Hillen St. The nearest church at this time was the present St. Vincent's Church, on Front St. Here, in 1846, when mother was 7 years old, the Sisters of Charity opened a school for girls, and it was probably here that mother received her elementary education. That she attended St. Vincent's Church I know from an incident she relates of her childhood days. One Sunday morning during the children's mass at this church, the children cried out with one voice: "Oh! Father———" Unfortunately I do not remember the name of the parish priest who had died but a short time before. Sometime later she attended St. Alphonsus School, on Saratoga St. which was then taught by the Sisters of Notre Dame. Shortly after making her First Holy Communion at St. Alphonsus, Mary Rosina being the oldest of the girls, was kept at home in order to assist her mother, in the management of the household. Though she was thus deprived of the advantages of a High School education, she assisted the younger children in the preparation of their lessons, always preserved a taste for good reading, and was both gentle and refined in her manner.

In sharing the duties of the household, she was fitting herself in a thoroughly practical manner for her future station in life. At the age of 20, Nov. 24, 1859, she was happily married at St. Alphonsus Church, by Rev. Geo. Ruland, C.SS.R. The marriage was witnessed by Peter and Margaret Kunkel, my father's eldest brother and his wife. My parents took up their residence on the corner of Pierce St. and Chatsworth St. (now Myrtle Ave.) It was here that my oldest brother Frederick was born. What were the labors and anxieties of those early years, when father had

37

THE HOME OF FRANZ MAI IN 1926
FREUDENBERG, BADEN
Birthplace of the Kern and Kerchner Family

not yet mastered the intricacies of the English language and was only beginning to establish himself in business, only a devoted wife and mother of a large family can appreciate. She was a real helpmate, and by her thrift and household economy, enabled father to develop his business and to meet his ever increasing obligations. In the care of her growing family she was indefatigable. By her sewing and mending, by her industry in putting up home fruits and vegetables for winter use, she merits to be called in the words of Scripture: "A valiant woman. . .one who ate not the bread of idleness. . .and her children rose up to bless her." What an inspiration for the girls of such a household, to be brought up in this school of domestic science, under so capable and devoted a teacher.

Notwithstanding her many duties, she assisted at daily mass when it was possible. The morning paper was scanned for a Requiem Mass and her marketing was done in the neighborhood where she could hear Mass. She invariably took one of the children not yet of school age and thus instilled into their tender hearts a love for God's house and the Holy Sacrifice of the Mass. She lived her religion in her home, and seasoned all her labors with prayer. As the children grew older and she was able to absent herself from household duties, she would visit the sick and by her charitable services bring comfort to the unfortunate. With what loving devotion have I seen her at the bedside of the sick, reciting the prayers for the dying, and whispering in their ears the sweet names of Jesus, Mary and Joseph, urging them when possible to repeat with her these and other pious ejaculations. To the sick in their last hour she was truly a ministering angel.

She was also a tireless and efficient church-worker. And that, not only for her parish church, but also for St. James Home for Boys, St. Joseph's Technical School and for the Christian Brothers when they were planning the present Calvert Hall, at the corner of Cathedral and Mulberry Sts. But all these activities in a mother of 12 children, gradually undermined her health, which was never at any time robust. After she had suffered from one or two minor strokes of paralysis, it was decided that she and father would take a trip to Europe, in the hope that it would help to restore her health. According to the month of July, 1905, they embarked from Baltimore for Hamburg. It was father's first return to his Vaterland and mother's first trip across the ocean. Little did they anticipate what sorrow was in store for them. as they prepared themselves for this long journey. On the morning after their arrival in Germany, just as they were entering the Capuchin Church in Aschaffenberg to hear Mass she was fatally stricken. It was fully two months before they were able to undertake their return journey and then with serious misgivings whether she would be able to stand the ocean voyage. We can imagine what a sore trial this must have been for my father, then in his 76th year. That both father and mother accepted this visitation of Divine Providence in a Christian spirit and bowed submissively to the Divine Will, there can be no doubt.

At the end of October they were again in Baltimore, when mother was brought from the steamer to the home on Hanover St. and placed in bed from which she was never again to rise. For 3 months, Sisters of Bon Secours tenderly cared for her day and night until she was called to her eternal reward. On the morning of Feb. 3, 1906, fortified by the rites of the church she so ardently loved and of which she was a shining example, surrounded by her sorrowing husband and children, she gently slept in the Lord.

[Continued on Page 41]

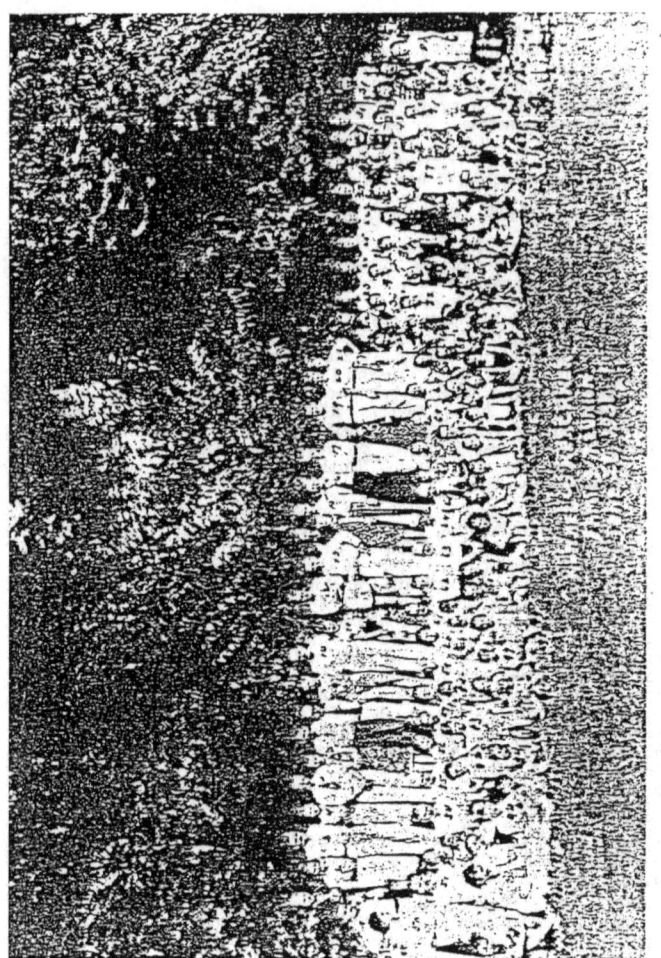

Kunkel & Kirchner Family Reunion June 1973

OUR KERN ANCESTORS

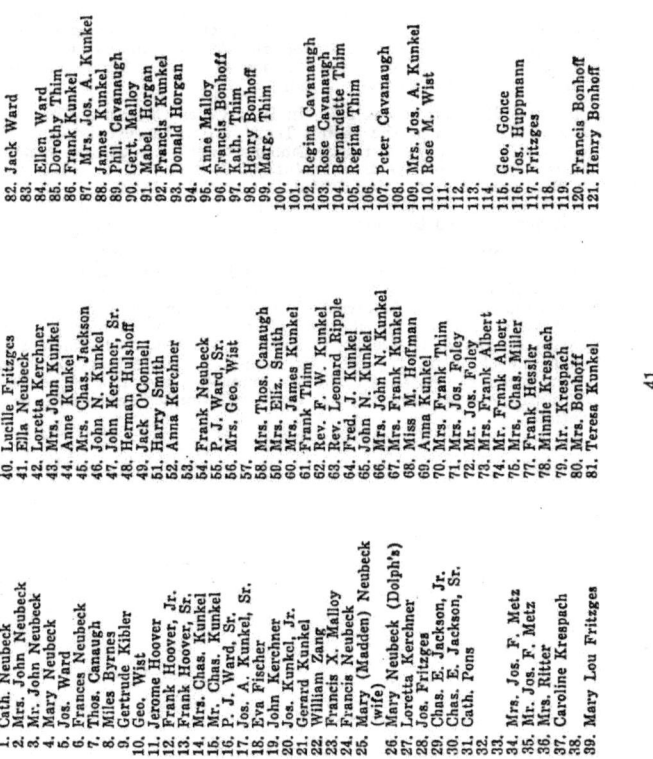

1. Cath. Neubeck
2. Mrs. John Neubeck
3. Mr. John Neubeck
4. Mary Neubeck
5. Jos. Ward
6. Frances Neubeck
7. Thos. Canaugh
8. Miles Byrnes
9. Gertrude Kibler
10. Geo. Wist
11. Jerome Hoover
12. Frank Hoover, Jr.
13. Frank Hoover, Sr.
14. Mrs. Chas. Kunkel
15. Mr. Chas. Kunkel
16. P. J. Ward, Sr.
17. Jos. A. Kunkel, Sr.
18. Eva Fischer
19. John Kerchner
20. Jos. Kunkel, Jr.
21. Gerard Kunkel
22. William Zang
23. Francis X. Malloy
24. Francis Neubeck
25. Mary (Madden) Neubeck (wife)
26. Mary Neubeck (Dolph's)
27. Loretta Kerchner
28. Jos. Fritzges
29. Chas. E. Jackson, Jr.
30. Chas. E. Jackson, Sr.
31. Cath. Fons
32.
33.
34. Mrs. Jos. F. Metz
35. Mr. Jos. F. Metz
36. Mrs. Ritter
37. Caroline Krespach
38.
39. Mary Lou Fritzges
40. Lucille Fritzges
41. Ella Neubeck
42. Loretta Kerchner
43. Mrs. John Kunkel
44. Anne Kunkel
45. Mrs. Chas. Jackson
46. John N. Kunkel
47. John Kerchner, Sr.
48. Herman Hulshoff
49. Jack O'Connell
51. Harry Smith
52. Anna Kerchner
53.
54. Frank Neubeck
55. P. J. Ward, Sr.
56. Mrs. Geo. Wist
57.
58. Mrs. Thos. Canaugh
59. Mrs. Eliz. Smith
60. Mrs. James Kunkel
61. Mrs. Frank Thim
62. Rev. F. W. Kunkel
63. Rev. Leonard Ripple
64. Fred. J. Kunkel
65. John N. Kunkel
66. Mrs. John N. Kunkel
67. Mrs. Frank Kunkel
68. Miss M. Hoffman
69. Anna Kunkel
70. Mrs. Frank Thim
71. Mrs. Jos. Foley
72. Mr. Jos. Foley
73.
74. Mr. Frank Albert
75. Mrs. Chas. Miller
78. Minnie Krespach
79. Mr. Krespach
80. Mrs. Bonhoff
81. Teresa Kunkel
82. Jack Ward
83.
84. Ellen Ward
85. Dorothy Thim
86. Frank Kunkel
87. Mrs. Jos. A. Kunkel
88. James Kunkel
89. Phil. Cavanaugh
90. Gert. Malloy
91. Mabel Horgan
92. Francis Kunkel
93. Donald Horgan
94.
95. Anne Malloy
96. Francis Bonhoff
97. Kath. Thim
98. Henry Bonhoff
99. Marg. Thim
100.
101.
102. Regina Cavanaugh
103. Rose Cavanaugh
104. Bernardette Thim
105. Regina Thim
106.
107. Peter Cavanaugh
108.
109. Mrs. Jos. A. Kunkel
110. Rose M. Wist
111.
112.
113.
114.
115. Geo. Gonce
116. Jos. Huppmann
117. Fritzges
118.
119.
120. Francis Bonhoff
121. Henry Bonhoff

41

Note that Herman Hulshoff is #48 in this index; other family members in the Hulshoff, Kerchner and Kern families appear as well.

► 189 ◄

[Continued from Page 39]

During that long period of physical pain, she was likewise tortured by the thought of her utter helplessness. She who had throughout the years, been to her husband a constant helpmate, his devoted partner in every duty, toil and burden, can now but lie still and suffer him to bear the burden alone. Instead of sharing his burden, she is now only an added burden. But the true husband falters not in his love; rather is he the more solicitous to comfort the ever faithful spouse; and his love grows deeper and more tender, because rooted and founded in divine charity. The devoted husband finds even sweeter joy in serving her in her pain and anguish, than in being served by her.

A Requiem High Mass was sung in Holy Cross Church on Tuesday, Feb. 5th by Father Damer, the pastor. Testifying to the esteem in which she was held, His Eminence Cardinal Gibbons together with a large number of clergy were present in the sanctuary, and the body of the church was well filled with relatives and friends. Very Rev. E. R. Dyer, S.S. of St. Mary's Seminary and Rev. Father Haug, S.S., an esteemed friend of the family, accompanied the remains to Holy Cross Cemetery.

This brief notice of my dear mother, very sketchy at best, is intended to be read in conjunction with that of my father. The one is necessarily a complement of the other, for those two great Catholic hearts beat as one. They cooperated in all the concerns of the family, in the Christian education and religious training of the children, in the family prayers, gatherings, and home amusements; in the religious and charitable activities of their church, in making this Christian home a sanctuary of peace, joy and contentment. This good father and mother have thus bequeathed to their children a memory worthy of being transmitted from generation to generation.

42

Letter of Card. Gibbons to Francis W. Kunkel.

Cardinal's Residence,
408 N. Charles St.
Baltimore.

July 27 '92.

My Dear Frank:

Your letter informing me [that] you desire & intention to become a priest [has] given me surprise, [and] satisfaction [also]. I have also seen to whom [I] have spoken ([ ]me some experience) the wisdom of [ ]taking to the new undertaking.

Though I have hoped to see you laboring as a priest in the [diocese], you will be doing a more important work in devoting yourself to the sacred ministry.

You have my best [wishes], & I hope you will receive the blessing of your parents.

Affectionately
+ James Card. Gibbons

Remember me kindly to your uncle & aunt.

(South Baltimore 'Messenger', Saturday, July 16, 1898.)

Father Kunkel's First Mass

Will Celebrate at HOLY CROSS

An event of great interest in Catholic circles—Sketch of the young priest— Was baptized in the church where he will celebrate Mass—Educated in Baltimore and ordained in Paris.

An event of great interest in Catholic circles will take place tomorrow morning. Rev. Frank W. Kunkel will celebrate his first Mass at 10:30 A.M. at Holy Cross church, at which church Father was baptized.

He is the son of Mr. and Mrs. John N. Kunkel, well known residents of South Baltimore who live at No. 614 Hanover St. Rev. Frank W. Kunkel was born on Lee St., July 9, 1870. He received his early education at Holy Cross school. From there he went to Calvert Hall College graduating at that Institution in 1887. In September of 1887 he entered St. Charles College where he remained 5 years and graduated with high honors. He next entered St. Mary's Seminary where he spent 4 years. In the fall of 1896 he went to Paris and entered the Seminary of Saint Sulpice, and finished his preparation for Holy Orders. He was ordained in Paris, June 4, 1898.

He has received an appointment as Professor at St. Charles College, Ellicott City, where he will remain the ensuing year, assisting in the preparation of candidates for the Priesthood. He joined the Sulpician Order in Paris. His brother Wm. F. Kunkel, Director of the Mozart Orchestra, will have charge of the music at the church tomorrow.

Although Father Kunkel has been absent from this section for several years, his friends and neighbors have affectionate and pleasant recollections of him. After the ceremony the visiting clergy and friends will be entertained at the home of Mr. Kunkel on Hanover Street.

44

Sister Johannetta

Sister of Christian Charity, Daughter of Mr. and Mrs. John N. Kunkel entered the Convent May 5, 1892 and will celebrate her Golden Jubilee next year-1942.

Black Veil Bestowed on Many Candidates at Malinckrodt Convent. Rt. Rev. Bishop Hoban Officiated—Many Friends Attend.
August 12, 1896

Special Dispatch to "The Press"

Wilkes-Barre, Aug. 12. At the Malinckrodt Convent, this city, the motherhouse of the German Catholic Sisters of Mercy, of this continent, twenty-seven young ladies took the white veil, this morning, and thirty renounced the world to become the bride of Christ, by taking the black veil. The beautiful and impressive ceremony was witnessed by a large number of people, relatives of the sisters and the novitiates who came from all over the country.

The ceremony began at 9 o'clock this morning and was conducted by Right Rev. Bishop Hoban, the following priests being in attendance. Father Simeon, S.J., Buffalo; Very Rev. P. C. Nagle, Fathers Bidlingmaier and Von Welden, St. Nicholas Church, Wilkes-Barre; Rev. J. Koeher, Williamsport; Rev. Charles Damer, Baltimore; Rev. P. Christ and Rev. G. Stopper, Scranton; Rev. J. Steinkerchner, Luzerne; Rev. Wm. Brehl, Pittston; Rev. T. Hanselman, Brooklyn; Father Longinus, Pottsville; Father Lenfort, Bastross; Rev. N. Forve, Hazleton; Father Preiser, Syracuse, N.Y.; Father Huber, Danville; Father Dassel, Honesdale; Brother Arnold, Troy, N.Y.

The acolytes who served at the Mass were Mr. Frank Kunkel, Baltimore; Louis Schmidt, Adam Sceidel, Peter Forve, Messrs. Kellar and Jaeger, Wilkes-Barre.

45

FRED J. KUNKEL
b. 1860

Mr. Fred J. Kunkel Is Octogenarian

Pioneer Member Of St. Dominic's Parish Celebrates At Home Of Son

Fred J. Kunkel, one of the pioneer members of Saint Dominic's parish, recently celebrated his eightieth birthday. Mr. Kunkel, who is still vigorous, now lives in Saint Francis of Assisi parish.

Mr. Kunkel was an esteemed friend of the late Father John B. Manley, who established Saint Francis of Assisi parish. Mr. Kunkel's wife, Katherine Bush Kunkel, died in 1934 within a few months of their golden anniversary.

Mr. Kunkel is the brother of the Rev. Francis W. Kunkel, S.S., Saint Mary's Seminary, Roland Park, and Sister Johannetta of the Sisters of Christian Charity, now stationed at Villa Immaculata, Wilmette, Ill. He is also the father of Sister Philomena of the Good Shepherd Convent in Washington.

His son, John N. Kunkel, is well known as the archdiocesan president of the Holy Name Society and is the owner of the Kunkel Automobile Accessories and the Kunkel Super Service Filling Station in Bel Air with a branch in Chestertown on the Eastern Shore. His son John was formerly mayor of Bel Air.

Two other sons are Charles J. Kunkel, with law offices in Bel Air, and Francis W. Kunkel, associated with his brother in the automobile accessories business.

A daughter, Mrs. Charles Miller, resides in Baltimore. Mr. Kunkel also has three grandchildren and four great-grandchildren.

Last Monday evening Mr. Kunkel was the guest of honor at the home of his son John in Bel Air. Among those who attended the celebration were:

Mr. and Mrs. John N. Kunkel, host and hostess; Father Kunkel, Mr. and Mrs. John A. Kunkel, Mrs. Charles Miller, Mr. and Mrs. Charles J. Kunkel, Mr. and Mrs. Francis W. Kunkel, Mr. and Mrs. Adolph Pons, II, and Mrs. and Mrs. J. Carvel Archer.

46

Good Shepherd Nuns Pronounce Their Vows

DAUGHTER OF MR. AND MRS. FRED. J. KUNKEL

Archbishop Presides At Ceremonies, Says Mass And Delivers Sermon

October 12, 1928

Archbishop Curley spent the morning of Columbus Day, his own birthday anniversary, at the House of the Good Shepherd, Mount Street, where he received the final vows of Sister Mary of the Holy Spirit and the first vows of Sisters Mary of Saint Benedict, Mary of Saint Philomena, Mary of Our Lady of Perpetual Help and Mary of the Blessed Sacrament.

His Grace said Mass at 8 o'clock, in the convent chapel, during which the sisters' choir sang: "Suscipe Domine," "Tu Gloria Jerusalem," and "O Sacrum Convivium." After the Mass the Archbishop received the final vows.

Represent Five Parishes

These young sisters represented five parishes. Sister Mary of the Holy Spirit was known in the world as Miss Nell Campbell of Saint Martin's.

The four novices who made their Holy profession were: Misses Mary Hebrank of Saint James', Lydia Kunkel of Saint Dominic's, Anna Cahill of Saint Patrick's and Elizabeth Riley of Saint Paul's.

Solemn Benediction was given. The clergy present were: Monsignor M. F. Foley and the Rev. Louis O'Donovan, Ecclesiastical Superior of the Convent; J. J. Feldmann, C.SS.R.; L. M. Braun, C.SS.R.; F. X. Bader, C.SS.R.; John H. Eckenrode, R. J. Barron, J. J. Russell, L. L. Otterbein, H. J. Wheeler, Walter J. Hayes, W. Paul Smith and Peter J. Quinn, the last-named of Altoona, Pa.

His Grace preached the sermon.

47

WILLIAM F. KUNKEL

At the time of his death (1907) was organist at St. Patrick's Church, Baltimore, Md.

48

William F. Kunkel

At the time of his death January, 1907 was organist at St. Patrick's Church, Baltimore, Md.

Married at St. Patrick's Church—A Pretty Wedding.

St. Patrick's Church, Broadway and Bank Streets, was on Thanksgiving Day, the scene of a beautiful and impressive spectacle, Miss Mary T. Becker, daughter of Mrs. Josephine T. Becker, becoming the bride of Mr. Wm. F. Kunkel, son of Mr. and Mrs. John N. Kunkel.

A solemn nuptial Mass was celebrated by Rev. James F. Donohue, pastor of the church, assisted by Revs. Richard O'Neill and M. A. Ryan, respectively, as deacon and subdeacon. Mr. Joseph A. Kunkel, brother of the groom, acted as master of ceremonies, and his nephew, Mr. John N. Kunkel, as thurifer. The solemnity of the occasion was further increased by the presence of his Eminence James Cardinal Gibbons, who at the end of Mass bestowed on the happy couple the nuptial blessing and addressed them a few salutary words of counsel. The Cardinal was attended by Revs. Charles Damer, of Holy Cross Church, and Ferdinand Litz, of St. Michael's Church. Other clergymen who were present in the sanctuary were Revs. William A. Fletcher, rector of the Cathedral; Caspar P. Elbert, of St. Katharine's; Father McNamara, of St. Bridget's, and Father Barre, of St. Joseph's Church. The seminarians present were Messrs. John F. and Ferdinand H. Angel, Leonard Ripple and T. W. Brown.

The bride presented a most comely appearance, wearing a beautiful gown of white crepe de chine over white taffeta, ornamented with clusters of pearls, and a tulle veil held in position by a handsome sunburst diamond, the gift of the groom. She carried a bouquet of Bride roses. Miss Mary Schoenlein acted as maid of honor and Mr. George Becker as groomsman. Messrs. Joseph Cooper, George Deeder, Frank Neubeck and Joseph Frank attended as ushers.

The music of the occasion was certainly a prominent feature. Prof. F. X. Hale directed a choir composed of nearly fifty voices, which Prof. Fisher's orchestra accompanied throughout the Mass. The main quartet consisted of Mrs. George J. Coy, soprano; Miss Anna E. Hyson, also; Mr. Charles A. McCann, tenor and Mr. Edward Geis, basso. Mr. Schenuit presided at the organ.

It may not be inappropriate to mention here that the groom is organist at St. Patrick's Church, and under the direction of his widely known musical abilities the choir maintains an enviable reputation. A luncheon followed the ceremony at H. Y. M. Hall, Baltimore and Bond Streets, and a german was held there in the evening. At the luncheon toasts were drunk and many speeches were made. The many handsome presents of which they are the recipients are manifest proofs of the esteem in which they are held by their numerous friends.

After the reception Mr. and Mrs. Wm. F. Kunkel left on an extended tour North, after which they will reside at 2202 East Lombard Street. Too much cannot be said in praise of a ceremony in which the spiritual and temporal were so well commingled that it will never be forgotten.

MR. AND MRS. JOSEPH A. KUNKEL

Kunkel---Becker

One of the prettiest of the early July weddings took place Thursday last at St. Michael's Church, when Miss *Dorothy Eva Becker* and *Mr. Joseph Anthony Kunkel* were united in the holy bonds of matrimony. The bride is the daughter of Mrs. Josephine Becker, while Mr. Kunkel is the senior member of the William F. Kunkel Piano Company, and is a son of Mr. John Kunkel, president of the Kunkel Wagon Co.

The ceremony was performed by Rev. Frank W. Kunkel, brother of the groom, of St. Patrick's Seminary, Menlo Park, Cal. Father Kunkel celebrated Nuptial Mass at 9 o'clock.

Mr. Louis Becker, brother of the bride, was master of ceremonies, and Mr. John N. Kunkel, nephew of the groom, was thurifer.

The bride wore a princess gown of white liberty satin, over taffeta, trimmed with duchess lace, a tulle veil and diamond brooch, the gift of the bridegroom. She carried a shower Bouquet of bride roses. Miss Mary Cecelia Dutousch was maid of honor. She wore a princess gown of pink radium silk and picture hat, and carried a bouquet of La France roses.

The ushers were Messrs., Marry A. Frosch, of Philadelphia; George Becker, brother of the bride; Louis Sellmayer and John Hohman. The church was decorated with 1,000 electric bulbs and palms and roses in profusion. Lillies were formed by clusters of electric bulbs. The music was under the direction of Prof. Chas. F. Mutter. Among the members of the clergy present were: Very Rev. Dr. E. R. Dyer; Rev. John Norton and Rev. John B. Manly, of St. Dominic's, Hamilton.

Mr. and Mrs. Kunkel were the recipients of a number of beautiful presents among them being a handsome cut glass punch bowl from the employees of the Kunkel Piano Company.

After the cermony a wedding breakfast was served at Congress Hall, Baltimore and Bond Streets. In the evening a reception was held at the same hall.

Mr. and Mrs. Kunkel left late Thursday evening for a trip to Atlantic City and Niagara Falls. Upon their return they will live at Hamilton.

Among the out-of-town guests, all of whom were from Philadelphia, were: Mrs. Emma Reihling; Miss Mamie Frosch; Messrs. Andrew Frosch, Frederick Kunkel, Charles Born, Caspar Kunkel.

50

Young Jesuit To Say Goodbye To Native Land
August 11, 1933

Eight Scholastics Will Take Part In Departure Ceremonies At Saint Aloysius'

VOLUNTEER FOR SERVICE IN PHILIPPINE ISLANDS

Three Of Number, Messrs. Bradley, Brew And Kunkel Are From This Archdiocese

EIGHT young Jesuit scholastics, who have volunteered to serve as members of their order in the Philippine Islands, will take part in a departure service at Saint Aloysius' Church at Washington at 7:30 o'clock next Tuesday night.

Three Are Sons Of Archdiocese

The eight are Messrs. Kyran Egan, Robert Reilly, Nicholas Kunkel, Frederick A. Brew and Walter Hogan, from the Jesuit novitiate, Saint Andrew-on-the-Hudson, and Messrs. James Keller, Lee H. Bradley and Francis Renz from the Saint Isaac Jogues' Novitiate, Wernersville, Pa.

Three of the eight young scholastics are sons of the Archdiocese of Baltimore. The three are Mr. Brew, of Saint Joseph's parish, Washington; Mr. Bradley of Saints Philip and James' parish, Baltimore, and Mr. Kunkel, of the Shrine of the Sacred Heart parish, Mt. Washington.

The Most Rev. James F. G. Hayes, S.J., newly-consecrated Bishop of the Diocese of Cagayan, the Philippine Islands, will preside at the ceremonies. The Rev. James Cotter, S.J., of Saint Aloysius' Church, will preach the departure sermon.

Bishop Hayes may accompany the young scholastics when they sail for the Philippines about the middle of August.

The Benedictus and other hymns will be sung by a select choir under the direction of Miss Catherine Rupert, organist. The soloists will be Mrs. Agnes Whelan McLoughlin and Miss Mary O'Donoghue, sopranos; Mrs. Irene Fitzhugh, contralto; Mr. Gerald Whelan, basso, and Mr. Bernard Fitzgerald, tenor.

Benediction of the Blessed Sacraments will bring the ceremonies to a close. After the service Bishop Hayes and the young missionaries will hold a reception in the Aloysian Club rooms.

Records To Be Proud Of

The young scholastics from the Archdiocese of Baltimore who will go to the Philippines are sons of parents who believe in giving their children a thoroughly Catholic education.

Mr. Kunkel is the son of Mr. and Mrs. Joseph A. Kunkel, Mt. Washington. He is the nephew of the Rev. Francis W. Kunkel, S.S., treasurer of Saint Mary's Seminary, Roland Park. He has been for 28 years a priest of the Society of Saint Sulpice.

His father's sister, Sister Johanetta Kunkel, is a member of the order

51

of Sisters of Christian Charity. She is stationed at the Maria Immaculate Convent, Wilmette, Ill.

One of his sisters, Miss Genevieve L. Kunkel, will be professed as a member of the order of School Sisters of Notre Dame at the Institute of Notre Dame, Baltimore, on August 8.

Made Wonderful Record

Miss Kunkel was educated at the Institute of Notre Dame, Notre Dame of Maryland High School and Notre Dame of Maryland College. She was graduated from Notre Dame of Maryland College with high honors. She was winner of the second prize in the national essay contest conducted in 1931 by the Catholic Press Association of the United States.

The announcement of the prize-winners was made at the Baltimore convention of the Catholic Press Association.

Mr. Nicholas Kunkel, the scholastic, was educated at Saint Michael's School, Mount Saint Agnes' Country School for Boys and Loyola High School. Following his graduation from Loyola High he entered the Jesuit novitiate at Saint Andrew-on-the-Hudson three years ago.

Believe In Catholic Education

Mr. Kunkel's other sisters and brothers and the Catholic educational institutions which they are attending are:

Dorothy Margaret Kunkel, class of 1934, College of Notre Dame of Maryland; Marie Josephine and Annie Marie Kunkel, Notre Dame of Maryland High School, class of 1934; Barbara Irene Kunkel, Notre Dame of Maryland High School, class of 1936; Theresa M., Joseph A., and Francis X. Kunkel, pupils of the Cathedral School.

52

LETTERS

of

MRS. ROSINA MUSSIG KERCHNER (1778-1855)

to

her son

MICHAEL ANTHONY KERCHNER (1804-1857)

1. Safe Arrival of Mich. A. Kerchner, Wife and Children William and Fred.

Freudenberg, Jan. 6, 1833.

        Joint letter of David Kerchner
        Dominic Kern, Anthony Mussig,
        Sister Margaret, and Mother Rosina.

Dear Brother:

 We were anxiously waiting for a letter and so on the 4th inst. we received your letter telling us you and your family had arrived safe. This gave great pleasure not only to ourselves but to all your friends. We are glad to know that you are well. Dear Brother since you made the dangerous journey so successfully, and have found your happiness *Dominic* (Kern) and myself are determined to start off after Easter. Please give us all the details necessary for the voyage. I can say that none of the other Freudenbergers except yourself have written. We also received your 2 letters from Bremen.

              David Kerchner.

2. Dear Brother-in-law:—

 I wish to let *Jos. Anthony* know about our going but don't know if he is still in Hanover, so can't say if he will go with us. I should also like to know why *Susanna* did not write us along with your letter. Can we buy property in your neighborhood? Write before Easter if possible; if we do not hear from you we shall have plenty to do this summer. My family all well and send greetings to your family and Susanna.

              Dominic Kern.

 Greetings from your devoted friend *Anton Mussig* and myself. I wish you a Happy New Year. *Ti?* (Anton's Wife?)

3. Greetings from Anna and Margaret.

Dear Brother:—

 I again beg you to write at once, I can hardly wait for your answer. Your father gave me property worth 300 Gulden. I shall sell this and engage a man for 200 Gulden (R 11 hundert Gulden). I shall get 200 Gulden from my Butcher. Tell me if this is sufficient for I have also a young son, *John Henry David Kerchner.* Write me for my wish is to join you. I shall end my letter in tears and greet yourself, wife, children and friends with wishes as numerous as the stars of the firmament and the sands of the seashore. Heart too full to write more.

      Your devoted and true brother,

              J. David Kerchner.

4. My best wishes to you and your whole family. I wish you all health and happiness and particularly my dear William, for I cannot dismiss you from my thoughts. I must close my heart is too sad, my eyes are blinded with tears. I recommend you all to God and remain your ever devoted and loving mother *Rosina.* Write soon again.

5. To M. A. K. July 8th. Before David Kerchner's death.
    1834 David and Michael quarrel.
    Mary Anne's 'baas' very sick.

Dear Son:—

The usual greetings, etc. *Mary Ann's 'baas'* Mrs. Michnel Ebert (aunt or Godmother) is quite sick, and can not survive the fall. Peter Andrew's Franz has bought her house for 300.50 Gulden, she has her chair in the lower room. Your letter of 1st of February gave me more pain than joy, since you are not living at peace with *David.* I wrote him at once of his duty as a brother and it would grieve me if you did not receive my letters which I wrote with such difficulty. I told you that *Margaret* was *married.* I addressed David's letter to you because I don't know whether he is in Philadelphia or not, therefore let him know that I have written to you. *Kuhnel Michel* also wrote but his letter was a year in coming. He bought as much land for 100.50 Gulden as would have cost him here 3000 Gulden, but he is far from you. I waited a long time for your last letter so write at once on receipt of this. Do not write until you find whether *David* is in Philadelphia or not, then send a joint letter to save the P. O. stage. Dear M. it would have been better for you to have remained in Germany. Since you left we have fruit and wine in abundance every year, in Winter a good crop of Wheat and Rye. All is fine since bread is 9 tis. as dear and potatoes 4 to 5 tis. as dear; and this is not so good for us, since we can not sell much and have plenty of work and heavy expenses. But day laborers and mechanics have good times. I can find no joy when I think you have been deprived of your children. *Where are they whom you have brought up with such great care and in the Christian religion? Such thoughts disturb me day and night. My last words are fear God and keep the Commandments. We shall not again meet in this world, but may we meet one another in heaven. Greetings.

                                                                        M. R. K.

David and Michael quarrel.   *Where are the children?

6. Nov. 28, 1834   Dom. Kern & Regina Kettinger Mar. 9-18-34
    Letter of Dom. Kern

Dear Brothers, Sisters & Brothers-in-law:—

Usual greetings. I was married to my neighbor *Regina Kettinger* Sept. 8th. All our friends gathered together and we danced till 5:00 A.M. Three weeks later *Gerhard (Kern)* mar. *Gertrude* daughter of *Alois Müssig,* and the same friends gathered again. Many sad things took place this year. Gerhard (Kern) lost his wife, *Alois Mussig's* son *Lawrence* drowned, our youngest sister *Regina* died of dysentery; *Dorothy Kern* wife of *Mich Ebert* died Sept. 17, Mrs. Peter Vaeth died on Gerhard's wedding day.

Jos. Anth. wrote me about year and half ago (see Letter No. 29 J. A. K. in Canada) from Hamburg. Does this correspond to Copy of Sautter which states that a letter was received from Hamburg in 1828?) I always wanted him to remain at home, but it was useless to advise him. Matthew has put off his departure to the Spring and Dorothy is still with Mich Ebert. The little brothers and sisters are all well and greet you.

                        Dominic Kern and Regina nee Kettinger.

Note:—Dorothy Kern, wife of Michael Ebert, was the godmother of Dorothy Kern, who later married Valentine Ruppert.

7. Freudenburg, February 8, 1835

    1. Exhortation of a Christian Mother.
    2. Advice to Father and Mother.
    3. Margaret mar. Jakob Mai, Sept. 18, 1834
    4. A very dry summer, failure of crop.

Dear Son:—

Glad to hear you are well again. God has visited you with sickness; He is an allwise Father; who leads us at times over rough ways, through sickness and adversity, to try our patience, to keep us from the path of sin, to lead us to the practice of virtue and to perfection of life.

Dear Michael, I am sorry I cannot speak to you face to face. Bring up your children in the true faith and in the love and fear of God. Let these treasures which God has placed in your hands, be ever dear to your heart. Fulfill your duty as a father, by giving your children a good example, and instill in their tender hearts piety and religion, so that you may rejoice on the day of judgment. For it would be better not to have children than to leave godless children behind you.

Dear Anna Maria:—Be a devoted and faithful wife, but above all be careful of your morning and night prayers. I have written out for you my beautiful morning prayers also several other prayers. Prayer is the source of all blessings of the home. Where there is no prayer there cannot be the blessing of God. Each morning recommend your children to God and to the holy Archangel Raphael so that as he conducted young Tobias safely on his journey, he may be a guardian to your children in their wanderings. Then God will be in your midst, all your years will be filled with benediction. God's blessing, peace and joy will abide with you. *Margaret married Jakob Mai, Sept. 18, 1834.* They live with us. We work and eat together; as long as it seems too good to them, and as soon as they wish to go elsewhere, they will receive their patrimony as the rest of the children.

We might have had servants like others for some years; but there is no getting along with strangers, for they do with your father what they wish. We have been fortunate this year in our fruit and grain, and made some wine; but cattle fodder was scarce this year. From Easter to August we had no hay or grain. When it rained it penetrated the soil only an inch. The wheat stands on dry soil and the grass is dried up. One can scarcely describe the conditions. Water for the grain was carried into the fields in wagons, but it was useless as the ground was like a hot stone. What was watered in the morning was dried up in the afternoon. There was no cabbage, no turnips, nothing in the line of vegetables. But potatoes were in excess. They came late but were more abundant than ever before.

My best wishes, may God keep you in body and soul, your wife and children and yourself. Dear Michael, I can not forget you. You are always before my eyes. I am now robbed of every joy. Your friendly countenance, your love for me bring tears to my eyes. May the love of God be always with you and your devoted wife. Do not forget me.

                                                    R. M. K.

8. Dominic Kern to Michael A. Kerchner, March 10, 1835.

Dear Brother-in-law:—

.... Matthew (Kern) can't come as yet, because he can't get his money before he is 20 years old. Dorothy is still with Michael Ebert. When Matthew is 20 I think they will both come. Have not heard anything of Joseph Anthony Kern for 2 years (See letter No. 4, he was then in Hamburg).

Greetings, Dominic Kern

This year's wine is very good. When a man has taken 3 glasses they have to take him home. You can be glad you are not here, for you would have to drink yourself to death. Good wine is a misfortune for both the living and the dead. Amand Michael died a few days ago, also the wife of Furnbach Balz.

Dominic Kern.

9. Letter of Matthew Landkammer, June 16, 1835

Wabaukaneta, Mo. (?)

Advises M. A. K. against going West.

Dear Friend Kerchner:—

I received your letter of December 16th, and am glad that you are well including your youngest son who had been seriously ill. I am well and hope this letter will find you also well. I wrote you a letter to which I expected a reply but to date none has come. Regarding the purchase of property here in view of establishing a shoe-store, I would dissuade you from doing so. Your family is young and would find the journey long and difficult; besides the stores here usually get their shoes from New York or Philadelphia. My friends are coming over, they left home about Easter. I hope they will come soon for I have built a house on the property I bought and am living alone. I have saved enough and planted enough for my old age.

Your sincere friend,

Math. Landkammer.

To Herrn Mich. Anton Kerchner
4th near Cock & Lion Hotel, Phila., Pa.

10. Letter of Grandmother Mussig, Aug. 15, 1835

1. Daily prayer.
2. Exhortations to rear his family in a Christian manner.
3. Evil of Drink.
4. She longs to see her children.

Dear Son Michael:—

I pray for you daily that you may bring up your family in a Christian manner, - - - All at home are well yet there are many difficulties and contrarieties which I will not mention. As to news it will not be necessary to write, since *Michael Mussig and Grandmother (Kern) (Susanna*

57

Ziegler) are coming to you. They will tell you personnally all I had to suffer. Dear Michael you were drawing on your imagination if you thought your mother had forgotten you, and would no longer write to you. She would indeed be an unnatural mother, who could forget her children; I would no more do this than forget God. I have suffered, because having written you last Easter, and that with great fatigue to my eyes, besides the other weaknesses of my body, and yet have no reply. Each time I gave you all the news from home. If you did not receive these letters I am greatly grieved because my letters contained personal matters which I did not wish to fall into the hands of strangers.

I wrote again only a short time since and addressed it to the same Hotel as formerly. Also wrote *David* (Kerchner) but have not received any answer from him. I do not know if I had the wrong address or whether it was the fault of the postman. You wrote us that you bought a beautiful large *Saloon*. God grant you success in your undertakings for success depends on God's blessing. You should begin and end each day with prayer. Say rather with Solomon:—Lord help me in my youth and foolishness, that I may act as a faithful householder and rule over my possessions." Beware of the harmful vice of intoxication. Be particularly mindful to bring up your children in the Christian religion, and in the fear of God. This is the essential duty of parents to whom children are given as a precious trust from God who will ask them of your hands on Judgment Day. We are not created for this world; but to serve God, and save our souls. Dear Michael you wrote that you intended to return for a visit after 3 years. But put this from your mind. I could not encourage you to do this, for you have a large family, demanding your care. If your business suffered on this account or misfortune came to your family, or should something happen to you on the journey to prevent your return, I could not forgive myself for encouraging you to do so. I would rather come to you, were this possible. It would give me no greater pleasure in this world, than to see my children again, and press them to my heart. Dear children should we not meet again in this world, may we one day meet at the right hand of the Father. Greetings, etc. Anthony's cousin intends to go to America in the Spring. I believe Dorothy will also accompany him. He went with his wife and children to Wertheim to make arrangements. Your father remains obstinate and will not be advised.

M. R. K.

11. Freudenberg, Nov. 16, 1835.
        M. A. K. thinks of moving West.
        See Letter No. 5 of Landkammer, 1835.
        Margaret is with child.
        She was married in 1832?
        Troubles with Schulreter.
        David still living.

Addressed to Phila., North 5th Street near Cock and Lion Hotel, Phila.

Dear Son and all the Family:

How wonderful it is that though we are so far apart we can still write to one another. And yet if we were together we could speak mouth to mouth. Tears of joy stream down my cheeks, as I learn from your letter, you are all living in peace and harmony, young and old in fraternal charity.

58

Dear Michael you tell me of your trouble with Schulreter. I sympathize with you, but be at peace with him and forgive him, and God will reward you in some other way. I also had to suffer a great deal from him, because I tore up his letter of hate. Now he will write his mother a letter full of hate, scolding and lies. It is a shame, for he spoke so badly of America, that I am ashamed when I hear of it. And now the blacksmith of Dresden has come back. He was 14 days distant from David, spent all his money and is now a day laborer. He made such a disturbance that no one now wishes to go to America. Dear Michael I understand you intend to move West where there are no churches or schools. Do not go in the wilderness, but be concerned about the religious training of your children. And then what would become of my letters where there are no Post Offices. So many letters were sent to Johann J. Mussig and to David and they were not received. The papers which you sent last year came to the church. There were great disturbances in the Saloons. They drank the Post money. Each one had to pay a fine of 9.30. Do not write to these people again and send nothing that may not go through the P.O. Mary Anne's Aunt (Mrs. Michael Ebert) has been sick for a whole year. She made her will and left everything to me. This year has eaten up considerable of the property. Peter (Andrew's son) bought the house but the servants will not let him keep it. They wish to keep the house and the furniture as their own. Anton M—— her attorney does not care, because there is so little left. So I have become the only nurse day and night for 6 weeks. But she can not last much longer. I shall write you after her death. You wondered why Jakob Mai gave you no news in the last letter. But Dominic Kern, your Father and Jakob are in Frankfurt. Margaret Mai is again with child. Pray for her happy delivery. Anna will make her first Communion at Easter.

Your loving mother R.

Note:—Best wishes to Michael, David, Anna Maria, Christine and your children from your loving sister *Margaret Mai*.

12. February 5, 1836.
       1. Rosina K. to M. A. K.
       2. Joseph Michael Mussig, cousin of M. A. K.
       3. Dominic and Regina Kern
       4. Matthew Kern, Sr., father of Matthew, Jr., and Dorothy.
       5. David Mussig

(a) Dear Son and all the Family:—

Health, success, happiness and blessings. It is my wish and daily prayer that God will keep you all in good health, that you may take care of your home and bring up your children in a Christian manner... Dear Michael, I wrote you twice last summer, August 2nd and again a little later, but received no answer. I understand that you did not receive my letters for which I am very sorry. I wrote many things which I can not repeat because of my poor eyesight, and will not write till I hear from you.

Rosina (Müssig) Kerchner.

(b) Dear Michael Kerchner:—

I can't resist writing you and David a few lines, because my stepbrother, John Joseph Mussig, did not reply to my three letters. So I beg you my two friends to let me know if I should go to America. I know what the wages are and rely on your good judgment. I have a son and 3 daughters, have sold my house and will not buy another till my mind is made up. Greetings to your wives and children. Your friend,

Joseph Michael Mussig.
(*Brother of Rosina Kerchner*).

Feb. 6, 1836

(c) Dear Brother-in-law, Brothers and Sisters:—

I shall be glad if this letter finds you in good health. I received your letter the 2nd of this month but learn you did not receive your mother's letter. Your mother and myself are anxiously waiting for an answer to her letter, and can't understand why you did not receive it. There is nothing new except that my wife gave birth to a daughter July 28, 1835. Matthew left in the fall to go to America. Joseph Anthony Kern wrote 8 days ago from Hamburg, the first time he has written in a year. Dorothy is still with Michael Ebert, our mother, Susanna (Ziegler), Ehrhard and Josepha are well; Joseph Anthony Kettinger is dead.

Dom. Kern. (Husband of Regina Kettinger.)

(d) Dear Brother-in-law:—

I should like to receive a positive answer for myself, Kern's Frank, Matthew Kettinger, David Mussig and your Sister Dorothy all wish to come to America, if you can promise them something good. Times are so bad here we can't live as ordinary human beings. I shall send Matthew and Dorothy at all events. So write us how things are with you; if I can practice my trade in the country or in the city, or would it be better to go further West, and how much money would be required for the land on which to make a living. I have 3 more good friends who would go with us if they knew they could provide for their families. We can bring 6000 or 7000 Gulden, if you think we can undertake something. Write us at once the particulars so that we may prepare for the journey. I should like to come one year before the others so as to prepare the way for the others. They tell me it is better further West where land can be had cheap. Michael Kerchner told me he had bought a fine piece of land in Missouri, St. Genevieve on the Missouri River. Tell the truth and don't give us any lies; we have enough misery right here. Greetings to you, your wife, David and his wife, Susanna and her husband, and all my acquaintances. *Matthew Kern and Regina* (Dom's wife).

Feb. 6, 1836.

(e) Dear Michael:—

My wife gave birth to a daughter, Rosina, May 24, 1835. Let me know if it is better where you are, or if it would be better to join you rather than to go West. But tell us the truth. Greetings.

Your loving godfather,
David Mussig.

(f) Dear M.—

I wrote in a hurry on February 5th, because we were anxious to answer your letter which Dominic received on the 2nd. On February 6th just as we were closing your letter we received a letter from John Joseph

Mussig, which gave us great joy, because it told us you were all well and living in peace and harmony. I am pained that David did not enclose a word. Best wishes from your loving mother. Greet David and his wife Christine for me. Best wishes from Franz Brand; he married Miss Wolf and wishes he were with you.

                    Mother Rosina.

See Letter No. 3.

13. Letter May 15, 1836

Dear Children and the entire Family:—

It is a long time since I wrote you and yet there is no reply. I do not understand how my letters are undelivered for a whole year. Have I the wrong address or is it the fault of the P.O.? We wrote at the beginning of February and *Dominic* and *Anthony's cousin* and *Dot* are anxious to hear from you, for they wish to go to America if they get favorable news. Emigration, especially from Bavaria, is very great this year. *Barth. Gross, Ziner's Hannes, Joseph Michael Mussig, Kasper Kettinger* and his son want to leave. *Peter Vaeth* sold his house and goods and went to considerable expense; but it is now impossible for him to leave for his children are too young. Many others would also leave if they could get together sufficient money for the voyage. And we can not blame them for it is impossible for a property owner to exist. All rights are denied us and worthless new laws imposed on us. We can not enter the forest, to cut wood, taxes are so divided that the beggar gets as much as the property owner. We get scarcely enough for a horse and have to pay very dear for goods from people who have no cattle. The same holds good for wood, for it has become as dear here as in the cities. We have a forest guardian who is more like a tyrant than a friend of mankind. He sticks to the laws and if he finds anybody in the woods he fines them without mercy, so that we have to buy all our wood and that is forcing many people to America. This is the reason *Dominic* wishes to leave. We can not charge anymore for our work, but have to pay three times as much for our wood. The Reichstag takes place every 2 months. Whoever violates the forestry law is obliged to pay all the fines or go to the workhouse. We have just received another notice; all Bake ovens not located below the ground floor must be removed. All wash kettles must be bricked in. We have to remove our bake oven and may not wash in the kitchen. If we carry out the instructions it will cost us more than 100 Gulden. Father is going to visit his Rev. Cousin (Michael Rauch) Pentecost. He is not very well, and is sparing in his benefactions to us, since Kettinger died. It would be better for us if Kettinger had not died. Greetings. Margaret is again with child and this is the fifth month. N.B.—We sent the letter to Wertheim but they would not take it because the address was not in English.

ITEMS:

1. Dominic, Anton's cousin, Dorothy Kern, intend to sail.
2. Bart Gross, Ziner's Hannes, Joseph Michael Mussig, *Casper Kettinger* and Son, also.
3. Margaret with child.
4. Kettinger's death.
5. Higher Taxes.

61

14. Freudenberg—March
   Anna Maria's 'baas' (aunt) Mrs. Michael Ebert dies 1835.
   Margaret has a son, Francis Louis.
   Paul Kerchner has a bad foot.
   Death of Michael Anthony's Adrian.
   Anna Maria's First Communion, 1835.

Dear Sons;—and all the Family:

There was reason for my not writing for so long a time. The hand of God was laid heavily upon us this past winter. Yet, will I say with Job: "The Lord hath given, the Lord hath taken; blessed be His Holy Name." December 10th Mary Ann's 'baas' died. She was my best friend whom I can never forget. She was buried on December 12th, and there was no rest in the house, for on the same night Margaret was in labor, and on the 13th a son was born. She needed help and there was no one to help her. She had a hard time and was confined for 8 weeks. Scarcely was this past, when your father had a very bad foot. He would have died, had we not gotten a very good surgeon. He was in bed for 4 weeks. With all this worry, and without rest at night or day, I became *seriously ill* and was in bed for 3 weeks. All despaired of my recovery. So it was the whole winter. We still have two beds in the room, making it look like a hospital. I am now up for a few days, but still weak and unable to work. My dear children you must have been very anxious, for I thought of you always. Do not forget me in your prayers, as I never forget you. Dear Michael, you wrote that you lost a child. (Adrian died 1834). Now you can rejoice that you have an angel in heaven. Margaret also has a dear child and whenever I take it in my arms, I think of your children and fold them to my heart. I could write a great deal more, but my eyes are weak dear Michael. Let me know how David is. If only I could, I would leap over the ocean and bring back my children to the Fatherland. There would be no greater joy in this world than to behold my children again. Yet, conditions are so bad in Freudenberg, I could not wish you to be back here where a decent man can hardly earn a living.

R. M. K.

Anna Maria—Dear Brothers: (Michael A and David).

I am making my First Communion at Easter and will remember you in my prayers. I enclose best wishes and it is the wish of your little sister Anna, that you are all well.

Margaret—

I had a hard winter and thought I would never see you again. I greet you heartily and wish you health and happiness. Your loving sister Margaret.

R. M. K.

15. Letter May 18, 1838.
   Great Grandmother 61 years.
   M. A. Kerchner moved to Wilmington.
   Written after David's death.

Dear Son and all the family:—

Have been waiting for an answer to my letter of last December. I now acknowledge receipt of two letters, one from yourself, the other from

62

Christine. I at once sent a letter to Philadelphia and would be grieved if my letter fell among strangers for there were many things of a personal character, and for your special benefit. Dear Michael please write me fully how Christine and her children are doing, and if you handed her my letter. (Christine was David Kerchner's wife). Why did you move to Wilmington? Perhaps because your brother David is buried there and you can better bring up your children. This would be a great consolation for me. It is a matter of anxiety for me how your children are being brought up, and if they are being taught the same religion I taught you. I lay it down as a duty for you to be concerned about the education of your children. When they need advice take them by the hand and by advice and counsel you will accomplish more than by scolding. If only I could speak to you personally. There is so much to say and it is so difficult to express in writing what is in my heart. I had often consoled myself that we would see each other once more but I realize that this is now impossible. God grant that we may one day meet in heaven. Many persons of different ages died this past winter, but now death is taking the children. I am not now sick but many cares weigh heavily upon me. So that I am now as useless as a piece of decayed wood.

We have a great deal of work with no income and no money to procure help. We must worry ourselves about all this and yet no one can persuade your father to go to America. If he felt as I do we would be with you, and then I would have seen for myself how David lived and died. I suffer from the thought of it every day, that I was not there to prepare his soul for eternity. But I must keep silent, for the thought of it brings the tears to my eyes. Dear Michael I am now 61 years old. God alone knows how much longer I may be able to write. See that my counsels sink deep into your heart. Your greatest concern, as it was my own, must be to bring up your children in the fear of God, that none of them be lost through your fault. I must close as my eyes are getting weak. I could tell you all sorts of news but it is too painful for me.—R. M. K.—Greetings and best wishes to all the family.

My Dear Brother:—

My one wish would be to be with you and join you in song and mirth. I think I am still young and it is possible that when parents are dead you may forget me. But do retain some affection for me.

Your Sister Margaret also greets you. She has two sick children and I do not know how they are just now. The *nurse* died.

Anna Maria.

16. Fragment 1838 after David Kerchner's death.

First part is the end of a letter of Grandmother to (M.A.K.)

Then follows a note to Dominic Kern.

Best wishes to you and your wife Regina (Kettinger) Dearest friend Dominic Kern:—Do me the favor of handing this little note to my son Michael. I am living in great fear and anxiety since I saw in a letter of *Anna Wolf* to her parents, that David was dangerously ill. I must have the truth.

Dear Michael:—Received your letter of July 31st. I will not write again till I hear about Dorothy's inheritance of which I wrote you July

63

1st. Tell me the truth about David. He has not written me for a year. I greet you all, the names too numerous to mention. R. M. K.

17. Letter to M. A. K. next to Cock and Lion Hotel, No. 4th St. Phila.

No date. But evidently before David's death in 1838. O Michael! If I had only one hour's chat with you. You are constantly in my thoughts and I have no news from you. What a sad mother. What a sad lot has been mine, to be robbed of my children and grandchildren. How often do I remain buried at home, and call out grief-stricken to Michael, and David. "Where are they? I may never see them again." I must again tell you that you have a mistaken judgment of David, as I see in your letter. We are often mistaken in our judgments. Your father made little money this fall. In Rossbach we had lots of apples and gathered them in the fall before time, so they might not be stolen. In addition he bought 200 Gulden worth, and built a new boat, and remained in Frankfurt the whole winter. At last when he returned the apples were worthless and shrivelled and he had little money. He had no confidence in the day laborers and to satisfy his debt against them stripped them even of their shirts, for they had not a Kreutzer on them. When they came home they went to Wertheim and lodged a complaint against him and he had to pay a pretty sum to satisfy the costs.

In Wertheim they pay little attention to the mail. They accept the money and then forget about it. Michael Mussig complained a number of times to the P.O. but it was useless. Many young people have died. Schulreter's Michael, his brother Solad, and his mother. *Gerhard Kern's* wife, Andrew Rossbach's wife, John Joseph Müssig's wife, Val. *Bechtold, Matthew Langinger,* Geo. *Jos. Keck's* wife, *Joseph Karl's* wife, and *Kilian Grein.*

    1. Cries for Michael and David.

    2. Business bad.

18. No date. To M. A. K.

1840 or 1841

Jakob Mai buys Michael Ebert's house.
Franz Anton Mai wishes to come to U. S.
Grandparents would come but do not wish to leave Fr. Rauch.
Mr. Haas comes on a visit from U. S.
Rosina born Aug. 9, 1839.

Dear Son and all the Family:—

I hope my letter will find you in good health which will give me pleasure. I pray daily that God may give you continuous good health, so that you may rear your children in a Christian manner. We are all well thank God, though age and the weakness of my body, is for me a sickness Dear Michael, your old mother had to bear great afflictions this winter. Your father and the plough-horse were in Frankfurt all the winter, selling fruit and the earnings were little. I had to remain at home with the little *Kormann*, whose health is not good. We have him with us since his mother died. I received your letter and understand that you will sell your house. I hope you will succeed and have good luck, and that it will be for the best. There was another reason for my delay in writing. I was disturbed and had many interruptions on account of *Margaret's* children and wanted to put it off because *Jakob Mai* had been negotiating with *Alois Kern* for the purchase of Michael Ebert's house. They have concluded the deal for 510 Gulden, though the house will need many repairs. Jakob Mai and Leonard Mai spent the winter together because there was no other business. I hoped he would join you in the United States, but he did not wish to do so because his family is young and numerous, and produce is not bringing much. As the year was bad *Franz Anton Mai* wanted to go to America to his brother-in-law Anthony Kerchner. But business is bad. Many householders left Burgerstadt this year.

Three weeks ago a former citizen of Ebenheit named *Haas* returned from America. The horse was with him in Ebenheit. But he could only say that he met you once casually. He intended to return in the fall bringing his sister with him. *Mr. Gerber* of Hartheim was also on a visit but to all appearances he is in debt. He had already sold his property and would go to his brother-in-law in America. I showed him the letter in which you spoke of the happy day you spent with *Baumann* and it gave him great pleasure. But now his wife heard that a ship was lost last fall and many people of our own neighborhood were lost. So he is now doubtful about going. Dear Michael, we would have left long ago, Father would have sailed with Dorothy and *Anthony's* cousin, but did not wish to sadden his *Rev. Cousin*. It would be too hard for him to leave so good a friend. He did more for us this year than a father for his children. He gave us a beautiful picture in memory of an old friend who lived to be 125 years old. When his Bishop asked him to what he attributed his long life, he said he had always feared three deadly sins: impurity, drunkenness and anger. Our Rev. Cousin also possesses the same kind of a pure heart, and is enriched with God's blessings and a ripe old age. Father and the horse are at present on a visit to him (Pentecost). I am going to finish as I am coming to the end of my paper. Best wishes to yourself, wife, family and friends. May *God bless your dear little daughter, who bears my own name* (*Rosina*) born Aug. 9, 1839. May God bless you and keep you from all evil and grant you increased happiness. I am happy that my name and memory is being perpetuated in America. And you dear Sons, live well and happy, and grow in grace and wisdom as the child Jesus, before God and man. This other sheet send to my brother *David Mussig*. He told me in his last letter I should send it to you. So please attend to it, because I don't know his address. Give the other page to *Lawrence Mussig*.

19. December 30, 1839 or 1840.

    David Kerchner's sickness or death.
    Dorothy Kern's inheritance.
    Mass for Regina (?).
    Dorothy and Matthew Kern received 200 Gulden from Fr. Rauch's housekeeper.
    Lawrence Wolf, Dom. Ebert, young Denmar died.
    Margaret has 3 children—Louis age 5, Joseph age 3, and Edward age 1.

Dear Sons and Family:—

Another year has passed away and we are nearer to eternity. Many sad and black clouds have passed over our heads, many sufferings and adversities have afflicted us during the past year. Yet with God's help and with resignation to His holy will, we have borne them and still exist. We are now entering a new year and take a firm resolution, should God give

65

health and strength to enter this new year for His honor and the salvation of our souls. I shall not, dear children, give you any news or stories, of which there is an abundance, but they are not worth the paper on which they are written. My sole wish and longing is to give you wise counsel from my heart; to instill in you the love of God and neighbor, and ask you to say your prayers faithfully and conscientiously. Dear children God has placed us in this world to serve and save our souls and thus merit heaven. We have but one soul and should we lose it, we should lose all. Above all pray to God the Holy Ghost to enlighten you with His heavenly light, that you stray not into dark paths which lead to temptation and damnation. Dear Michael in spite of all my love and solicitude for you, you do not carry out my wishes. For more than a year I have not heard a word from you, in spite of all my letters which cost me no small effort. Every mail day I look in vain for a letter. I do not know what to think unless my many letters annoy you. If this is so, you should have told me, for I have no intention of annoying you. It seems to me you ought to be happy for every word received from your old mother. God alone knows how long I may still be able to write you. Most people of my age already lie in the cemetery. I scarcely survived the past winter for the news of your brother David nearly brought me to my grave. I can not dismiss him from my thoughts and must therefore be silent about him.

Why does not your brother-in-law Ruppert (married to Dorothy Kern) say where to send his money, for it is lying useless while we are waiting for an answer. A few days ago a woman from Sommerau, who has a sweetheart in Philadelphia, visited us and had a letter saying she should bring along 25 Gulden from Paul Kerchner. It appeared to me strange, since we had no advice from Ruppert, and we shall not give her a Kreutzer. I had a letter from my brother David Mussig, saying I should have a Mass read for his Regina. If such is the custom, Dominic still has plenty of money, so I got 5 Gulden from Kettinger and had Masses read. But, now the case is quite different. Dorothy and Matthew received 200 Gulden from the old cook, which Kettinger wished to send to America. Now Kern blamed the old cook for this, so the money has been placed at interest until her death. I had to give back to her the 5 Gulden, you can tell my brother. We are now keeping 5 Gulden out of Dorothy's money.

I am living alone since St. Martin's day, and it will likely be three weeks, because father with the horse, is in Wurzburg seeing nuts. They sold very well because this year fruit is scarce. Hoof and mouth disease attacked the cattle this year. Milk could not even be fed to the hogs, and had to be poured out in the fields. We could neither harness nor milk our cattle for three weeks. There was neither milk nor butter. I believe this was the reason why so many people died last winter.

The Eheleitern and shoemaker Schloer became reconciled in the spring, but now in the fall they began to quarrel again. Lawrence Wolf, Dominic Ebert and young Denmar, as well as Mrs. Rebein died.

Greetings, but I can not single out my brother Anton, for a greeting, for he does not write. I wrote my brother David Mussig in August; let me know if he received my letter. I should like to know if the aged grandmother is still living (Susanna Ziegler?). Your sister Margaret greets you. She has three children, Louis age 5, Joseph age 3 and Edward age 1. Hand the enclosed to Lawrence Mussig. I no longer send letters by Wertheim, so my brother Rochus sends them by Hundheim.

R. M. K.

GG

20. Letter to David Mussig, May 5, 1841.

  An unusual snow storm lasting 6 days.
  Eve, Sister-in-law to David Mussig marries.
  Kern's Dorothy dies. (Mrs. Michael Ebert)
  Dorothy Zingelein, wife of Alois Hess, dies.
  L. M.'s Teresa with *Christine*.

Dear Brother:—

  Received your letter of last winter, and understand you will live on your property in the spring. You can be glad you left Germany for conditions are very bad, especially for property owners. Last winter was the most severe in many years... was lost in the snow for 6 days. Grape vines frozen, apple trees must be replanted, all potatoes in storage were frozen. We had no rain all during May. For the last 8 days we had a prayer hour at 8:00 P.M. for rain and trust the good Lord will have pity on us. We had to sell all our cattle for lack of food, and fodder was scarce last year; yet we had considerable straw and bran, but this year we have nothing. Yet we will trust in the Lord and rely on His goodness. I shall write you about *Eve* your sister-in-law. She has married and lives in Kammerhof. Two years ago she visited us just as your letter came. With tears in her eyes she wishes she had taken passage with you. She is not doing well. Kern's Dorothy (Mrs. Michael Ebert) died and was buried in April. Dorothy Zingerlein, my neighbor Grim's daughter, was married 11 months ago to *Alois Hess*, and died in childbirth. You told me your Teresa was with Christine, but said nothing about her children, whether they are still Catholic or went back to Lutheranism as their mother was formerly. I can not help writing about it my heart is full of anxiety. Greetings, etc. Your true and devoted sister unto death. Best wishes to brother Anthony. M. Rosina Kerchner.

21. Praised be God.

  As Letter No. 22 was addressed to M. A. K. in Baltimore and refers to the departure of Mr. Wolf, the date may be after 1844. Also Margaret married in 1833, has her fifth child.

    Reproaches for neglect to write.
    She sent a letter with Wolf in June.
    Peter Vaeth and Blatz Son going to America.
    Anton Kerchner's brother-in-law is going to live near Frank
     Kettinger.
    Margaret has another son—David.
    Refers to David Kerchner's death, his wife and children.

Grandmother to M. A. K.

Dear Son:

  Letter writing is all the more painful when letters are not answered. I am forcing myself to write and trying to persuade myself that all mother love has not died out in your heart. You give me no proof to the contrary. Yet, moved by my love for you and by the two presents you sent me, I am urged to honor you with a letter. May it find you in health and happiness.

  Dear Michael you may imagine what pleasure the presents gave me, and your two sisters, whose cheeks were flushed with joy, not merely be-

67

cause of the presents, but because of the love you manifest through the presents. We rejoice that you now have a more comfortable living than in **Freudenberg**, as is evident, since you cannot give unless you have to give.

Nevertheless, I am grieved that you did not enclose one syllable in Ruppert's letter, or even sign your name. One might think you had taken an oath not to write. Yet, you have a wife and children who might have written that you have received my letter. I also gave a letter to Mr. Wolf who left for America last June.

The latest is that Peter Vaeth is going to America and Andrew Blatz's son is going to live near Frank Kettinger. The latter wrote that he has succeeded very well and that he had a visit from Dominic Kern. They told Kettinger that the old blacksmith had lost everything and is moving away. Anthony Kerchner also gave us good news. His brother-in-law will likely join him at the latest in the spring.

Dear Michael I have many things to say, but owing to lack of time and pressing affairs cannot do so. Father is again engaged in selling fruit, and the horse had to go with him. Margaret gave birth to another child September 14th and named him David. He is strong and healthy and the image of your brother David, whom I cannot forget, and bewail his early death. His wife (Christine?) has not written us since his death. I would like to know if she has married again, and how her children are.

R. M. K.

22. Freudenberg, May 13. To M. A. K. addressed to Baltimore after 1844.

Dearest beloved Children and Relatives:—

Generalities.

We are getting old and our work must be done by strangers, which we can scarcely afford. Tried to get along with a smaller house but cannot persuade your father, and must let him have his own way. As long as God permits us to live together I shall try to live peaceably with him. It takes all our strength and understanding to bear with all the adversities. We have so many bad years, fruits turned out bad, potatoes rotted and many people became sick on that account. *Anna Maria* does not wish you to return to Germany, as things are getting worse every year. More than a hundred people have left Frankfurt this year. I am sending you a letter *Christine's* husband sent me 3 years ago when they were going to California. It says that Henry went to Philadelphia to learn his trade with his brother *Jakob Herz*. *Anna Wolf's* husband who lives in Philadelphia was suffering from T. B. and did not think he would return to America alive. I gave him a letter but as I did not hear anything I am sending you a letter for *Jakob Herz*, and please see that he gets it, because he ought to be able to give the best information about *Christine and her husband David Kerchner*. We are old people I wish I were ready to appear before God. Let Adam, Clara, Susan Huguenin and Dorothy Ruppert, write. We do not know how soon death will take us. Greetings.

Rosina M. Kerchner.

68

23. September 22, 1844?
>   M. A. K. recently moved to Baltimore.
>   1. Disapproves of his desire to go West.
>   2. Warning against saloons.

Dear Son and Family:—

I wrote last year earily in April, and addressed the letter to Wilmington thinking you were still on the Brandywine. I included a note to Lawrence Mussig from his mother, to which he at once replied though I did not hear a word from you. I have been anxiously waiting for an answer. This year again May 15, I sent you a letter to the Brandywine address. Yesterday I received a letter which gave me an awful shock, when I read of the Mexican War. I have been suffering from fear and anxiety for a whole year and my sleep has been disturbed with unpleasant dreams. I pray daily dear M. that you may be able to bring up your children and not leave them orphaned. I can give you no better advice than to fear God. God resists the proud and gives His grace to the humble. Do not undertake more than you can manage. Stick to your business and by it support your family. I have no use for Taverns. There is nothing to be gained from strangers; we have been deceived on every side. You say you wish to go further west. Are you not ashamed to think of dragging your wife and family into the wilderness and have your children grow up without religion? Baltimore is one of the finest cities for your business. It is certainly better than in Germany. We have suffered heavy losses in the last 3 years, in the loss of cattle, through sickness and other misfortunes. Anna is now married to Leonhard Mai, son of Francis Michael Mai. He is a fruit dealer and lives with us. Margaret has had bad luck with her boy Edward, whose eye was put out by a boy with a stone. She has now 2 boys and a girl, having lost 2 children. They spent a hundred Gulden in Doctor Bills, and sacrificed their house through a suit they entered in order to get damages. She is returning here about St. Martin's Day. Jakob Mai and Leonard Mai are in business together and have a hard time. It is hard to earn a living; there is too much lying and trickery. If a person is not economical and does not work night and day he can not make ends meet. Many persons once well off have been ruined. Egidius Kerchner (see letter No. 25) was one time in comfortable circumstances, but has been reduced to misery. His house and goods were sold, and he has been reduced to want, after leaving his wife and 10 suffering children. He beat his wife day and night, and 3 weeks ago she nearly died. He then left her intending to go to America. If he comes to you, you will know how to deal with his lies. Many others have lost everything, while some through thrift and economy have improved their condition.

Dear Michael, let me again warn you against your desire to wander; it is your greatest fault. Keep a quiet and restful spirit, and take care of your family. If a father has raised his children well, he is by no means ruined. Children can learn nothing good in a tavern, and there is no time for prayer. Where there is no prayer there can be no blessing. Easy come and easy go, is always true. Although you brought little money with you to America, you fared well, and you should have enough at present to get along. Remain in the city where you are and do not move about, otherwise I must suffer with anxiety. If things are not so good now, they will be better later. God strikes and heals. He has deposed Kings and Emperors from the thrones, when they sinned through pride. Begin an entirely new manner of living and keep all strangers from your home, especially those who buy on credit. We have had our own sad experience in this regard.

We are only 2 old people and have to worry about many things. Two cows do our plowing and we no longer have any help. Nothing gave better returns this year than Potatoes, Apples and Wine, though the summer was cold and wet. Kilian Kerchner died and left everything to his widow. We did not get as much as a kreutzer. Our Rev. Cousin's old cook died, and himself is failing. I do not think he can last long. The young people do with him what they like; he now has an assistant since he is too old to look after the mission. It was because of his old age that we did not leave for America. I was constantly after your father to leave, but he would not be moved. I am now ashamed to mention America for your father is not to be moved. I hardly dare show anyone a letter from America. Michael Mussig recently wrote us; also Neilerman (?) that he has married. My brothers have not written for a long time, and I have not heard from Christine since David died. (Christine the widow of David Kerchner). Keep well and do not move again until after our death. We are both old people and know not what help we may need. After our death all shall be shared with each one equally. She then addresses herself to the children and begs them to be obedient and respectful to their parents; to love them, to strive after virtue and holiness, to pray to the Holy Ghost to enlighten them in all that is good and holy, not to abandon God or His holy religion; for He will not abandon anyone who puts his trust in Him. Your loving and devoted mother unto death.

Rosina M. Kerchner.

No. 24. Copia. June 14, 1845. Bretten. Witnessed, Phila., Feb. 3, 1846
Joseph Anthony Kern (?)

Dear Brother-in-law:—

I did not send you word of your inheritance sooner because I was waiting to give you more definite information, and send if possible a portion of your inheritance. I recd. your power of attorney at the end of April of this year I at once applied to the Courthouse and govt. officials for your release from allegiance to this country. Also advertised in the Anzeigerblatt and the Karlsruhe paper to give opportunity to anyone to file possible claim against your portion. After 6 weeks it was possible to obtain permission for division and distribution. Eberhard (could this be Eberhard Kern) and myself paid 150 pf. to Masterturner John Doll on your account. I also wrote your 2 brothers-in-law Fred Eck and Pfinniger in Switzerland, that they should refund your share. Only after repeated writing, they sent 140 pf. which was sent to John Doll, so that you now have credit of 290 pf. Brother-in-law Stauffer after repeated reminders promised to pay you 81 pf. after the harvest. I hope to make a settlement at the latest by St. Martin's day, 1845. I regret that you did not advise me of your address sooner, and avoid the necessary expense of redistribution. The additional expense must naturally be borne by yourself, since the last time I heard from you was through your letter sent from Hamburg in 1828. It was filed at the Courthouse but the claim was too old before the law. You will not receive the 102 pf. due you from the Solomon children, since this has been consumed. The oldest son has been in the army for 1 year; the 2nd son is learning the linen business; in Karls-

70

ruhe; the 2 oldest girls are in domestic service; the youngest has been with me for 3 years, and the second youngest is being cared for by Bernhard at our expense. It will be a long time before the latter will be able to earn their living, which means 4 or 5 years. I trust therefore that you will not take the bread out of the mouths of these poor children of your brother Solomon, but cheerfully make the sacrifice of the last amount. Your devoted brother-in-law Sautter.

No. 25. Dec. 14, 1845

> M. A. K leaves Wilm. for Balto. Sept. '44
> Fr. Rauch dies Nov. 5, 1844 His will.
> A disastrous flood.
> Anna Maria's first child.
> Egid. Kerchner leaves wife and 10 children.
> Margaret's son Edward loses his eyesight. They begin a suit for damages, and after 3 years lost and had to pay the charges.
> Condemns taverns.

Dear Son:—

Glad to hear you are all well. Dear M. you ask me if I am still alive or whether I don't care to write to you again. I am surprised at you. The last time you wrote me, was in September and you were leaving for Baltimore and the children were suffering with fever. I at once wrote you a letter of sympathy, to which I received no reply *Christine's* (2nd) husband wrote me last spring the first time in 6 years. He tells me he is a devoted father and the children are good and obedient. He was also in Germany with little Lawrence, but did not visit us. He is now in Newark. Our *Rev. cousin* died Nov. 25, 1844 aged 86 years, 2 months. He left after him a blessed memory and might have left a large fortune, had he not been a father to the needy and unfortunate. He left a number of bequests and made several foundations.—thanks to God and himself. R.I.P. Last winter was bearable, but in the spring there was more snow than had been seen for centuries. When it began to melt the Main overflowed and caused great damage. Trees were uprooted, barns and houses washed away, men and beasts drowned. On Whitsunday the children could not go to mass, as the water stood in the churches. I never saw the like misery. The cattle had to remain in the woods as the town was under water. Margaret's beautiful home was in the middle of the flood, and we thought it would be swept away any moment. Though it escaped, it cost as much to repair as a new house. A second flood was almost as bad as the first, and considerable sand was deposited in the fields. The next year things were not much better because the summer was wet and cold. Winter grain was about normal, but the wet ground damaged the wheat. Lentils and beans rotted in the ground, and the potatoes spoiled in the cellar. A loaf of bread cost here 20 kreutzerand even more elsewhere. Our Nange (Anna Maria) married *Franz Mai's* second son, *Leonard* and already has a beautiful son, Joseph. I would thank God if we could meet one another again, for your father and mother are now old while you are still young.
TO THE GRANDCHILDREN. Dear Children be mindful of the fourth commandment; respect your parents in all that is right and honorable, especially in what concerns your faith and religion. The blessing as well as the curse of parents falls on their children. This is the advice of your grandmother given you from her heart. I am glad that you assisted

at the beautiful ceremony of the blessing of your church and that you received the sacrament of Confirmation. It is a means to strengthen your faith which ought to be particularly dear to you. Dear children there is so much I would like to say to you, but my paper is too small. In the meantime live virtuously and piously and the blessing of God will remain with you. It will be with you in this world and also in' eternity. Goodbye dear children, live in peace with your dear parents, and relatives, and do not forget me when I am gone. I am already old and feeble for old age is already a sickness and I do not know how long I may yet be able to write. Sincere good wishes from your devoted grandmother and your friends and relatives in Germany. Write me very soon.

Dear M. I will now give you news about our Rev. Cousin's last testament. Your father went as usual on the anniversary of the dedication of the church. Finding him very sick he remained with him to the end. He had made his will 12 years before, when in sound mind. His whole estate amounted to more than 13,000 Gulden, at which everybody was surprised, because he had been so good to the poor. The estate was divided into 3 parts; the first for your father, the second for Frank, and the third for the parishes of Freudenberg, Euerfeld and Liebergau. This last bequest was to teach poor boys a trade and for an anniversary mass for himself and the Rauch family. The half-sisters of your father and Frank were to receive no more than 15 Gulden, with which sum they were dissatisfied, and refused to accept. The bequests amounted to 700 Gulden and the housekeeper received a nice sum. Each schoolteacher, caretaker, baptismal and confirmation sponsor, received a remembrance. The Tombstone and Funeral amounted to more than 2000 Gulden, for which the 2 parishes were assessed as a condition for receiving the foundation. Since he made his will he wrote down all that he had given. We had to state what we had received and this was deducted from our bequest. We then bought the fine field which had belonged to Egidius Kerchner, (letter No. 23) for 500 Gulden, and from Zoeller the Hirtenstein, next door to us. Egidius is entirely ruined; there remain only his wife and the 10 children. He stays mostly with the woman tavernkeeper; to say more would be too scandalous. In the same way, 3 months ago the son of Walter Sheurig became bankrupt and left his wife and family. There is so much of this shameful news these days; I must say no more.

Dear M. I wish to make one more request. Please be more steady; and give up this desire for moving from one place to another. You must already know from past experience what little profit there is in moving about. From what I understand you are now in a beautiful city, (Baltimore) and have all the advantages of schools and religion, which ought to be highly esteemed specially where there are children. So be contented; you already have grown childrn, who can come to your assistance if need be, though you ought to be able to care for yourself with your business. I have no use for Saloons, where there is too much lying and deceit. There can be no blessing in Saloons which leave no time for prayer, where the children may hear all kinds of scandalous talk and will learn nothing good. Children well brought up are the greatest riches, and their training should be your greatest concern. Jakob and Margaret have suffered great reverses this year. Their home was greatly damaged by the flood and now after 3 years their suit for damages, on account of the injury to their boy's eye has been lost. Greetings from your 2 Sisters, relatives and friends.
R. M. K.

No. 26. Dec. 5, 1847

                      Will of Fr. Rauch
                      Jakob needs help
                      Floods 1845
                      Heat and drought 1846
                      High price of food, thieving, beggary
                      3 vineyards, new wine vats,
                      Grandmother 70 years old-born in 1777.

Dear son, wife and family:—

    Usual greetings. I am well, but old age is itself a sickness. Are you still living in Baltimore, or have you again given way to your wanderlust? In my last letter I gave you details about the will of our Rev. Cousin Father Michel Rauch. I took great pains to do so, and yet I have no answer. Dear Michael, do you believe I have forgotten you, or that I have no mother love? May such be far from me. There is not a moment when I do not think of you, and then the tears stream down my cheeks. If you would generously come to the assistance of Jakob, it would be an act of charity. He is in great need with his large family and has suffered adversity the last few years. The floods of 1845 did great damage as you likely saw from the papers. In 1846 prices of foods were greatly advanced because of the heat and drought and the failure of the crops. The same was true of wine. We paid 24 Gulden for 2 bush. of seed corn, for our own was useless for sowing. Summer fruits dried on the trees and the potatoes rotted in the ground. Few hogs could be raised because feed was scarce. Consequently the price of everything was high, and the most careful man could scarcely earn sufficient to buy bread, and the lazy and worthless give themselves to begging and thievery. The roads are so full of idle working men, that it arouses pity. . .A 6 lb. loaf costs 45 pf. and a peck of potatoes as much. From morning to night 2 or 3 beggars come to the door. Many lock their doors to escape from them, but I gave what I could. Many persons died in Oberwald. Those who could, hastened to the banks of the Main, and these bothered us the most. Finally the beggars stormed the Courthouse, demanding bread. Food supplies from the surrounding country were brought here and distributed. As the money had to be raised out of the forests, we could not cut wood. May we never see the like again. Hunger has now thank God disappeared, but the price of a loaf is 16 pfennig. The potato crop has again failed and the people are suffering from sickness. But fruit is abundant and serves to take the place of ordinary food. Everywhere, even where the soil is poor, the fruit is plentiful. Much of it remained on the trees till St. Martin's day, and considerable was trodden under foot. As tonebreaker on the road earned more in one day than the man who raised apples. There are some who have 100 or even 200 acres of apples and can't raise a pfennig of credit. Those whom we helped promised to repay, and some were not willing even to do this. We were afraid to demand payment, as some of them are quite bad and worthless.

    Dear M. you did not like it because we bought more land. Had we more money invested in land we would at least have something. We were afraid of losing our money and so invested it in land. We still have fine property including 3 vineyards. Last year and this year we had a fine fall and have stocked our cellars, and spent 150 Gulden for wine vats. They were as dear as formerly, because there is considerable demand for wine. Our casks are full of wine and cider and it cost considerable for help. We

73

still have our tavern and keep a barmaid. You may think we are having good and peaceable times, but what we are once used to we can not easily do without. I am now 70 years old and the first to rise and the last to retire. If I could have luxuries I would still do so; but I cannot, and do not live on the best as some people do. We have our coffee in the morning, our meat at noon, and visit the cellar in between. We live after the manner of old people, cost what it may. There is a great deal of news but of such kind that, it is not worth spoiling the paper. Greetings. Write soon, Your devoted and loving mother until death. Good wishes from your 2 sisters and brothers-in-law.

Rosina (Mussig) Kerchner.

No. 27. Feb. 25, 1848

Eberh. Kern, Rochus Mussig, intend to go to Amer.
Mrs. Grimmien, & Kilian Keck (husb. of Kath. Kettinger died.
Anna Maria's oldest boy Joseph dies.
Lawr. Mussig's wife died. Dec. 3, '47
Marg. has 5 children living, 6th expected.

Dear Son:—

Complains of not receiving a letter for 2 years. Eberhard Kern, and Rochus Mussig intend to visit Lawrence Mussig and if they like it there, will remain. They are fine young men; see if you can give them work. A large number of unmarried persons are going abroad. They tell many wonderful stories; but—beware of false prophets. Many people died here this winter, including our neighbor *Mrs. Grimmien*. Our cousin *Kilian Keck*, husb. of *Kath. Kettinger* also died. Anna Maria's oldest boy, *Joseph*, died. Fruit dealers are having a hard year. Bread and meat are dear in Frankfurt. Leonard remained there the whole winter and hardly earned a penny. My brother Anthony wrote that *Lawrence Mussig's* wife died (Dec. 3, 1847) Anton tells me that many steamships come to Wilmington. But that is nothing new here; we can go daily and in a short time, to Frankfurt or Würzburg, if we have the money. My eyes are growing weak and I must close. I would like to embrace my dear grandchildren and give them a thousand kisses. Your 2 sisters and Margaret's husband greet you. Margaret has now 5 living children, and is expecting a 6th.

Your devoted mother Rosina.

No. 28. 1848?

After Fr. Rauch's Jubilee in 1837, 5 years after the real anniv. 1832 Rochus Mussig & E. Kern coming to America. See No. 25.

Dear Son and Family:—

No need to give you news since our friends Eberhard Kern & Rochus Mussig (Letter No. 25, 1848) are coming to see you. This departure makes us very sad, having our friends and relatives leave us here alone. I would like to go along with them, for I shall never again have so good an opportunity. But your father will not be persuaded; the one argument is Fr. Rauch whom he does not wish to leave and sadden in his old age. Yet I can't complain for he is an honor to our family, and worthy of our esteem. He celebrated his golden jubilee on Epiphany, and it is impossible to describe the joy and solemnity of the occasion. The King

74

of Bavaria presented Father with a Gold Medal of great value. The celebration should have taken place 5 years ago, but he was afraid of the excitement. He had a gold reliquary made for the true cross and gave a souvenir to all the children. He was told by the King not to part with the Medal. Great numbers came from Würzburg and the surroundings. The procession was headed by a band and the children carried the jubilee crown. Joy and jubilation was everywhere, and the ceremony was concluded with a splendid banquet.

Dear M. I showed him your last letter and he remarkable you had never written to him. Now please enclose a nice letter to him in your next, and I will see that he gets it. My brothers Rochus and Michael will give you all the news. I would like to send some eatables but they are already weighed down with their baggage. I am sending you 2 blessed medals, 2 beautiful books, some dried Prunes with all the good will and love of a mother's heart. Do not forget me in your prayers and be sure to use the books in honor of Our Blessed Mother, for she is the Mother of Grace and the Refuge of sinners. Make the books known to your friends; they are very recent and very little known. They became known for the first time here this winter. I do not think we shall see each other again, for weakness has taken hold of me. Yet I had often thought of coming to you, and even asked how old people stood the voyage. I am growing dizzy and must stop. Bring up your children in virtue and piety and they will be your joy in old age. Live in peace with one another and the blessing of God will abide with you. When our friends come to you, they must write and give us news, and let me know if you received my letter addressed to David (Mussig) in March. May love to you all.

Rosina.

No. 29. July 20, 1848 or 1849

      War. Liberty, Fraternity, Equality
      Christine & husb. in Calif.
      Anna Maria Kern's 'baas' dies
      Wife and mother of Kilian Keck die.

My dear Michael:—

I see that you are concerned over our situation, but thank God we are still free from the murderous war, which has destroyed so many human beings and property. It may yet reach us; all sorts of rumors are spread through Bavaria. Neither people from other countries or soldiers have been quartered with us. May God protect us from it though it may still happen. We have suffered very much during the past 2 years. Professions and industries are idle and our people are suffering from hunger and misery. We have had our 'Strauswirth' for 1 year, and what business we did in that time could have been done in 2 months. People are dishonest, and whoever can trick another considers it something honorable. No one knows what he wants. The situation is a punishment of God. Last year they started a society here, and who ever did not join, was persecuted and slandered. Everybody has to shout 'Viva Liberty, fraternity, equality'. There is a rumor that Baden is lost and we don't know to what country we belong. May the Lord help us.

Dear M. I received a letter from *Christine and her second husband, a short time ago. They went to a distant country (See Letter No. 15) to seek their fortune and took little Lawrence with them. They sent their

75

son to Philadelphia to learn his trade. Your aunt **Anna Maria Kern (grandmother Kerchner's aunt) was buried 8 days ago. (Letter No. 22) She was blind and bed-ridden for many years. R.I.P. Kilian Keck who married B. L. Kettinger (Letter No. 26) also died. He was a handsome young man. His wife died 4 months later and shortly after that his mother. They left behind them a boy 8 years old, delicately raised and he must now be brought up by strangers. Margaret has another boy, making the 9th child 6 of whom are living. Anna M. is again with child. Fear God and keep his commandments. Write soon. Live in peace. Your loving mother, Rosina.

*Christine, widow of David Kerchner.
**Anna Maria Kern—sister to John Dominic Kern (1781-1826).

No. 30. Jubilee Wishes of Grandmother Mussig to Fr. Rauch, 1844.

Unending thanksgiving to an all wise and overruling Providence, who has appointed over us so wise and kind a friend and father, and endowed him with so many gifts and graces. May God's wisdom and providence be praised and blessed, since we can not, dear father, thank you sufficiently for all the benefits you have conferred on us, still less can we hope to repay you. So we turn to the Heavenly Father and pray Him, to shower His graces and blessings on you, for your spiritual and temporal welfare, and for the fruitfulness of your ministry as a good shepherd. We are most grateful to God our most dear Father, for permitting you to celebrate this Golden Jubilee of your priesthood, and to enjoy the honors of this celebration. May the good God grant you many more years of peace and happiness, and we pray that when the final summons comes you will receive the reward which God has promised to a good and faithful servant.

Be pleased to receive the good wishes and congratulations, of all our family and believe me your most devoted and loyal friend,

Rosina Kerchner

Dear Rev. Cousin:—I am enclosing herewith a short letter which Mich Anthony sent in haste to his parents, that we might share with him the joy he experienced in the safe arrival of his friends. I am also sending you his address, trusting you might find it possible to send him some words of kindly advice, for his spiritual benefit.

Dear Michael:—

As our Rev. Cousin asked to see your letter I took the liberty of sending it to him, with the above little note. Rosina.

No. 31. John D. Kern to Grandmother M. A. Kerchner.

St. Genevieve, Mo. July 8, 1850

Dear Sister:—

I received your letter of April saying your husband had written me several times without receiving a reply. I also wrote twice to him, and *David Mussig* said he wrote twice and received no answer about the Herman lots. This is why I did not write again. I now have information about the lots. *David Mussig* has taken one of them for which I gave the

76

papers. He says he can't take the other because there is no deed. He took the papers to a certain place and they told him the lots were not worth much, and not worth bothering about. *Teresa Mussig's* husband was in Herman a few days ago, and brought the news that your lot was sold, the day before, but could still be redeemed. So I had a clerk write to Jefferson City and bought it back again in your husband's name. The Taxes are about $3.00. I don't know what David spent on it, and he tells me that one of the papers for the deed of sale is missing.

You may have it yourselves, for I have not seen it. As regards my family all are well, I have 3 sons and 3 daughters and live here in the city. You might call it a German village; but I will not live here much longer. I intend to go further up the Missouri River where there is better land, and better business than here. (i.e. St. Genevieve). All the other Freudenbergers who live here are well except *Kasper Kettinger* who died last year. Brother Matthew lives here and has a Hotel and restaurant at the landing place. He is married and has 3 children. I have already written to Stuben and received no answer. I also wrote to Germany, but it is useless because they do not answer.

      Greetings to you all. John D. Kern.

    (Note. John Dom. Kern married Regina Kettinger.)

No. 32. Nov. 18, 1854.
    Michael asks for assistance from his parents.
    Loss of money through the Winery. Bad times, bad people.

Dear Children and Relatives:—

There was a good reason for my delay in writing, for my eyes gave me great pain and prevented me from sleeping at night. I was thinking night and day how I might assist you. We have lost much this year and have earned nothing. We are 2 old people useless for any sort of work, and the day laborers cost us more than they can earn. We had neither fruit nor wine this year and the little wine we did store was sour. I wanted to give up the winery (The Strauswirth) but your father would not be persuaded. He said he would rather die than give up any of our property as long as we live. Our property suffered great loss because of the bad year. I consider it a divine punishment for the insolent letters you wrote about Germany. I am ashamed when America is mentioned, and Lawrence Mussig's letter almost made me feel you were a beggar. His mother is carrying it about with her, and I am ashamed of being seen anywhere. You will still receive a respectable portion from us and in this I have nothing on my conscience. I shall soon be 77, and it can't be long before the end, and we can't take anything with us. Yet I will trust in God; He will deal with me according to His wisdom, for the best. Dear Children I wish to speak quite plainly. It is a saying 'Easy come, easy go' "wie gewonnen, so geronnen." What your father intended, he has done. He bought a place installed new casks, and expensive wines, the whole installation costing considerable money. I was always opposed to this, and consequently there was a quarrel; he would not be advised and so the blessing of God is not with us. You can understand how we have gone behind. He could neither read or write and the winery was far from the house. The rascals stayed the whole night and paid nothing. At this particular time we dare not speak our mind to any one. Everything is Liberty, Fraternity, Equality. Judging from the noise, I often thought the tavern would be wrecked. We had to be satisfied if we spent the day without receiving blows. We have wicked people who rob one another, and even if the Prussians had not come we would have suffered all the same. We must be grateful that we still have some property.

This will remain; we shall give none of this away yet many day we haven't a kreutzer and don't know where to borrow. God be with you all.

Your loving mother, Rosina.

INDEX to the *Letters* of *Rosina Kerchner* addressed principally to her son Michael Anthony Kerchner. The Numbers refer to the number of each Letter.

Arrival of M. A. K. and family in America; 1.
Balz, 9
Baumann, 18
Blatz, 21
Brand, Franz, 12(f)
Cattle, hoof and mouth disease, 19
Children, duty of, towards parents, 25
Children, duty of parents towards, 5, 7, 10, 12, 15, 25.
Crops, bad, 7, 12(d), 14, 17, 25, 26
Crops, good, 5.
Drink, evil of, 8, 10
Ebert, Michael, 6, 12, 18, 19
Eve, 20
Flood disastrous, 25, 26
Forestry laws, 13.
Gerber, 18
Grandmother Rosina, K. wishes to come to America, 15, 18, 23, 26
Grimmien, 27
Gross, Barth. 13
Herz, Jakob, 22
Hess, Alois, 20
Jubilee, Golden, of Rev. Michael Rauch, 30
Kerchner, Anna M. 4, 11, 14, 15, 25, 27, 29
  Christine, 5, 12, 14, 20, 22, 25, 29
  David, 4, 5, 10, 16, 17, 19
  Egidius, 23, 25
  Kilian, 23
  Margaret, 4, 5, 7, 11, 13, 14, 15, 18, 25, 27, 29
Kerchner, Michael A. 7, 11, 13, 15
  Rosina, 18
Kern, Alois, 18
  Dominic, 4, 9, 11, 13
  Dorothy, 6, 8, 10, 12, 13, 16, 18, 19
  Eberhard, 24, 27
  Jos. Anthony, 4, 6, 8, 12

Matthew, 6, 8, 10, 13, 18 19, 31
Susan, 4, 20
Kettinger, Joseph A. 4, 12
Kaspar, 13, 19, 31
Katharine, 27
Matthew, 12
Regina, 4, 6
Kuhnel, Michel 5
Landkammer, 9
Letters, neglect of M.A.K. to answer, 21, 26
Liberty, Fraternity, Equality, in Germany, 29, 32
Long life and virtue, 18
Mai, Franz, 14, 25
Jakob, 7, 12, 18, 23, 25, 26
Leonard, 5, 18, 23, 25, 27
Michel, Amand, 4, 5, 10
Mussig, Alois, 4, 6, 12
  David, 12, 20, 31
  John Jos., 11, 12
  Lawrence, 13
  Michael, 10, 12, 18, 23, 28
  Rochus, 27
New Year Resolutions 19
Prayer, recommended, 7, 23
Rauch, Rev. Michael, 13, 18, 23, 25, 26, 28, 30
Saloon, evils of, 10, 23, 25
Schulreter, 11
St. Genevieve, Freudenberg of America, 31
Times, hard, 13, 15
Vaeth, Peter, 6, 13, 21, 30
Wanderlust disapproved 23, 25, 26
Wash Kettles and sanitary laws, 13
Wolf, Anna, 16, 22
  Lawrence, 12, 19
Ziner, Johann, 13
Zingerlein, Dorothy, 20
Zoeller, 25

REV. MICHAEL RAUCH (1758-1844)

In the Letters of my great grandmother, Rosina Müssig Kerchner, there is frequent reference to 'our Rev. Cousin'. For a long time I was convinced that 'our Rev. Cousin' was Rev. Father *Vaeth*. But then I was faced with the problem of his relationship. I was led to believe the name was Vaeth because the mother of Anna Maria Kern (my grandmother) was Margaret Vaeth. Letter after letter of inquiry was directed to Germany without result, until I finally addressed a letter to the Rev. Chancellor of the Diocese of Würzburg in which diocese the Parish of Freudenberg is located. To my great satisfaction the name of 'our Rev. Cousin' was definitely established by the Rev. Dr. Franz Bendel, Chancellor and Archivist of Würzburg. Below is a copy of his letter.

Office of the Diocesan Chancery   Würzburg, Dec. 17, 1937
In Ref. to your Nov. 28, 1937
    To
        Rev. F. W. Kunkel, S.S.
        St. Mary's Seminary

"The priest in question is not Father Vaeth, but Rev. Michael Rauch. He was born in Freudenberg a. Main, Nov. 2, 1758 and died as Pastor of Euerfeld, Nov. 25, 1844. I am sending you a copy of my Essay in which you will learn something of his activity. In regard to information concerning his family it will be necessary to address yourself to the Rev. Pastor of Freudenberg."

                              Signed—J. A.
                                  Dr. Franz Bendel,
                                      Archivar

The title of the pamphlet sent me by Rev. Dr. Bendel reads as fol.:

"The Diary of a Pastor of Lower Franconia. Notations of Rev. Michael Rauch, Pastor of Euerfeld (Dio. of Würzburg) concerning events in Franconia at the beginning of the 19th century."

Published by Subscription. Dr. Franz Bendel.

REV. M. RAUCH (2)
(Below follows the first paragraph of the Chronicle)

"Parish Chronicles ordinarily and quite naturally deal only with what concerns the Parish. The Pastor will not lightly consider it either a duty or a pleasure, to write the history of his country or of the world. Under certain circumstances, however, it might be most interesting to chronicle world happenings, as viewed from the belfry of a village church, provided the chronicler has the necessary breadth of view, an unshakable love for the truth, and is capable of giving a faithful narrative of the events. Rev. Michael Rauch has, happily, these three qualifications. It is a simple matter to give here a brief outline of his life. Born Nov. 2, 1758 in Freudenberg a. Main, ordained in Würzburg Dec. 21, 1782, he served for 15 years as assistant in Obersinn, and was then appointed Pastor of Euerfeld, with a mission at Biebergau.

He was Pastor of Euerfeld from 1797 to 1844 a period of 47 years. In the 62 years of his priesthood he had therefore only 2 appointments, one as assistant and the other as Pastor. As Pastor of Euerfeld he was Dean of the Dettelbach Deanery for 34 years. He died at the age of 86 and was active to the end of his life. To each of the 2 Parishes of Euerfeld and Biebergau he left the sum of 11,000 Florins to assist boys of the Parish in learning a trade."

(See Letters No. 25, 28 of Rosina Kerchner for reference to the Golden Jubilee of Father Rauch and an account of his will.)

Family of Rev. Michael Rauch

Father—Andreas Rauch

Mother—Margaretha Hockin

Children—Anna Maria,   b. 1745
         John Gabriel   1747
         Jos. Andrew   1750
         Jno. Ignat.   1754
         Anna Kath.   1756
         Michael (Rev.)   1758
         M. Barbara   1761

REV. M. RAUCH

The relationship of Father Rauch with the Kerchner family.

(1) Kasper Kerchner (b. 1751) mar. (2) Katharine Rauch (b. 1756)
(3) Paul Kerchner (1782-1826) mar. (4) Rosina Mussig (1778-1855)
(5) Michael A. Kerchner (1804-1857) mar. (6) Anna M. Kern (1806-1870)
(1) was the grandfather of my maternal grandfather (5)
(2) was the sister of Rev. Michael Rauch

The parents of Father Rauch were Andreas Rauch and Margaretha Hockin.

(2) Katharina Rauch (b. 1756, Sister of Rev. Michael Rauch was the maternal grandmother of MICHAEL A. KERCHNER, maternal grandfather of F. W. Kunkel.

Descendents of

MR. AND MRS. EMILE ULISSE HUGUENIN

to the

SIXTH GENERATION

Emile Ulisse Huguenin
(1810-1880)
Susanne Kern Huguenin
(1807-1896)

82

Baptismal Certificate of Emile Ulisse Huguenin

Emile Ulisse Huguenin Jean, son of Pierre Frederic, son of Gaspar Huguenin Jean, deceased, and of Augustine, daughter of Daniel Sandos Otheneret, his wife, born the eighteenth of June, 1810 (1810) has been baptized the 11th of August following.

    Godfather—Charles Daniel Saugy
    Godmother—Marie Esabeau Saugy, wife of Godfather.

The 25th day of December, 1828, Christmas day at the morning service, Emile Ulisse, son of Pierre Frederic Huguenin Jean, born at Locle, the 18th of June, 1819, baptized the 11th of August, has made a ratification of the baptismal promises and has been admitted to Communion.

    Certified

    Seal   Favre, Pastor.

Locle 20th of March, 1830.

Citizenship papers of *Emile Ulisse HUGUENIN*

    The Corporation of Locle, Principality and State of Neuchatel, Switzerland certifies that the bearer Emile Ulisse Huguenin Jean, son of Pierre Frederic, son of deceased Gaspard Huguenin Jean, Burgess of Valengin. Born in 1810, single man, is and will be at all times recognized as a member of said Corporation, which declares consequently that the above said member will be received by it at all times and in all circumstances.

    In faith of which the present act of origin has been sent him by the undersigned and following the deliberation of the Corporation in date of this day.

    So done at Locle, the 7th of March, 1830 by order
        The Secretary of the Corporation
        Prre. Fic. Huguenin, Jr.

The Officer of the jurisdiction certifies the authenticity of the above signature at Locle, the 8th of March, 1830. In absence of his Honor the Mayor, M. J. Flouriet, Lieutenant.

    As the Governor and Lieut. Gen. for his Majesty, the King of Prussia in the Principality and State of Neuchatel and Valengin in Switzerland. While recommending under offer of reciprocity the bearer to the good will and protection of the respective authorities, we certify that M. J. Flouriet, who has signed the above Declaration is Civil Lieutenant of the jurisdiction of Locle, and that all acts sent by him in that capacity, full and entire faith can be had, as well out of court as in court. We also declare that stamped papers and the control are not in use in this State.

Given in the Castle of Neuchatel 9th of March, 1830.

    By order of His Excellency the Governor

    The Secretary of State Council

    August de Montmollein.

EMILE U. HUGUENIN

RES. E. U. HUGUENIN
Cote Brilliante Ave., St. Louis

Jewelry Store
E. U. HUGUENIN & SONS

Death of E. U. Huguenin

(St. Louis—*Globe Democrat* 9-26-1880)

Cote Brilliante, St. Louis has lost one of its best citizens in the death of Emile U. Hugunin, who died on Saturday, September 25th, and now rests in Calvary Cemetery. He was a watchmaker in this city for nearly thirty years, and was so talented and successful a mechanic that he was pronounced the best watchmaker in St. Louis. He numbered among his numerous patrons many of the oldest and wealthiest families of the city, and by them, and all others who knew him, he was held in the highest esteem for the integrity of his character and his unhesitating opposition to everything mean and dishonorable.

He was in his seventy-first year. Born in the town of Locle, canton Neutchatel, Switzerland, celebrated for its families of Huguenins and others engaged in watchmaking, he emigrated to this country, arriving in Philadelphia about the year, 1830. Three years after this, he married Miss Susan Kern, who is now his widow and was all these years emphatically his best friend, counsellor and helper. On the day after his marriage he began business in a moderate style, but his premises being soon thereafter cleaned out by burglars who carried off his entire stock of goods and all his tools, he moved to Delaware. Thence he went to Maryland, doing business at Princess Anne and Cambridge. In these places and in Baltimore he will be remembered by old residents as a desirable citizen and a mechanic of great skill. His reputation was so great that watches and guns were sent to him for repair from distant places.

When he left Cambridge, it was to go to Ste. Genevieve, Mo., and there he remained for about two years. He then came to St. Louis. The first store he opened here was on Washington Avenue, between Seventh and Eighth Streets, where now stand some of the finest buildings.

Dr. R. M. Swander was his physician and friend.

The remains of the deceased were buried last Sunday, September 26th, and were followed to the grave by a large number of friends and relations. Messrs. M. A. Wolff, B. A. Hickman, E. P. Gray and C. F. Walther acted as pallbearers, and the funeral services were conducted in the church of the Holy Ghost, Parson Street, by the Rev. Mr. Busch, who delivered an appropriate sermon. He knew the deceased personally—his virtues and the exemplary life he had lived; a good man is dead, but his virtues are as lasting as time. We were intimately associated with him for a long period, and our tears testify to our love and respect.

But, E. U. Huguenin no longer suffers pain, nor will his grand soul ever again be penetrated with sorrow and sympathy for the misfortunes of others.

Will of Susanna Huguenin. The will of Susanna Huguenin, widow of the late Emile U. Huguenin was yesterday filed for probate. She leaves to her son Fred all her interest in the jewelry business, and bequeaths the homestead at 4570 Taylor Avenue to her daughter, Elladine, with all the household goods in this residence. Other real estate in St. Louis and a farm of 320 acres in Reynolds Co. are left to Julia C. Ryland, wife of A. L. Ryland, Fred U. Hugunin and Millard Filmore Hellery, son of Zelline Hellery.

85

MR. AND MRS. FRED U. HUGUNIN

FRED U. HUGUNIN AND FAMILY
*Mr. and Mrs. Fred U. Hugunin, Emil U. Bertha May,
Ethel Zelma, Grandson Hugunin Miller.*

86

ZELLINE HUGUENIN HELLERY (1838-1904)
(Funeral notice local paper)

The funeral of Mrs. Zelline Hellery, mother of M. Filmore Hellery, who died Wednesday afternoon, will take place at 9:30 o'clock this morning, at the new Cathedral chapel, Maryland and Newstead Aves., Rev. Francis Gilfillan officiating. Mrs. Hellery was the widow of Henry Hellery who died in 1880, after having been for many years connected with the steamboat business on the Mississippi. She was born in Delaware City in Delaware in 1837 and came to St. Louis in 1852 with her father, Emil U. Hugunin. She married Mr. Hellery 3 years later. She leaves four daughters. They are Mrs. John I. Haynes, Mrs. Chas. H. Stevens, and Misses Clara and Mamie Hellery. Mrs. Hellery's death was due to pneumonia.

M. FILMORE HELLERY (1851-1903)
(Notice of St. Louis Globe Democrat).

M. Filmore Hellery for years known as 'Fil' Hellery, proprietor of a restaurant and buffet opposite the Merchants Exchange, has been unconscious since last Friday and sinking rapidly at his residence, 4010 Olove Street. Dropsy and complications have kept him confined to his bed for the last 2 weeks. The last sacraments were administered by Rev. Father Francis X. Mara Thursday evening. Mrs. Chas. H. Stevens, wife of the paymaster of the Iron Mountain Railroad is rushing home from a tour of the Rockies to reach the bedside of her brother before he expires. Dr. Wm. F. Kier informed the relatives that his death is probably a matter of hours. The house is guarded against visitors as the relatives do not wish the patient to be disturbed. At the bedside of Mr. Hellery are his wife and 3 sisters, Mrs. John I. Haynes, wife of the architect, Mrs. Fred D. Marshall wife of a police sergeant, another sister, Miss Mary Hellery, residing at Leechburg, Pa., has been notified. Mr. Hellery has been engaged in business in St. Louis for more than 30 years. His buffet at 312 No. Third Street has long been the rendezvous for members of the Exchange, among whom Hellery made many friends. High Mass was sung at the College Church. Several hundred business men attended the services.

87

FREDERICK ULISSE HUGUENIN (b. 1851)
Up to May 1941 Chief Time Inspector for the Wabash R.R.
From "The Wabash Club News" June 1941

Mr. F. U. Huguenin our General Time Inspector celebrated his 90th Birthday, May 28th. Mr. Huguenin is remarkably alert and active, attending his duties at his office in the Railway Exchange Building every day.

His employees surprised him with a little party and a big cake.

We hope that the Goddess Atropos will continue in her benign mood.

88

MRS. CLARA MARSHALL
Wife of Fred Marshall (1862-1926)
Daughter of Henry Hellery and Zelline Hugunin.

89

JOHN I. HAYNES

"Fifty years ago, Geo. D. Barnett and John I. Haynes, architects and draughtsmen, in the Office of Commissioner of Buildings, Furlong of St. Louis, resigned to go into business under the firm name of BARNETT & HAYNES, ARCHITECTS." The St. Louis, *Star Times*, Sept. 28, 1939.

Mr. John I. Haynes, born in 1860, is now in his eighty-first year. Although he has retired from the architectural business, he is nevertheless actively engaged in an enterprise that promises to revolutionize the automotive industry. The firm of Barnett and Haynes was responsible for the Transportation Building of the St. Louis International Exposition of 1893, Hotel Jefferson, the Adolphus Hotel of Dallas, Tex., many smaller Hotels, Apartment Houses and Business Buildings from Coast to Coast. He supervised the construction of the magnificent St. Louis Cathedral and built many Catholic Churches, Hospitals and other Catholic Institutions in various parts of the country. He was happily married to Miss Harriet Hellery, daughter of Henry and Zelline Huguenin Hellery, who died in 1932.

90

DESCENDENTS OF
SUSANNA KERN and EMIL ULYSSE HUGUENIN

I. Generation	II. Generation	Birth-Death
	HUGUENIN	
1. Susanna Kern (1807-1896)	3. Uline Constance	1834-1926
2. Emil U. Huguenin (1810-1880) St. Louis	4. Mary Marg.	1835-1904
	5. Zelline	1838-1904
	6. Josephine	1845-1929
	7. Elladine	1848-1923
	8. Frederick	1851-

II. Generation	III. Generation	
	RYLAND	
3. Uline Constance Huguenin (1834-1926)	10. Olivia S.	1862-1920
9. Alston L. Ryland (1829-1899) St. Louis	11. Laura I.	1864-1876
	12. Richard	1865-1865
	13. Robert R.	1866-1940
	14. Uline C.	1869-
	15. Cecelia	1870-
	16. Edw. Alston	1872-1936
	JAQUES	
4. Mary Marg. Huguenin (1835-1904)	18. Ida	1858-1935
17. Chas. B. Jaques Chicago	19. May	1860-1886
	20. Charles	1861-1880
	21. Guy	1863-
	22. Edgar	1871-1906
	HELLERY	
5. Zelline Huguenin (1838-1904)	24. Millard Filmore	1856-1908
23. Henry H. Hellery (1835-1880) St. Louis	25. Elladine M.	1858-1860
	26. Clara	1860-
	27. Henry Huguenin	1862-1887
	28. Marg. Mary	1867-1935
	29. Harriet	1869-1932
	30. Susan	1871-1916
	31. George	1873-1880
	KEUTHAN	
6. Josephine Huguenin (1845-1929)	33. Louise H.	1861-1929
32. John H. Keuthan (1843-1878) St. Louis	34. Henry E.	1865-
	35. Anne Belle	1870-1929
	36. Joseph H.	1878-1937
	HUGUENIN	
8. Fred. Ulysses Huguenin (1851-	38. Emil H.	1873-1922
37. Kath. Everett Liggett (1853- St. Louis	39. Bertha May	1881-
	40. William F.	1887-1893
	41. Ethel Zelma	1890-
	42. Edward	1890-1893

III. Generation	IV. Generation	
	MILSTER	
14. Uline C. Ryland (1869-	44. Arthur N., Jr.	1902-
43. Arthur N. Milster, D.D.S. (1867-1901) St. Louis		
15. Cecelia Ryland (1870-		
45. Richard S. Standish (1877-1935) St. Louis		

91.

III. Generation	IV. Generation	Birth-Death
	RYLAND	
16. Alston Edward Ryland (1872-1930)	47. Alston L.	1901-
46. Celestine B. McLin (1877-1930) San Francisco	48. Lyda E. 49. Robert D. 50. Uline C. 51. Henrietta R. 52. Garland C.	1902- 1904- 1906- 1909- 1911-
	COULSON	
18. Ida Jaques (1858-1935) 53. Benjamin Coulson (1852-1893) Houston, Texas	54. J. Arthur	1889-
19. May Jaques (1860-1886) 53. B. Coulson (1852-1893) Houston, Texas	COULSON 55. Vaughn le Compte	1885-
21. Guy Jaques (1863- 66. Sophie Scharle (1873- Chicago	JAQUES 57. Lillian 58. Norman 59. Joseph 60. Katherine 61. Ruth	1895-1915 1897-1922 1900- 1904-1911 1906-
22. Edgar Jaques (1871-1906) 62. Gertrude Mazander (1878- Chicago 24. Millard Filmore Hellery (1856-1908) 64. Lillian Getty St. Louis 26. Clara Hellery (1860- 65. Fred Marshall (1862-1926) St. Louis	JAQUES 63. Myrtle	1898-
27. Henry Huguenin Hellery (1862-1887) 66. Clara F. Peckham (1863- St. Louis 29. Harriett Hellery (1869-1932) 69. John I. Haynes (1860- St. Louis 30. Susan Hellery (1871-1918) 70. Charles Stevens St. Louis	HELLERY 67. Zelline 68. Georgeanna	1884- 1886-1929
33. Louisiana Keuthen (1861-1929) 71. Geo. W. Reuter, Sr. (1863-1935) St. Louis	REUTER 72. Lillian B. 73. Geo. W., Jr. 74. Anne E. 75. Ida Mae 76. Robert R.	1888- 1889- 1892- 1896- 1901-

III. Generation	IV. Generation	Birth-Death
	KEUTHAN	
34. Henry E. Keuthan (1865- 77. Ada May Turner (1875- St. Louis	78. Ella	1897-
	STILLMAN	
35. Anna Belle Keuthan (1870-1929) 79. James Walter Stillman (1867-1929) St. Louis	80. James Curtis 81. Josephine Clara 82. Wm. Walter 83. Marion Albert 84. Robert Bailey 85. Eliz. Belle 86. Joseph Martin 87. Arthur Sidney 88. Thomas Clarence 89. Edward Lawrence	1888- 1891- 1893- 1895- 1897- 1899- 1901- 1903- 1906- 1906-
38. Emil H. Huguenin (1873-1922) 90. Alma Schulenberg St. Louis		
	MILLER	
39. Berthia May Huguenin (1881- 91. Aug. Julius Miller St. Louis	92. Fred. Huguenin	1907-
IV. Generation 44. Arthur N. Milster (1902- 93. Ruth Murdock (1902- St. Louis 47. Alston L. Ryland (1901- 94. Lillian Bell (1901- St. Louis	V. Generation	
	HAMILTON	
50. Uline C. Ryland (1906- 95. Murray Hamilton Redwood, Calif.	96. Robert E.	1930-
	FRANCIS	
51. Henrietta R. Ryland (1909- 97. Gerald C. Francis (1908- Detroit	98. Gerald A.	1931-
	COULSON	
55. Joseph A. Coulson (1890- 99. Ida Howard (1892- Houston, Texas 57. Lillian Jaques (1895-1915) 100. Elmer Wulfmeir (1894- Chicago	98. (a) Violet	1909-

IV. Generation	V. Generation	Birth-Death
	JAQUES	
58. Norman Jaques (1897-1922)	102. Norman, Jr.	1919-
101. Clara Valeria (1898- Michigan City, Ind.	103. Vernon	1922-
	JAQUES	
59. Joseph Jaques (1900-	105. Joseph	1938-
104. Ruth Pettle Chicago	105. (a) Andrew Gale	1941-
61. Ruth Jaques (1906-		
106. Andrew J. Doyle (1912- Chicago		
	FRIEDE	
63. Myrtle Jaques (1898-	108. Myrene	1918-
107. Myron Friede (1888- Chicago	109. Jane	1920-
	DOUGLAS	
67. Zelline Hellery (1884-	111. John Henry	1911-1913
110. Holme Douglas (1884-1926) St. Louis	112. George Albert	1913-
	MAGILL	
72. Lillian B. Reuter (1888-	114. Georgia	1908-
113. Charles Magill (1875- St. Louis	115. Dorothy Jane	1920-
	REUTER	
73. Geo. W. Reuter (1889-	117. Ralph	1913-
116. Anna Ploch (1893- St. Louis		
	WHITNEY	
74. Anne E. Reuter (1892-	119. Marg. Louise	1913-
118. Wm. Henry Whitney, Jr. (1890- Pine Lawn, Mo.		
	FIELDS	
75. Ida Mae Reuter (1886-	121. Jessie May	1917-
120. Guy B. Fields (1891- St. Louis	122. Clara Bell	1923-
	123. Guy B., Jr.	1926-
	124. Grover	1928-
	125. Roy Raymond	1930-
	126. Jackie	1932-
	127. Joan	1933-
	128. Jean Fay	1936-
	129. David Lawrence	1940-
76. Robert Ray Reuter (1901-		
130. Esther Louise Flottmann (1901- St. Louis		
80. James Curtis Stillman (1888-		
132. Mary Nixon 1902- St. Louis		

94

IV. Generation	V. Generation	Birth-Death
	WEISS	
81. Josephine Clara Stillman	134. James Thomas	1915-
1891-	135. Elmer Albert	1918--1919
133. Thomas Ely Weiss	136. Robert Wm.	1920-
(1891-	137. Helen Josephine	1929-
St. Louis		
82. Wm. Walter Stillman		
(1893-1938)		
138. Norine Mulken		
St. Louis		
83. Marion Albert Stillman		
(1895-		
139. Esther Miller		
St. Louis		
84. Robt. Bailey Stillman		
(1897-		
140. Bessie Dath		
St. Louis		
85. Eliz. Belle Stillman		
(1899-		
141. Edward Cornish		
St. Louis		
87. Arthur Sidney Stillman		
(1903-		
142. Juanita McManamee		
St. Louis		
	MILLER	
92. Fred. Huguenin Miller, Sr.	144. Fred Huguenin, Jr.	1939-
(1907-		
143. Ruth de Bow		
(1908-		
Los Angeles, Calif.		

V. Generation	VI. Generation	
	BROWNHILL	
98. (a) Violet Coulson	146. Robert	1930-
(1909-	147. James	1932-
145. Eable F. Brownhill		
(1908-		
Houston, Texas		
102. Norman Jaques, Jr.		
(1919-		
145. Lona Edwards		
Chicago		
109. Jane Friede	WEBER	
(1920-	147. Joel Ralph	1939-
146. Ralph Fred. Weber		
(1920-		
Chicago		
114. Georgia Magill	COOK	
(1906-	149. Thomas, Jr.	1924-
148. Thomas Cook, Sr.		
St. Louis		
117. Ralph Reuter		
(1918-		
149. Mary Single		
(1908-		
St. Louis		

V. Generation	VI. Generation	Birth-Death
	MC CREA	
119. Marg. Louise Whitney	151. Gloria	1929-
(1911-	152. Beverly	1934-
150. Ray McCrea	153. Margie Anne	....-
(1909-	154. Mary Anne	1937-
St. Louis		
	MILLER	
121. Jessie May Fields	* 156. Ray, Jr.	1940-
(1917-		
155. Ray Miller		
St. Louis		
134. James Thomas Weiss		
(1915-		
158. Bernice Laura Fuches		
(1915-		
St. Louis		
136. Robt. Wm. Weiss		
(1920-		
159. Evangeline Kruzick		
(1919-		
St. Louis		

96

II Generation

KERN

I Generation			
5. Dominic Kern	27. Wilhelmina	(1835-1913)	108 descendents
(1811-1871)	28. John Edward	(1839-1877)	62 descendents
Regina Kettinger	29. Mary	(1840-1918)	12 descendents
(1812-1886)	30. Charles	(1844-1911)	31 descendents
	31. William	(1847-1891)	53 descendents
	32. Josephine	(1850-1935)	24 descendents
	33. August	(1853-1939)	22 descendents
	34. Julia	(1856-1914)	41 descendents

97

Original letters in German of Dominic and Regina Kern in the possession of Rev. F. W. K.

Freudenburg, Jan. 6, 1833.
Dominic Kern to Michael A. Kerchner

Dear Brother-in-law:

I wish to let Joseph Anthony Kern (1809-1848) know about our going to America but don't know if he is still in Hamburg, so can't say if he will go with us. I would like to know why Susanna did not write us at the same time that you wrote. Can we buy property in your neighborhood? Answer before Easter if possible; but if we do not hear from you we shall have plenty to do this summer. My family are all well and send greetings to yourself and family and to Susanna.

(signed) *Dominic Kern.*

DOMINIC KERN 1811-1871

Dominic Kern to his relatives in America.
Freudenberg, Nov. 28, 1834.

Dear Brothers, Sisters and Brothers-in-law:—

I was married to my neighbor, *Regina Kettinger*, September 8th. All our friends gathered together and we danced till 5:00 A.M. Three weeks later Gerhard Kern married Gertrude Müssig, daughter of Alois, and the same friends gathered again. Many sad things occurred this year. Gerhard Kern lost his wife, Lawrence, the son of Alois Mussig, was drowned, our youngest sister Regina died of dysentery, the wife of

98

Michael Ebert died September 17th and Mrs. Peter Vaeth died on Gerhard Kern's wedding day. Joseph Anthony wrote to me about a year and a half ago, from Hamburg. I always wanted him to remain at home but it was useless to advise him. Matthew (1816-1893) has put off his departure to the Spring, and Dorothy (1820-1903) is still with Michael Ebert. The little brothers and sisters are all well and send greetings.

(Signed) Dominic and Regina Kern.

Dominic Kern to Michael Kerchner
Freudenberg, Mar. 10, 1835.

Dear Brother-in-law:—

Matthew Kern can't come yet because he is not able to draw his money before the age of 20. Dorothy is still with Michael Ebert. As soon as Matthew reaches his 20th year I believe both he and Dorothy will come. I have not heard of Joseph Anthony for 2 years.

(signed) Dominic Kern.

REGINA KERN
1812-1886

Another letter of Dominic and Regina Kern to Michael Kerchner
Freudenberg, Feb. 5, 1836.

Dear Brother-in-law:

I shall be glad if this letter finds you in good health. I received your letter the 2nd of this month, but hear you did not get your mother's letter. Both she and myself are anxiously waiting for an answer to her letter, and can't understand why you did not receive it. There is nothing new except that my wife gave birth to a daughter (Wilhelmina) July 28, 1835. Matthew left in the fall to go to America. Joseph Anthony wrote 8 days ago from Hamburg, the first letter in a year. Dorothy still with Michael Ebert, our mother Erhard and Joseph are well. Jos. Anth. Kettinger died.

(signed) Dominic and Regina Kern.

Obituary Notice—Mrs. Regina Kern (nee Kettinger)

Ste. Genevieve, Mo.—Sept. 18, 1886.

JOHN DOMINIC KERN (1811-1871)

(The Baltimore 'Sun')

News from Ste. Genevieve near St. Louis, Mo. mentions the death of John Dominic Kern, a well known farmer, whose extensive lands adjoin Ste. Genevieve, a number of whose relatives reside in Baltimore. Deceased was nearly sixty years of age. It is mentioned that one of his sisters is the wife of a well known watchmaker of St. Louis, who was a long time resident of Cambridge, Md. whence he moved West about 1852 and was a subscriber to *The Sun* for upwards of 15 years.

MRS. JOHN DOMINIC KERN (1812-1886)

On Saturday, Sept. 11, 1886, at the residence of her daughter Mrs. Max Bader of Ste. Genevieve, after a long and painful illness of 49 days, Mrs. Regina Kern nee Kettinger at the age of 72 years, 5 months and 1 day. The funeral preceded by a solemn Requiem Mass in the Catholic Church, took place in the Valle Spring Cemetery on Monday and was marked by an extraordinary number of mourners who had assembled to attend the remains to their last resting place.

The departed was born in Freudenberg, Baden, April 10, 1814 was married to John D. Kern and followed her husband to America, where he had resolved to make his new home. After a sojourn of several years in the East the couple came to Ste. Genevieve County, July 22, 1840, where they lived the rest of their days honored and respected by all. More than 15 years ago Mr. Kern preceded his wife in death. As fruit of the happy union there are still living seven children, two in California, 1 in Texas and four in Ste. Genevieve, and 38 grand-children. The deceased was a good Christian, a kind mother and a faithful wife. May she rest in peace.

100

WILHELMINA ETTER (1835-1913)

THE MOTHER OF ALBERT F. ETTER

Mrs. Wilhelmina Kern Etter, A Model Mother

From the San Francisco "Monitor"—Jan. 25, 1913.

On the evening of the 17th inst. there passed away at Ferndale, Humboldt County, a woman remarkable in many ways. Mrs. Wilhelmina Etter, the mother of thirteen children, twelve sons and one daughter, ten of whom survive, was not only one of the best known, but also one of the very best and most charitable women in Humboldt County.

Born in Baden, Germany, nearly eighty years ago, she was brought an infant to the United States. Her parents settled in St. Genevieve, Missouri, where she grew to womanhood and married Mr. Benjamin Etter in 1854. In the early sixties the family moved to Placerville, California, where they remained till the spring of 1876, when they went to Humboldt County.

Since then the members of this family have been widely identified with the agricultural development and interests of the county. The nine surviving sons are not only prominent farmers owning large tracts of land, but also among the most skilled horticulturists in the northern part of the State.

Mr. Albert Etter, always in great demand at the Agricultural Institutes, may well be styled the Burbank of Northern California.

The father of this distinguished family having died nearly twenty-five years ago, the training and management of the family devolved almost entirely on Mrs. Etter.

How well she performed her duty may be inferred from the fact that the children never moved far away from her, and were as obedient and submissive to her in their mature years as in childhood.

Her strong Catholic faith characterized her everywhere she went and all her children are equally devoted to the practice of the ancient faith.

Mrs. Etter was widely known for her charities, and her great generosity to the poor. During all her years in Humboldt County she supplied her parish church with flowers raised under her personal supervision in her own beautiful garden. The Ferndale parish will miss her. Her sympathies were as broad as human needs.

For more than a quarter of a century she was the chief solicitor for St. Joseph's Union in Ferndale, and her success indicated how zealous she was in the cause of the homeless boys.

Mrs. Etter belonged to a generation of sturdy Catholics who are fast passing away, with the one difference that she has left behind her those who are proud of her faith and good works, and will likely follow her footsteps to the end.

The Monitor, to which she was a subscriber for many years, extends its sympathy to Miss Etter and the other members of the bereaved family. May the soul of Mrs. Wilhelmina Etter rest in everlasting peace.

DESCENDENTS OF WILHELMINA KERN

II. Generation	III. Generation	Birth-Death
	ETTER	
3. Wilhelmina Kern	12. Benjamin	1856-1862
(1835-1913)	13. Louise	1858-1935
11. Benjamin Etter	14. Emil	1861-
(1822-1889)	15. Jules	1863-1937
	16. George	1866-1930
	17. William J.	1867-1886
	18. Fred	1869-1938
	19. Albert F.	1872-
	20. August	1875-
	21. Francis	1879-
	22. Louis	1879-1937
	23. Walter	1882-

III. Generation	IV. Generation	
	ETTER	
14. Emil Etter	25. Mary	1889-
(1861-	26. Joseph	1891-
24. Minnie Schallard	27. Gertrude	1895-
(1866-	28. Charles E.	1900-
Upper Mattole, Calif.	29. Benjamin	1903-
	30. Raymond	1908-1918
	ETTER	
15. Jules Etter	32. William	1901-
(1863-1937)	33. Norine	1904-
31. Genieve Haley	34. Genevieve	1906-
(1877-	35. Wilhelmina	1909-
Mrs. Genevieve Morse—2d Mar.	36. Marie Jos.	1913-1926
Orick, Calif.	37. Edward Jules	1915-
	ETTER	
16. George Etter	39. Anna	1894-
(1866-1930)	40. Eleanor	1896-
38. Margaret Hogan	41. Clarence	1899-
(1875-1929)	42. Verna	1901-
	43. Cecil	1904-
	44. Adrian	1905-
	45. Eldred	1908-
	46. Marjorie Dol.	1910-
	47. Hermione	1913-
	ETTER	
18. Fred Etter	49. Leo	1912-
(1869-1938)	50. Cyril F.	1914-
48. Margaret Bailey	51. Bernard F.	1917-
(1880-		
Ettersburg, Calif.		
	ETTER	
19. Albert F. Etter		
(1872-		
52. Katherine A. McCormack		
Ettersburg, Calif.		
	ETTER	
21. Francis X. Etter	54. Alma T.	1906-
(1878-	55. Donald E.	1908-
53. Dora Hill	56. Keith T.	1909-
(1882-	57. Edgar L.	1912-
Petrolia, Calif.	58. Frances M.	1917-

103

III. Generation	IV. Generation	Birth-Death
	ETTER	
23. Walter B. Etter		
(1882-		
59. Anna M. McAllister		
(1895-		
Weotty, Calif.		
	SHINN	
25. Mary Etter	61. Evelyn	1911-
(1888-	62. Mary	1913-
60. Vernile Shinn	63. Margaret	1915-
(1886-1930)	64. Alice	1917-
Honey Dew, Calif.	65. Vernon E.	1920-
	66. Anna	1923-
26. Joseph Etter		
(1891-		
67. Alice Glackin		
Honey Dew, Calif.		
	PETERSON	
27. Gertrude Etter	69. Paul	1918-
(1895-	70. Francis	1919-
68. Clyde Peterson	71. Clyde	1922-
Honey Dew, Calif.	72. Barbara P.	1929-
	73. Elizabeth L.	1935-
	74. Elbert A.	1935-
	ETTER	
28. Charles E. Etter	76. Delaria	1937-
(1900-	77. Edward C.	1939-
75. Jennie Peterson		
(1906-		
Honey Dew, Calif.		
	ETTER	
29. Benjamin Etter	79. Marrion	1933-
(1903-		
78. Eva Larkin		
(1908-		
Honey Dew, Calif.		
	ETTER	
32. William H. Etter	81. Richard William	1932-
(1901-	82. Raymond Kenneth	1934-
80. Dagmar Freeman		
(1907-		
Pittsburg, Calif.		
	WALUND	
33. Norine M. Etter	84. Doris	1922-
(1904-	85. Marjorie	1924-
83. John Walund		
(1903-		
R.F.D. 1, Box 76,		
Eureka, Calif.		
	DODGE	
34. Genevieve T. Etter	87. Lois Marie	1927-
(1906-1930)	88. Eugene L.	1929-
86. Wilmer Dodge		
(1905-		
Orick, Calif.		
35. Wilhelmina Ruth Etter		
(1909-		
89. Lester Steenfott		
(1904-		
Orick, Calif.		

104

IV. Generation	V. Generation	Birth-Death
39. Anna Etter (1894-) 90. Gaylord Dearborn Eureka, Calif.		
40. Eleanor Etter (1896-) 91. Joseph Hull Garberville, Calif.	HULL 92. James C. 93. Carol A.	1924- 1926-
41. Clarence O. Etter (1899-) 94. Katherine Goe Holmes, Calif.	ETTER 95. Gwendolyn	1926-
42. Verna Etter (1901-) 96. Jerome L. Carrow Kingman, Ariz.	CARROW 97. James J.	1931-
43. Cecil Etter (1904-) 98. Lola Cooper Star Rte. Eureka, Calif.		
44. Adrian Etter (1905-) 99. Gertrude Herman Briceland, Calif.	ETTER 100. Betty Jean 101. Harold Leroy	1933- 1936-
45. Eldred Etter (1908-) 102. Doris Sweet Fortuna, Calif.		
46. Marjorie D. Etter (1910-) 103. Ralph French Ettersburg, Calif.	FRENCH 104. Shirley 105. Glen 106. Jack	1926- 1929- 1931-
107. Fred Fearrien—2nd Mar. 47. Hermione Etter (1913-) 109. Nell Keith Eureka, Calif.	FEARRIEN 108. Richard D.	1936-
V. Generation 64. Alice Shinn (1917-) 110. Melvin Rynberg Upper Mattole, Calif.		

105

ALBERT ETTER (b. 1872)
Horticulturist of Ettersburg, Calif.

BEFORE THE REDWOOD PARK IDEA WAS BORN

Albert F. Etter

(From the Redwood Record, Garberville, Calif., Dec. 22, 1938)

    Everything in the way of progress has had to begin somewhere. Oftentimes the original conception that eventually developed into a big idea, is lost forever to the world.
    In the case of the Redwood Parks I, at least, know the inmost facts even to the beginning. Reared as a boy among the great trees that once made a mighty park of Eel River valley when the white man arrived I learned to love the forest. As these trees were felled one by one by the settlers in clearing the land I felt that we were losing something of beauty forever. Today even though the valley is worth more to man, it does not compare in beauty to the brush-wood and open park of 60 years ago, as I saw it when a small boy.
    It is self-evident when in 1904, I made a trip to visit the Louisiana Purchase Exposition, in St. Louis, the one thing I missed was real forest trees. To my notion I saw no trees worthy of being regarded as forest trees. On Nov. 21st, I was a dinner guest of Mr. Henry Baumann of Ste. Genevieve, Mo., one of the quaintest and oldest towns of the Mississippi valley. Naturally our conversation drifted to trees and I learned from my host that he had never seen a tree over 100 feet high and may be 2½ feet in diameter. Mr. Baumann wanted me to tell him what a redwood tree looked like. The only object to which I could compare a redwood tree was the brick tower of Union Station in St. Louis. I remarked that that big tower looked like the trunk of a redwood tree but it was but a third as high. So he asked me how the great buildings of Forest Park impressed me. I told him I had failed to find any forest in Forest Park, and as for getting a thrill out of them, after having once walked through a redwood forest, was like to comparing a wigwam with a great cathedral.
    But it was only when I arrived back in Humboldt that I realized the real magnificence of our forest trees and felt sorry for the millions who never saw a real forest such as we know it. I felt we really had the eighth wonder of the world and should use it as a boosting asset as well as a source of lumber.
    It was, I think in 1907, that the Eureka Chamber of Commerce called delegates from all over the country to boost for a railroad to Eureka. I was not among the delegates nor did I attend the meeting, but I wrote my friend Geo. H. Kellogg, Secretary of the Chamber of Commerce to stress the idea that if a railroad was built, our redwood forest would be a genuine drawing card to induce tourists to travel over our railroad and visit us to our advantage, for where many come always a few stayed. I suggested that we have one of our best groves set apart as a State Redwood Park. My letter was read before the delegation but no action was taken. It was the first public appeal for a Redwood Park.
    A year later another meeting of delegates was called to promote the idea of building a railroad to connect Eureka with the outside world. I again wrote to Mr. Kellogg and enlarged on the idea of a Redwood Park. This time I asked that we start the ball rolling to establish a great national redwood park, and carry our campaign back to Washington. I felt we could get a lot of good publicity in such a campaign. My idea was

put into a Resolution and acted upon. A committee was appointed including Miss Laura Perrott, Frank Stern and others I do not remember. Thus under this redwood park committee, active work was begun to get a Redwood Park for Humboldt.

As late as 1914 realizing that the Redwood Park idea was making slow progress, while in San Francisco I had published in the San Francisco Chronicle an article trying to help the cause along by suggesting the idea of Memorial Parks, such as we now have. I went further by suggesting the purchase of a tract in trust, the same to be paid for by individuals who would purchase trees therein as "family trees" each tree being marked by the name of the purchaser of same.

Herein we have the most intimate facts relating to the early history of our Redwood Parks for record. I pioneered the way like 'a scout in the wilderness' for others to follow up. I was never asked for advice or help to get the parks. Fittingly my name means 'pioneering the way' or 'the beginning of progress'. In this manner I played my part.

(Note. In submitting the above, Albert Etter, the author does not do so with any desire for credit or publicity, but only as a matter of history, as the origin of the Redwood Parks idea, has never been published, he states.)

BREEDING THE APPLE. A LESSON IN INDUSTRY

LIFE'S WORK ON A FARM BRINGS MANY RESULTS

ALBERT F. ETTER

(From the Humboldt Times, Sept. 24, 1939).

A PERSONAL NOTE

In writing this article it is my desire to put some historical facts on record, rather than indulge in self-adulation. Most people in Humboldt know something about Ettersburg, but few if any know very much about it. In as much as I am the only person, able to write the whole story I will assume all the responsibility and take all the blame.

In the beginning Ettersburg was all a dream of an enthusiastic youth who was willing and anxious to pit mother wit and studied program to develop observation and originality of mind against the wisdom of ages and the training as represented by the universities.

The lineup in the contest was about as we boys used to run up against in school: "Carthage, old, rich and crafty—Rome, young, poor and robust." The subject was to solve the age old apple riddle: "From where did our apples come and how to breed them." The contest began in the early '90's and is still going strong.

Far from being a haphazard start with all the science on the side of the University Experiment Stations, as time goes on it would seem the most scientific thing that could be done to insure a favorable outcome was the wisdom of selecting Ettersburg as the site for an apple breeding station.

From the beginning I felt that I should win, and today as one surveys the outlook here, and notes what the universities have accomplished as the Year Book records, it would seem an 'old hill billy' reading first-hand from the book of nature, has a favorable outlook indeed, to lead the way as decisively as he did in strawberry breeding.

108

When Prof. E. J. Wickson, dean of the Agricultural College of the University of California, first heard of my ambition to start experiments in apple breeding in the hopes of cracking the apple riddle, away back in 1897 he fell for it at once and did all he could to help me get started on a long apple trail that might lead on for a lifetime. He not only sent me all the material available in apple varieties, over 600 varieties, but gave me personal encouragement as well. Blessed indeed the young man who could count on the approbation and counsel of a man as wise as Prof. Wickson.

A WARNING OF PROF. WICKSON

One evening as I talked to the old Professor he told me that if I actually discovered worth while lanes leading to success, I would meet with opposition I did not dream of—something I did not then dream was possible. The status was simply that of the old Maine farmer who told in court that a neighbor threatened to knock a bale of hay out of him. He declared "from a 'theological' point of view the threat didn't amount to much, but since he actually did do it, the fact should be considered by the court."

In writing the article about Strawberry Breeding, in the Year Book, Dr. Darrow gave credit for the work carried on at Ettersburg. But in apple breeding at Ettersburg, Prof. Magnuss made no mention whatever, though it is not possible he could have been ignorant of what had been going on, because the information asked for had been forwarded to Dr. Darrow as requested.

PROF. WICKSON'S PROPHECY OF 17 YEARS AGO

The following is copied from the Pacific Rural Press in 1922. "To the Editor:—I am sending a selection of some of my new varieties of apples. I have pried the lid up enough to peek under it and it looks good to me—a veritable treasure house that is going to give new varieties of apples by the hundred. The prospect looks so good to me that I am proceeding to develop thousands of seedlings. The preliminary work is now done and the light good enough to go ahead at full speed. The whole problem is now as simple as breeding up a good herd of dairy cows when one has a good herd to begin with. I have probably 50 varieties as good as those I am now sending because they are now ripe. I will send more varieties as they ripen. Albert F. Etter.

"The foregoing is a personal note which we take the liberty of printing because it reveals the spirit and enterprise of the writer better than we could describe them in a column of type. The apples which came through the parcel post, as sound as a shipment of base balls, show a basic shipping quality like our best winter apples which is invaluable in a lot of apples ripening so early.

"They are remarkably beautiful, juicy and crisp, which they must be to be really good. There is a great variety in solid lines, and in stripes and they have a clear waxen finish which is noticeable in a bunch of apples grown so near the coast. It seems to us Mr. Etter has the stuff in himself and in the strains he is working with to mark the apple list of the next generation all over with California varieties. And fortunately he is still young enough to do this before he can get old and lazy." Eds.

And a few weeks later on receipt of a new lot of these seedling apples, Prof. Wickson wrote and published as follows: Mr. Etter's seedlings which we have examined with much interest, and kept on exhibition in our office since arrival, certainly justify much more than he has claimed to have attained in his preparatory sketch. They have very striking and novel characters, external and internal. In our judgment he has already attained things which generations of apple growers have not developed. We are glad to put on record this early report of his work which will some day be looked upon as of great historic interest.—Eds."

When Prof. Wickson had published the two comments quoted above, his employer, Frank Honeywell, asked the old professor why a man of his characteristic conservativeness should make such prophetic editorial comments, he replied: "I have followed Mr. Etter in his work for many years. His method tackle and perseverance leave no room for failure."

The progress attained in developing new varieties in the last 17 years is almost incredible. Today the whole setup is so well understood, the quest for new and more different varieties, could easily be turned to mass production. Since the whole work has been carried on without money the cost is a minor problem, while the benefits would be great indeed.

REAL PROGRESS

Unless one has originated varieties that are different and superior in quality to existent forms he hasn't really gotten anywhere. When one compares new forms that seem to outclass existing forms so that a child could pass judgment, there can be no argument as to progress being made. In strawberry breeding at Ettersburg, new elements were added to broaden the foundation. But in the apple it was necessary to analyse the species that were in the bloodstream of a variety so it could be intelligently mated to a variety of dissimilar origin to get best results.

In his article in the Year Book Prof. Magnuss makes the statement that primitive crabs cannot be used in breeding because the progeny lack so much in size as to make the varieties of little or no value. Under the intense light and deep blue skies of Ettersburg the ultraviolet rays are so strong that the progeny of such a cross can reach almost any size fruit. It is this element here at Ettersburg that makes it such a favored region for plant breeding.

This may be just a hillbilly theory, but it apparently works. When one can take a tiny crab about twice the size of a shoe button and by hybridizing it produce from its seeds a variety that has actually produced fruit 464 times as heavy as the mother species' fruit, it is going some. This was done with our own native wild crab.

One really cannot comprehend what that increase in size means without comparison—let it be a little mother showing off her son. She weighs 130 lbs. while her son tips the scales at 414 times that, or 60,320 lbs. An ordinary cow would rear a calf that would weigh 150 tons, or a Rhode Island Red hen could have a chick large enough to pick up a full grown man and swallow him like an ordinary hen gulps down a grasshopper.

Of course this is not Dean Swift's dream in Gulliver's travels but real biology in apple breeding. Theory or what you may call it, it still remains we are able to get results in the elements nature offers us, and so long as this peculiar condition prevails, if there is only one Ettersburg in the world, we can be well satisfied if a hillbilly can drive it successfully.

THE ANSWER TO THE APPLE RIDDLE

It seems probable that somewhere else in the world at some remote time some other hillbilly had found conditions that were as favorable as those we find prevailing at Ettersburg, to promote this extraordinary development, in the size of hybridized primitive apples. At any rate a

110

horticultural writer in England in the 13th century was speculating on, whence did our large apples come from.

That marvelous old school master, J. M. Dickson of Ferndale, in the 90's used often to tell us that the answer to an apparently knotty problem was usually very simple. That instead of finding it in the depths of a dark well, we were more likely to find it in plain view on the front lawn. Apple breeders in the pride of their intellect set up an artificial standard. They were wont to place superior types in preference as stock to breed from. They could not believe such varieties as Baldwin, Jonathan and Wagener were half breed red Siberian crabs. It is a well established fact in the biology of hybrids that where selfed or crossed with a variety of similar parentage the progeny is usually inferior to the parent stock. But hybrids can be used most successfully when crossed with pure species or unrelated hybrids. For this reason such varieties as Manx Coddling, a little hybrid crab from the Isle of Man and Reniette Ananas, a little orange crab from Holland, but bearing a French name, have been so successfully used here at Ettersburg. Neither of these varieties are closely related to any of our common apples.

When once the apple breeder casts 'superior' types to the winds, and relies on blood lines, the breeding of superior types becomes very simple. At any rate it is true here at Ettersburg. Where a really good variety appeared once in a while, among seedlings of our best varieties, under an intelligent mating so many good varieties appear, it is difficult to know what to do with them. At present no one can really guess the future of the apple; they will be so different and varied from the present day varieties.

ETTER BROS. CREATE EARTHLY PARADISE

WORLD RENOWNED HORTICULTURIST CONDUCTS AMAZING EXPERIMENTS ON BEAUTIFUL ETTERSBURG RANCH. "HUMBOLDT STANDARD," EUREKA, CALIF.—JUNE 23, 1934.

Article by E. F. Flaherty

"Etter, a German word meaning a little patch of cultivated land in a fallow and sparsely inhabited region, the same surrounded by a broad, unhewn stone wall."

Many years ago a famous scientist friend told Albert Etter, world renowned horticulturist of Humboldt County, the definition of his family name. It is a definition that has become a symbol of Etter's life work. For in the midst of a wilderness surrounded by a wilderness, he and a brother, August, have created an earthly paradise, the workshop in which they play strange tricks upon the flora of the world. In this workshop involving a few acres of southern Humboldt land, the brothers have labored and experimented for close on a half century, pitting their ingenuity and patience against nature in a new 'origin of species'. Hardly pitting—that word is a misnomer. Rather they work with nature, make nature their partner in this intriguing enterprise in which they have found life careers.

Here in the workshop where grow the amazing examples of their ingenuity, you will find blood-red crab apples as large as California grape fruit which trace their ancestry to a tiny species imported from a 2-mile high wind-swept plateau in Mongolia; a golden apple as rich in promise

111

as that which tempted Atalanta; plums that taste more like apricots than apricots themselves; strawberries whose ancestors 14 generations ago grew in an ancient garden in Cathay; apples so sweet that they may be used for the manufacture of champagne. You will see several hundred species growing peacefully together on the same tree. You will find fat cows contentedly munching away at the foliage of locust trees, instead of hay or corn fodder.

You will see all these and thousands of other species, whose ancestors gathered from the four corners of the earth, comprise a veritable horticultural melting pot. Only a month's visit, and an exhaustive review of 40 years of experimental work, would enable the curious visitor to canvas the work that has been done in this strange workshop. It was more than 40 years ago when Albert Etter shouldered his gun one fine morning in January and sauntered up a canyon leading from the little mountain crossroads hamlet now known as Ettersburg. But that is getting slightly ahead of the story.

To start at the proper place Albert and August Etter, the two brothers whose names have become famous in modern horticulture, were born at Placerville in El Dorado Co. of a pioneer family, of German-Swiss extraction. The elder Etter had always played with the idea of plant breeding, but was held down by the business of raising sons. From his father Albert Etter had inherited his love of plants and his insatiable interest in experimentation. Even as a young man he had begun to dream of solving the "Apple riddle". The apple, he explains, although cultivated for centuries, has undergone but little improvement from the early species. Etter arrived at the belief that this was because growers had always relied on the same species, incapable of improvement in themselves without the aid of new influences. In other words nature had arrived at the deadline in the development of the apple.

Much of his success in plant breeding, Etter attributes to an interest sponsored in his youth by a teacher named "Jim" Dickson, pioneer California educator, who afterwards achieved considerable success as a dairy rancher in Oregon. Realizing young Etter's natural bent the teacher furnished much of the inspiration that led to the lad's subsequent career.

CHANCE DISCOVERY

It was quite by chance that Etter discovered the site where his ranch is located, in the Mattole about 5½ miles from the ocean near the Mattole River. He had gone on a fishing trip with a party of young men. Instead of going fishing, one morning, he shouldered his rifle and took off up a deep ravine by himself. Climbing to the top he discovered the little table land upon which the ranch lies. Immediately he sensed that this was the place where he could carry out his long cherished ambitions in plant breeding. But at that time he was too young to file on a homestead. Nevertheless he began to make investigations how it might be acquired. Meanwhile another party had also discovered the little flat, and Etter learned that he had a competitor for the land. Accordingly as soon as he became of age he set out for Eureka—a long and arduous trip in those days—and filed claim on the parcel of land now known as the Etter ranch. Subsequently his brother August joined him in the enterprise.

But although well located, Etter soon discovered that the land was not as productive as he had anticipated. Consequently he wrote to the University of California for advice as to how to improve its productivity. He was told to apply lime to the fields. The advice he received did not,

112

however, prove successful in practise, so he decided to do some experimenting on his own.

CRYSTAL WATER

The world "Mattole" Etter explains is the term for crystal water in the language of the Indians originally inhabiting that region. Indeed the crystal like clarity of the water is a characteristic of that district. In his studies Etter deduced that the reason for this clarity of the water lay in the absence of bacteria in the land drained by various streams. Thus he came to the conclusion that the land was going back to stone. Which meant that since nature had reversed her processes in this region, that she must again be induced to return to normal characteristics if the soil were to be made productive. And—strange to say—it was to the lowly angleworm that Etter turned in his search for a means of enriching the soil.

Man, Etter firmly believes, is grossly lacking in his appreciation of the lowly angleworm. In that respect he quotes Darwin who once said that "man has to thank the angleworm most for making the world a fit place to live in". The angleworm he eplained further, plays an important role in soil building. Not only does the angleworm keep the soil aerated, through constant burrowing under the surface, but furthers needed bacterial growth through its digestive system. The angleworm which Etter used in building up the soil of his ranch is an eastern species, differing from that commonly found in the west. To the lowly worm he attributes much of the outstanding success on the Etter ranches.

500 ACRE RANCH

The Etter ranch embraces some 500 acres in all. Only a relatively small part is used for experimental purposes, the remainder being pasture for sheep and cattle. In this small plot, however, hundreds of thousands of experiments have been conducted, including the breeding of almost every variety of berry and fruit.

As it was the riddle of the apple that first lured the Etters into the field of plant breeding, so it is that much of their work has been devoted toward the improvement of that fruit. Attacking the problem they decided they must get down to basic principles, and if they hoped to succeed where others failed, they must go directly to nature for their solution. Consequently they decided to start right from the beginning, with wild species of the fruit.

Growing in the yard surrounding the special ranch house, there is a tree bearing a fruit that resembles diminutive cherries, no larger than ordinary peas. The fruit however is a true apple, and according to brother Albert is the original apple—the great ancestor of them all. This tiny fruit has figured largely in the experiments, being used to breed many of the hybrid species. Etter explained also that all apples were originally crab apples, and that the apple as it is generally known is simply a development of the original species. One of the types of crab apple that he has used to considerable advantage in his experimental work is a species grown at a two-mile elevation in Mongolia. It is this crab apple that is the parent of his famous "All Gold" apple, one of his proudest achievements.

It would be impossible to enumerate the hundreds of types of hybrid species of apple that have been developed by the Etter brothers. They themselves are not able to give a definite figure. Albert Etter states, however, that if all the hybrids developed during the past 40 years, were planted close together in one row, they would stretch from Ettersburg to beyond San Francisco.

113

SEVENTY-FIVE VARIETIES

Out of these types the Etters have developed some 75 varieties of apples which they believe are the best in the world today. Even yet the work is not finished. They believe, however, that at last their work has shed enough light on the subject that it is now possible to breed with the hope of really arriving somewhere.

Another field of deciduous fruit in which the Etter Brothers have done outstanding work is that involving the plum. Here again they have gone back to basic principles and crossing wild species with cultivated types, have originated hundreds of new varieties. Their search for types has led them far afield—to the eastern and western parts of the United States; to Europe and other remote places. One variety has been developed to a stage where it tastes more like an apricot than apricot itself. Their aim with plum development has been largely concerned with the elimination of the acid characteristic of that fruit, an ambition in which they have succeeded to an astonishing degree.

HEAVILY LADEN

In both the apple and plum orchards, the visitor is confronted with trees so heavily laden that it would be impossible to find room for more fruit on the same tree. The amazing thing is that on the same tree, hundreds of different varieties grow side by side, furnishing odd contrasts in shape and color and general characteristics. From the native wild California grape, that grows along the creeks and branches of the Mattole River, the Etters are now at work on the hybrids of that fruit. Several hundreds of variation of the wild grape crossed with cultivated species, grow in a couple of rows planted in a corner of the field.

Another field in which the Etters have achieved great success is that of the strawberry. The most famous variety developed at Ettersburg, is the "Golden Gate" which has been adapted to the commercial field in California and Oregon. The "Golden Gate" represents the fourth generation of the hybridization involving crosses with a parent Chinese strawberry known as the Duchesne. Another Berry "Ettersburg No. 1" known as the best berry for canning is a cross between the little Alpine strawberry of Europe and a wild Mendocino berry.

EXPERIMENTAL PLOT

Surrounding the experimental plot are hundreds of chestnut trees, representing as many different hybrid types. The Etters are great believers in the chestnut tree and have devoted considerable time to their improvement. Commenting on their experimentation in this field, Albert Etter revealed that oddly enough, their work has been patterned after an example set by Napoleon. Relating Napoleon's influence in this field, Albert Etter pointed out that following his campaigns in Europe, the 'little emperor' set out to make France a self-sustaining country. In several provinces he ordered that the fields be plowed under and given over to the cultivation of chestnut trees. As a result these self-same provinces still grow chestnuts as the chief crop, and the people are among the most happy, contented and most prosperous folk in France.

As with other most numerous trees and plants which have lent themselves to hybridization, the varieties of chestnuts on the Etter ranch represent unending experimentation. And so it goes from the far ends of the earth, from the wild varieties developed by nature through the ages and from the cultivated types grown by man the Etter brothers have recruited the parents for their hybrid species. In each instance they have

114

gone forward from the point where nature halted. But, as stated before they have made nature their partner in their work. As put by Albert Etter: "We simply set the stage; the insects and nature do the rest." A modest admission, certainly, but such is the way of genius.

MANY INQUIRIES

From throughout the world come inquiries relative to the plant breeding work. The same mail brings letters of inquiry and letters attesting success with varieties that have been commercialized in many climes. And from as many corners of the earth come scientists, fruit and berry growers, and others interested in this field. It is a pleasant visit that awaits the visitor to the Etter ranch. First there is the long trek through the mountains from the Redwood highway, via roads branching off either at Garberville, or at Redwood. They are to be true mountain roads; but fairly well improved. Beyond the historic little hamlet of Ettersburg the visitor fords a little creek where the brilliant sunlight glints on Mattole river—crystal clear. Beyond that a steep winding grade to the flat above, along the brink of a precipitous canyon. And then suddenly the visitor comes upon the spacious, comfortable ranch house, built on the very edge of the canyon which constitutes a natural ventilating system.

WIDOW OF EDWARD J. KERN (1869-1938)

Mrs. Leah Kern taken by Death

Fort Madison, Iowa, March 23, 1940

(Clipping from local newspaper)

Mrs. Leah Fusch Kern of St. Louis, Mo., died here (Fort Madison) at the Sacred Heart Hospital after an illness of about 8 months. During the past year Mrs. Kern made her home with her sister Mrs. Bertha Clarke, 1134 Ave. D. She was the daughter of Christopher and Catherine Degenhardt Fusch was born in Fort Madison, Oct. 2, 1875. Her parents were among the pioneer residents of Fort Madison and North Lee Counties. She attended the parochial schools here and was a talented musician, receiving her musical education from her mother and her elder sister.

Mrs. Kern was united in marriage to Edward J. Kern in the Immaculate Conception Church in Monmouth, Ill. June 10, 1914. The couple made their home in St. Louis until the death of Mr. Kern, Feb. 3, 1938 and since then has spent most of her time in Fort Madison. She underwent an operation last August from which she never fully recovered.

Surviving her are one sister Mrs. Bertha Clarke of Fort Madison, 2 brothers, L. H. Fusch, San Bernardino, Calif. and Robert Fusch, Monmouth, Ill., a step-son Mr. Harold O. Kern of St. Louis and several nieces and nephews.

115

REPRODUCTION OF FR. KUNKEL'S MANUSCRIPT

MR. ALBERT F. ETTER
and
MRS. KATHERINE MCCORMICK ETTER

DESCENDENTS OF JOHN EDWARD KERN

II. Generation	III. Generation	Birth-Death
	KERN	
1. John Edward Kern (1839-1877)	3. Henry	
2. Philomena Govro	4. Emily	1864-
	5. Edward J.	1869-1938
	6. Leonard R.	1871-
	7. Dominic J.	1873-
	8. Louise	1875-

III. Generation	IV. Generation	
4. Emily Kern (1864-		
9. Charles Evans		
	KERN	
5. Edward J. Kern (1869-1938)	11. John Edward	d. infant
10. Sophia Bisinger—1st. Mar.	12. Harold O.	1898-
14. Leah C. Fusch—2nd Mar. (1875-1940)	13. Ralph C.	d. infant
	KERN	
6. Leonard R. Kern (1871-	16. George	d. infant
15. Fannie Lindsay	17. Austin	1900- d. infant
	18. Franklin	1903-
	19. Anna	1906-1921
	20. Laura	
	KERN	
7. Dominic J. Kern (1873-	22. Alan	1901-
21. Emma Weber	23. Edwin	1903-1926
	24. Pearl	1904-
	DUNAWAY	
8. Louise Kern (1875-	26. Ethel	1895-
25. Charles Dunaway	27. Ruth	1896-
	28. Charles R.	1899-
	29. Thomas J.	1900-
	30. D. Milburn	1902-

IV. Generation	V Generation	
	KERN	
12. Harold O. Kern (1898-	32. Harold O., Jr.	1920-
31. Marie Breslin	33. Betty Jane	1925-
	34. Edward J.	1929-
	35. Leroy T.	1933-
	KERN	
18. Franklin Kern (1903-	37. Dolores L.	1929-
36. Bernice Kadel	38. Emily Anne	1930- d. infant
	39. Marylin Milders	1931-
	40. Franklin, Jr.	1937-
	KERN	
22. Alan Kern (1901-	42. Kern	1929-
41. Ella Summann	43. Raymond	1931-
	44. Norman	1933-
	45. Marie	1934-
	46. Mildred	1938-
	BRANNEKE	
24. Pearl Kern (1904-	48. Robert	1928-
47. Harry Branneke	49. Peggy	1931-

117

IV. Generation	V. Generation	Birth-Death
	JONES	
26. Ethel Dunaway	51. Dorothy	1916-
(1895-	52. Evelyn	1918-
50. P. Jones	53. Mildred	1920-
	54. Arlita	1922-
	55. C. M. Jones	1924-
	56. Raymond	1927-
	DEVER	
27. Ruth Dunaway	58. Olita G.	1922-
(1898-		
57. Edward M. Dever		
	DUNAWAY	
29. Thomas J. Dunaway	60. Clarence	1927-
(1900-	61. Clarence	1930-
59. Marg. Kelley	62. Darline	1937-

118

DESCENDENTS OF MARY KERN

II. Generation	III. Generation	Birth-Death
	KOEHLER	
1. Mary Kern	3. Emma	1864-1892
(1840-1918)	4. Chas. Emil	1808-1871
2. Herman Koehler	5. Sidney A.	1870-1884
(1841-1911)	6. Walter Dom.	1876-1911
	7. Nora	1880-

III. Generation	IV. Generation	
6. Walter Dominic Koehler		
(1876-1911)		
8. Pauline Glaser		
St. Louis		
	HICKS	
7. Nora Koehler	10. Dorothy	1901-
(1880-	11. Marjorie	1924-
9. Roy Hicks		
(1875-		
St. Louis		

IV. Generation
10. Dorothy Hicks
(1901-
12. Arthur Rich. Karr
(1900-
St. Louis

MRS. MARY KERN KOEHLER
(1840-1918)

The remains of Mrs. Mary Koehler nee Kern, who died at the home of her daughter Mrs. Roy Hicks, in St. Louis, Monday, July 29, 1918, arrived here Monday morning at 10:00 o'clock and were taken to the Catholic Church where funeral services were held after which the body was laid to rest in the Valle Spring Cemetery. The deceased was a daughter of the late John D. Kern, and Regina Kern of St. Genevieve. She was 78 years old and was well known here having lived in St. Genevieve until 15 years ago. Her husband Probate Judge, Herman Koehler preceded her to the grave 7 years ago. She is survived by one daughter, Nora, Mrs. Roy Hicks and 4 grandchildren, and many relatives and friends who will learn of her death with sorrow. Roy Hicks, wife and daughter, Miss Dorothy, Mrs. Pauline Koehler, Mrs. Nancy Kern and daughter, Miss Agnes accompanied the remains to St. Genevieve. (St. Genevieve, July 31, 1918).

EMMA KOEHLER

At her parental home in St. Genevieve died on Sunday evening, Feb. 28, 1892, the oldest daughter of Judge of Probate, Mr. Herman Koehler, at the age of 28 years, 5 months, and 13 days. The funeral took place in the Valle Spring Cemetery on Tuesday morning and a large concourse of friends and neighbors followed the remains to their lasting peace. Miss Emma was all her life more or less sickly and for the past 10 months was confined to her bed a confirmed invalid.

119

MR. CHARLES KERN

Mr. Charles Kern (1844-1911) in the late 60's drove to California from St. Genevieve, Mo. in a covered wagon. He moved from El Dorado Co., where he first landed as far south as Orange Co., and returned to the East through Texas where he met with an accident, causing the loss of his left hand. Four of his daughters (Louise, the eldest, died 1939) conduct a successful Dress Making Establishment in St. Louis. They have likewise produced some artistic Church vestments.

120

DESCENDENTS OF CHARLES KERN

II. Generation	III. Generation	Birth-Death
	KERN	
1. Charles Kern	3. Mary Teresa	1871-
(1844-1911)	4. Louise Margaret	1873-1939—single
2. Mary Arnold	5. Josephine Antoinette	1875- single
(1845-1928)	6. Henry	1877-1882
	7. Agnes Regina	1879- single
	8. Emma Sophie	1881- single
	9. Caroline	1883-1884
	10. Catherine	1885- d. infant
	11. Julia Angeline	1886-

III. Generation	IV. Generation	
	NAUMANN	
3. Mary Teresa Kern	13. Myrtle T.	1895-1896
(1871-	14. Earline	1896-
12. John Naumann	15. Elmer	1899-1900
(1873-1931)	16. Albert	1901-
St. Louis, Mo.	17. John Emmet	1913-1924
	JOHNSON	
11. Julia A. Kern	19. Eugene	1906-1930
(1886-	20. Sidney	1908-
18. Walter Johnson	21. Gertrude	1909-
Weston, Mo.	22.	1912-
	23. Marrion	1915-

IV. Generation	V. Generation	
20. Sidney Johnson		
(1908-		
24. Gertrude Rothburg		
	STRASSER	
21. Gertrude Johnson	26. Teresa Marie	1931-
(1909-	27. Eugenia Gert.	1933-
25. Carl Strasser		
(1909-		
22. Charles Johnson		
(1912-		
28. Ruble Blair		
	KNOWLES	
23. Marrion Johnson	30. Charles Horace	1937-
(1915-	31. Myriel Irene	1939-
29. Weston Knowles		

121

DESCENDENTS OF WILLIAM KERN

II. Generation	III. Generation	Birth-Death
	KERN	
1. William Kern	3. Mary L. E.	1873-1874
(1847-1911)	4. Wm. Anthony	1875-1879
2. Justine Thomure	5. Wm. Justin	1878-
(1850-1878)		
2nd Mar.		
6. Caroline Meyer	7. Louis Philip	1881-
(1857-1926)	8. Elizabeth Regina	1882-
	9. John Hilary	1883-
	10. Henry Joseph	1885-1932
	11. Anna Caroline	1887-
	12. Mena Josephine	1888-
	13. Leo August	1890-1916
	14. Joseph Anthony	1893-
	15. Francis Xavier	1895-
	16. Regina Cecelia	1899-1901

III. Generation	IV. Generation	
	KERN	
7. Louis Philip Kern	18. Myrtle M. Caroline	1904-
(1871-	19. Raymond Geo.	1907-
17. Emily M. Gisi		
(1879-		
St. Genevieve		
	GETTINGER	
8. Elizabeth R. Kern	21. Edgar Wm.	1906-
(1882-	22. Harry Jos.	1908-
20. Peter J. Gettinger	23. Francis Anth.	1909-
(1882-	24. Clarence Columbus	1911-
Festus, Mo.	25. Leonard Adolph	1913-
	26. Helen Marie	1915-
	KERN	
10. Henry Jos. Kern	28. Wm. Michael	1915-
(1885-1932)	29. Henry Anth.	1917-
27. Nellie M. O'Hearn	30. Mary Marg.	1919
(1882-1937)		
12. Mena J. Kern		
(1888-		
31. Herbert M. O'Leary		
(1882-1937)		
Los Angeles, Calif.		
	KERN	
14. Joseph A. Kern	33. Rosalie Eulalia	1917-
(1893-	34. Theo. Milton	1918-
32. Mary T. Gisi		
(1893-		
St. Louis, Mo.		
	KERN	
15. Francis X. Kern	36. Michael Leo	1921-
(1895-	37. Marie Sylvia	1922-
35. Ann Marg. O'Hearn	38. Thos. Edward	1924-
(1892-1931)	39. Francis Jos.	d. infant
2nd Mar.	40. Helen Marg.	1927-
41. Augusta Cath. Wilson	42. Anna Mae	1929-
(1907-		
St. Genevieve, Mo.		

122

IV. Generation	V. Generation	Birth-Death
	GOLDKAMP	
18. Myrtle M. C. Kern	44. John D.	1931-
(1904-	45. Richard	1933-
43. Urban R. Goldkamp		
(1901-		
St. Charles, Mo.		
	GETTINGER	
21. Edgar W. Gettinger	47. John Wm.	1937-
(1906-	48. Robert Jos.	1938-
46. Mary Rose Burke		
(1909-		
University City, Mo.		
	GETTINGER	
23. Francis A. Gettinger	50. Eliz. Frances	1933-
(1909-	51. Glennon A.	1936-
49. Alpha Cornell Aubuchon		
(1913-		
Overland, Mo.		
	BRENNAN	
26. Helen M. Gettinger	53. Peter John	1938-
(1915-		
52. Ambrose C. Brennan		
(1909-		
Dallas, Tex.		

123

JOSEPHINE KERN MONTGOMERY and SIMEON MONTGOMERY
(1850-1935) (1838-1924)
Their daughters Sister Felix and Sister Ignatia, both of the
Sisters of St. Joseph of Orange, Calif.
*Picture taken at the Golden Wedding Anniversary of
Mr. and Mrs. Montgomery*

MRS. SIMEON MONTGOMERY nee JOSEPHINE KERN

(1850-1935)

It was from the lips of a Franciscan Father that I first heard of this staunch Catholic mother. She took care of the decoration of the altar and the cleanliness of the sanctuary in the little church at Lakeport, Lake Co., Calif. In this respect she resembled her elder sister Mrs. Wilhelmina Etter who from her own garden decorated the altars of the parish church in Ferndale, Humboldt Co., Calif. Some of Mrs. Etter's dahlias supplied the main chapel as well as that of the Sisters' chapel of St. Patrick's Seminary, at Menlo Park for years. The Montgomery's lived for many years in Lakeport, but on the death of their son John, who died in the flu epidemic of 1918, they moved to Bayside, Calif. and lived with their son Felix, at that time engaged in the dairy business. Felix married Miss Margaret Friel, and of this happy union there were born 11 children, 3 of whom have entered religion—Sister Felix, Superior of the parish school in Corpus Christi Church, San Francisco, Sister Ignatia, assistant mistress of novices at the Motherhouse of the Sisters of St. Joseph in Orange, Calif. and Sister Alice at the time of this writing is a novice with the Sisters of Mercy, at Burlingame, Calif. I remember on one occasion being seated at the family table, with the grandparents, parents and children, with great edification to myself as well as to Monsignor P. G. Moriarty, St. Ann's Shrine, San Francisco, who accompanied me and in later years frequently referred to this happy gathering.

Both Mr. and Mrs. Simeon Montgomery lived to a ripe old age, the former being 86 at the time of his death while Mrs. Montgomery was 85.

124

DESCENDENTS OF JOSEPHINE KERN

II. Generation

1. Josephine Kern
(1850-1935)
2. Simeon Montgomery
(1838-1924)

III. Generation

4. Felix Montgomery
(1873-
6. Marg. Anna Friel
(1874-
Eureka, Calif.

III. Generation

MONTGOMERY
3. Josephine   1871-   d. infant
4. Felix   1873-
5. John   1875-

IV. Generation

MONTGOMERY
7. Mary   1897-   Sister Felix
     St. Joseph of Orange
8. Joseph   1899-
9. Margaret   1900-
10. Ida   1902-   Sister Ignatia
     St. Joseph of Orange
11. Felix   1905-
12. Josephine   1907-
13. James   1909-
14. Catherine   1911-   d. infant
15. Nell   1912-
16. Anna   1915-   Reg. Nurse
17. Alice   1918-   Sister of Mercy

Sister Felix is at present Superior of the Corpus Christi Convent in San Francisco.

Sister Ignatia is assistant Mistress of Novices, of the Sisters of St. Joseph of Orange.

Anne Montgomery is a registered nurse, St. Mary's Hospital, San Francisco, Calif.

Alice Montgomery has entered the Motherhouse of the Sisters of Mercy, Burlingame, Calif. (January 6, 1941). Sister Mary Pius.

IV. Generation

8. Joseph Montgomery
(1899-
18. Ruby Giacomini
Los Angeles, Calif.

11. Felix Montgomery
(1905-
21. Lois Otis
(1915-
San Francisco, Calif.

12. Josephine Montgomery
(1907-
23. Kenneth Jorgensen
Los Angeles, Calif.

15. Nell Montgomery
(1912-
24. Irene Mitchell
Berwyn, Ill.

V. Generation

MONTGOMERY
19. Catherine
20. Frances

MONTGOMERY
22. Jean Marie

Birth-Death

1921-
1923-

1940-

125

DESCENDENTS OF AUGUST KERN

II. Generation	III. Generation	Birth-Death	
	KERN		
1. August Kern	3. Nettie	1881-	single
(1853-1939)	4. Raymond	1882-	d. infant
2. Sarah Frary	5. Katherine	1883-	
(1857-1930)	6. Rachel	1886-	single
St. Genevieve, Mo.	7. Fred A.	1889-1896	
	8. Nicholas J.	1892-	
	9. Hilbert	1894-1940	
	10. Filmore	1894-	single
	11. Edna	1899-	single

III. Generation	IV. Generation		
	LALUMONDIERE		
5. Katherine Kern	13. Lloyd	1908-	
(1883-	14. Glennon	1911-	
12. Jules Lalumondiere			
(1881-			
	KERN		
8. Nicholas J. Kern	16. August W.	1930-	
(1892-			
15. Bertha Schindler			
(1892-			
	KERN		
9. Hilbert Kern, Sr.	18. Hilbert, Jr.	1934-	
(1894-1940)	19. Mary Ann	1939-	
17. Helen Daniels			
(1908-			

IV. Generation	V. Generation		
13. Lloyd Lalumondiere			
(1908-			
20. Elizabeth Rhodes			
(1907-			
	LALUMONDIERE		
14. Glennon Lalumondiere	22. Glennon J.	1939-	
(1911-			
21. Adele Heil			
(1913-			

126

DESCENDENTS OF JULIA KERN

II. Generation

1. Julia Kern
   (1850-1914)
2. Max Bader
   (1845-1927)

III. Generation

3. William F. Bader
   (1877-1930)
12. Rose Klein
    (1877-

4. Bessie Bader
   (1880-1935)
13. Joseph G. Rehm
    (1881-
    Ste. Genevieve, Mo.

5. Chas. Jos. Bader
   (1883-
18. Edith Larkin
    (1887-
    Mendota, Ill.

6. Anna Bader
   (1885-1941)
21. William Marquis
    (1884-
    Ste. Genevieve

7. August Edwin Bader
   (1887-
22. Helen Blass
    (1895-
    Earlville, Ill.

8. Oliver John Bader
   (1890-
26. Winifred Donnelly
    (1893-
    Princeton, Ill.

10. Susan Bader
    (1894-
29. Bernard L. Schwartz
    (1891-
    Freeport, Ill.

11. Mary Ellen Bader
    (1898-
33. Ben H. Miller
    (1899-
    Ste. Genevieve, Mo.

III. Generation   Birth-Death

BADER
3. William F.   1877-1930
4. Bessie   1880-1935
5. Charles Jos.   1883-
6. Anna   1885-1941
7. August Edwin   1887-
8. Oliver John   1890-
9. Jules   1892-1899
10. Susan   1894-
11. Mary Ellen   1898-

IV. Generation

REHM
14. Norman   1906-
15. Myriel   1908-
16. Edward   1910-
17. Derrill   1912-

BADER
19. Donald Larkin   1917-
20. Clifton Jos.   1923-

BADER
23. Aubrey   1917-
24. Ruth   1921-
25. Elizabeth   1932-

BADER
27. Edward J.   1920-
28. Max Oliver   1929-

SCHWARTZ
30. Glenn   1916-
31. Herbert   1917-
32. Dorothy M.   1925-

127

IV. Generation	V. Generation	Birth-Death
	REHM	
11. Norman Rehm	35. Dolor	1931-
(1906-	36. Victor Julian	1936-
31. Margaret Basler		
(1907-		
Ste. Genevieve, Mo.		
10. Edward Rehm		
(1910-		
37. Erma Figge		
(1912-		
Ste. Genevieve, Mo.		
	REHM	
17. Derrill Rehm	39. Darryl	1938-
(1912-		
38. Margaret Duval		
(1911-		
Ste. Genevieve, Mo.		
	BADER	
19. Donald Larkin Bader	41. Donald James	1939-
(1917-		
40. Lucille Hanley		
(1918-		
Mendota, Ill.		

128

HOTEL STE. GENEVIEVE, MO.
Matthew Kern (1816-1893) was for a long time Proprietor of Hotel Ste. Genevieve.

REV. F. W. KUNKEL ON PORCH
Taken by Louise Kern, July 4, 1937.

DESCENDENTS OF MATTHEW KERN

OBITUARY NOTICES

George W. Kern, 4126 Lexington Ave., St. Louis, Mo. eldest son of Emil and Charlotte Dinsbier Kern, beloved husband of Clara T. Kern (nee Ritscher) dear father of Helen May and James W. Kern, our dear brother, brother-in-law, uncle and great uncle—entered into rest Sunday, Nov. 17. 1940, 12:30 P.M. Funeral, Wednesday, Nov. 20, 2:00 P.M. from Matthew Hermann & Sons' Chapel. Interment Laurel Hill Cemetery, member of Painter & Decorators Local Union No. 115.

Margaret P. Kern, in her 88th year, beloved sister of Emil Kern and the late Josephine, Alice, Fred, Henry, and Frank Kern, dear friend of Josephine Schaefer. Funeral from Arthur J. Donnelly Parlors, Tuesday, April 9, 1940 to St. Rose's Church. Interment Calvary Cemetery.

I Generation	II. Generation	Birth-Death
	KERN	
1. Matthew Kern	3. Henry	1845-1881
(1810-1893)	4. Josephine	1849-1936
2. Johanna Fitzkam	5. John	1852-1889
(1824-1889)	6. Margaret	1853-1940
	7. Emil	1856-
	8. Frederick Louis	1858-1934
	9. Alice	1863-1932
II. Generation	III. Generation	
	KERN	
3. Henry Kern	11. Anna	d. Infant
(1845-1881)	12. George	d. Infant
10. Mary Eliz. Naumann	13. Mary Elizabeth	1878-
(1846-1920)		
	KERN	
5. John Kern	15. Lallah	
(1852-1889)	16. Fred	
14. Margaret Spiess		
	KERN	
7. Emil Kern	18. George W.	1880-1940
(1856-	19. Edwin C.	1883-1940
17. Charlotte Dinsbier	20. Grace O.	1885-1935
(1860-	21. Albert B.	1888-1933
St. Louis, Mo.	22. Harry J.	1894-
	23. Charles E.	1898-
	KERN	
8. Frederick Louis Kern	25. Harry Frederick, Sr.	1880-1937
(1858-1934)	26. William Arthur	1885-
24. Lucia Medora	27. Olive	1892-
(1863-1938)		
Denver, Col.		

130

III. Generation	IV. Generation	Birth-Death	
	BAUMANN		
13. Mary Eliz. Kern (1878-	29. Agnes	1898-1922	
28. Edward J. Baumann (1872- Ste. Genevieve, Mo.	30. Austen	1903-	single
	31. Glennon	1912-	d. infant
	KERN		
18. George W. Kern (1880-1940)	33. Helen May	1917-	
32. Clara Ritscher (1889- St. Louis	34. James William	1921-	
	KERN		
19. Edwin C. Kern (1883-1940)	36. Edwin C.	1914-	
35. Johanna Zachow (1894- St. Louis	37. Albert C.	1919-	
	GATZKE		
20. Grace O. Kern (1885-1935)	39. Elmer K.	1907-	
38. William Gatzke St. Louis	40. Ethel G.	1909-	
21. Albert E. Kern (1858-1933) 41. Louise Fitzpatrick St. Louis			
23. Charles E. Kern (1898- 42. Viola Hoyer (1900- St. Louis			
	KERN		
25. Harry Fred. Kern, Sr. (1880-1937)	44. Harry Fred, Jr.	1911-	
43. Alice Robertson—1st Mar. Denver, Colo.	45. Betty Jane	1915-	
46. Oral Peck—2nd Mar.			
27. Olive Kern (1892- 47. Emmet Earl Hussey Denver, Colo.			

IV. Generation	V. Generation		
	GATZKE		
39. Elmer K. Gatzke 1907-	49. Jacqueline Edna	1937-	
48. Edna LaBorenz 1909- St. Louis			
	GENTRY		
40. Ethel G. Gatzke (1909-	51. Carole Grace	1937-	
50. Ivan Wm. Gentry St. Louis	52. Richard Wm.	1939-	
44. Harry Fred Kern, Jr. (1911- 53. Janet McKenzie New York, N. Y.			
45. Betty Kern (1915- 54. Humphrey Ireland New York, N.Y.			

Emmet E. Hussey (47) with "Ideal Cement Co." Denver, Colo.
Olive Kern Hussey (27) Sec. of Denver Red Cross.
Harry Fred Kern, Jr., (44) Asst. Foreign Editor, "Newsweek," N.Y.

Dorothy Kern Ruppert

DOROTHEA KERN—BAPTISMAL CERTIFICATE

Den eilften Oktober Eintausend acht hundert und zwanzig Abends neun Uhr ist geboren und den zwölften Mittags zwölf Uhr getauft worden, Maria Dorothea Tochter des Dominikus Kern, Wagner, und Margaretha Väth. Witnesses: Johann Joseph Höpfner und Michel Ebert.

Freudenberg den 16ten. August, 1836.

                Hormuth, Pfarrer.

The eleventh of October Eighteen Hundred Twenty at 9.00 P.M. was born and at noon of the day following was baptized Mary Dorothea, daughter of Dominick Kern, Wheelwright, and Margaret Vaeth.

Witnesses: John Josp. Hoepfner and Michael Ebert.

Freudenberg, Aug. 16, 1836.

                Hormuth, Pastor.

PASSPORT—JULY 18, 1836

After *Dorothea Kern*, of Freudenberg, had appeared before the below mentioned parish authorities and stated that she wishes to go to Philadelphia, in North America, in order to visit her relatives and for this purpose has need of identification and declaration of her personal belongings, we hereby testify that she is the legitimate daughter of Dominick Kern, wheelwright of this place, and Margaret Vaeth, that she is rightfully a member of this parish and therefore as such may at any time return to this parish, unless in disregard of the law duly made known to her, she would marry without due permission of our authority, in which event she would forfeit all her rights to citizenship in the Archduchy of Baden.

She has in her possession

   250 fl. family inheritance, 100 fl. personal earnings, besides 129 fl. gifts.

         Witness: Knoepp, Burgermeister
               Hoepfner, Parish trustee

July 18, 1836.   _____, farmer.

133

DESCENDENTS OF DOROTHEA KERN

I. Generation	II. Generation	Birth-Death
	RUPPERT	
1. Dorothea Kern (1820-1903)	3. Adam	1838-1873
2. Valentine Ruppert (1801-	4. John Valentine	1847-1910
	5. Adolph Edward	1849-1900
	6. Alphonsus	1855-
	7. Fred. Louis	1857-1931
		N.B.—Several children born 1838-1852 died as infants.

II. Generation	III. Generation	
	RUPPERT	
3. Adam Ruppert (1838-1873)	9. Henry	1861-1926
8. Margaret Woelfel (1838-1919)	10. John Valentine	1863-1931
	11. Joseph	single
	12. Frank A.	1868-1917
	13. Frederick	1870- d.infant
	14. Mary Margaret	1871-1902
	15. Alphonsus	1873-
	RUPPERT	
4. John Val. Ruppert (1847-1919)	17. Mary	1871- single
16. Mary Weber (1851-1915)	18. Francis	1873-1926
5. Adolph Edward (1849-1900)		
19. Mary Weller		
6. Alphonsus Ruppert (1855-		
20. Rebecca McGee		
	RUPPERT	
7. Frederick Louis Ruppert (1857-1931)	22. Matthias	1884-
21. Barbara Wagner (1857-1931)	23. Dorothy	1885-1907
	24. Charles H.	1887-1936
	25. Alphonsus	1887-1888
	26. Herman	1890-1915
	27. Henry Louis	1892-
	28. Louis Joseph	1894-
	29. Joseph Alphonsus	1896-
	30. Mary Ruth	1897-
	31. Francis Wm.	1904-

III. Generation	IV. Generation	Birth-Death
	RUPPERT	
9. Henry Ruppert (1861-1926)	33. Teresa	1891-
32. Frances B. Delchelbore (1867-	34. Margaret	1893-
	35. Julia	1896-
	36. Mary	1900-
	37. Frances	1904-
	RUPPERT	
10. John Valentine Ruppert (1863-1931)	39. Margaret	1888-1920
38. Agnes Kalberloge—1st Mar.		
40. Anna Schubert—2nd Mar. (1863-1928)	41. Frank	1893-
	42. Alphonsus	1895-
	RUPPERT	
12. Frank A. Ruppert (1868-1917)	44. Mary	1893- d. infant
43. Eva Shaub (1868-1927)	45. Louis	1894-

III. Generation	IV. Generation	Birth-Death	
	HUBER		
14. Mary Marg. Ruppert (1871-1902)	47. Harry	1893-	
46. Henry Huber (1865-	48. Francis	1895-	
	49. George	1895-1908	
	50. Margaret	1897-	
	51. Mary	1895-1910	
	52. Dora	1898-	d. infant
	53. Gertrude	1901-	
	54. Agnes	1902-	
	RUPPERT		
15. Alphonsus Ruppert (1873-	56. John	1897-	
55. Katharine Dietz (1864-1932)	57. George	1898-	
	58. Margaret	1900-	Sr. Alfred, R.S.M.
	59. Mary	1902-	
18. Francis Ruppert (1873-1926)			
60. Mary Ann Smith			
22. Matthias L. Ruppert (1884-			
61. Anita O'Neill (1883-			
24. Charles H. Ruppert (1857-1936)			
62. Grace Marie Martin (1884-			
	RUPPERT		
27. Henry Louis Ruppert (1892-	64. Henry Louis, Jr.	1916-	
63. Myrtle Eckardt (1894-	65. Joseph E.	1917-	
	66. Mary Virginia	1922-	
	RUPPERT		
28. Louis Joseph Ruppert (1894-	68. Louis F.	1917-	
67. Catherine Raymer (1900-	69. Robert	1923-	
	70. Catherine	1927-	
	71. Vernon	1933-	
	RUPPERT		
29. Joseph Aloysius Ruppert (1896-	73. Elsie Josephine	1916-	
72. Mary Alger 1st Mar. (1896-	74. Doris E.	1919-1922	
75. Virginia Jones, 2nd Mar.	76. Jos. Travers		
	77. Noel Laurenston		
	MURRAY		
30. Mary Ruth Ruppert (1897-	79. Barbara Anne	1929-	
78. Charles Athey Murray (1893-	80. Mabel Athey	1931-	
	81. Martha Ruth	1933-	
	82. Joseph Athey	1935-	
	RUPPERT		
31. Francis Wm. Ruppert (1904-	84. Francis Wm., Jr.	1923-	
83. Elizabeth Brempker (1903-	85. Prunetta Eliz.	1926-	

IV. Generation	V. Generation	Birth-Death	
36. Mary Ruppert (1900-			
86. Raymond K. Johnson (1889-			
	WILLS		
37. Frances Ruppert (1904-	88. John	1926-	
87. Vincent Wills (1903-	89. Robert	1929-	
	MC GRANN		
38. Margaret Ruppert (1888-1920)	91. Julia	1918-	
88. William McGrann (1883-	92. Teresa B.	1920-	d. Infant
	RUPPERT		
45. Louis C. Ruppert (1894-	94. John F.	1919-	
	95. Marie E.	1921-	
93. Anna Schmidt 1898-	96. Barbara M.	1923-	
	97. Francis A.	1925-	
	98. Teresa M.	1928-	
	99. Henry L.	1930-	
	100. Joseph L.	1933-	
	HUBER		
47. Harry Huber (1893-	102. Henry	1918-	
101. Anna Stilbert	103. Leonard	1920-	
	HUBER		
48. Francis Huber (1895-	105. Marie	1918-	
104. Mary Pich (1897-			
50. Margaret Huber 1897-			
106. Runge			
	HEAPS		
53. Gertrude Huber (1901-	108. Henry	1920-	
107. Otho Heaps 1st. Mar.			
109. William Cornell 2nd Mar.			
	BUEHLER		
54. Agnes Huber (1902-	111. Anna Rose	1927-	
	112. George	1928-	d. Infant
110. James Edwin Buehler (1905-	113. James Edwin, Jr.	1930-	
	114. Agnes	1932-	
	115. Marie	1937-	d. Infant
	RUPPERT		
57. George Ruppert (1898-	117. Joseph	1920-	
	118. George	1922-	
108. Anna McGowan	119. Alfred	1925-	
	120. Francis	1927-	
	121. Mary	1929-	
	122. Dolores	1931-	
	123. Elizabeth	1934-	

136

UNCLAIMED MILLIONS

The following letters of Francis L. Neubeck, an attorney of Washington, D.C., and a cousin of Rev. F. W. Kunkel, and another letter of the Rev. Joseph A. Meck of Mannheim, Germany written in 1888, refer to a secret loan made by three members of the Kern family to the government of Holland, over a century ago. In 1912, Mrs. Mary Koehler, a cousin of St. Louis, wrote to Father Kunkel about this claim and he in turn referred it to his cousin, Mr. Neubeck, as may be seen from the letter. Acting on the advice of Mr. Neubeck, Father Kunkel wrote to the Pastor of Freudenberg in 1912, and at the same time communicated with several relatives in the ancestral village, but was unable to locate the missing bible.

In a visit to Germany in 1926, Father Kunkel spent a week in Freudenberg, but no one was able to give him any information either about the loan, or the family bible. Inquiries made in this country brought out the statement that the book had been entrusted to a relative leaving Germany for the United States, and it was unfortunately lost on the way. Thus it is that unless we locate the Kern Family Bible in which the secret transaction was recorded these untold millions must forever remain unclaimed.

FRANCIS L. NEUBECK
ATTORNEY-AT-LAW
BOND BUILDING

Washington, D.C. Mar. 18, 1912
Commissioner
U. S. Court of Claims

Dear Father Frank:

As you doubtless know I have been investigating the supposed claim of the Kern family against the Government of Holland, but so far I am not able to get any trace of it, though the matter has been superficially inquired into by a very prominent attorney at the Hague. The difficulty is that we have no definite data on which to work, which difficulty is increased by the fact that the loan is said by our cousin to have been a secret loan.

In her letter to you dated June 4, 1910, Mrs. Mary Koehler wrote to you as follows:—

"There were 3 brothers, one a priest, one a merchant and one your and my mother's great grandfather who made the secret loan to the government of Holland, and the secret was left in an old family bible that was kept by the priest. After the priest's death the bible was held by our grandfather John D. Kern. He was told by the priest to take good care of the book, as through it they (his descendents) could claim his millions. When your and my grandfather died the book was given to Joseph who had 2 daughters Margaret and Teresa. These sisters married brothers by the name of Keck. One brother died in Holland and the other came to the United States. The bible was left with relatives of Keck by the name of Emerick or Emerich. This was 57 years ago, but I think that as it was a bible and from a priest, it was taken care of and can be found. It is the only thing that will give us a chance to get the money. Please write to the priest of the parish in Freudenberg and ask him to try to find the book."

Francis L. Neubeck.

N.B.—I wrote to the Parish Priest of Freudenberg and even visted him but could learn nothing of the Bible. F.W.K.

137

Erhard Kern was a foster-brother to Mrs. Susanna Kern Huguenin. That is, he was a son of John Dominic Kern and Susanna Ziegler, his second wife. Of this marriage there were a son and a daughter, Erhard and Josepha Maria.

This is a free translation by Captain Bauer and A. L. Ryland, of the Tax Collector's Office of St. Louis.

Freudenberg, Mar. 12, 1883.

To Susanna (Kern) Huguenin.

Dear Sister Susanna:—

I have often been thinking of you in the past and wondering if you were still alive and well. Now I see from your letter that you and your family are well, which gives me great pleasure. I am, thank the Lord pretty well. My youngest daughter is Maria Teresa Kettinger. I have 4 children happily married. The eldest, a daughter is married to the son of Michael Keck. The other daughter is at home with myself. Of my two sons, one has been just discharged from the army while the other is still in military service. They have cost me considerable money. The oldest is in business with myself. I have a large Furniture Factory and my business covers the surrounding territory within a radius of from 100 to 140 miles.

My hair has already turned gray. When my youngest son is discharged from the army I shall take him into the business and retire, for I have many offices of honor. My sister Josepha is still alive and has two children, Rev. Joseph Meck and Mary. Her son is a priest in Basle, Switzerland and the daughter has been a widow for the past 12 years but is comfortably situated.

You ask me what relatives are still alive. They are, Michael Keck, Peter Joseph Kern, Franz Matthias Keck, Antonio Keck and my wife's sister Barbara who was married to Franz Kern. All the others of your time are dead. If my sister-in-law has sent Dominic's picture, then you can judge of me, for I have the same gray hair.

I am enclosing photo of my youngest son. If I were younger I would pay you a visit. If we do not meet again we shall meet in eternity. Greetings from myself and my family to yourself and your family and to all our acquaintances.

I sign myself
Your foster brother,

Erhard Kern.

Letter of Rev. Jos. Meck, Professor in Mannheim written 1888.

"The writer of this letter is the son of **Erhard Kern's** (d. 1887) sister. Our uncle Kern died Sept. 1887 very suddenly while visiting his vineyards. Only my mother is still living, Maria Joseph Meck, widow, maiden name Kern. My mother, born in 1824, and my sister Maria are with me in Mannheim. I am Professor in the Gymnasium and Resident Chaplain in the County Jail. I was ordained 13 years ago and have been in Mannheim for the past 7 years. I did not know of any letter in 1886. The son of Erhard Kern sent me the same last week. Today the priest, Rev. Father Butz of Freudenberg, sent me the letter of Uncle Dominic's children in America.

138

"I at once took all the necessary steps to get all the details of the affair. I entrusted it to the Dutch Consul General residing here. He will inquire officially in Holland and will get all the facts in the case. Should there be $1,200,000(?) waiting for us then I would have the best possible chance to follow up the affair and make further inquiries. I will do my duty and you can assure yourself that if anything is to be gotten out of the affair, my inquiries are the safest to obtain results. As soon as anything turns up I will let you know at once. Please give best regards to my beloved relatives from my mother, especially Aunt Dorothy and Uncle Matthias and Aunt Susanna.

"My mother has had no chance to correspond with her relatives, because letters were exchanged only between uncle Erhard and America. I left home very early to study and hence heard very little of my relatives in America. I should be very happy whether on the way to millions or not if a livelier and friendlier correspondence would result. I ask you kindly to notify the children of uncle Dominic (dec.) who wrote to the priest in Freudenberg that I have made inquiries about that fortune. Many regards to you, your beloved mother and good sisters."

From your cousin,

Joseph Meck, Professor.

P.S.—There are only two married sons and two married daughters of uncle Erhard living. His widow is still living.

139

DESCENDENTS OF ERHARD and MARY JOSEPHA KERN

After the death of Margaretha Vaeth **DOMINIC KERN** married Susanna Ziegler. Of this union a son and daughter were born—Erhard and Mary Josepha.

I. Generation	II Generation	Birth-Death
	KERN	
1. Erhard Kern	3. Maria	1848-1922
(1822-1887)	4. Theresia	1850-1933
2. Maria Teresa Kettinger	5. Erhard	1852-1924
(1824-1897)	6. Franz	1861-
II. Generation	III. Generation	
	KECK	
3. Maria Kern		
(1848-1922)		
7. Hermann Keck (his 2nd Mar.)	8. Anna	1880-
(1837-1937)	9. Leo	1885-
4. Theresia Kern		
(1850-1933)		
10. Leo Wolf		
	KERN	
5. Erhard Kern	12. Franz	1888-1914
(1852-1924)		
11. Mary Hoffmann—1st Mar.		
(1856-1891)		
13. Christine Grimm—2nd Mar.	14. Joseph Anton	1895-
(1855-1932)	15. Margarethe	1897-
	16. Karl	1899-
	KERN	
6. Franz Kern	18. Maria	1889-
(1861-	19. Rosalinde	1891-
17. Beata Deckert—1st Mar.	20. Erhard	1893-
(1845-1898)	21. Johanna Amanda	1897-
22. Katharina Hoffmann—2nd Mar.	22. Richard	1899-
(1870-	23. Anton	1902-
	24. Anna	1904-
	25. Elizabeth	1913-
I. Generation	II. Generation	
	MECK	
1. Maria Josepha Kern	3. Joseph Anton	1851-1915 Ord. Priest 1875
(1824-1902)		
2. Johann Michael Meck	4. Anna Maria	1862-1911 single
(1820-1866)		

Note—On a visit to Mannheim, Germany in 1897 I saw Aunt Mary Meck, Rev. Father Meck, and cousin Anna Meck. F. W. K.

140

*** END OF FR. KUNKEL'S KERN MANUSCRIPT ***

www.ingramcontent.com/pod-product-compliance
Lightning Source LLC
Chambersburg PA
CBHW071422150426
43191CB00008B/1009